The kitchen in catering

The kitchen in catering

by the late Joan Walley

completely revised by
Judith Evans

Constable London

Published in Great Britain by
Constable and Company Limited
10 Orange Street London WC2H 7EG

First published 1953
Second edition 1958
Reprinted 1961
Reprinted 1963
Third edition 1970
Fourth edition, completely revised by Judith Evans 1979

ISBN 0 90 462340 6

Set in Monophoto Times New Roman 10pt
Printed in Great Britain by
BAS Printers Limited, Over Wallop, Hampshire

Contents

List of figures

List of plates

List of tables

Preface to the fourth edition

When Joan Walley prepared the third edition of *The Kitchen in Catering* in 1970 she devoted the final chapter to the subject of New Trends. By now these trends have become established methods of catering, and, as such, have been integrated into the fourth edition. One of the first tasks has been to define the systems of catering now available from which the caterer may make his choice, provided that he takes into consideration the questions of cost-effectiveness and suitability to his clients' needs and tastes.

But much in catering remains the same. In particular, the principles enunciated by Joan Walley, and expressed with clarity, precision and unhurried logic, have not changed and are now restated in the fourth edition.

Judith Evans
October 1978

Metric international system
The Metric International System (SI) has been used. This has involved a certain amount of conversion of Imperial weights and measures, and some rounding-off has been necessary.

Acknowledgements

The fourth edition of *The Kitchen in Catering* owes a great deal to the kind and generous help given by many people and organisations. Acknowledgements and thanks go to the following for providing information: Air Products Ltd; Applied Chemicals Ltd; Automatic Vending Association of Britain; The British Gas Corporation; Calor Gas Ltd; Cleveland Public Schools, Food Services Dept, Ohio, USA; Crypto Peerless Ltd; The Department of Employment; The Department of Health and Social Security, Catering and Dietetics Branch; The Distillers Company (Carbon Dioxide) Ltd; Diversey Ltd; The Electricity Council; The Flour Advisory Bureau; GEC-Xpelair Ltd; The Hobart Manufacturing Company Ltd; The Hotel and Catering Industry Training Board; Kalamazoo Ltd; The Meat and Livestock Commission; The New Zealand Lamb Information Bureau; The Solid Fuel Advisory Service; Stotts of Oldham; Warwickshire County Council, Trading Standards Department; The White Fish Authority; and the Wine and Spirits Education Trust.

Acknowledgements and gratitude are also due to those who kindly supplied either drawings for the figures or photographs for the plates as follows:

Automatic Vending Association of Britain: figures 53, 54.
British Gas Corporation: figures 24, 25, 26, 27, 29b, 31, 32, 33a–b, 36b, c, d, 37, 38a, 39, 43. These drawings, except for figure 26, are taken from *A Student's Guide to Gas Catering* obtainable from British Gas, Marketing Division, 326 High Holborn, London WC1V 7PT. Figure 26 is taken from *Systematic Layout Planning for Commercial Catering*.
Crypto Peerless Ltd: figues 16, 38b, 49.
Electricity Council: figures 3, 8, 19, 20, 29a, c, 30, 33c, 35, 36a, e, 38c, 41, 42b, d, 44, 50, 51, 52, 55, 68.
Paul R. Doyen, Director, Food Operations, West Jersey Hospital, New Jersey, USA: Plate 1.
Glynwed Domestic and Heating Appliances Ltd: figures 21 and 28.
Hobart Manufacturing Company Ltd: Plates 2, 3, 4, 5, 6, 7, 8, 9.
Meat and Livestock Commission: figures 64, 65, 66.

Neff-Werke, Vertriebs-KG, Germany: figures 23, 34, 36f, 38d.
Régéthermic UK Ltd: figure 22.
G. K. N. Sankey Ltd: plate 10.
Temprite International Inc.: figure 42c.

The Department of Health and Social Security, Catering and Dietetic Branch, has allowed information from DHSS publications to be used in Table 8 and Appendix 3. The Controller of Her Majesty's Stationery Office has given permission for the reproduction of material as follows: figure 57, Appendix 1, Appendix 3.4, 3.5, 3.6, 3.7.

Special thanks go to Mr Colin Andrews of Air Products Ltd, Mr R. E. Lambe of the British Gas Corporation, Mr Douglas Owen of Crypto Peerless Ltd and Mr David Taylor of the Electricity Council for reading sections of the text and making suggestions. The help given by Miss Mary Smith who typed the manuscript is greatly appreciated.

Chapter 1

Introduction to catering

Successful catering is dependent upon the selection of a system that is suitable to the needs and demands of potential clients, and appropriate to economic circumstances currently and in the foreseeable future. If the system chosen is not appropriate, the undertaking is doomed either to failure or to a very limited degree of success, however good the standard of day-to-day management may be.

The need to be sensitive to the client's demands has always been self-evident so far as the commercial sector is concerned, but this has not always been so in the case of welfare catering—and perhaps it has not always been true. But lately people have become more individual in their tastes, and consumerism has increased in power. Also there is a greater knowledge and awareness of the variety of individual biological needs—one man's slimming diet is another's road to obesity. So this truth about sensitivity to the client's needs and wishes applies to the welfare section of catering, with which this book is primarily concerned. It follows that the caterer must study his market. He must look also at systems, which are briefly defined and described below.

1. *Conventional catering*

Food enters the kitchen in a raw state, not oven-ready, and is then prepared and cooked in individual pieces of equipment and served shortly afterwards.

2. *Cook-freeze systems*

Food is prepared and cooked in a similar manner to conventional catering, after which it is quick-frozen and stored at a low temperature until needed. The food is then regenerated (*i.e.*, receives its final cooking or heating) and served.

3. *Cook-chill systems*

The procedure is similar to cook-freeze, but instead of the food's being frozen it is cooled rapidly under controlled conditions and is kept chilled (for a maximum of three days) until it is regenerated before service.

4. *Finishing kitchens*

In these kitchens most of the food used is prepared frozen food of the type obtained either from a cook-freeze production unit functioning as described in (2) or from a manufacturer of prepared frozen foods. Other items used are those needing little or no preparation—*i.e.*, convenience foods such as canned and dehydrated goods.

5. *Snack bar and call-order catering*

The so-called 'fast foods' are the basis of this method of catering. Many of them are manufactured (*e.g.*, beefburgers, sausages) or ready-prepared (*e.g.*, chipped potatoes), but they are not by any means all frozen. The basis of this system is that simple food is freshly cooked to the client's requirements.

6. *Systems based upon continuous cooking operations*

In these systems, either food may be freshly cooked in a variety of apparatus, through which the food proceeds on a conveyor belt, or chilled food may be regenerated in a continuous operation on a conveyor belt passing through a microwave oven.

7. *Automatic vending*

Catering systems may be built round the use of automatic vending machines.

8. *Combined systems*

Any of the above systems may be used in combination.

From these brief descriptions it will be seen that methods of catering vary intrinsically in cost. It is obvious that some of the equipment mentioned will be very expensive to buy, but that not many staff will be needed to run the system. Again, where manufactured frozen foods are bought, these are almost certain to be dearer than raw foods because the manufacturer's costs have to be included in the price. But the caterer who buys them will save on his staffing costs because the food has already been prepared. When the management of a catering concern looks at several possible systems and tries to find out which will be the most cost-effective, account is taken of all the costs that would be involved in each of the systems: how much they would take to set up, and how much they would take to run. It might be the case that a capital-intensive scheme would justify its initial expense over a period of years because its running costs were low. The question of cost-effectiveness will be discussed in more detail in Chapter 22, and reference will often be made, directly or indirectly, to this fundamental subject.

Throughout the book we shall be talking about various catering systems, describing how they operate, and how they affect the design of the premises, the choice of equipment and the number and quality of staff employed.

Chapter 2

Sites and buildings

It does not fall to the lot of every food services manager and administrator to take a share in planning kitchens or selecting suitable sites. But senior officers in large catering organisations, and advisers to manufacturers and other bodies, may find that kitchen planning forms an important part of their responsibilities. Those not concerned with planning new establishments may, as food service managers, spend much of their working lives in catering premises whose design could be improved by either simple or radical alterations; this is especially likely to be so if in the course of years the style or system of catering has been altered.

It follows that questions of site and building affect, either directly or indirectly, all those concerned with catering management, and they are therefore fundamental to the main theme of this book.

Site considerations

It is not unusual for a kitchen building to be detached, built either on the same site as the establishment it serves or some distance away. An example of the former is a refectory designed to cater for students and staff on a university campus; an example of the latter is a cook-freeze unit built on an industrial estate and sending frozen meals out to surrounding schools. In the vast majority of cases, however, kitchens form part of the buildings they have been designed to serve. There are certain important site requirements.

(a) The site should if possible be level. Kitchens can, of course, be built on sloping sites, but this adds considerably to their cost, since foundations will have to be excavated or built up. At the same time it is necessary to have a fall between the kitchen and the main sewer to permit a natural flow. The ideal site is therefore on a flat plot of land at a slightly higher level than the main sewer. One small advantage arises from a moderate difference in the levels when the foundation has been built up so that the kitchen entrance is higher than the surrounding land: it is easy to provide a loading platform for the use of suppliers.

(b) Mains services—piped water, main drainage and electricity—

are usually considered essential, though there may be exceptions in remote areas. The proximity of these services is therefore a major consideration in choosing a kitchen site, and, if gas is preferred, its availability and proximity is also a factor. Laying on services to a site is a major expense, which can be minimised by choosing a site near existing services.

(c) Access should be easy. It must be remembered that a kitchen is visited by a number of heavy road vehicles during the week, usually including articulated lorries, and also refuse must be collected. It is therefore important that the site should be easily accessible from the public highway and as near to it as possible, so as to minimise the expense of laying a drive to the kitchen suitable for carrying this sort of traffic. Unless a one-way system with a separate entrance and exit is planned, there should be adequate turning space for the largest vehicle likely to make deliveries; it is wise to make precise checks about this.

(d) Planning permission from the local authority is needed for the erection of any building. A proposal to build a kitchen in a residential area may not be acceptable, and may lead to objections to the planning authority from local residents on grounds of the building's appearance, noise (*e.g.*, from ventilation plant) and cooking odours. The planning authority may require a more expensive type of construction in a residential area than would be the case on an industrial estate. The architect and other specialists will have planning considerations in mind when they advise on the suitability of a site.

The location of the kitchen

We must now consider the various factors that influence the location of the kitchen when it is not an independent unit but forms part of a larger building.

(a) *Relationship between kitchen and dining room*

Except where cook-freeze or chill-freeze systems are used, it is obvious that kitchen and dining room should be adjacent, on the same level, and easily accessible one from the other, but, for one reason or another, this does not always happen. For example, there may be constraints imposed by the site that prevent kitchen and dining room from being on the same floor, or the kitchen may be designed to serve meals to more than one dining area and it may be feasible to site only one of them close to the kitchen. A decision to site the dining area away from the kitchen is not one to be taken lightly: it should be borne in mind that the quality of the food served may suffer as a result, and that running costs will be greater because of the extra time and effort required from the staff.

(b) *Access for delivery purposes to kitchen and stores*

As already mentioned, the kitchen premises must be readily accessible from the outside for the delivery and collection of goods. This point needs special thought when the location of the kitchen within a larger building is being considered. The ideal arrangement is, of course, to have the storerooms situated as near as possible to a door opening directly on to the area into which delivery vehicles can drive. It is undesirable, on hygienic grounds, that those making deliveries should enter the preparation areas of the kitchen. This is particularly important in the case of those delivering vegetables, because 'dirty' foods such as these should be kept away from 'clean' foods. For this reason it is often the practice in large kitchens to have a separate entrance directly into the vegetable store. Access to the kitchen should be such that other users of the building are not inconvenienced or endangered by the traffic of goods to the kitchen. The safety of pedestrians—especially children—should be considered.

Forethought about ways of reducing the distance goods have to be carried may achieve a considerable saving of time and energy. When kitchens are not on the ground floor, arrangements fall far short of the ideal. In such cases a service lift is desirable. Similar considerations apply about easy access from outside to the lift. Where a kitchen is serviced by a lift problems of food hygiene can arise, and suitable solutions for these should be worked out at the planning stage.

If the kitchen is large and the intake of goods heavy, the provision of an unloading platform (already mentioned) may be an asset. A suitable height is 1·07 m or, if most lorries are low-loading, 610 mm. However, many heavy vehicles are fitted with automatic devices, and trolleys are used. Here, entry at ground level is more convenient.

Where the opening hours of the kitchen are relatively short it may be an advantage to have a self-contained reception area within the kitchen premises to which suppliers may have access at times when the kitchen is closed. Such an area might well be equipped with a low-temperature unit where the supplier may leave perishable foods. The supplier benefits by this arrangement because he can deliver at off-peak periods, and thus plan his deliveries more economically. He can be expected to pass on some of his savings to the customer.

(c) *Aspect*

This is a vital consideration in planning storerooms. The vegetable store, the general store and the larder must all be kept cool, and should therefore be planned to avoid direct sunshine at least during the hottest part of the day. Thus a northerly or easterly aspect is desirable for storerooms, while storerooms facing south should, for obvious reasons, be avoided. Considerations of aspect, however, do not apply where the only form of natural lighting is through a domed roof light. The design should then be such that the roof light is in shade from some other part of the building during the late morning and afternoon.

The aspect of the kitchen windows is important, particularly where there are large windows immediately above preparation benches. Excessive heat and glare make working conditions trying for the staff, and certain cooking operations (*e.g.*, rolling pastry) suffer. A little sunshine is, however, welcome, particularly in the early morning.

(d) *Natural lighting and ventilation*

Lighting and ventilation, which will be dealt with at some length in a later chapter, are mentioned here as they must be considered in the initial stages of planning. Unless the question of good natural lighting is discussed at an early stage it may be overlooked. Special attention should be given to natural lighting in preparation and washing-up areas. Forethought is needed also where ventilation is concerned, for, although some degree of artificial ventilation to extract cooking fumes is usually essential, it must be planned in relation to natural ventilation, which should be the best possible. Where complete mechanical systems are installed, natural ventilation is unnecessary.

(e) *Which floor level?*

In a building of several storeys the question arises as to which is the most suitable floor for the kitchen. Given a free choice there is no doubt that the ground floor would be chosen, and the top floor would be the next best. The top floor possesses many advantages that make for comfortable working conditions. It is easy to arrange good natural lighting and ventilation, and cooking smells do not permeate through the whole building. But there are also serious disadvantages as compared with the ground floor, and these are shared with all the intermediate floors. Delivery of stores and disposal of waste will be inconvenient, and may create problems. Extra costs will be involved in providing utility services, and in reinforcing the floors to carry the load of equipment. Also there will be the expense of installing and maintaining the necessary service lift. However, it must be borne in mind that there will be other claims for the available accommodation besides those of the caterer.

It is seldom easy to decide where to locate a kitchen in a new building of any type, but perhaps it is even more difficult when a hospital is concerned, the problem being chiefly one of food distribution to the wards. In recent years several new systems have been evolved in an attempt to overcome this difficulty. Thought should be given to the system to be used at the very earliest planning stage.

While discussing this subject it is interesting to consider the case of a two- or three-storied building devoted entirely to use as a restaurant, such as one might find on a university campus. The question will arise at an early stage as to whether the kitchen should be on the top or the ground floor. The main arguments are those previously enumerated, but there is one additional factor to be considered: the type of stairway needed to the top floor. In a building not entirely devoted to catering large stairways to the top floor are needed in any case, but in a building where only the kitchen and ancillary rooms are on the top floor a narrow stairway for staff use will suffice. Thus it might prove to be the least expensive arrangement to put the kitchen at the top and the dining rooms below.

The building

A discussion of the style of building, its construction and the materials to be used is clearly outside the province of this book. Nevertheless, it is appropriate to mention here some aspects of the subject which are closely associated with comfortable and convenient working conditions, with hygiene and with maintenance costs.

(a) *Height of ceilings*

Those who have worked in low-ceilinged kitchens know only too well their disadvantages. They quickly become oppressive, and, as a rule, only an efficient artificial ventilation system makes working conditions tolerable. A lofty kitchen is certainly desirable, but one that is too lofty has serious disadvantages, besides costing more to build. It is essential for the walls, ceilings and fittings in the kitchen to be kept scrupulously clean, and the difficulties and cost of cleaning and redecorating increase with the height of the ceiling. Unless tiling or other durable permanent surfaces are installed at the outset, kitchens will need complete redecoration at frequent intervals, the actual period depending chiefly upon the type of surface and the nature and volume of work done in the kitchen. It is obvious that this work will be more costly in a very lofty kitchen than it would be in one of moderate height. When a kitchen is in constant use (as in the case of a hospital), costs will be enhanced because work has to be undertaken at awkward hours and at higher rates of pay. Very high ceilings may also cause problems of acoustic control. Suitable heights from floor to ceiling are from 3·6 m to 4 m. Ceiling heights for storerooms may be lower than for the kitchen, and this may be used as a means of allowing clerestory lighting and ventilation where kitchen and stores adjoin.

(b) *The surfaces of walls and ceilings*

When walls and ceilings are considered, several requirements should be borne in mind:

1. The surfaces should be as smooth as possible, and without ledges, cracks or exposed pipes where dust, grease and insects can lodge. (Pipes may also produce condensation, with the consequent nuisance of drips.)

2. It is an advantage if the wall surfaces are washable up to a height that the staff may reasonably be expected to clean. (There may be little advantage in having higher areas finished with washable material, since there is usually not much difference in cost between having walls washed by a contractor and having them redecorated.) Glazed wall tiles and laminated plastic in the form of sheets or tiles are suitable washable surfaces for lower wall areas of a height up to, say, 2 m. Wall glazement (a treatment that is sprayed on to the wall after plastering to give a hard, impervious surface) and anti-condensation paint are also easily cleaned.

3. The surface must be resistant to the steamy atmosphere of the kitchen. Finishes such as distemper, which are liable to flake, offer a considerable risk to the purity of the food served. It is advisable to prevent condensation as far as possible by the use of lining materials of low thermal capacity, giving good thermal insulation of the walls.

4. A fourth point deserves consideration. No matter how smooth or clean a surface may be, or how resistant to disintegration, the nuisance of condensation and consequent streaming and drip formation is liable to occur at certain times unless some form of surface heat insulation is adopted. The object is achieved by applying to the surface some such poor conductor of heat as cork. Hence the use in kitchens of anti-condensation paint, containing a substance that is a poor heat conductor. Very often wall tiles or other impervious materials are used to a height of, say, 2 m, and anti-condensation paint is used above. The question of minimising condensation should be considered also in relation to the system of ventilation and extraction.

5. A further point concerns the acoustic quality of the materials used. Kitchen machinery is often noisy: hygienic, impervious materials such as stainless steel used for equipment and working surfaces have poor acoustic properties. The same is true of cutlery and many other table appointments, and hence there are special problems of noise in kitchens and dining rooms. This subject is dealt with in more detail in Chapter 3.

(c) *Kitchen floors*

It is far easier to enumerate the essential requirements for a satisfactory kitchen floor than it is to give examples of floorings that meet all of them; the ideal kitchen flooring has yet to be found. It should be hard-wearing; impervious; easy to keep clean; non-absorbent to grease; non-slippery when wet or dry; not liable to damage or discoloration by hot utensils, by standard cleaning processes or by the weight of heavy equipment; and, for the comfort of the worker, it should have a certain degree of resilience. A further point is colour; a brightly-coloured floor has a good psychological effect and encourages cleanliness.

Terrazzo flooring meets all requirements except that it may be slippery when wet. An important point about terrazzo tiles is that they are precision-made, and this means that joints between tiles can be reduced to a minimum; this is an obvious advantage in relation to hygiene. Ceramic floor tiles, vitrified or semi-vitrified, also meet most requirements; the semi-vitrified version is less slippery. Several anti-slip surfaces are available in quarry tiles—for example, studded, shot-faced, ribbed and grooved—but all these are less easy to clean than the smooth-faced variety. Their use might be indicated in areas of especial hazard. Another type of safety flooring contains metallic chips, and this can be obtained with a roughened surface; the latter is safer, but less easy to clean. Skirtings should be coved in the interests of hygiene.

Thermoplastic tiles and sheeting, when in good condition, give a hygienic, impervious surface that is easily cleaned, and they have a certain degree of resilience. They may be slippery when wet, and are usually considered unsuitable for heavy duty. The advantage of tiles over sheeting is that damaged ones are easily replaced.

Chapter 3

The working environment: ventilation, lighting, heating, acoustics

Ventilation, lighting and heating are important features in the planning of a kitchen. They contribute to good working conditions, which, in their turn, have a positive effect upon the health of the staff and also upon their output of work. Good lighting is essential to the maintenance of adequate standards of hygiene, and for the exercise of craft skills. Poor ventilation can be a cause of high maintenance costs. The topics of ventilation, lighting and heating are closely related, and the influence of one upon another must be constantly borne in mind. At the same time each has its own problems, which we shall consider separately.

Ventilation

Good ventilation consists in maintaining a suitable atmosphere by the admission of fresh air and the removal of vitiated air. A suitable atmosphere is one that provides conditions of comfort, is not detrimental to buildings or plant, and is not deleterious to standards of quality and hygiene.

Among the factors that may detract from comfort are excessive humidity, the presence of cooking smells, unsuitable temperatures, and draughts. The ventilating system in the kitchen must therefore be capable of controlling—or helping in the control of—any and all of these factors so as to contribute to the comfort of the occupants.

Let us consider first the question of humidity, which is, perhaps, more than any of the other factors, a cause of discomfort. When water is kept at or near boiling point, water vapour is constantly given off into the atmosphere. Boiling pans, steaming ovens and heated rinsing sinks—which use large quantities of water—are the main sources of steam in a kitchen, but hot water taps discharging into sinks, and the contents of any sink when it is full of hot water, also contribute. Much of this water vapour is taken up by the air, and the hotter the air the more vapour it can hold. The increase in the humidity of the air reduces the rate of evaporation of moisture from the skin, and this is the fundamental cause of discomfort. (The chef's cotton kerchief to absorb perspiration was one answer to a problem that has in recent years been exacerbated by the wearing of overalls made of non-absorbent man-made fibres.)

Saturation point is reduced when hot air meets a cold object (*e.g.*, walls, ceilings, metal service pipes and struts), and condensation takes place. The resulting moisture streams down walls or drips from pipes and ceilings, causing decorations to deteriorate, certain metals to rust, and possibly food to be contaminated or damaged. Occasionally one sees clouds of steam in kitchens, which may be so serious as to interfere with visibility; this occurs especially on days when there is no wind, and even more during fog, when the atmosphere is already so heavily laden with moisture that it cannot carry the heavy loads imposed upon it by cooking processes. This is the extreme case, which produces very unpleasant conditions and must obviously be guarded against, but a good ventilation system provides for more than the avoidance of the extreme. Comparatively dry atmospheric conditions are most conducive to comfort, and the system should therefore be designed to keep the moisture content of the atmosphere low. (At the same time, kitchen staff should be encouraged to play their part by using equipment correctly to avoid unnecessary production of steam, and by operating natural and mechanical means of ventilation effectively.)

The elimination of all cooking smells is, of course, impossible, and indeed undesirable—the cook's sense of smell is an important tool of trade. It is only when odours linger and become stale, or when they spread to other parts of the building and surrounding areas, that they become a source of annoyance. A good ventilation system is one that avoids these defects. Frying, and particularly deep-fat frying, is one cooking process that may load the atmosphere unpleasantly with cooking fumes even for those working in the kitchen, and very efficient ventilation is needed to ensure that the atmosphere, and the clothes and persons of the staff, do not become permeated with this particular smell. Some items of equipment, *e.g.*, continuous fryers, incorporate their own ventilation and cooling systems. Adequate ventilation, however, is not the whole story: the frying medium and the way in which it is used also enters into the picture.

Although the prevention of uncomfortably high temperatures will be discussed later, it is convenient to consider here the joint effects of temperature and draughts. Heat is constantly discharged into the atmosphere by cooking processes, and, as a result, the staff may become too hot and thus very sensitive to draughts. This should be remembered when a ventilating system is being planned. It is difficult to provide for adequate circulation and exchange of air without creating draughts, and when this happens staff may be reluctant for the ventilating system to be used. Excessive draughts may also cause cooked food to cool rapidly during the dishing-up or service period, and may also affect the performance of cooking equipment.

The measurement used in assessing the capacity of a ventilating system is based upon the number of air changes in one hour. From what has already been said one would expect a higher target figure for a kitchen than for the general run of rooms, and this is the case. Ventilating systems designed to give change rates up to 30–40 an hour are generally recommended, but higher rates may be necessary in cases of low ceilings or restricted space. These high rates of change should ensure good ventilation, but care should be taken to avoid cooling the kitchen too much in cold weather. It is an advantage if the rate of air change can be varied according to conditions in the kitchen.

Methods of ventilating kitchens

In kitchens with a small output of meals, say fewer than 50, it is possible that natural ventilation may be adequate, but a great deal depends upon the type of equipment installed. In such kitchens, if there is good cross-ventilation and if the equipment is placed so that the steam and cooking smells have easy exit, satisfactory conditions can be maintained for most days of the year, but trouble may be experienced on damp, misty and warm, still days. However, if the equipment includes a fish fryer, a heated rinsing sink, a boiling pan or a steaming oven, mechanical ventilation is almost certain to be necessary.

Care must be taken in planning kitchens to ensure that windows are not so placed that whenever they are opened wind—and wind-borne dust—blows on to the food in its various stages of preparation. Thought should also be given to ease of cleaning from both inside and outside, and ease in opening and closing. Where windows open at a high level, easily-operated opening gear or equipment should be provided. In the case of single-storey buildings, lighting and ventilation are often provided by either lantern lights or clerestory windows. These, when open, allow the escape of rising steam and hot air. Fresh air is then drawn in through opening windows at a lower level. In large kitchens windows should be widely distributed to ensure natural ventilation in all areas.

It is common practice in kitchens to group cooking equipment in blocks and to install canopies over them. Steam and hot air emitted during cooking rise into the hood and escape to the outside with the help of the fans. Where there is more than one canopy each may have its own fan, or there may be ducting from each leading to a common fan. Grease and dirt tend to collect on extractor fans, and this is particularly so where fish fryers are concerned. To reduce this, grease filters are often fitted; otherwise grease on the fan impeller can become a fire hazard. It is important that grease filters are easy to remove for cleaning. Canopies should not block the light, and should be made of a material that, in the event of fire, would be self-extinguishing. Corrugated self-extinguishing fibre glass is suitable. It is usual to provide a gutter to a canopy, so that moisture condensing from the steam produced during cooking collects there and eventually evaporates; thus condensation drips are avoided.

The position of the canopy in relation to the block of equipment it covers, and the height of the lower edge from the floor, are points to be considered. The height above the floor must allow the staff to stand underneath the canopy in comfort; 2 m is adequate.

Canopies are designed to extend beyond the cooking apparatus with a minimum overhang of 450 mm where equipment doors open, and 300 mm elsewhere.

An alternative to the provision of a canopy with extractor fans is a general controlled system for the whole kitchen area. The method is to install at appropriate points powerful extractor fans that create vigorous air currents and draw steam and hot air out of the kitchen. This system can be efficient, and it is an advantage visually not to have a canopy; also there is no canopy to be cleaned. But it often happens that odd fans are installed here and there to produce air movement without attention having been given to the fundamental principles of ventilation, and then results are not satisfactory. Fans vary in power, and are rated according to the number of cubic metres discharged in one hour. They should not be too noisy, or staff will be reluctant to use them.

Where mechanical ventilation is limited to extraction, fresh air to replace that extracted enters through open windows and other apertures and is drawn from other parts of the building. In other systems provision is also made for the mechanical control of incoming air: fans force fresh air into the kitchen at selected points. Incoming air is warmed to between 15° and 18° Celsius, and doors and windows are kept closed. The advantage of this system is that draughts are avoided. It is important that the fresh-air input does not exceed 60 to 80 per cent of the maximum extraction rate, so that a negative air pressure is maintained within the kitchen. The maintenance of a negative pressure prevents cooking smells from spreading to other parts of the building, and prevents moist air from penetrating the stores and causing condensation there.

The use of input and extractor fans sounds ideal, but even when these have been installed conditions are not always satisfactory. Conditions vary from kitchen to kitchen according to the amount of equipment installed, the amount of heat it radiates, the amount of steam produced during cooking and other factors. It is sometimes held that a more powerful ventilating system is necessary for a kitchen in which gas is used for cooking than for an electric kitchen; this is because water vapour is one of the products of combustion. In practice, however, the increase in power required is too small to be significant. Ventilation systems should be planned by an expert, and any problems should be referred to an expert for advice.

Ventilation of ancillary rooms

Storerooms

Good ventilation is needed in storerooms, but, as the atmosphere in them is not affected by cooking processes, mechanical systems are unnecessary except in those rare cases where it is not possible to provide natural ventilation. Care should be taken, however, to ensure that storerooms do not become pockets in which the hot, steamy atmosphere of the kitchen can collect. It is obvious that stores should be kept cool; if steam from the kitchen can enter it will condense in the cooler atmosphere, and streaming surfaces and moisture droplets will result. Natural ventilation should be at both low and high level; air bricks or other ventilators are often fitted low down where windows are high. Windows, roof lights, air bricks and ventilators for food stores are especially designed with suitable screening so that when they are open rats, mice, birds, flies and other insects are unable to enter. Windows should be placed so that they do not limit unduly the amount of wall space available for shelving.

Offices and staffrooms

Natural ventilation should be provided, and no mechanical means should be necessary.

Sanitary conveniences and adjoining rooms

It is essential that rooms containing sanitary conveniences should be ventilated. Where natural ventilation is not possible, special extractor fans ventilating to the outside air are installed. These are designed to operate automatically for a predetermined period when the light to the w.c. compartment is switched on. Rooms containing sanitary conveniences should not lead directly off the kitchen, and the intervening room (which is usually a staff cloakroom) should be ventilated separately, preferably by natural means. The Food Hygiene (General) Regulations, 1970, paragraph 16, refer.

Dining rooms

The question of the ventilation of large dining rooms is for the most part outside the range of the present discussion. It is interesting to note in passing, however, that when numbers of people are collected in a comparatively small space the air temperature slowly rises—the heat generated by 10 human beings is equivalent to that given out by a one-kilowatt electric fire, and also a certain amount of heat is emitted by the dishes of food served. The period of use of a dining room may extend over two hours for main meals, and call-order and snack meals may be served continuously. Hence it is clear that in a large dining room a controlled system of ventilation may be necessary to maintain comfortable conditions.

Lighting

All kitchen operations rely a great deal upon the use of the eyes, whether it be for finding an insect in a cauliflower or deciding upon the delicate degree of browning needed in potato straws. Even though operations such as rolling pastry and mixing puddings do not require so high a degree of visual discrimination and judgment, the eyes are constantly being used, and efficient illumination is necessary at all points in the kitchen where work is in progress; this is critical in the maintenance of high standards of cleanliness and hygiene.

Reasons for good lighting

(a) It is essential that absolute cleanliness be maintained in all parts of the kitchen and all equipment used. Although this is obvious, it cannot be too strongly emphasised. When kitchens and storerooms are inadequately cleaned, rats, mice and insect pests may be attracted by particles of food left on floors or tables. Also, dust and dirt harbour bacteria, some of which may be harmful. Thorough cleaning depends upon a combination of several factors, but one of the more important is the ability to see clearly what has to be cleaned. For instance, it is impossible to clean a large milk boiler without frequent and careful examination to see whether further friction is needed. For this, as for all cleaning processes, the standard of lighting must be good.

Furthermore, cleanliness in kitchen work extends beyond the cleaning of premises and equipment. Some foods—for example fresh vegetables—must be cleaned before they are used, and a close watch for foreign bodies must be kept on all foods.

(b) It is well known that any work is done more efficiently when conditions are comfortable and convenient. Less strain, both physical and mental, is placed on the worker who is able to get on with the work more quickly, and the onset of fatigue is considerably delayed. There must be a good light on any work that needs careful watching; a dim light, or one so placed that the worker's shadow falls on the working area, are constant sources of irritation. Admittedly he may be almost unconscious of the effect because over a long period he has become inured to conditions that are far from ideal. But as soon as conditions are improved he realises how unsatisfactory they were before, and finds that he can now carry out the operation much more easily and efficiently.

(c) An attractive appearance in the finished article is one of the aims of all good cooks. This applies equally to the delicate colourings and careful piping on an iced cake for a special occasion, and the browning of the potato crust on a cottage pie. If the lighting in the kitchen is poor, it is probable that the cook will be dissatisfied with both these products when they reach the bright light of the dining room. The carefully blended colours on the cake may appear crude when they are correctly illuminated, and the cottage pie may turn out to have been over- or under-browned.

Natural lighting

There are two very good reasons why there should be good natural lighting in kitchens. In the first place, it is well known that daylight is more conducive to good work than is artificial lighting, partly for psychological reasons. In the second place, unnecessary expense is involved where no use is made of natural light. To use artificial lighting continuously when this could have been avoided at the design stage is clearly bad policy, and an unjustifiable additional charge on running costs.

Lighting levels and their effects are discussed in Chapter 16, but at this stage it is appropriate to note how the shape, size and placing of windows influence the intensity of illumination and the penetration of daylight. A tall, high window gives much greater light penetration than does a long, low one, while clerestory lighting is better still in this respect. Upper-floor windows admit more light than those on the ground floor or in the basement, which are often obstructed by other buildings, nearby walls at right angles to the plane of the window, or overhead balconies. Another factor that influences light distribution in a room is the height of the sill in relation to any adjoining working surfaces such as tables, benches or sinks. A high sill will cast a deep shadow across the surface; this is particularly noticeable in a deep sink. It is therefore advisable that the sill should not be more than 150 mm above the top of the sink.

Heating

The problem of temperature control

The problem of maintaining a satisfactory working temperature in a kitchen is more complicated than is the provision of adequate heating in classroom or office. This is mainly because in the kitchen there are many pieces of equipment which during operation contribute various amounts of heat. The total amount supplied varies from hour to hour according to how much equipment is in use and the rate at which the heat is produced. Also, the efficiency of the insulation of equipment makes a difference.

The problem of heat from cooking equipment is complicated because the heat comes from three different sources: direct radiation from oven walls, hot cupboards and solid-top boiling plates; steam from boilers and steaming ovens; and the convection of hot air round appliances. When both temperature and humidity are high discomfort is experienced by workers because natural evaporation from the skin is diminished. Thus at peak cooking periods the problem of maintaining a satisfactory temperature is likely to be one of cooling rather than heating. Ventilation is important, and management should ensure that staff play their part by carefully regulating the controls of such equipment as steaming ovens and boiling pans so that excessive steam is not produced, and by turning or switching off cooking appliances when they are not in use. An increase in the number of air changes per hour at peak periods can do much to help, but this alone clearly cannot produce a cool kitchen on a day when the outside temperature is higher than that considered satisfactory for kitchen work. In these conditions a kitchen with a controlled system of ventilation and air conditioning has an advantage.

So far the kitchen has been considered as though all parts were affected by cooking equipment, but this is not always so. For example, it is not very likely that heat from cooking equipment will reach the vegetable preparation section, and the staff working here are particularly liable to feel the cold because of the nature of their work. This area needs special consideration when the heating system is being planned.

Temperature requirements

There are two separate issues to be considered when deciding the temperature requirements in the kitchen during working hours. The first relates to the staff, and the second to the materials handled. A person doing active or moderately active work can do such work comfortably at temperatures ranging from 13 to 20° Celsius, and even up to 23° little discomfort is felt. Much of the material used in the work of preparation and cooking is also handled satisfactorily at these temperatures. However, perishable foods such as meat and fish should be kept as cool as possible during preparation, and pastry requires the lower range of temperature for best results. On the other hand, yeast mixtures are better dealt with at the higher temperatures, which are also more suitable in post-cooking preparation areas and in the servery, where food should not be allowed to cool unduly. It is usual to site preparation areas for pastry, meat and fish in comparatively cool parts of the kitchen.

Type of heating required

It is evident that the heating provided in kitchens should be available early in the morning, and should be capable of quick adjustment later in the day when cooking equipment generates a considerable amount of heat. Special facilities should be supplied in the vegetable preparation section. If adequate heating is not provided, staff will be inclined to use cooking equipment for space heating, and this is extravagant. During the winter months, heat should be provided to maintain a temperature of not less than 10° Celsius outside working hours. This will prevent pipes from freezing during frosty spells, and will keep the fabric of the building warm, thereby minimising problems of condensation at the start of the working day.

Acoustics

Much thought has been given to the acoustic qualities of buildings, and, although a great deal of this work has been directed towards the quality of sound for speech and music, the control of noise has also received attention. In general the kitchen tends to be a noisy place, partly because of the nature of some of the work, but also because, for reasons of hygiene, most surfaces are hard and shiny, and therefore not sound-absorbing. This applies to walls, floors, working surfaces, equipment, utensils, cutlery and ceramic tableware. The noisiest areas are those devoted to dishwashing and panwashing. There are also noise problems in dining rooms, but, because it is possible to use materials with sound-absorbing properties such as curtains, carpets and acoustic tiles, it is easier to find a solution there. In dining rooms difficulties may arise on two counts. At meal-times the sound level of conversation often rises to a high pitch to overcome the noise and clatter of dishes and cutlery, and the general level may become unacceptable. On special occasions, such as formal dinners, the penetration of noises from the kitchen may make it difficult for speeches to be heard.

Practical measures for dealing with noise

In Chapter 16 consideration is given to the measurement of noise levels and the effects of noise on people. Here we shall look at some practical measures for dealing with noise, remembering that sound waves are transmitted by air, that all material substances can transmit sound waves to a greater or lesser degree according to their nature, and that sound waves are reflected when they meet rigid obstacles.

So far as noise penetration from kitchen and dining room is concerned, serving hatches and counters used for cafeteria service create a particular problem. One method of dealing with this is to have the service counter opening not into the dining room itself but into a service area adjoining the dining room, and this serves to isolate the noise to some extent. (See Figure 18 for one such arrangement.) Another method is to provide double shutters to the serving hatch to create a sound barrier, but this, of course, is effective only at times when meals are not being served, and so it is of value chiefly when the room is being used for purposes other than dining.

In the dining room sound-absorbing materials may be used to reduce noise coming from the kitchen area and from within the room itself. If these are used for walls, floors and ceilings, noise that would otherwise be reflected off these surfaces will to a large extent be absorbed. An acoustic tile has a mainly non-porous surface, drilled with holes. Sound passes into the holes and is absorbed by the walls, which are porous. Curtains, carpets and other soft furnishings have sound-absorbent qualities. Carpets, which at one time were rarely used in institutional buildings, are now being fitted in dining rooms. Acrylic fibres, of which heavy-duty carpeting is often made, can be scrubbed by machine as well as being vacuum cleaned, and where carpet tiles are used worn or damaged tiles can easily be replaced. Hence, the use of carpeting in institutional dining rooms for acoustic reasons is a more practical proposition than it used to be. A point to note in the use of acoustic materials is that maximum benefit is achieved if they are placed as near as possible to the source of noise. It is not uncommon to see screens placed in dining rooms a few metres away from service counters. The intention is partly to screen the kitchen from the clients' view, but if the screen is made of sound-absorbent material it also limits noise penetration.

It is necessary to consider at the planning stage the question of noise transmission from the kitchen through the fabric of the building to adjacent rooms other than the dining room, and some special measures to reduce this nuisance may be needed.

Although almost all materials used in kitchens have poor sound-absorbing properties, some measures can be taken to reduce noise from these sources, and rubber and plastic may be used to good effect. Rubber bumpers as well as rubber tyres reduce the noise of trolleys, and plastic-coated baskets for rinsing crockery and cutlery are much quieter in use than are all-metal ones. This applies also to plastic tableware as compared with ceramic, which may be a factor influencing choice. Where a large surface is concerned, such as a stainless steel bench, vibration may be a cause of noise, and this can be lessened by stiffening the surface with struts. A coating of heavy bituminous material on the underside of such benching is often useful in reducing noise.

Chapter 4

Questions of space

One of the early planning decisions to be made concerns the total floor area needed, and its allocation between the various sections of the kitchen and storerooms. The efficiency of the kitchen is impaired if the area is inadequate, or, as happens less often, if the kitchen is larger than it need be for the amount of work to be done there. Both mistakes are costly. It is a waste of capital to build a kitchen that is too large, and running costs are needlessly high. On the other hand, it is extremely expensive to enlarge later on a kitchen that has proved to be too small.

The difficulties in a kitchen where the working area is insufficient are mainly caused by congestion. Equipment, utensils and staff all occupy a certain amount of floor area, and unless there is also sufficient space for the free movement of staff (who will at times be carrying food and equipment or pushing trolleys) and the operation of equipment, work will take more time and energy than it should; there will also be an increased likelihood of accidents. Cleaning operations may be difficult because of congestion, and consequently standards of hygiene may suffer. Other difficulties may arise with ventilation and temperature control. Many caterers are only too familiar with the discomfort caused by high temperatures and steam-laden atmospheres in overcrowded kitchens, and those who have tried to improve conditions know that this is not easily done.

Too much floor space presents different problems. Extra demands are made upon the time and energy of staff by the distances to be covered. Nearly all kitchen work, however well planned, entails a considerable amount of walking, carrying and trolleying, and obviously if the lines of communication are unnecessarily long the energy expended and the time taken for each section of the work will be greater. The increased expense that results from the extra cleaning, lighting, heating, maintenance and staff hours needed is a major disadvantage of an over-large kitchen.

The previous remarks refer only to the actual working space in a kitchen, and not to the storeroom areas. Because there is usually pressure to keep down building costs it is unusual for stores to be excessively large. On the other hand, the problems of inadequate stores are so obvious that there is scarcely need to point them out.

Certain rules of thumb have been evolved as a result of experience for estimating the size of kitchens and ancillary rooms, and these are very helpful at the design stage. But numbers of decisions have to be made and a considerable amount of data is required before these rules of thumb can be applied, and they have to be modified to suit individual circumstances.

Factors affecting the amount of floor space needed

(a) The nature of the establishment for which the kitchen is designed to cater

These fall into three main categories:

Residential establishments, such as boarding schools or halls of residence, at which residents are expected to take all, or nearly all, their meals;

Non-residential establishments, such as day schools or factories, where the main commitment is to provide midday meals with, possibly, beverages and light snacks at break periods;

Institutions where a full range of meals is offered to residents and non-residents alike. Universities often come within this category and may provide, as well as main meals, snacks and light refreshments throughout the day and evening.

Where there is a varied type of commitment, or where full board is provided, one would expect more space to be needed in relation to the number of persons to be catered for, since a wider variety of equipment and tableware will be necessary and stocks of food have to be larger.

(b) The number of meals to be served

This factor is of prime importance, and it is usual to describe a kitchen as having a capacity of x number of meals. But in arriving at this figure one must be quite clear as to what is meant by it. In the case of a residential establishment offering inclusive board-residence terms it is not usually difficult to determine numbers in advance, though one must be clear as to what is meant by the number of meals. Confusion could arise if the total daily number of meals were stated rather than the number to be catered for at any one meal, and it might be better to use the term 'number of residents' rather than 'number of meals'. But this figure alone is not likely to be sufficient, for there would almost certainly be non-residents who wanted a midday meal. An estimate should be made of these additional meals to arrive at a figure for the largest number of meals that will be needed at any one time, and the capacity of the kitchen should be based on this figure. Where it is not the intention to provide meals as part of board-residence or other all-in terms, it is much more difficult to estimate demand. Usually statistics for similar establishments or catering services are studied, but it is not easy to find examples that are comparable in every way with the new undertaking. Also many circumstances may arise, outside the control of the planners, that will affect demand. For example, in schools a decision to have a shorter school dinner hour could increase the demand for meals because fewer pupils would have time to go home for a meal. In an industrial canteen a reduction in the level of subsidy of the catering account could involve a fall in demand that could not have been foreseen at the planning stage.

(c) The choice of catering system

This is a fundamental consideration. For example, if it is intended to buy ready-prepared vegetables, hardly any vegetable preparation area will be needed (but facilities for preparing salads may still have to be provided). If a system based upon ready-prepared frozen foods is proposed, a kitchen area about 40 per cent smaller than that needed for a conventional kitchen is appropriate, because there will be less equipment and fewer staff to be housed.

(d) Style and type of meal

Less equipment and fewer staff will be needed to produce meals of two courses only than for three- or four-course menus. If a choice of dishes is to be offered, the effect can be a reduction in the amount of equipment needed, though this does not always follow. This point is discussed in Chapter 14.

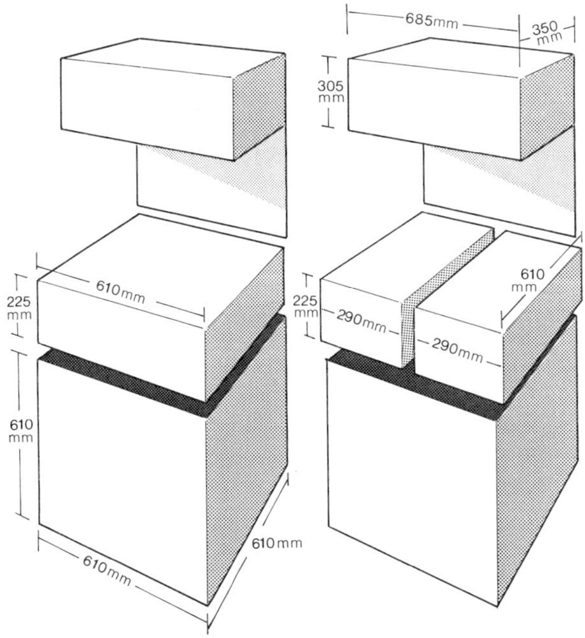

Fig. 1 Modular cooking equipment
(a) based on standard dimensions

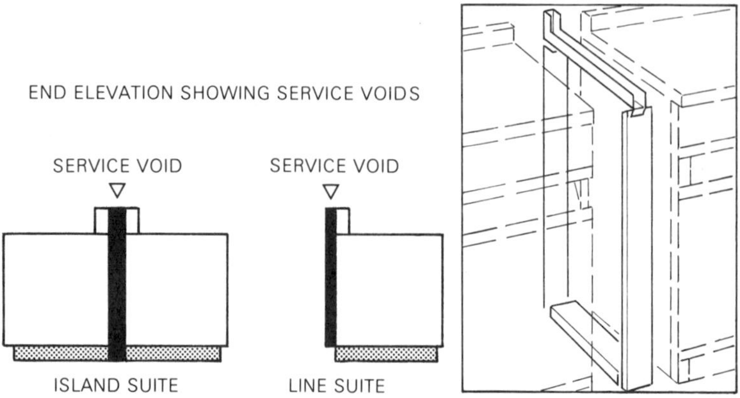

(b) with service voids at back to enable equipment to be fitted back-to-back or flush against wall

(c) with special jointing arrangements to enable items to be fitted side by side without gaps

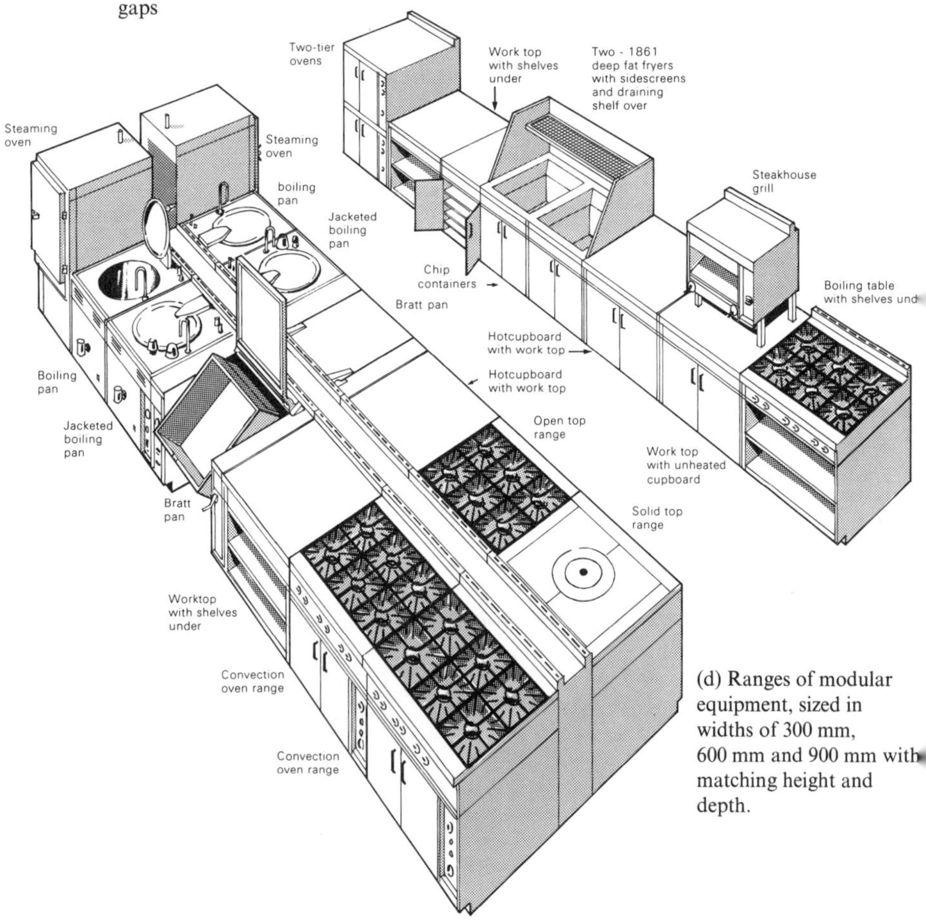

(d) Ranges of modular equipment, sized in widths of 300 mm, 600 mm and 900 mm with matching height and depth.

(e) Type of equipment

Items of cooking equipment that are designed as modules to fit flush with each other without intervening gaps save floor space (see Figure 1). So does multi-purpose equipment, such as the bratt pan, but for a different reason: the number of appliances installed can be reduced. Some equipment saves floor space because it operates at very high speeds, and so the ratio of output to floor space occupied is high. This is true of high-pressure steaming ovens.

(f) Method of service

Some service methods need considerably more space than do others. Linear counters designed to offer a wide choice of menu items and free flow service systems (see Figures 2 and 3a–b) occupy a great deal of space, while waiter service and carousel service units (see Figure 4) need very little.

(g) Requirements for ancillary rooms

When considering the overall space, it is important to take into account the demands for such ancillary rooms as staff dining rooms, offices, cloakrooms and lavatories, and to ensure that adequate floor space is allowed for these if they are to be provided within the total space allocated for kitchen use.

(h) Nature of the space available

If the space allocated for kitchen premises is an awkward or unsuitable shape, the total area needed is likely to be larger than it would be in standard conditions. This may happen in new buildings when supporting pillars or other objects project into the room, but it is much more common when existing buildings are adapted for use as kitchens. For example, where walls are knocked out to give larger working areas or stores, it may not be possible to remove them completely, and thus there may be small recesses of little use included in the overall area. The total space requirement in such cases would be greater than that which would be satisfactory without these inconveniences.

There is also the point that some widths of buildings are more suitable for kitchen planning than others. If the width of building is unsuitable, a greater area will be needed because there will be some wasted floor space. For example, dimensions may be such that the circulation space between a central island of equipment and working surfaces fitted along the wall is wider than necessary, and so space is wasted. Problems arise also when a space is too narrow to be used to best effect. The most convenient kitchen is rectangular, with the length not more than twice the width. Much, however, depends upon the skill of the architect and his specialist adviser; ingenuity and imagination can overcome many apparent difficulties about dimensions, and can even use them to advantage.

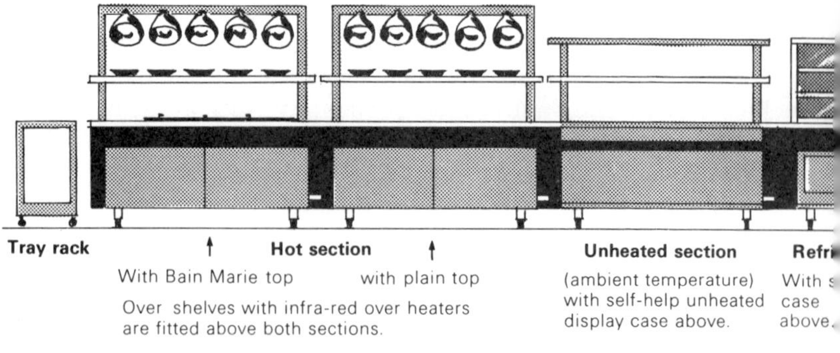

Fig. 2 Cafeteria catering counter

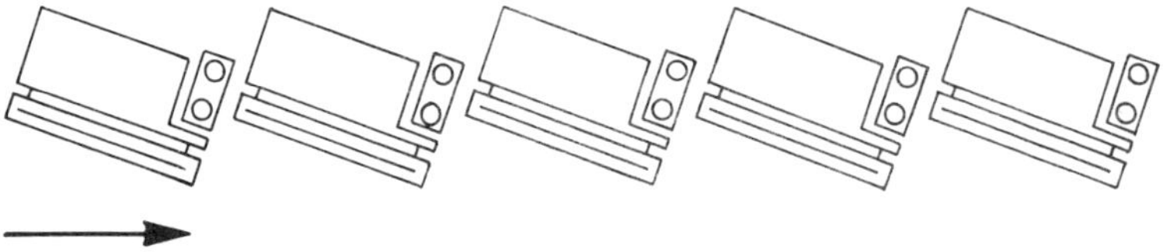

Fig. 3 Examples of free-flow method of service
(a) free-standing service units arranged in echelon
(b) free-standing service units arranged in U-shape

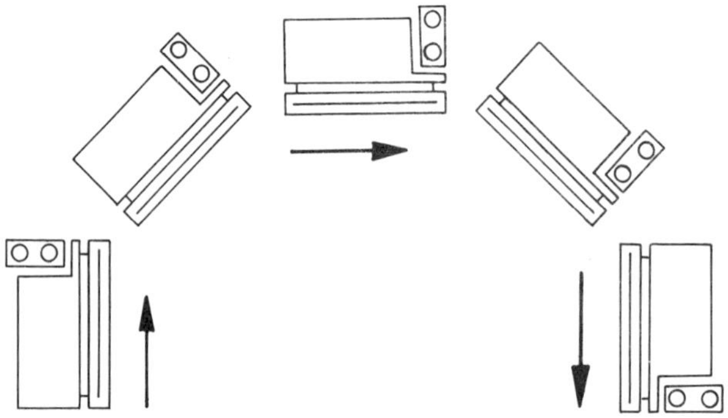

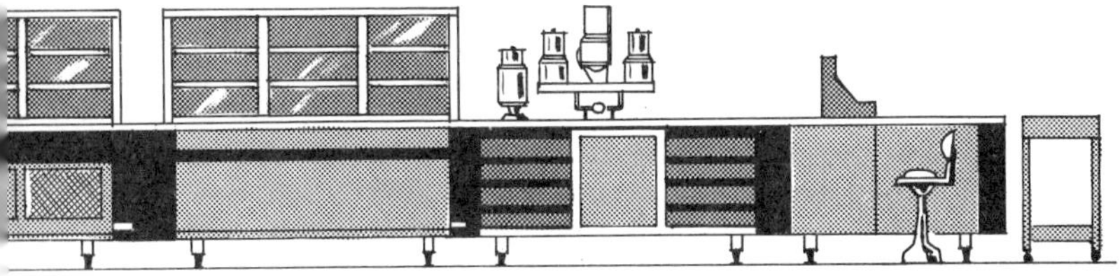

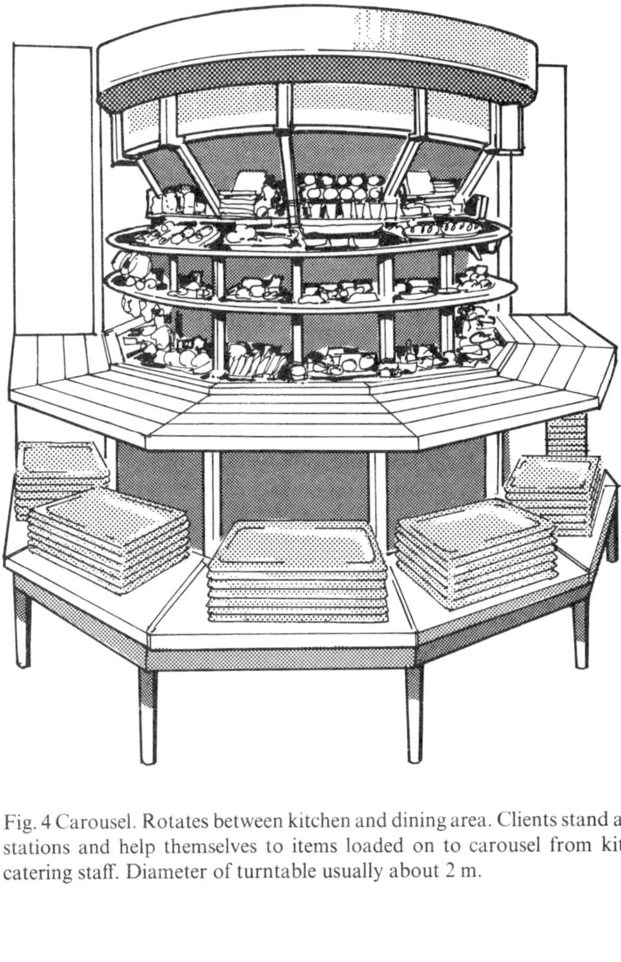

Fig. 4 Carousel. Rotates between kitchen and dining area. Clients stand at any one of 6 stations and help themselves to items loaded on to carousel from kitchen side by catering staff. Diameter of turntable usually about 2 m.

Allocation of the total area

Having considered factors affecting the kitchen area in general, the next point to look at is the allocation of floor space to the various ancillary rooms and the kitchen itself.

Ancillary rooms

The number and use of these rooms vary according to the size and requirements of the kitchen. Thus, in a small kitchen only two food stores may be necessary—one for vegetables and one for other foods—whereas in a large establishment separate stores may be provided for the following: vegetables, dry goods, bread, wines, china, brooms and brushes, cleaning materials, and empty cartons and cases. (In a small kitchen some of these would be accommodated in cupboards rather than storerooms.) Again, in a small kitchen the only staff accommodation needed will be a small cloakroom and lavatory. But in a large kitchen cloakrooms, lavatories, dining rooms, and sometimes a rest room, are provided; also, office accommodation will be needed for the supervisor or manager and any clerical staff employed.

All kitchens must have some refrigerated storage facilities for perishable foods, and most will need storage for frozen foods also. But, whereas in the small kitchen perishable and frozen foods are stored in free-standing refrigerators, in large ones walk-in stores are often found.

Considerable variation occurs in the type of storeroom provided in large kitchens. There may be several chill stores (or the chill store may be supplemented by refrigerators), so that meat, fish and other perishables may each be stored separately at the temperature most appropriate to its category. (The range of temperatures suitable for different foods is dealt with in Chapter 11). There may also be a chilling room for the rapid cooling of cooked food. If a large quantity of dry goods is kept, it is convenient to have two separate rooms so that the bulkier goods in sacks and boxes may be stored separately from smaller articles. Sometimes a separate store is provided for goods issued from the main store that are to be used during the day; this is known as the daily-issues store.

The whole question of the amount of space needed for food storage is dealt with in detail in *Residential Catering, University Building Notes*, 1966, and recommendations are made for supplies for young people for three meals a day seven days a week. The total floor areas are given for dry store, bread store, vegetable store, cool store, chill store and storage for frozen foods. Graphs summarising these recommendations are shown in Figure 5a–c. Lists of storage requirements for food and other items expressed in metre runs of

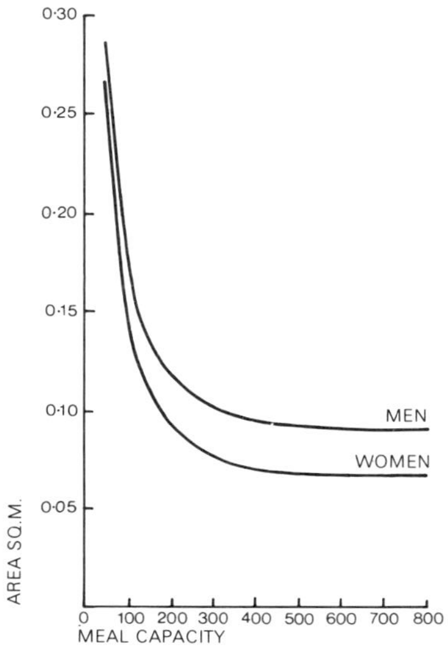

(a) Maximum areas per person expressed in m²

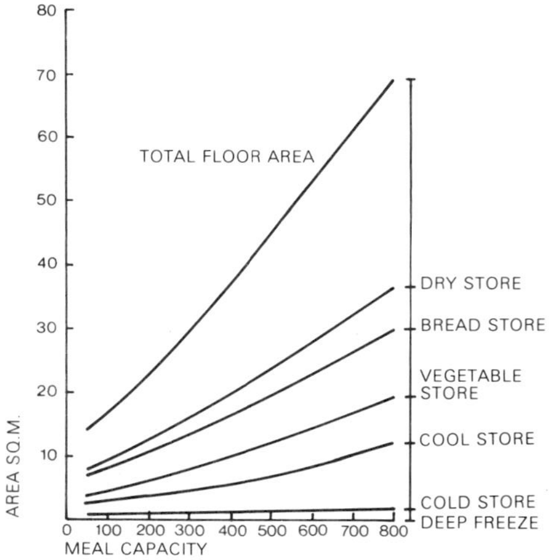

(b) Men: total requirements

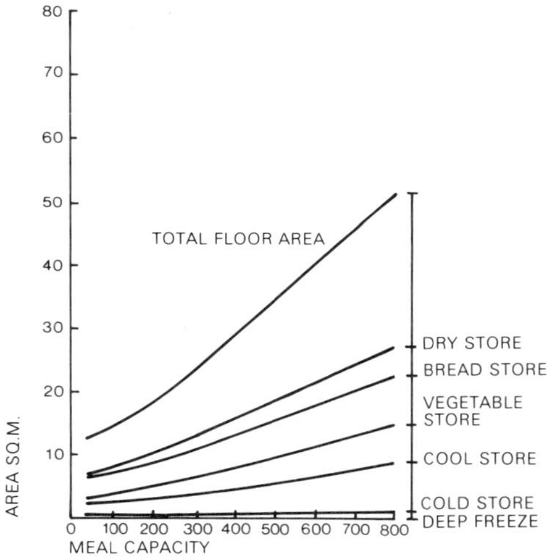

(c) Women: total requirements

Fig. 5 Space needed for food stores in residential establishments.
(From *Residential Catering*, University Building Notes, 1966).
In calculating requirements, note has been taken that men have higher energy needs than women

shelves are given in *School Kitchens*, Educational Building Note 14, Scottish Education Department, HMSO, 1976 (see Appendix 1). These figures apply to simple two-course meals served once a day for a five-day week. The amount of floor space necessary to accommodate this area of shelving will depend upon the arrangement of the stores. In the case of prepared frozen foods a useful rule of thumb is that 4·5 kg of food can be stored in 0·003 m^3; this figure allows for access and stock rotation. Given a figure for the average weight of frozen food to be served per meal (340 g is an average amount) and the expected frequency of delivery, a working figure for the cubic capacity of storage space may be calculated, but for a more accurate figure it would be necessary to know the dimensions of packages and the way in which the accommodation is to be arranged. Allowance must, of course, be made for reserves of stock. Appendix 2 includes details of the cubic capacity of deep-freeze storage units suitable for finishing kitchens providing simple two-course meals.

The kitchen

The space allocated for the preparation, cooking and serving of food, and for washing up, must allow for the following:

1. The placing and operation of all the equipment and fittings to be used, including tables, work benches and trolleys;
2. Staff to work in safety and comfort at their various stations;
3. Sufficient circulation space.

In some kitchens the various preparation processes are separated from each other and the main kitchen area by dividing walls. This arrangement has some advantages:

1. The kitchen is given a tidier appearance;
2. Noise from the potato peeler, and the general dampness associated with vegetable preparation and washing up, are kept away from the other work of the kitchen;
3. Circulation areas are less likely to become cluttered, and this is important for both convenience and safety.

There are, however, disadvantages:

1. Dividing walls, unless they are of the dwarf variety, may cut off light and interfere with ventilation;
2. Staff supervision is more difficult;
3. Dividing walls make the kitchen more difficult to run;
4. A greater area is needed.

Whether or not dividing walls are used, it is usual to plan so that preparation work of various types is carried out in different parts of the kitchen. The number of such sections will vary according to the scale and complexity of operations, but it is essential on hygienic grounds to keep raw vegetables away from other foods during the course of preparation, and to keep preparation areas for raw foods such as meat and poultry away from cooked food.

The service area

Opinions differ as to whether the service area should be separate from the kitchen or not. Where the servery is separate, it has the advantage of cutting off the view of the kitchen from the dining room, and it also helps to isolate some of the noise, but more floor space is needed. In small catering units, separate serveries tend to be wasteful of space and staff hours. In any circumstances it is essential that the relationship between the areas where cooking, post-cooking preparation and serving take place should be closely-knit if energy and effort are to be saved.

One way of achieving close integration between the kitchen and the servery without having the kitchen exposed to view is by the provision of heated and unheated pass-through cabinets in the dividing wall, or free-standing equipment may serve the same purpose. The hot cabinets may consist of small compartments with doors on each side fitted with viewing panels. By these means only small quantities of food are exposed to cooling when doors are opened, and the contents can be seen without the doors having to be opened. In the case of cold cabinets it is an advantage if they are designed to be used in conjunction with mobile racks that can be loaded with dishes such as cold desserts and salads before they are pushed into the cabinet (see Figure 6).

Fig. 6 Hot and cold push-through cabinets, offering convenient arrangement between kitchen and service area
(a) Cold cabinet (b) Heated cabinet

When recommendations are made on the size of the servery, two main points must be considered where a linear service counter is concerned: its length and its width. The length is related to some extent to the number of meals served, but where the client (rather than a waiter) is to use the counter and choose from a display, the number and type of items to be displayed and served, and the number of serving staff to be accommodated, are major considerations. Where no choice of menu is offered, a counter 3·6 m long would be about the minimum. Otherwise, lengths range from about 6 to 15 m. A counter 9 m long would allow a good selection of dishes to be displayed, and would provide working stations for 12 staff; this may be regarded as a useful average length. When seating accommodation in the dining area exceeds 300, it is preferable to have an extra servery rather than to increase the length. The counter is usually divided into hot and cold sections. Beverage service may be included in the main counter or it may be at different counters separated from each other, so that those taking beverages do not have to join the main queue. The width of the servery consists of: the depth of the service counter (0·6 m to 0·8 m); the serving aisle used by staff (1·2 m to 1·4 m); and the back counter, if needed (0·6 m). The efficiency of a service counter may be judged by the speed of client flow, which can range from 7 to 14 a minute, with 10 being a good average. The capacity of the dining room and the speed of service should be related; otherwise clients served with food may be unable to find seats.

One way of reducing the length of a service counter is to incorporate a roundabout device at counter level, which is filled on the servery side of the counter and rotates before the customer, who makes his choice as it appears before him. Instead of being used as an adjunct to a linear counter, the roundabout or carousel may be used as the chief means of dispensing food. In this case the client and serving staff have no direct contact, and the client helps himself to all he wants. Figure 4 shows a carousel with 6 segments, so that 6 people may help themselves at a time. At the University of Stellenbosch in South Africa, 600 students an hour are served by means of a carousel.

Another method of service, the free-flow system, occupies a considerable amount of floor area. Several separate-service units are arranged either in echelon or in a more scattered way, and the client chooses what he wants as he would in a supermarket. By this means speedy service is given, and queuing is minimised. A service area of the kind shown in Figure 3a, designed to serve 1000 to 1500 meals in a two-hour period, occupies about 139 m^2.

Wash-up area

Space requirements for the wash-up, the planning of which will be dealt with in Chapter 5, are related to the number of meals served, the number of pieces of tableware used per meal, the type of equipment installed, the rate at which used crockery flows into the wash-up area, and the length of time available for dish-washing. Where there is no mechanical dishwasher, standard equipment consists of twin sinks with drainers. The first sink is used for washing and the second, which is usually heated, for rinsing (see Figure 7). With one such unit, dishes

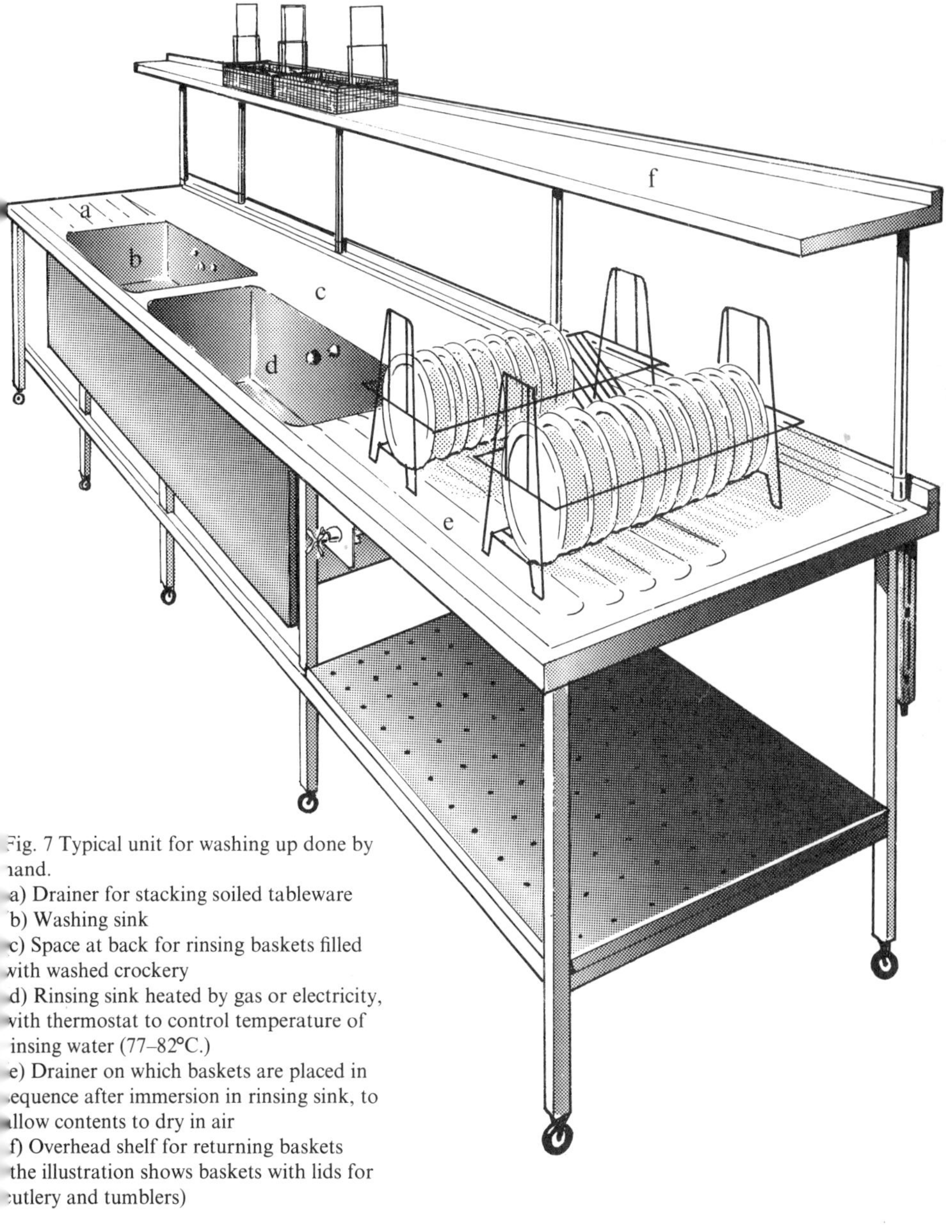

Fig. 7 Typical unit for washing up done by hand.
(a) Drainer for stacking soiled tableware
(b) Washing sink
(c) Space at back for rinsing baskets filled with washed crockery
(d) Rinsing sink heated by gas or electricity, with thermostat to control temperature of rinsing water (77–82°C.)
(e) Drainer on which baskets are placed in sequence after immersion in rinsing sink, to allow contents to dry in air
(f) Overhead shelf for returning baskets (the illustration shows baskets with lids for cutlery and tumblers)

from a simple two-course meal for 300 can usually be dealt with in a period of two hours. Two units (each 3·3 m × 0·7 m) installed on opposite walls, with an aisle of 1·5 m between, in an area about 4·6 m long, would be adequate for 500–600 meals and would occupy about 13 m^2. Mechanical dishwashers are usually installed away from walls, and typical lengths range from 1·5 m to 7·6 m. In addition to the space needed to accommodate them comfortably, an adequate surrounding area for stripping and sorting dirty dishes, stacking clean dishes and parking trolleys for carrying clean and dirty dishes is necessary. Small dishwashers are often sited in the kitchen, and no separate wash-up area is provided. For larger installations typical areas range from 14 m^2 for 500 meals to 50–85 m^2 for very large units. The area does not vary directly with the number of meals served. It should be noted that, where the 'flight-around' type of dishwasher is installed (see Figure 16), savings in space of up to 40 per cent are possible as compared with a linear model. It is advisable to consult the manufacturer of the dishwasher before making a final decision on the amount of space to be allowed for a wash-up area.

General recommendations on floor areas

So far we have discussed areas in very general terms, and have shown how requirements are affected by different factors. Some more definite recommendations on kitchen sizes must now be considered. Clearly it is not possible to lay down exact measurements, but experience has shown that there are certain figures that can be used as yardsticks, and as starting points when plans for individual kitchens are drawn up, but they must be applied with discrimination.

It is helpful to have in mind a figure for the amount of space needed per meal as an aid in determining the overall size of a kitchen. In general, the larger the capacity of the kitchen, the smaller the area per meal required. This is chiefly because in small kitchens the area necessary for ancillary rooms, access and circulation space is higher in proportion than for larger kitchens.

Conventional kitchens

An analysis of recommendations published in *The British Standards Code of Practice, C.P.3, Code of Basic Data for the Design of Buildings*, 1950, Chapter VII, Engineering and Utility Services, gives the following areas per meal, which generally accord with those suitable for conventional kitchens in residential establishments and others offering a good range of facilities:

Capacity of kitchen	*Area per meal*
100	0·697 m^2
250	0·48 m^2
500	0·46 m^2
750	0·37 m^2
1000	0·348 m^2
1500	0·309 m^2
2000	0·279 m^2

Plans published in *School Kitchens*, Scottish Education Department, Educational Building Note 14, relate to kitchens of various capacities designed to produce two-course midday meals five days a week, using modular equipment. An analysis of areas gives the following figures:

Capacity of kitchen	*Area per meal*
75	0·44 m^2
150	0·28 m^2
250	0·28 m^2
400	0·24 m^2
600	0·24 m^2
1000	0·205 m^2

Finishing kitchens

These are kitchens in which prepared frozen foods and other convenience foods predominate. The Electricity Council published a series of design studies in *Finishing Kitchen Planning Guide*, 1977, which gives an average figure per meal of about 0·28 m^2. (These figures relate to meals being served over a two-hour period with a maximum of three oven cycles, that is, three batches of food regenerated in the ovens.)

Cook-freeze production kitchens

Although quick freezing can be used in small catering operations, cook-freeze production units are often on a large scale. Three design studies of production units described and analysed in *Freeze Production Catering Unit Design Guide* by David Taylor (Electricity Council, 1975) give the following figures:

Meals per day	*m^2*	*m^2 per 1,000 meals*
A. 5000	557	111
B. 2500	242	97
C. 1000	168	168
D. 500	132	264

In looking at these areas it is essential to know what the meals figures are based upon, since the prime figure is the weight of food to be frozen per day. The number of meals is calculated on the basis that two portions of frozen food with an average weight of 170 g each will form part of each meal, and that these will be supplemented by commercially-produced foods. The outputs relate to an eight-hour working day. The weight of frozen foods the units are designed to produce per day are: A, 1701 kg; B, 850 kg; C, 340 kg; D, 170 kg. It is interesting to note that in this particular group of designs the largest unit does not give the most economical figure for floor area.

The design studies give a breakdown of the total area, and the following table is extracted from this information:

TABLE 1: Cook-freeze units of various capacities: percentage of total space required for main operational areas

Description	Capacity of cook-freeze production unit in kg of frozen food per day 1701	850	340	170
	Percentage of total space			
Storage of raw food	11·5	10·0	16·0	10·5
Production preparation:				
(a) before portioning and packing (pre-freezing)	27·5	21·6	23·0	28·0
(b) portioning and packing (pre-freezing)	10·0	8·6	10·0	8·5
Food preservation:				
(a) pre-cooking and/or pre-freezing holding	3·5	3·0	4·0	3·8
(b) cold storage (– 20°C or lower)	20·0	24·4	14·0	12·6
Final packing, etc.	10·0	8·6	8·0	10·6
General storage space (including packing materials and equipment)	7·5	6·6	6·0	5·0
Office and staff facilities	10·0	17·2	19·0	21·0
Totals	100	100	100	100

Figure 8 shows general space requirements in freeze production units expressed as a graph, and Table 2 gives optimum space requirements for various sections of units expressed as a percentage of total area. (Both figure and table are taken from *Freeze Production Catering Unit Design Guide*.)

TABLE 2: Optimum space requirements for a freeze production unit (% of total)

Section	*Description*	% *requirement of total area*
Raw material storage and preparation	1 Perishable meat and fish storage (5°C) including the preparation area	2
	2 General chill storage (5°C)	2
	3 Vegetable storage including preparation	4
	4 Dry goods storage	3·5
Main cooking and preparation area	5 Cooking equipment and food handling for product preparation	25
	6 Portioning and packaging, pre-freezing	10
Preservation	7 Pre-cooling/holding facility, pre-freezing	1·5
	8 Freezing (air blast at −35°C)	2
	9 Cold storage (−20°C)	20*
Final packaging, coding and distribution	10 General space requirements for handling frozen products during transfer into or out of cold storage	10
General storage space	11 Carton and general non-food goods storage	10
Office and staff facilities	12 Supervision 13 Cloakrooms 14 Staff space	10
	Total	100

* Based on the storage of a minimum of 10 day's production capacity with a maximum storage factor of 128 kg/m^3

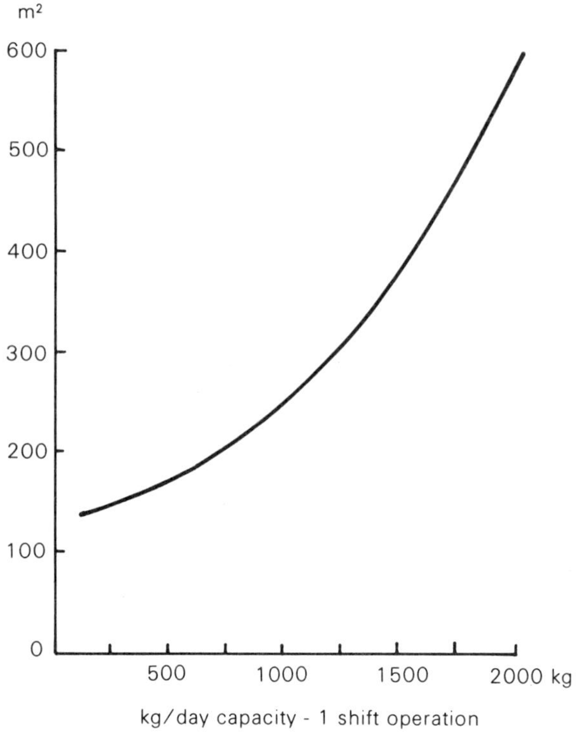

Fig. 8 General space requirements in freeze-production units (From *Freeze Production Catering Unit Design Guide*, Electricity Council, 1975)

Chapter 5

Kitchen design: General considerations

The design team

The design of a kitchen involves many considerations of a complicated and sometimes conflicting nature. It is essential to consider the functions and integration of various areas of the kitchen when plans are first drawn up, and to decide how various priorities may best be met. Many experts work together with the architect and catering specialist when a kitchen is being planned.

Large organisations employ their own catering experts in this field, part of whose job it is to keep abreast of material available from research and experiment, and of changes in the design and function of equipment. The catering expert should know also whom to consult for further information and guidance. An alternative to employing one's own expert is to engage a consultant, or it may be that an outside consultant will work side by side with the organisation's own expert. Consultancy services are available from the following: firms of kitchen planning consultants; the Electricity Council; the British Gas Corporation through the British Gas Commercial Kitchen Design Service; and some firms of equipment manufacturers. In the latter case the client is committed to buying most of the equipment from the firm concerned. The advantages of engaging outside consultants are that they are in an ideal position to keep in touch with the latest developments, they often have considerable resources, and they may employ architects and equipment engineers as well as catering experts. A disadvantage is that they do not necessarily understand the client's needs as well as might a person working inside the organisation—and the client does not always remove this disadvantage by making his needs absolutely clear. Some consultants not only offer services at the design stage, but also act as advisers when the kitchen is first opened, and this helps to ensure that the system is operated as planned, and that management is steered through some of the difficulties of the opening period.

Aims in kitchen planning

There are four main aims in kitchen planning, and the first three are to a large extent interrelated. These are:

1. Economy of time of operation
2. Economy of effort
3. Minimisation of cost
4. Minimisation of hygiene hazards.

It is unnecessary to enlarge upon these aims, for they are axiomatic, but from time to time one sees kitchens that fall far short of them. There are, of course, many influencing factors, some of which are not concerned with the layout, and others only partly concerned. In this latter group are choice and design of equipment and the provision of labour-saving devices, and these will be dealt with in later chapters. Here we shall deal with broad considerations.

The flow of work

A kitchen is like a factory in that materials—usually in a raw state—are received, processed and converted into a finished product. In the kitchen, as in the factory, raw materials enter at various points at one end of the building and pass along smoothly, ideally always proceeding nearer to the final point where the finished product is assembled and prepared for delivery to the customer. In the case of the kitchen, the final product reaches the dining room (or despatch area) as an assembly of various components that have travelled along different lines of progress through the various processes. If the kitchen is well planned, it will normally be the case that each time the material is moved it progresses towards the final assembly point—the serving counter or despatch point. In a factory, where several lines of production converge on one final point, it is important that these lines should not cross each other, for if they do loss of efficiency will result; this is equally true in the case of a kitchen. However, in kitchen planning difficulties arise because some pieces of equipment are used in more than one production line. Figure 11 shows some typical lines of progress in a kitchen, and indicates which items of equipment are used in more than one line. From this it is evident that complete separation of lines is not always possible without an expensive duplication of certain items. Even so, the use of common equipment must not interfere with the general lines of flow, and it is here that the planner's ingenuity is taxed. The placing of each item of equipment must be carefully considered so that maximum convenience may be obtained for all possible uses.

The work-flow diagram

Because the flow of work is fundamental to the design of a kitchen, a first step in planning the layout is to prepare a diagram showing this,

Fig. 9 First step in planning a kitchen is to prepare a flow diagram. Shows flow lines in typical conventional kitchen

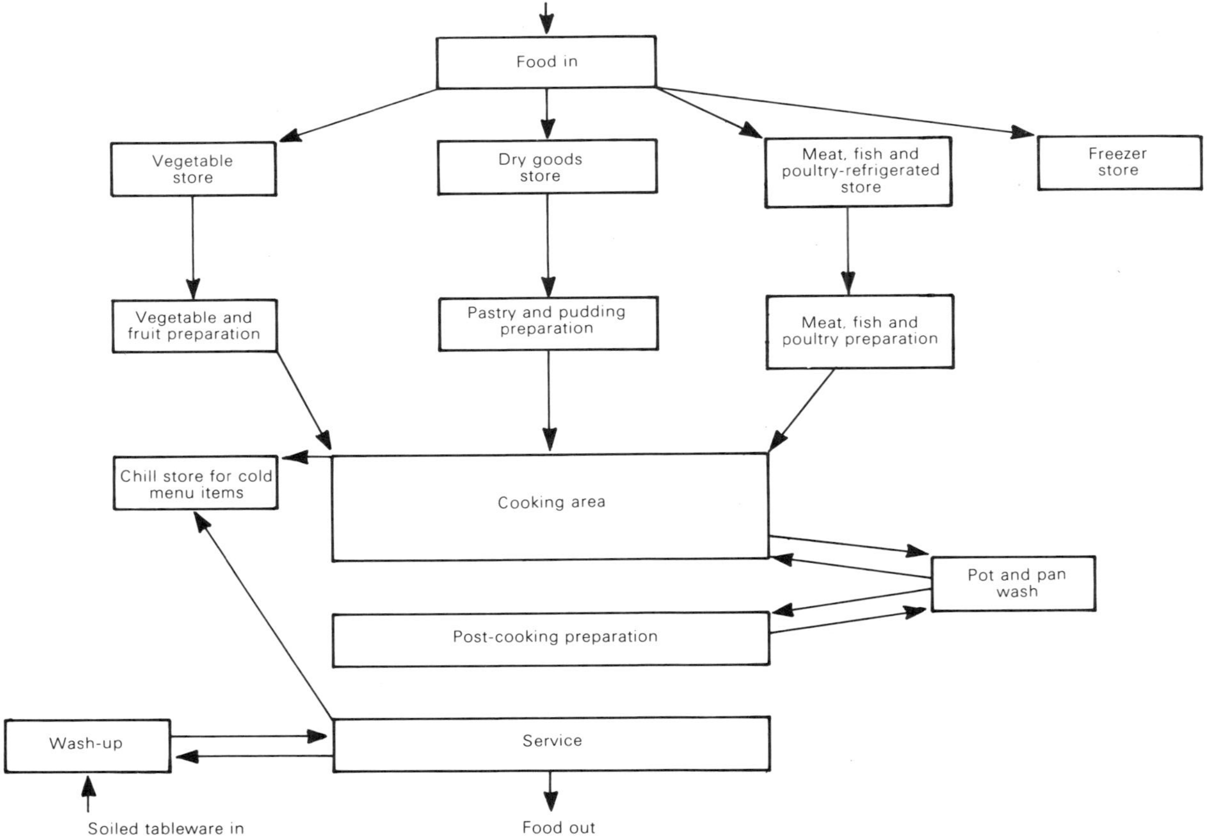

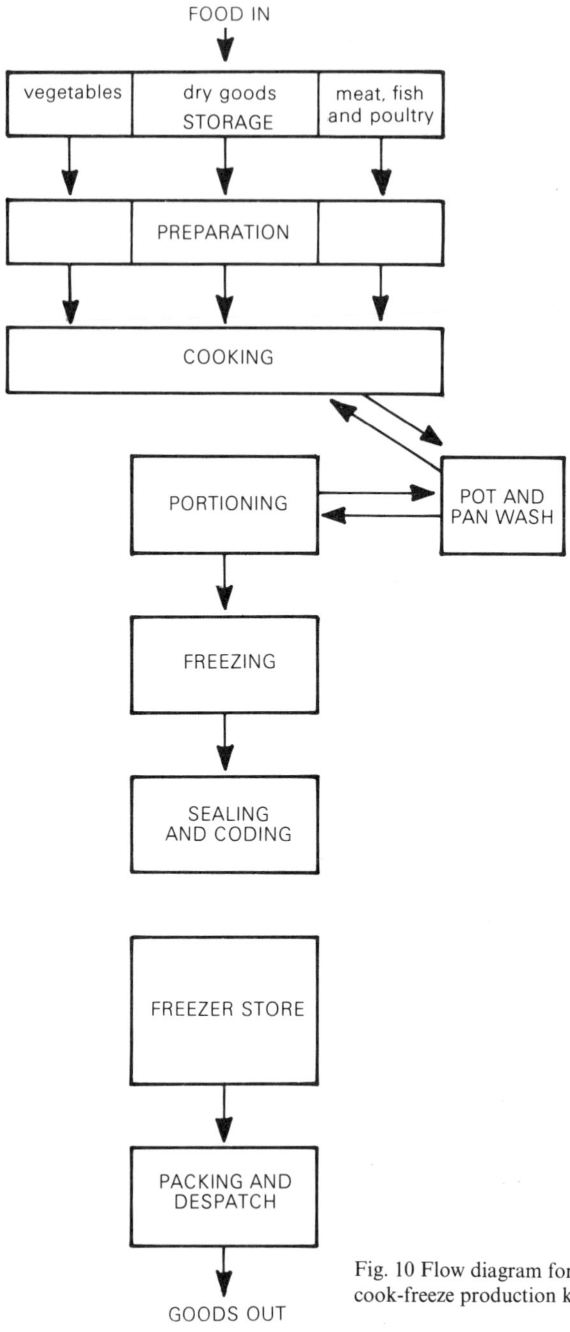

Fig. 10 Flow diagram for cook-freeze production kitchen

and indicating the relationships between the various areas. Figure 9 shows this for a conventional kitchen, while Figure 10 relates to a cook-freeze production kitchen. From these it will be seen that between some areas the flow is always forward; in others, chiefly where equipment is concerned, there is a return flow. The point has already been made that areas between which many journeys are to be made should be placed close together, and this applies even where quantities to be moved are small. (There are, however, ways of reducing the number of journeys, for example by the use of trolleys, or of eliminating them, for example by the use of conveyor belts—see Figure 23b). Where traffic between two areas is infrequent, even though the quantities to be moved may be large, propinquity is less important.

Lines of progress

Let us now consider in some detail the various lines of progress that one finds in a typical kitchen.

Goods reception

The starting point is, of course, the entrance where the goods are delivered. It is advisable to have one central receiving point where goods can be checked, and weighed if appropriate, before they are stored or used. One possible exception to this is vegetables, where it can be an advantage to have a direct entrance into the store, thus avoiding the carrying of sacks and crates inside the building. This means arranging for the vegetable store, as well as the main goods entrance, to open on to an area where delivery vans can unload. If the storekeeper, or whoever is responsible for checking deliveries, has an office, it should be near the goods entrance, and should preferably have a viewing window overlooking it.

Preparation and cooking area

Between the areas for preparation and cooking, movement will be mainly from the preparation bench to the cooking equipment. After cooking, the food will then go either direct to the service area or to a preparation area for final preparation—for example, slicing, portioning, garnishing. A better work flow is usually achieved if there are separate facilities for post-cooking preparation, and this is desirable, too, on hygiene grounds (see Chapter 23). The location of working surfaces in relation to items of equipment is important. It is an advantage to have a horizontal surface close to each piece of cooking equipment, but this need not be fixed, and in a large kitchen it would be impossible to have so many fixtures. More usually trolleys are used, many having been designed specifically for the purpose of loading and unloading ovens. The layout should be planned so that these trolleys may be used without impeding the flow of traffic, and parking space should be allocated.

The servery and the wash-up area

The service area (and also the dish-washing section) need considerable attention at the early stages of planning. Its position must be carefully related to the dining room as well as to the kitchen. In the case of self-service there must be suitable routes to and from the servery area, and cross-traffic is to be avoided. It is usually necessary to have some checkpoint at either the entrance to or the exit from the service area at the clients' side to ensure that:

(a) clients are identified as being entitled to a meal;

and/or

(b) they make any necessary payment to the cashier.

The siting of the dish-washing area, which must be related to both servery and dining room, is also critical. While it is best if it is immediately adjacent to the dining area, diners will not wish to see the interior while they are eating their meals; nor should noise from it cause a nuisance. If used tableware is to be collected continuously while meals are being served, the line of traffic to the wash-up should not cross lines to and from the service area. Where there are several dining rooms served from one kitchen, the question arises as to whether there should be several small washing-up units or one central area. If it is decided to have a central system with sophisticated machinery, trolleys or moving belts are likely to be needed to carry crockery and cutlery to and fro.

In hospitals food is likely to be served on several floors, when lifts or vertical conveyors are used for transport, and these must be conveniently placed. Where trolleys are used, their entire route must be such that that there are no steps and no steep ramps.

Sequence of arrangement of equipment

Figure 11 shows the main sections of work and the general items of large equipment needed in a typical kitchen for each section of work. To achieve an orderly flow of work, it is necessary to arrange this equipment in sequence. Figures 12, 13 and 14 show how this can be done in some sections, although, as we have seen, it is more difficult to arrange equipment in an ideal way when each section has to be integrated with the whole.

Vegetable preparation section. Figure 12 shows a layout for a vegetable store and preparation section. Goods can be delivered direct into the store, where sacks of potatoes and root vegetables are stacked on slatted floor racks, and green vegetables and salad items are on tiered mobile racks. Potatoes and other root vegetables which can be peeled by machine go from store into the potato peeler, which

KITCHEN FLOW CHART SHOWING ALSO EQUIPMENT USED

VEGETABLES	MEAT	FISH	SWEETS	TABLEWARE
Store	Refrigerator or Larder	Refrigerator	Dry Store	Store or shelves
Machine	*Mincer*	Slab	Refrigerator	*Hot cupboard* *Service Counter* Wash up
			Fruit and vegetable store	
Sinks	Prep. Table	Sink		
Shredder	Sink	Table	Ingredient cupboard	Store
Boiler	Slicing Machine	*Oven*	Preparation table	
Steamer	*Oven*	*Steamer*	*Mixer*	
Oven	*Boiler*	*Fish Fryer*	*Oven*	
Fish Fryer	*Steamer*	*Grill*	*Steamer*	
		Hot cupboard / *Tins and pan sink*		
Mixer	*Grill*		*Double boiler*	
Hot Cupboard	*Hot cupboard* / *Tins and pan sink*		*Hot cupboard* or *chill store* / *Pan sink*	
Service Counter	*Service Counter*	*Service Counter*	*Service Counter*	

Italics indicate equipment used in more than one line of progress.

Fig. 11 Kitchen flow chart showing equipment used

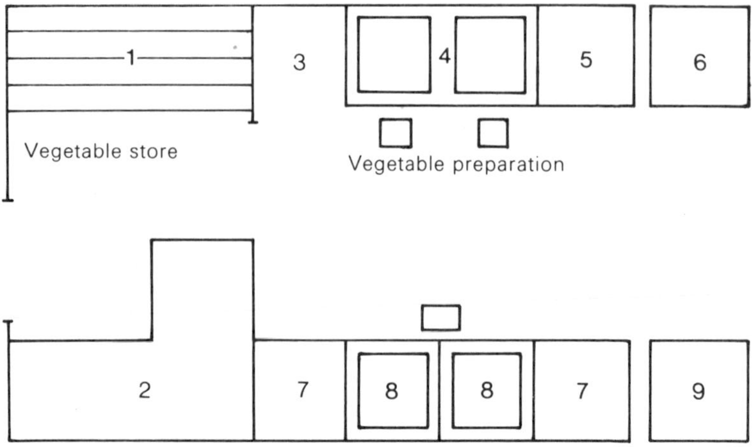

1 Slatted racks for potatoes and root vegetables
2 Mobile racks for green vegetables, salads, and fruit
3 Potato peeling machine
4 Twin sinks for preparation of potatoes and root vegetables
5 Mobile sinks
6 Potato chipping machine
7 Drainer
8 Sink for preparation of green vegetables etc.
9 Vegetable preparation machine

Fig. 12 Vegetable preparation section: arrangement of equipment in sequence

is so placed that the peeled vegetables are delivered directly into the sink for eyeing and any further trimming that may be necessary. When this process has been completed the vegetables are put into a mobile sink, by which means they are taken to the equipment in the cooking area (boiler, steaming oven, fryer, etc.). Where potatoes are to be chipped, this is done in the vegetable section using the chipping machine adjacent to the mobile sinks. Provision is made for the preparation of green vegetables on the opposite side of the section. A drainer provides a working surface for preliminary preparation work before washing, which is carried out in an adjacent pair of sinks, and the second drainer provides a further working surface for any preparation needed after washing. The adjacent vegetable preparation machine is used for shredding and slicing, and it should be noted that this will be used also for the slicing, dicing, etc., of root vegetables. Then prepared green vegetables are trolleyed to the cooking section, and prepared salad items to the final preparation area. It will be seen that up to the cooking stage this section is completely self-contained, but this would not necessarily be so if there were no vegetable preparation machine. In a smaller kitchen, instead of there being either a vegetable preparation machine or a chipper, attachments to the electric mixer might be used for these purposes, and the work-flow might then be rather less smooth.

Pastry preparation section. Figure 13 shows an arrangement for a pastry preparation area. Goods are collected from the dry store and cold store by trolley. The trolley, with its load of weighed ingredients, is parked next to the electric mixer, and post-mixing operations (rolling out, portioning, etc.) are carried out on the adjacent bench. Prepared foods then go to the cooking area, and the washing up to the cooks' sink.

The wash-up section. A layout for a wash-up section where the operation is manual is shown in Figure 14, but this would be suitable also for a dishwasher of the brush type, where plates are washed by means of mechanically-operated brushes in the washing sinks. The sequence of operations is as follows:

1. Soiled tableware is received at the hatch, where it is stripped and stacked, and then moved to one of the two adjacent drainers.
2. Items are washed in the first sink in the unit, placed in racks and immersed in the second sink for rinsing.
3. The racks of plates, etc., are then placed in sequence on the second drainer until the contents are dry.
4. Tableware is removed from the racks and carried by trolley to the service area, where it is stored.

A typical sequence of equipment where a dishwashing machine is used is shown in Figure 15. Here the soiled crockery is trolleyed into the wash-up area, after which the sequence is as follows:

1. Soiled ware and trays are removed from the trolleys, sorted and scraped. Operators scrape plates into a wide trough that is connected to a waste disposal unit. Cutlery is soaked, and items not to be washed immediately are stacked on the overshelf, except for trays, which go on the tray trolley.
2. After sorting and scraping, soiled tableware goes through the dishwasher.
3. Clean ware leaves the dishwasher, dries in the air and is stacked on trolleys for return to the service area.

It will be seen that the sequence here is similar to that shown in Figure 14. Where a flight-around dishwasher is used the arrangement is slightly different in that the machine may be loaded and unloaded at the same point (see Figure 16). It is important to note the considerable amount of ancillary equipment that is needed for large-scale dishwashing operations, and this must be fitted carefully into the layout.

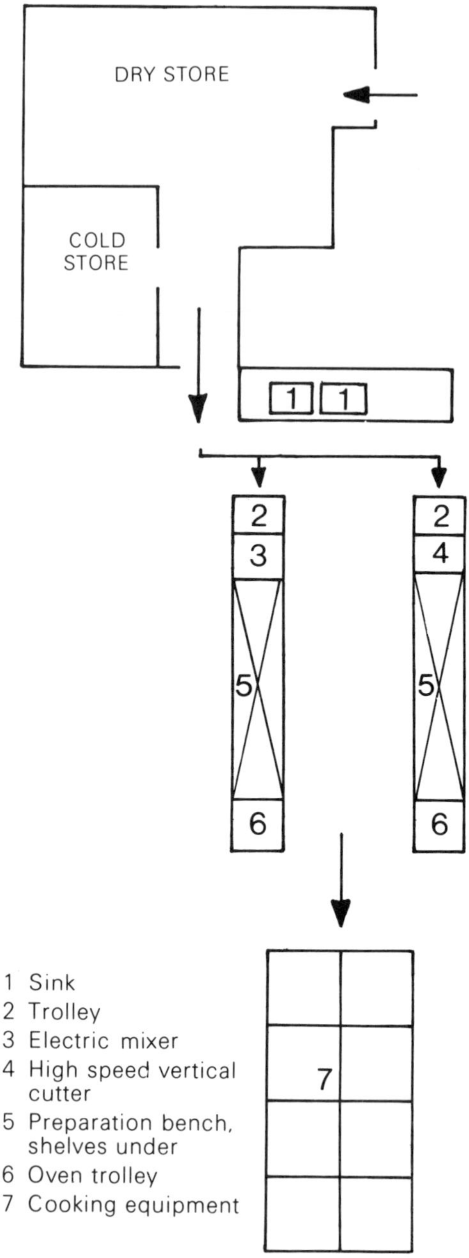

Fig. 13 Pastry preparation section: arrangement of equipment in sequence

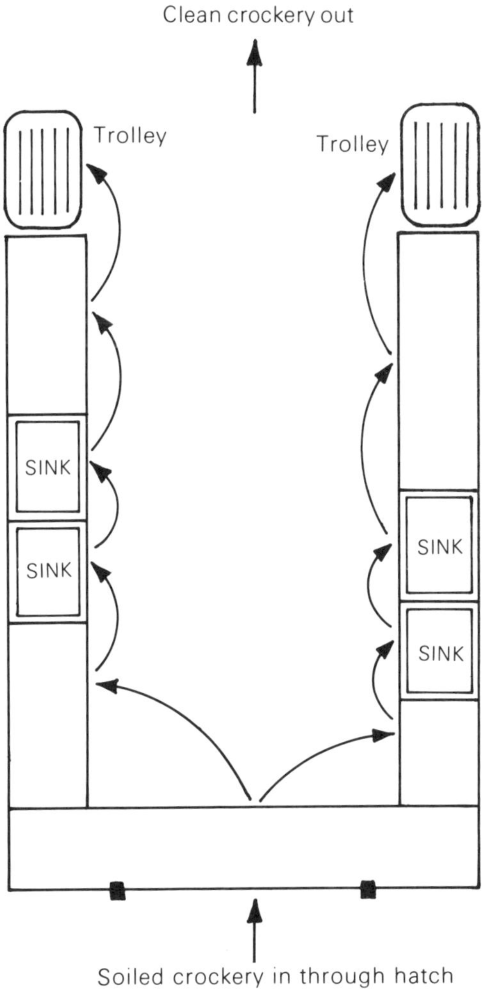

Fig. 14 Washing-up area fitted with 2 units each consisting of twin sinks. Soiled crockery enters washing-up area through hatch, and progresses through washing and rinsing sinks. Clean crockery is carried on trolleys out of washing-up area back to servery

The service area. It was appropriate to discuss types of serving arrangement in Chapter 4 because this determined to a great extent the area needed. Where the self-service counter is concerned, the sequence of equipment relates partly to the order in which the client likes to select his food, and he usually prefers to choose his main dish first. But there is also the question of the flow of items from the kitchen, and the convenient arrangement of heated sections of the counter. Cold items of a meal are often assembled in the same area of the kitchen. Hence a usual sequence in a linear service counter is as

Fig. 15 Washing-up area planned round flight-type dishwasher. Soiled crockery is removed from trolleys and prepared for dishwasher. Flight-type machine needs no baskets (except for cutlery), and crockery is loaded directly on to moving belt, which has pegs to hold it in place. After it has left machine it is air-dried, and is ready for stacking by time it reaches second operator. Clean tableware is carried on trolleys into service area

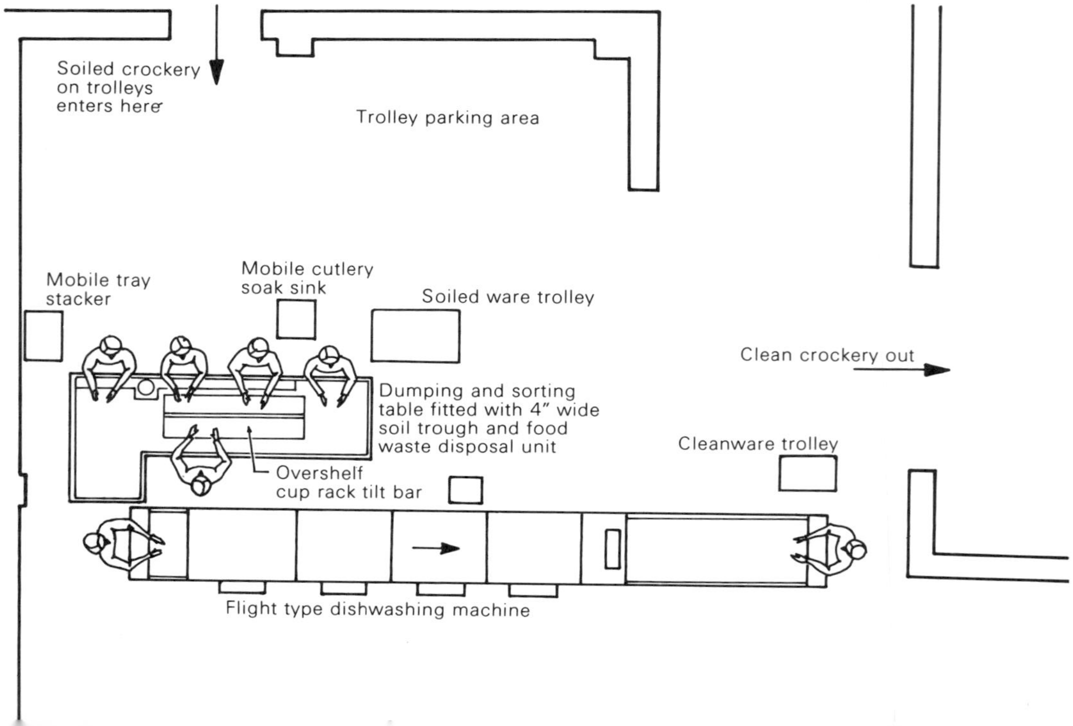

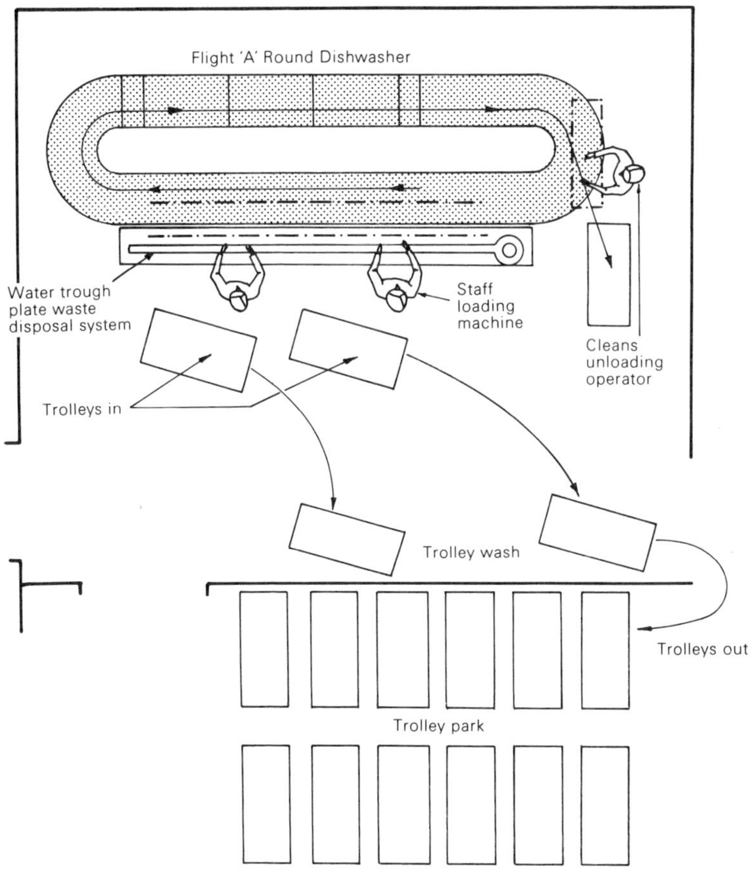

Fig. 16 Washing-up area with flight-around dishwasher. General arrangement here is similar to Figure 15, but dishes make complete circuit, thus saving space

follows: hot main course dishes; vegetables; sauces and soups; hot puddings; cold items; and beverages. The counter is arranged accordingly (see Figure 2). Where, for any reason, it is necessary or desirable to have two counters, a good flow of operations is achieved if the counters are placed back to back with an adequate space in between to accommodate serving staff. Food then enters the serving area at one point and is dispersed to either side. Where arrangement of hot and cold counters in a free-flow system is concerned (Figure 3a–b), similar considerations apply; heated counters for serving main dishes are best placed near the entrance area. The carousel method of serving (see Figure 4) involves all production lines converging into a relatively small area, and this is best achieved by the use of trolleys.

The relation of ancillary rooms to the main kitchen

The need for a smooth flow of materials through the processes of delivery, reception, checking, weighing, storage and issue of stores, preparation, cooking and serving has already been discussed, and it has a bearing upon the siting of some of the ancillary rooms.

The dry goods store

There are two points for consideration here:

1. It should be as near as possible to the reception area of the kitchen in order to avoid transporting goods a long distance either within the building or from an outside store. Trucking and trolleying take time and energy, and so add to costs. If goods are left unattended while they await transport there is the possibility of pilfering; also, the conditions under which they are left may be unhygienic. Although, as has already been said, short journeys are less important where movement of food is comparatively infrequent, it is an advantage to keep journeys as short as possible.

2. The store should be as near as possible to the part of the kitchen where the main bulk of its contents will be used. Although certain items may be issued to a subsidiary store within the kitchen, the general system is for the principal goods to be issued daily from the main store. Since these goods may be both bulky and heavy, it is desirable that they should be carried or trolleyed for the shortest possible distance.

Cooling rooms

In many kitchens there is a need for a cooling room where cooked food that is to be served cold may be cooled rapidly before it is transferred to the service area or refrigerator. (The Food Hygiene [General] Regulations, 1970, require that cooked or partly cooked food shall either be kept at a temperature of not less than 62·7° Celsius until it is required for serving for immediate consumption, or be cooled to a temperature below 10° Celsius as quickly as reasonably practicable.) This room, which is often kept cool by mechanical means, should be conveniently near to the cooking area and also to the servery, since it will occasionally happen that there will be some unserved food that could be served cold at a later meal, and therefore needs rapid cooling.

Refrigerators, chill rooms and freezer stores

A chill room may be used not only for keeping foods cold but also for chilling cooked foods. Hence, if it is the only refrigerator facility, it should be conveniently placed with regard to the goods entrance, the meat and poultry preparation area and the cooking and service sections, in that order. Where there is no chill room, it is better to have two refrigerators, because this makes it easier to ensure that cooked foods are kept away from raw foods, which is an essential hygiene requirement. The refrigerator allocated for raw foods should be near the reception area, away from the flow lines of 'dirty' foods such as unprepared vegetables, and handy for the meat and poultry preparation section. In those large kitchens where it is the practice to carry out butchering operations there may be separate sections for meat and fish, in which case each will have its own refrigerator or chill store. A useful arrangement is to have the chill room with goods-in and goods-out doors. Access to the chill room can then be direct from both delivery and preparation areas.

When manufactured frozen foods are used, a freezer storage unit (either free-standing or built-in) will be needed and may also be necessary for storing raw frozen foods such as meat, poultry and fish. Siting considerations here are similar to those applying to the refrigerator, but as it is likely to be opened far less often its position would have a lower priority. In cook-freeze production kitchens the deep-freeze stores lead directly off the post-freeze packing and/or assembly areas, and they are also near the goods-outwards section (see Figure 19). In some layouts it is an advantage to have goods-in and goods-out doors in the freezer store. Other points on the location of refrigerators are referred to in Chapter 11.

The supervisor's office

A good position for the office is one that allows a view of the general work of the kitchen, and also of the goods entrance area. It should also give some degree of privacy, because it is part of the supervisor's duties to interview staff and visitors. There may be a conflict between the first two and the last requirements, in which case the use of blinds, curtains or one-way glass may help.

Staff facilities

Lavatories and cloakrooms should be near the staff entrance, so that staff may leave their outdoor wear, don protective clothing, wash their hands and attend to their appearance before they enter food preparation areas. In addition to the wash basins located near the w.c.s, at least one basin should be available in the kitchen area for use during the course of work. The architect usually finds it convenient to arrange staff dining rooms and rest rooms *en suite* with cloakroom facilities, but this is not essential provided that they are reasonably near the kitchen.

Location of ancillary rooms in relation to kitchen windows

One general point arises in the location of ancillary rooms. Since these rooms are usually placed on the outside of the building for the sake of natural lighting and ventilation, it can happen that they occupy almost all the outside space available to the catering premises, leaving the main kitchen area hemmed in. Provided that the kitchen is either a single-storey building or is on the top floor, this does not mean that natural lighting and ventilation are precluded, because, as already stated, if the surrounding rooms are less lofty than the kitchen, clerestory windows and domed overhead lighting may be used to give both cross-ventilation and natural lighting in the kitchen. But it does mean that working conditions are less pleasant than they might be. It follows that it is desirable for the ancillary rooms to be arranged so that it is possible to provide viewing windows in the kitchen.

The placing of equipment

Although it is true that the flow of work is the main factor to bear in mind when deciding upon the general position of equipment, often there is a choice of two or more places where any piece could be fixed, each being more or less equally acceptable in relation to the general flow of work. The following points may have a bearing on the final choice:

1. *Cost and availability of services*

Cooking equipment must be connected with one or more services, and the main part of the fitting cost arises from the work of laying on and connecting the appropriate services. Thus, when boiling pans are fitted either gas, electricity or live steam is needed for heating; hot and cold water are necessary for the cooking process and for cleaning; drainage is needed for the easy removal of waste liquids. It is therefore common practice to locate all boiling pans together in order to minimise the cost of laying on services. In the case of boiling pans that are used solely for cooking vegetables this arrangement is satisfactory, but, if certain pans are used for milk puddings and sauces, it may not be convenient to have them in the vegetable cookery section. A choice then has to be made between cost and convenience. Siting roasting ovens presents fewer problems, because water and drainage are not needed, and it is only a question of providing a source of heat energy. Hence, if it is convenient to have ovens apart from each other to serve different sections of the kitchen (*e.g.*, pastry and meat), usually no significant extra costs are involved.

2. *Lighting*

Equipment should be fitted so as to gain best advantage from natural light. Ovens should be so placed that the state of the food in them may be easily seen when doors are opened. This will not be so if ovens are placed with their backs to the window, or if the doors of high-level ovens cut out the light when they are opened. However, if the ovens are fitted with internal lights no difficulty arises, and drop-down oven doors eliminate the latter problem. In the case of boiling pans with hinged lids, they should be located so that the lids do not cut off the available light when they are raised. Good natural light is needed also on sinks and work benches, which should be positioned accordingly. So far as artificial light is concerned, this is installed to suit the layout, and not *vice versa.*

3. *Different ways of grouping equipment*

In general there are two standard ways of placing equipment: in the first, equipment is placed along the walls, and work tables and benches occupy the middle of the floor; in the second, equipment is arranged in one or more banks in the centre space, and work tables and benches go against the walls or are fitted in bays. The banks may consist of single lines of appliances, or they may form a hollow square or rectangle with space for service pipes and for cleaning in the centre, or, in the case of modular equipment, items may be fitted back-to-back with a void for services (see Figure 1b). We shall look at the pros and cons of the two methods of arrangement.

Usually the work and cost entailed in laying the necessary services to cooking equipment are least if it is sited along the walls. All pipes may be run along the floor, or at a higher level, and the waste channels will usually have shorter runs before reaching the main outside drainage. Ventilation and temperature control may be simpler because of the natural outlets for steam and combustion products through adjacent windows. (But this is not invariably so, and outside air currents may blow steam back into the kitchen.) However, extractor fans—and possibly hoods—will be needed except where the items installed do not produce much steam.

With points of considerable weight in favour of having equipment against the wall, why is it that kitchen planners tend to favour central placing? There are three main reasons. The first is economy in floor space. In a large kitchen where all equipment is fitted in single lines against the walls, a great length of wall is needed, and, unless the kitchen is long and narrow, the necessary amount of wall space is not available. The second is concerned with planning to effect an easy flow of work. Figure 17 shows a working table for a pastrycook with two possible positions for the two ovens he will use. Either position would be convenient, and could be arranged to follow the natural flow of work. But, when one considers the steps the cook will take each time the oven is attended, it is clear that position CI is the better. This illustration simplifies the problem, but when planning a layout it is usually found that the various sections of work can be grouped more easily where equipment is arranged in central banks. In very

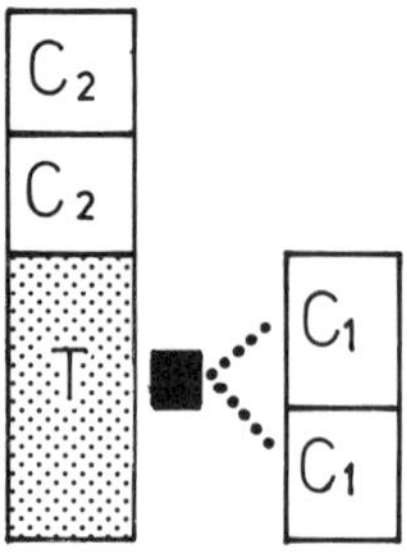

Fig. 17 Two arrangements for cookers near work table, allowing good flow of work between cookers and table. Cook will take fewer steps with Arrangement 1

large kitchens there may be several banks lined up precisely with the various preparation areas. Such an arrangement is indicated where continuous cooking equipment is concerned (see Figure 23a).

The third point relates to the position of the work benches. Positions near the wall usually offer more comfortable conditions for staff. This is mainly because of the light and air available, but there is also the advantage of being nearer to a view of the outside, which is usually more pleasant than the one in the centre of a large area. In a small kitchen, however, the cook may prefer to operate from a central position where he has the whole kitchen in view.

A further reason against installing equipment against the wall is that difficulties may arise about cleaning, but, as will be seen in the next paragraph, this depends very much upon the equipment chosen.

4. *Accessibility for cleaning*

Equipment should be fitted so that the cleaning of walls, floors, nearby pipes and the equipment itself, may be readily carried out. If cookers and other equipment are fitted too close together the result may be that it is not possible to clean either the narrow area of floor between them or the sides of the equipment itself. Similarly, when equipment is fitted close to a wall, it may be impossible to clean the area at the back, while in the case of pieces of equipment installed in a rectangular block there may be insufficient access to the area of floor and piping in the middle. These difficulties do not arise where modular equipment of the type illustrated in Figure 1 is shown, because special jointing arrangements allow them to be fitted side by side with no intervening gap, and, as we have seen, voids at the back for services enable them to be fitted back-to-back or flush against the wall. Other equipment is designed to allow it to be pulled out on rollers when necessary for cleaning. The question of access for cleaning must be considered in the early stages of planning so that, where necessary, space is allowed for access for cleaning. A suitable space between items that do not fit flush is 300 mm.

5. *Circulation areas*

In placing equipment and planning the layout, it is essential to leave enough space between items to allow adequate circulation space. Main walkways should not be narrower than 1·6 m. If, however, there is a work station situated on the walkway, or if equipment opens on to it, a greater width—a minimum of 2·2 m—is needed to avoid congestion and safety hazards. The minimum width of walkway is usually taken as 0·77 m. In deciding upon the width, account should be taken of the dimensions of trolleys to be used and the degrees through which they will have to turn.

6. *Dimensions of working surfaces*

It is crucial to the comfort and efficiency of operators that the heights and depths of working surfaces and equipment are appropriate. This will be discussed in Chapter 16.

Chapter 6

Examples of catering systems and kitchen designs

So far catering systems have been briefly defined, and design considerations have been dealt with in general terms. It is now time to look at some typical examples, and the circumstances in which they developed.

During the last two or three decades there has been a great increase in the number of people taking meals away from home. Much of this has been associated with the provision of catering facilities at schools, universities and other institutions of higher and further education, and at workplaces. Many of these institutions are very large, and hence there is a need to serve large numbers of people in a short time. One way of dealing with large numbers is to break them down into smaller units and to provide separate facilities for each group, but it is generally agreed that a large production unit is usually more economical to run than a series of smaller ones. Several of the examples that follow show different approaches to the question of how to obtain benefits of scale—which have been greatly enhanced by modern technology—and yet maintain speed of service and a high-quality end product. Each relates to a different type of circumstance.

The following are central points in some of the methods described:

1. The divorce of preparation and cooking from the service of the meal that is possible when either cook-freeze or cook-chill systems are used. This enables food to be served to small groups while gaining the advantages of large-scale production. Moreover, because production is not affected by mealtime peak demand, production can be planned in a completely logical way to make the best use of equipment and staff.

2. The use of a conveyor belt in kitchen, servery and wash-up areas to minimise staffing requirements and to give a smooth, continuous production flow.

3. The use of manufactured foods so that some of the work previously done in the kitchen now takes place in the factory.

4. The use of disposables to cut down the routine work of washing up and reduce the number of items in transit in the food service chain.

5. The use of the computer in a sophisticated food system.

6. Consideration of the individual's tastes, and medical needs. (The latter point refers particularly to hospitals.)

Example 1: Catering in a hall of residence for 250 students

Students and resident academic staff are catered for on board-residence terms. The method of service for students is cafeteria, and a limited choice of dishes is offered. Waitress service is provided for staff. The dining hall is used for formal and social occasions as well as for the day-to-day service of meals. Conventional methods of preparation and cooking are used, and there is no systematic use of convenience foods. The kitchen layout is shown in Figure 18.

Design features

1. Staff accommodation: a separate entrance is provided for staff, who do not enter the food area until they have prepared themselves for duty. Facilities, which include a shower and a common room, are good.

2. Dry store: this is near the entrance. The distance between the stores and the pastry and pudding preparation section, while greater than the ideal, is not unreasonable, especially as there is adequate space along the walkway for trolleys. The aspect is north-east.

3. Caterer's office: by means of an internal window the caterer has a good general view of the kitchen, and he is reasonably near the goods entrance although he cannot see it from the office.

4. Vegetable store and preparation area: this section is completely separate from the clean area of the kitchen, and the arrangement of doors to this and to the dry stores means that incoming vegetables, which take a very short route to the stores, do not cross the path of goods issued from the dry stores.

5. Preparation areas: separate preparation areas are allocated for meat, pastry and post-cooking operations, so that the possibility of cross-infection between groups of foods at various stages is minimised.

6. Servery: this is at right angles to the dining room, from which it can be shut off by means of twin doors. The arrangement has several advantages: it helps to isolate kitchen and servery noises from the hall; there is no view of kitchen and servery from the body of the hall; and the otherwise-necessary expense of providing shutters along the length of the service counter is saved.

7. Waitress service facilities: access to the staff table in the dining room is through a sliding door. Table appointments and a heated trolley are kept in the small store to which a sliding door on each side gives access.

8. Wash-up area: the route for the return of clean crockery to the

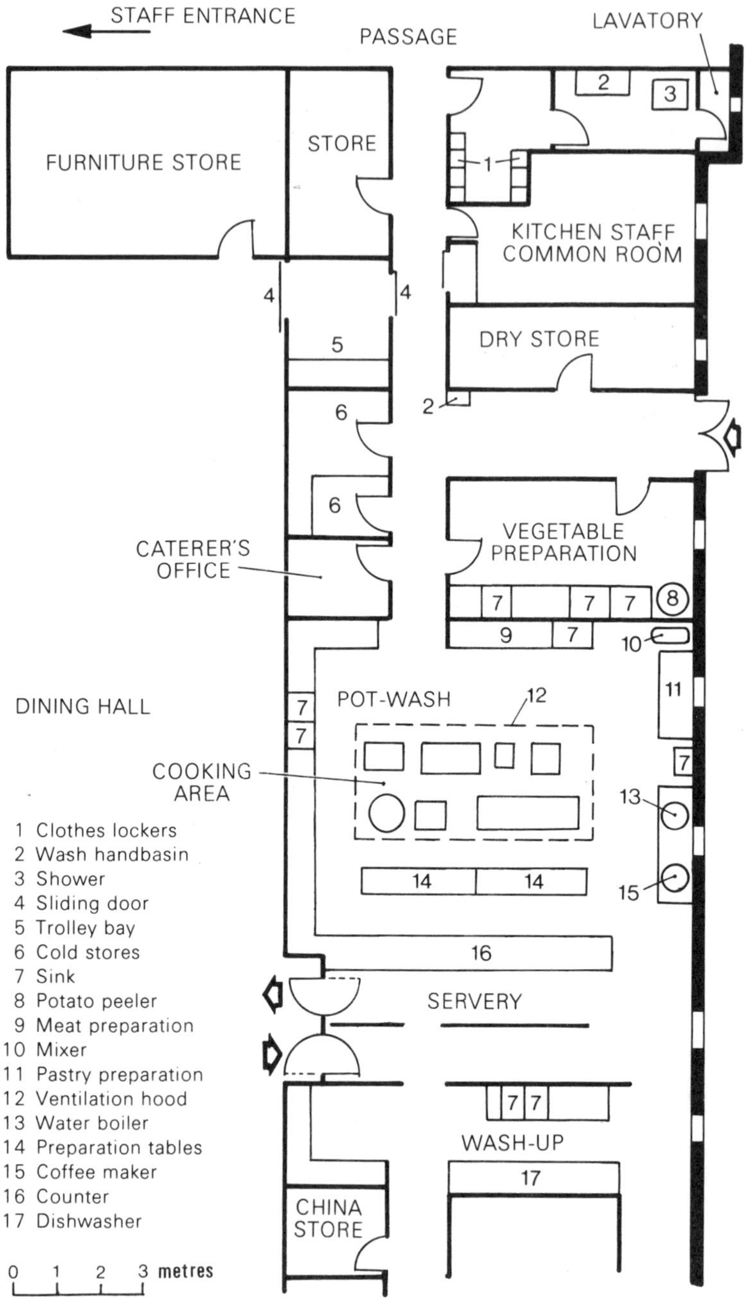

Fig. 18 Kitchen design for hall of residence with 250 students

service area is very convenient. Dirty crockery is not returned to the wash-up until the end of the meal (or, on more formal occasions when there is waitress service, at the end of each course), so that kitchen staff returning used crockery do not impede the progress of students who are collecting meals. Note the provision of sinks as well as the dishwasher for dealing with items of awkward size or shape.

9. Lines of progress: food progresses from store to serving counter in one direction only towards the service counter. Similarly, there is a smooth one-way flow of crockery after use from the dining room to storage areas in the servery. The exceptions to the one-way flow are: food and tableware for meals for the academic staff; cooked food that is taken from the cooking area to the chill store.

10. Natural lighting, ventilation and heating: in addition to the opening viewing windows, there is clerestory lighting above the centre of the kitchen and a roof light over the office. Steam is extracted by means of fans over the cooking area and the washing-up equipment.

Example 2: A cook-freeze system designed to cater for boarding and day pupils at a residential school

The cook-freeze production kitchen has the capacity to produce 3000 meals a day. The school's 800 boarders live in six houses and are provided with three meals each a day: breakfast, midday dinner and high tea. The 800 day pupils have a midday meal from Monday to Friday in the various houses. Meals for resident and non-resident staff are provided also. Other catering activities include conferences and courses held during school holidays, special functions, and meals-on-wheels service for old people. There is a special dining room for meals outside the normal run. Each boarding house and the special dining room has its own finishing kitchen.

The central cook-freeze kitchen (see Figure 19) produces all dishes that can conveniently be blast-frozen. Most vegetables are bought ready frozen. Ten days' supply of frozen food is kept in the cold store at the central kitchen, and other foods for issue to the house kitchens are stored there also. At the finishing kitchens the following are prepared: salads, most breakfast dishes, sauces and beverages.

The following processes take place at the freeze-production kitchen:

1. Food is prepared and cooked by the same methods that would apply in a conventional kitchen. Ready-frozen vegetables go straight to the freezer store.

2. After cooking, the food is portioned and packed as appropriate before it enters the blast freezer.

3. Batches of food are trolleyed into the freezer, which holds four trolleys.

Fig. 19 Cook-freeze production kitchen. Designed to produce 3000 meals (870 kg of frozen food) per 8-hour day. Total area 386 m²

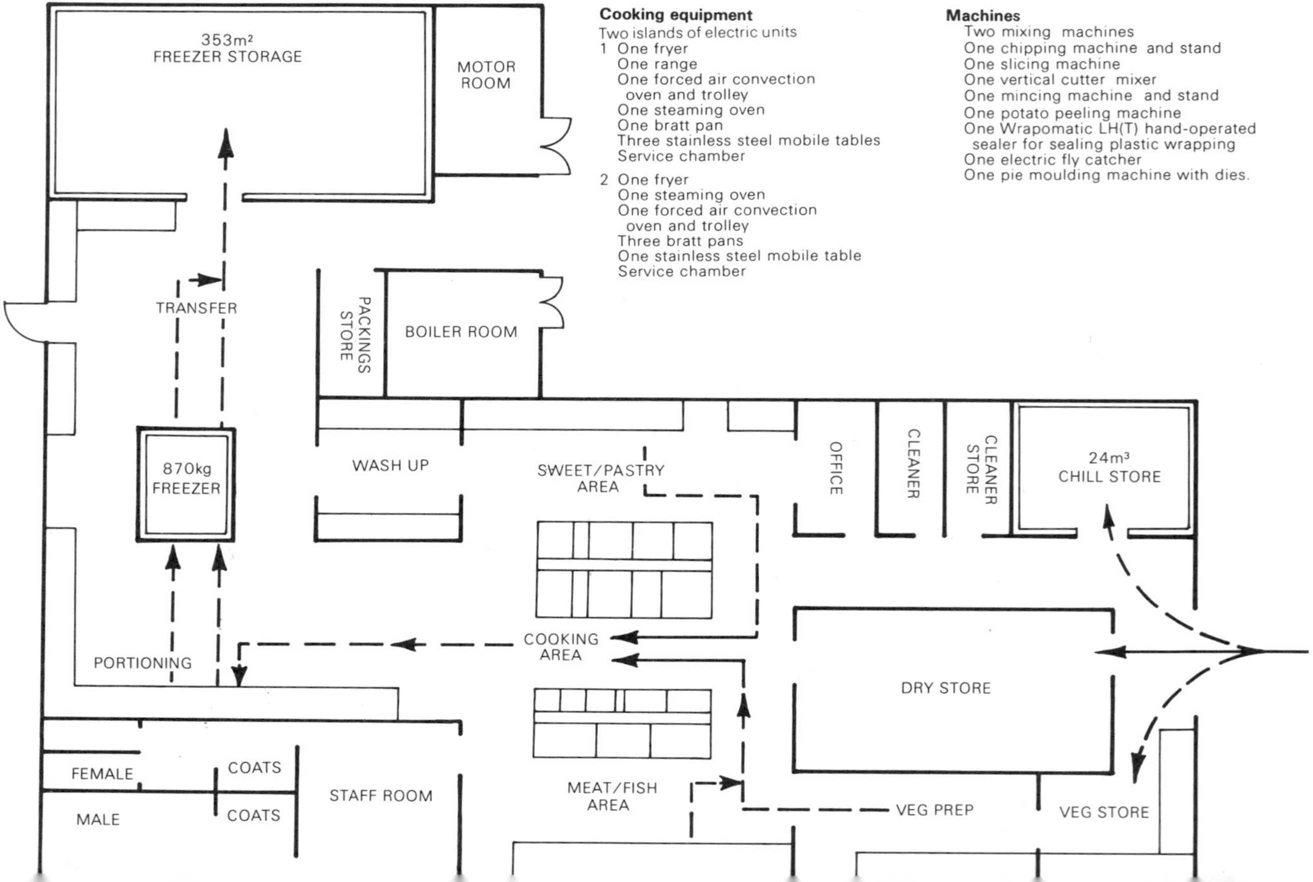

Cooking equipment

Two islands of electric units

1 One fryer
One range
One forced air convection oven and trolley
One steaming oven
One bratt pan
Three stainless steel mobile tables
Service chamber

2 One fryer
One steaming oven
One forced air convection oven and trolley
Three bratt pans
One stainless steel mobile table
Service chamber

Machines

Two mixing machines
One chipping machine and stand
One slicing machine
One vertical cutter mixer
One mincing machine and stand
One potato peeling machine
One Wrapomatic LH(T) hand-operated sealer for sealing plastic wrapping
One electric fly catcher
One pie moulding machine with dies.

4. After freezing further packing takes place if necessary, and packages are labelled and coded.

5. Food enters the freezer store (temperature −20° Celsius), where it stays for a maximum of six weeks.

6. Finally, food is transferred twice a week from the freezer store to the finishing kitchens, which have their own small freezer stores.

At the finishing kitchens, dishes from the central kitchen are supplemented as necessary to produce complete meals, and end-cooking of the frozen dishes takes place in forced convection ovens. The end-cooking process consists of reheating in the case of dishes already cooked, and cooking from raw dishes such as sponges and pastry that are frozen in the raw state.

Some points to note about the system are:

1. During the blast-freezing process food is cooled rapidly from 70° Celsius to −20° Celsius in 90 to 120 minutes. Rapid freezing prevents damage to the structure of the cells of food which occurs if it is frozen slowly.

2. Plastic reusable trays are used as containers during the freezing and storing process, so that expensive baking tins are not held for long periods in the chain of processes.

3. Food is carefully weighed and portioned into the containers, which are filled to a depth not exceeding 38 mm. (The depth of food is critical to the length of time taken for freezing.)

4. The blast freezer tunnel, 2 m × 2·75 m × 2·4 m high, is capable of freezing 870 kg per day, based on an eight-hour production day. The first batch of food is ready to enter the tunnel from one-and-a-half to two hours after production has started.

5. Although work is planned over a period to fulfil menu requirements, work for each day is not planned to meet a day's menu, but to make maximum use of cooking and freezing equipment and staff.

6. Because the work programme is not planned to meet mealtime deadlines, but proceeds steadily throughout the day, output is much greater than in a conventional kitchen.

7. Only 11 items of cooking equipment are used to produce over 170 menu items.

Design features to note are:

1. The smooth production flow lines, and the separate lines for foods of different categories;

2. The compact areas for preparation and cooking;

3. The considerable amount of space needed for portioning, packaging and freezer storage.

The cook-freeze system replaced one where each boarding house had its own kitchen, and where a separate kitchen and dining room was provided for day pupils. When the new system was introduced, substantial savings in staffing were made, which more than justified the capital expenditure involved. Other advantages were that it was easier to cater for special functions and holiday courses, and that quality and portion control could be maintained more easily than had been possible with six separate units.

Example 3: A cook-chill system designed to produce meals for a number of outlets on a university campus

This system is similar in many ways to the cook-freeze system described in Example 2. Food is prepared and cooked in a central food production unit or commissary. After cooking it is chilled rapidly and held in a chilling room to a temperature of 3° Celsius, after which it is despatched to the various outlets on the campus. The basic differences between this and the previous system are:

1. Food can be held for only a short time after chilling, the maximum being three days.

2. There is less reserve of cold in the cook-chill system: hence there is less margin for error.

3. If there is difficulty in determining accurately in advance what the demand for meals will be, there can be considerable waste, since once the food has been prepared and cooked it must be eaten within a short time.

4. Whereas the scheme in Example 2 could be used to supply meals to establishments some considerable distance away, the cook-chill system is less suitable for this purpose; but school and university campuses and hospitals lend themselves well to cook-chill.

5. Less capital expenditure is involved, because freezing equipment is unnecessary.

Example 4: A central kitchen producing frozen and chilled dishes for 180 units

A factory-style kitchen produces 100,000 meals a day for 180 schools in an area of the United States of America. These include meals prepared to a standard specification, *à la carte* dishes, and other refreshments such as filled rolls and sandwiches. There are two main production lines in the kitchen: one for frozen foods and the other for chilled. Each standard school meal consists of two packs, one frozen and the other chilled. After checking the packs are stacked on dollies and delivered to schools, where the dollies are transferred to cold stores in which a three-day supply of food is kept. Shortly before mealtimes those items that need reheating are transferred to oven dollies and wheeled into regenerating ovens. At mealtimes pupils collect all meal components themselves, except the packs of hot food, which are handed out by staff. Pupils eat direct from the packs, all of which are disposable.

The central kitchen has its own bacteriological laboratory, in which tests on samples of batches of food are carried out daily. There is a special kitchen for recipe development. Paperwork in this system

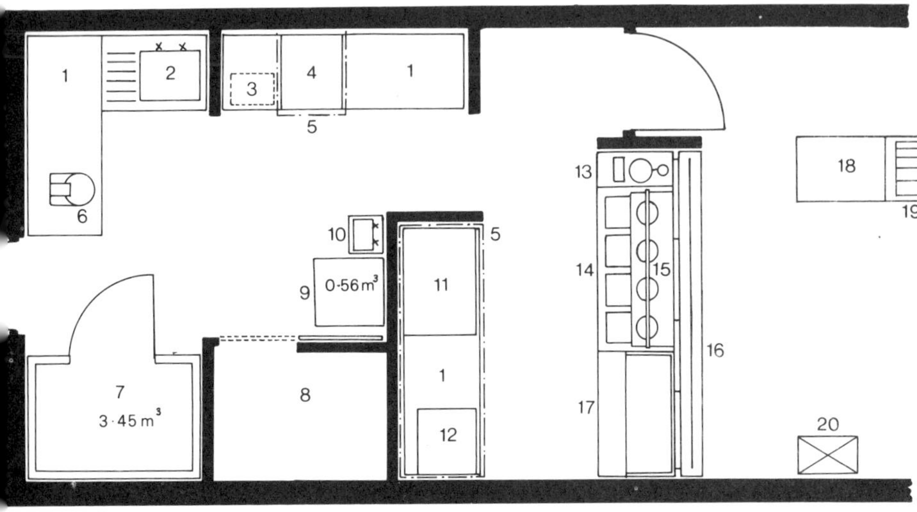

1 Benching
2 Sink
3 Refuse sack—under counter
4 Single tank spray dishwasher
5 Ventilation extract
6 Mixer—counter top
7 Cold store (-20°C)
8 Dry store
9 Reach-in chill store
10 Wash hand basin
11 Forced convection oven
12 Boiling table—counter top
13 Hot beverages
14 Hot cupboard with bain Marie top
15 Infra red lights
16 Tray rail
17 Refrigerated display above counter
18 Cash table
19 Cutlery dispense
20 Tray stand

Fig. 20 Finishing kitchen designed to produce 100 to 200 meals. For use of frozen and other convenience foods. Planned round package of regeneration/cooking equipment capable of producing 100–200 meals per 2-hour meal period, with maximum of 4 oven cycles

is kept to a minimum. Cooks at the schools telephone information about numbers of meals, etc., to a staff of telephone clerks. No stock records are kept at the schools.

The special interest of this scheme is the very high output of the production kitchen, and the high degree of automation achieved when so many outlets are involved. Once the food has left the assembly line in individual packs, very little handling is needed up to the point of consumption.

Example 5: A finishing kitchen designed to produce 100 to 200 meals

Figure 20 shows a finishing kitchen designed to use frozen and other convenience foods. The equipment is capable of producing 100 to 200 meals within a two-hour period. The ovens in which the frozen food is end-cooked are used for a maximum of four batches of food for any one mealtime.

The drawing shows how compact this sort of kitchen can be. Very little preparation space is needed, and very little equipment. Planning is easier because food goes through fewer processes, and separate progress lines are unnecessary. Apart from salad plants, food entering the kitchen is clean, and, on the whole, there is no longer any need to have separate areas to minimise cross-infection between different foods. It will be noted that no separate sink is provided for salad items, and, if these are not to be bought ready-prepared, the layout should be adapted to make this provision. In certain circumstances, where a big choice of dishes is offered, a longer service counter than that shown may be needed.

Example 6: Two methods of serving meals in hospitals

The service of meals in hospitals presents special difficulties, as has already been mentioned, because of the number of small units involved and the patients' lack of mobility. The trend nowadays is towards preparing trays individually in the catering department rather than sending food in bulk to the wards. This tends to make for more accurate portioning, helps to reduce waste, saves time in the wards, and makes it easier to cater for patients with special dietary needs. The question then arises as to how to load the trays quickly and efficiently, and how to serve the food hot.

In the Gannymede central tray system, plated food is kept hot by means of special heatstore plate bases. Heat-retaining material is an integral part of the base, which is double-sealed against moisture and may be heated safely to 120°C. Assembly-line techniques are employed for the service of patients' meals on to trays (see Figure 21), and the use of the heatstore bases ensures that food stays hot until it reaches the patient in the ward.

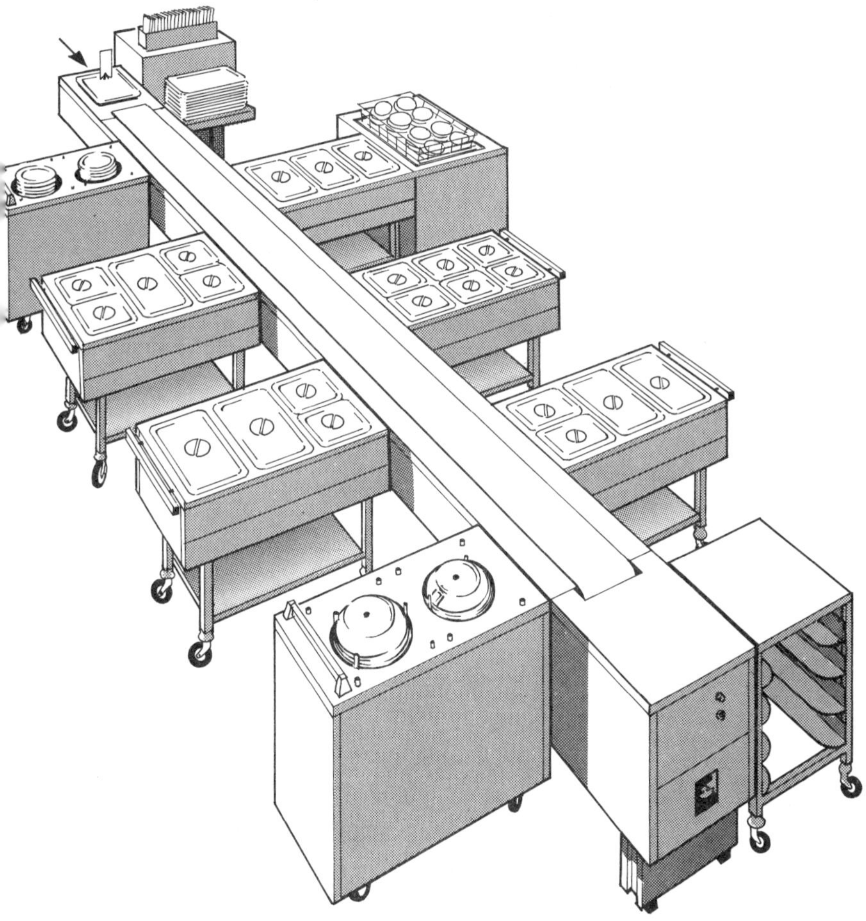

Fig. 21 *Ganymede* central tray service. Designed for hospital patients. Trays with individual menu cards are carried along conveyor belt, and food specified on card placed on tray as it passes appropriate service station. Trays, completed and checked, are put in ward trolleys. Heat-retaining bases are used for plates containing hot food

A feature of the system is the use of mobile equipment, which is wheeled into position as needed, at right angles to the conveyor belt. Electrically-heated mobile dry-well bains-marie are used for hot food, and there is similar unheated equipment for cold menu items. Mobile self-levelling equipment dispenses plates, other tableware and trays, so that items are conveniently to hand for serving staff. Electrically-heated self-levelling dispensers are used where hot plates are needed. Trays are trolleyed to the wards, and returned to a central wash-up.

A conveyor belt of this type is suitable for serving between 100 and 600 patients. Output per belt is about 8–10 trays a minute; the rate depends upon the speed and skill of the operators and the complexity of the menus. There are several variations of this system.

The *Régéthermic* system for hospital feeding is based upon cook-chill methods and the regeneration of food at ward level. Food is regenerated by means of infra-red tubes in a special cabinet after it has been plated on special porcelain plates under stainless steel covers. Trolleys with plated meals are pushed into the cabinets, which contain three different groups of infra-red tubes with different heating capacities, which decrease towards the top of the cabinet in order to ensure uniform heat distribution. The plate retains heat for some time, and the stainless steel cover is always warmer than the food. At the end of a timed period (about 12 minutes) the timer bell rings, power is automatically cut off, the trolley is uncoupled and a fresh trolley put in the cabinet if needed (Figure 22a–b). There are several variations of the *Régéthermic* system.

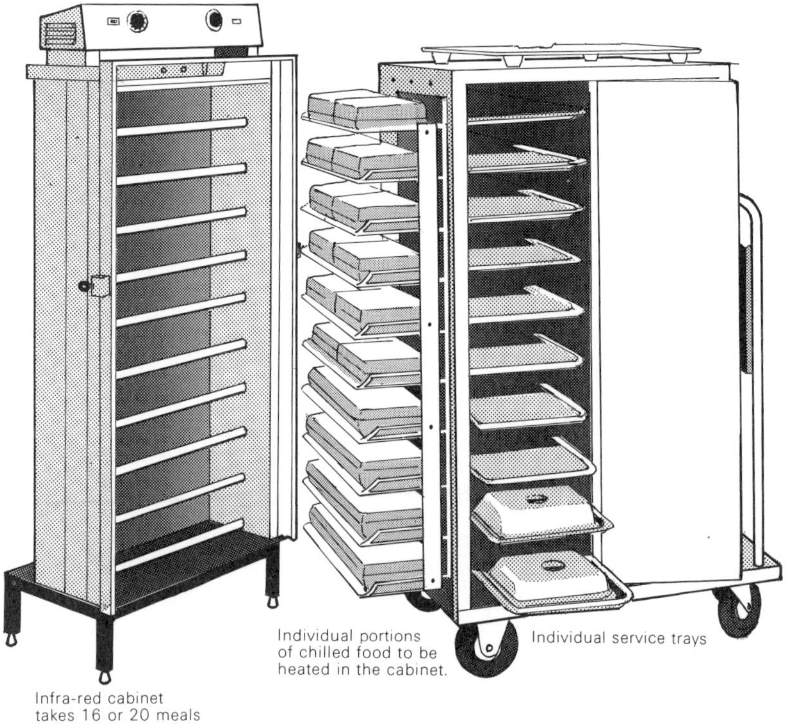

Fig. 22 Infra-red cabinet for heating chilled meals.
(a) In Régéthermic cook/chill system of catering for hospitals, individual meals are heated in a cabinet at ward level

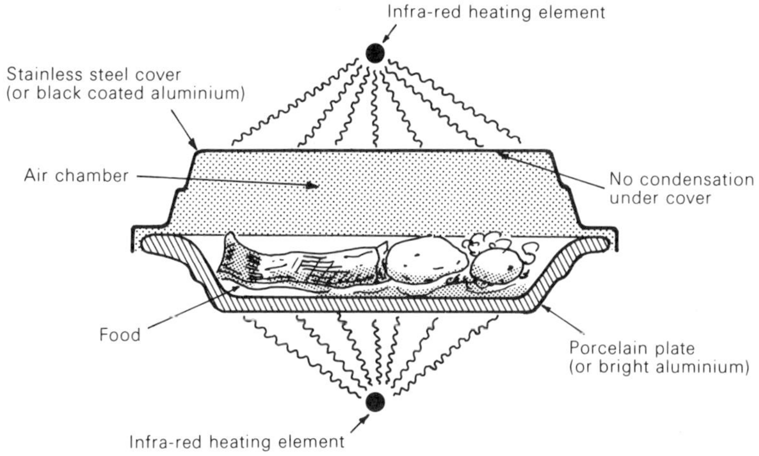

(b) Details

Example 7: A cook-freeze system associated with computer control

This highly sophisticated system operates in a group of three hospitals in the United States of America. It is designed round the use of a centralised food portion dispensing apparatus that is controlled electronically, used in conjunction with conveyorised microwave ovens. The food is prepared and cooked centrally, and then packed in individual portions. The next process is freezing by liquid nitrogen. Food passes through a vertical freezing tunnel on a conveyor belt. After having been sealed, labelled and coded—a system of colour coding is used to distinguish different diets—the dishes proceed to the storage freezer, where they remain until two or three days before they are to be eaten. At this stage they are placed in a tempering refrigerator, where their temperature is raised to 3° Celsius, and they are loaded into devices called cassettes. Before mealtimes the cassettes are loaded into ejecting devices known as magazines. At this stage catering staff order the meal components electronically according to what individual patients have chosen. This is done by means of a push-button control panel in the kitchen. As a result, dishes are ejected from the magazines, and if they are to be heated they are routed into the conveyorised microwave ovens; all foods proceed to the tray assembly point, where components are put into insulated trays designed with separately insulated compartments in which cold and hot foods will hold their temperatures for up to one-and-a-half hours. Catering staff deliver the trays on trolleys, and a beverage trolley goes with them. The same members of staff are

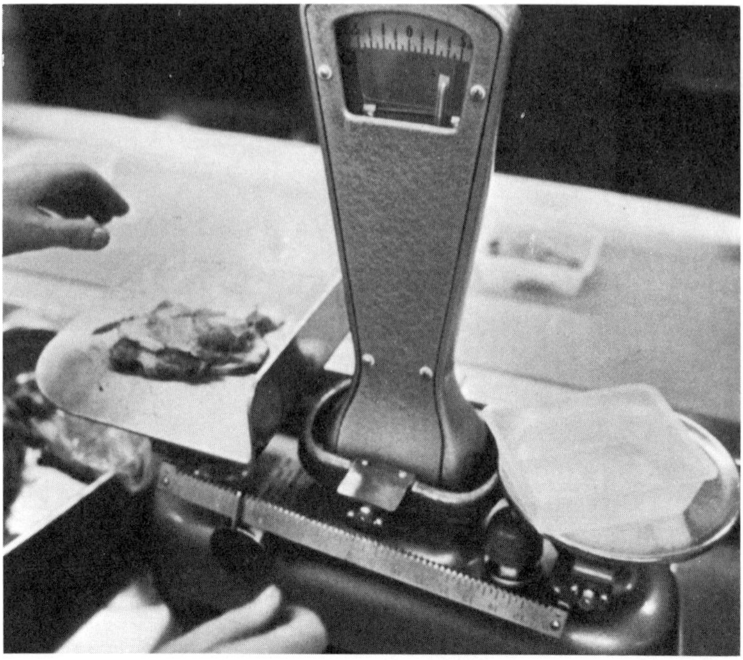

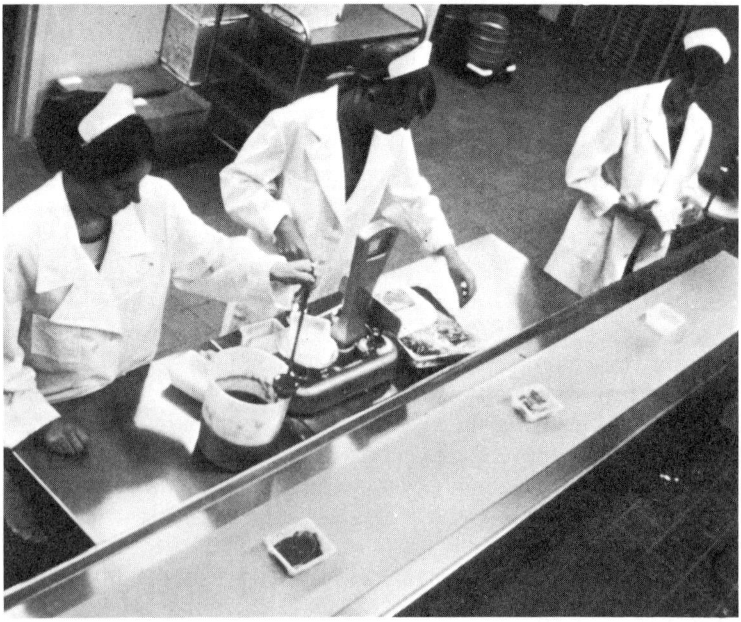

Plate 1 Various stages in catering system designed round use of centralised portioning dispenser that is controlled electronically
(a) Each package is carefully weighed for three reasons
(i) diet accuracy, (ii) portion control, (iii) weight is factor in microwave reheating
(b) Packaging assembly line

Plate 1 (contd.)
(c) Freezing process. Food is frozen by liquid nitrogen in vertical tunnel, where temperature is reduced from 49°C to −18°C in 20 minutes. Food is loaded on upper conveyor belt, and discharged on to lower belt

responsible for washing the trays and dealing with the disposable containers. Plates 1a–h show various stages in the procedure.

Example 8: A self-help system for hospital patients

A catering system recently introduced into hospitals in the Netherlands challenges the assumption that all patients need to take their meals in hospital wards. A central dining room is provided for all patients who are able to make their way there. In the dining room they are able to choose from a freezer cabinet individually-packed portions of frozen foods and put them in a 'posting box', from whence the food proceeds through a tunnel microwave oven and emerges in about five minutes' time into the dining room. In the meantime, the patient has helped himself to any cold items he would like. Therapeutic diets are included, and the patient can identify items suited to his needs by means of a colour-coding system.

Example 9: Catering system using continuous-cooking equipment

Such systems make it possible for clients to have freshly cooked food even though very large numbers of meals are served. The principle on which the equipment is designed is continuous-cooking in small quantities. Because food is cooked and served rapidly, loss of nutrients is minimised and the quality of the finished product is high. Food moves automatically through this type of equipment, which is available for steaming, boiling, frying and grilling. The system is suitable where 1000 or more meals are served in a central dining area

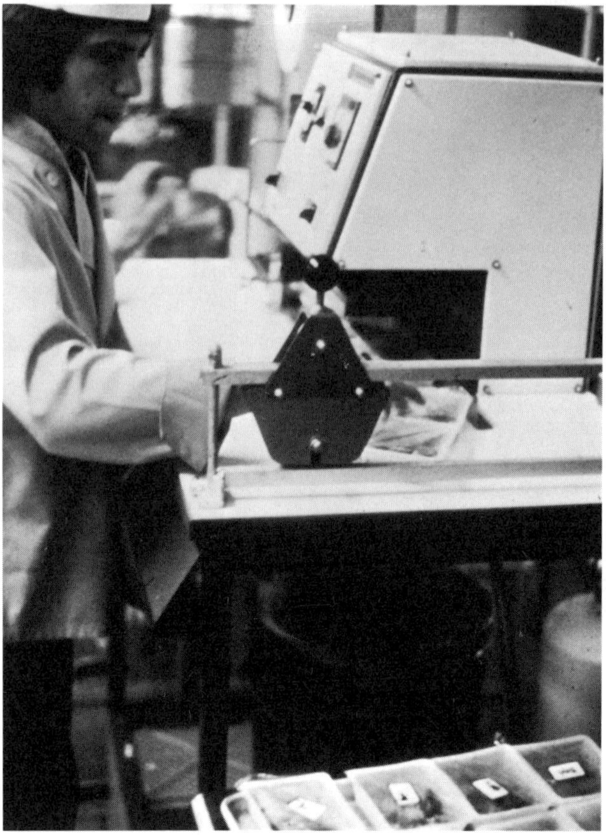

Plate 1 (contd.)
(d) Sealing and coding operation. After this, food goes to freezer store

close to the kitchen. This method may be compared with the cook-freeze and chook-chill systems described previously, where food is prepared centrally but is then dispersed to a number of outlets for service. Considerable use is made of systems based upon continuous-cooking equipment in Germany and other European countries at universities, factories and other large institutions. Figure 23a shows a typical layout for this type of kitchen. Food makes its way from the stores through the appropriate preparation area and then to the main cooking area, where the equipment includes a battery of continuous cookers. At the end of the automatic cooking process food is automatically deposited in stationary food service pans, from which it is portioned by catering staff on to meal trays, which run along a conveyor belt above above the service pans. The trays enter the service area on the conveyor, and clients help themselves to the trays. Cold items and other components of the meal are collected from different areas of the self-service counter. It can be seen from Figure 23a that several dining rooms are provided in juxtaposition to the service counter. Figure 23b shows the service arrangement in detail. Continuous-cooking equipment is used also in large-scale cook-freeze units.

Plate 1 (contd.)
(e) Two or three days before food is to be used, it is transferred to cassettes inside tempering refrigerator. See magazines (framework) and cassettes (shelf-like devices). Centre buttons enable system to be operated inside refrigerator

(f) Loading cassettes with food packages before cassettes are hung on upper part of magazine

Plate 1 (contd.)
(g) Meal components are selected electronically according to patient's choice b push-button con that ejects items from magazines. Here food is seen leaving refrigerat and falling on to another conveyo which takes it to microwave oven and then to trays for distribution to patients

(h) Microwave tunnel oven

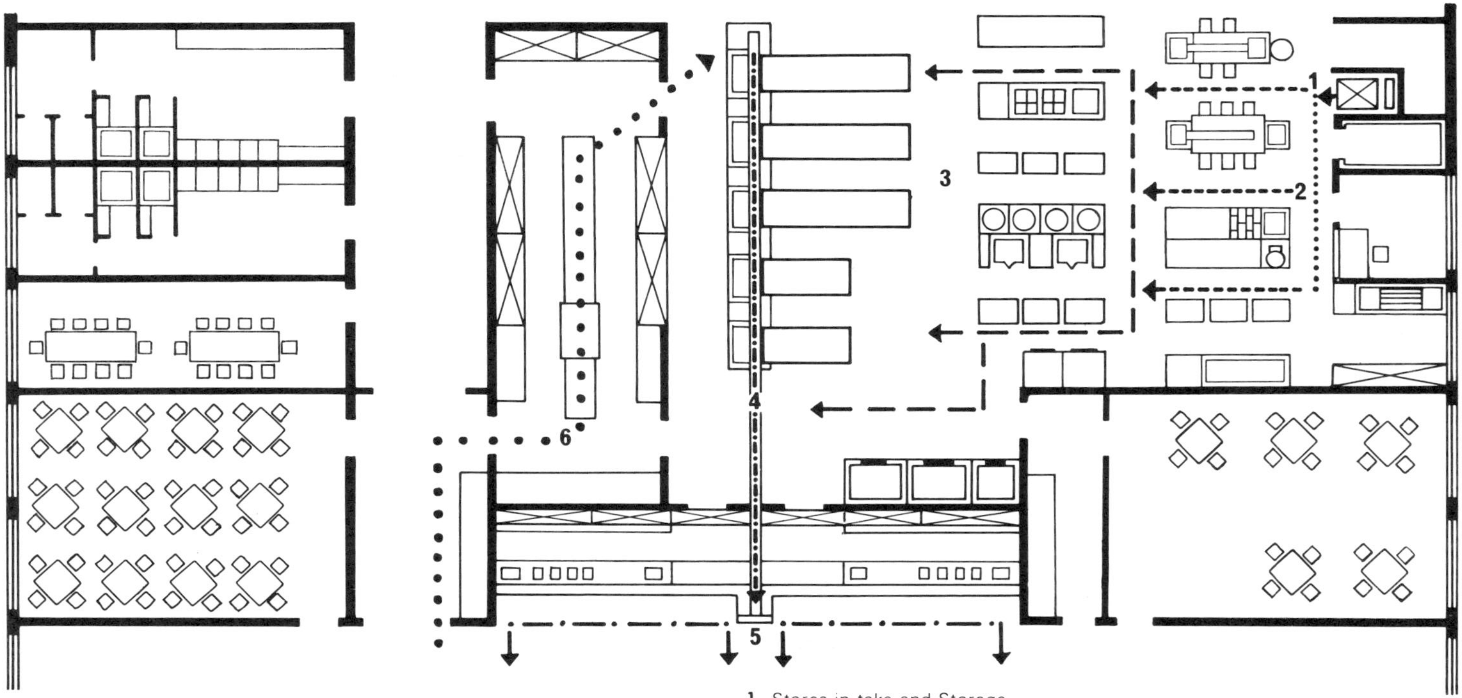

Fig. 23 (a) Typical kitchen layout using continuous-cooking equipment

1 Stores in-take and Storage.
2 Meat and Vegetable Preparation, Automatic Potato Peeling Machine.
3 Main Cooking: Battery of Continuous Cookers, Boiling Pans, Tilting Frying, Baking and Roasting Oven, Cooking Ranges.
4 Stationary Food Service Pans with Conveyor Belt over for portioning and transport of the meals.
5 Self-service Counters.
6 Dishwashing Area.

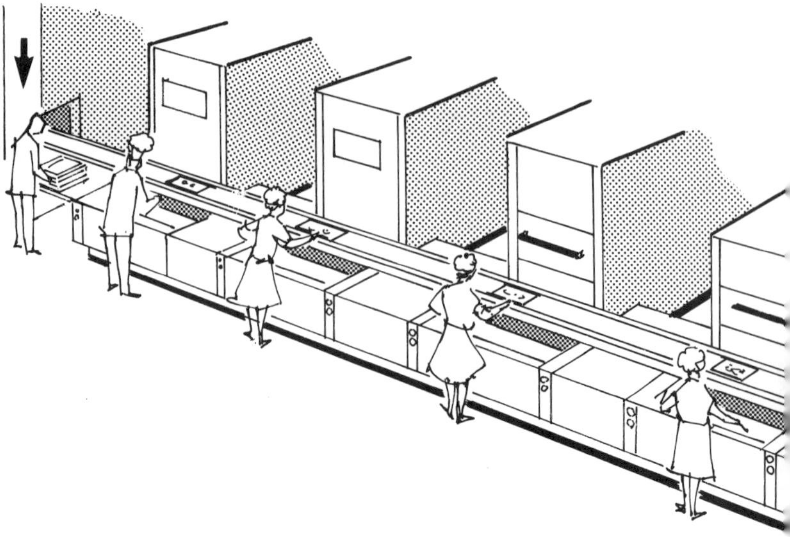

Fig. 23(b) Closer view of service arrangements. Catering staff dispense meals from containers into which continuous-cooking equipment deposits cooked food. Trays travel along assembly line and into dining area on conveyor belt

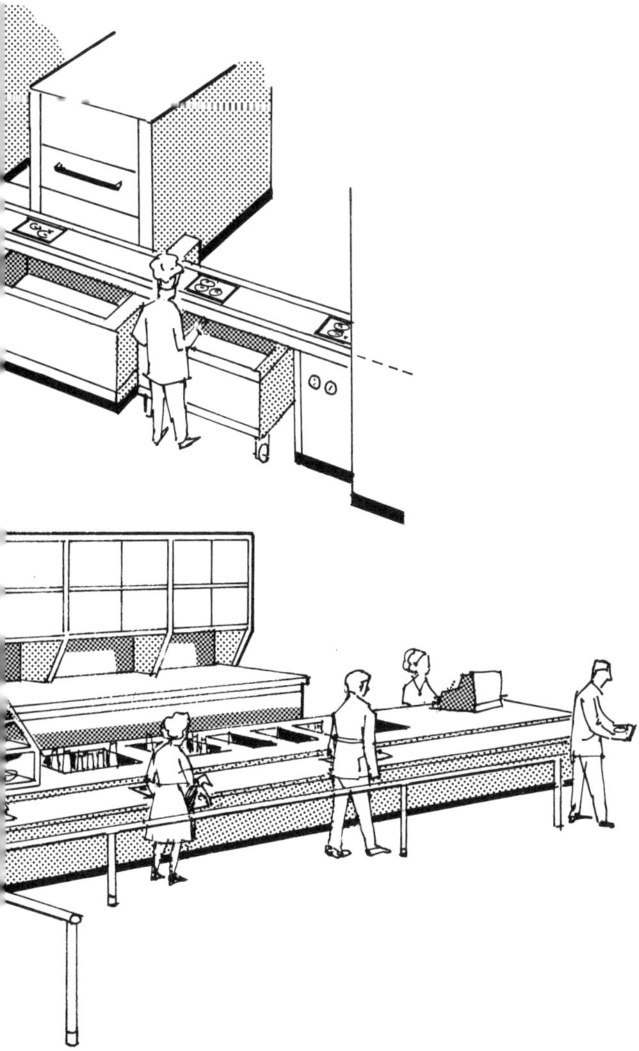

Chapter 7

Fuel and energy

Energy is required in catering for several purposes. For example, heat energy is needed for cooking and space heating; electrical energy is needed for operating machinery. In this chapter we shall be chiefly concerned with heat energy as used for cooking, and with heat sources: electricity, natural gas, liquid petroleum gas and other fuels.

Units of energy

Before we discuss sources of energy, it is necessary to look briefly at units used for the measurement of energy and heat. Under the International System of Units (SI), the joule is the unit used for all forms of energy and the unit of power is the joule per second (watt); this supersedes such units as the calorie, the Btu (British thermal unit) and horsepower. However, the Btu is still in use in Britain. Definitions are:

The watt: rate of working of one joule per second.

The kilowatt hour: the work done at a rate of one kilowatt (1000 watts) for one hour.

$$\begin{aligned} 1\ \text{kWh} &= 1000 \text{ watts for one hour} \\ &= 1000 \times 3600\ \text{J} \\ &= 3{\cdot}6\ \text{MJ} \end{aligned}$$

The British thermal unit: the quantity of heat needed to raise 1 lb (0·45 kg) of water at maximum density through 1°F. 1000 Btus are approximately equal to 1 MJ.

Natural gas

Until recent years the mains supply of gas in Britain consisted of town (manufactured) gas, but this has now been superseded by natural gas obtained from offshore undersea sources. The heat content of natural gas is approximately 1000 Btus per cu. ft (0·028 m^3). A unit of 100,000 Btus, known as the therm, is used as the basis of charge to the consumer, but from 1980 it is expected that the megajoule will replace the therm.

It is characteristic of the gas flame that it is speedy and easily controlled to give a wide graduation of heat. This is demonstrated particularly in the case of gas boiling rings, which can be readily adjusted to maintain temperatures suitable for simmering. Gas equipment should be serviced regularly. There are special features about controls fitted to gas equipment, some of which are described below.

Gas governors. Gas governors are fitted to individual pieces of equipment at the time of installation, with the object of maintaining an even pressure in the supply of gas by compensating for any inequalities of pressure in the mains supply. They are set to suit the needs of each appliance, and thus ensure consistent performance.

Ignition devices. The pilot light, ignited by means of a taper or other hand-held device, which then lights the main burner, is well known. As an alternative to lighting the pilot by hand, appliances may be fitted with devices that provide automatic ignition at the touch of a switch. These include filament lighters connected either to a battery or to mains electricity. When heated, the filament becomes incandescent and ignites the gas. Others ignite by means of a spark. The piezo electric igniter (Figure 24) generates electric current by means of pressure on a specially prepared crystal that produces a spark.

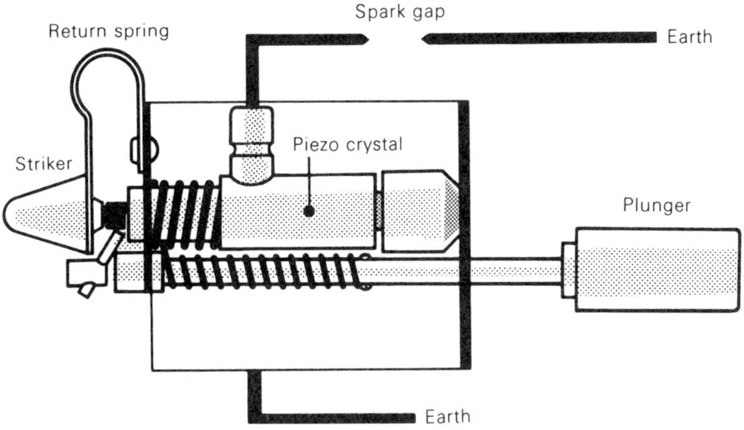

Fig. 24 Piezo electric igniter. For gas appliances. An electric current generated by pressure on specially-prepared crystal produces spark

Flame failure devices. If a burner fails to light a dangerous situation may result, especially if the burner's position is such that it is difficult to see whether or not it is alight. To guard against this, flame failure devices may be fitted, so that if the pilot fails the main gas supply is sealed off and unlighted gas is prevented from escaping. It is necessary to relight the pilot before the gas supply is restored. One type of flame failure device is shown in Figure 25.

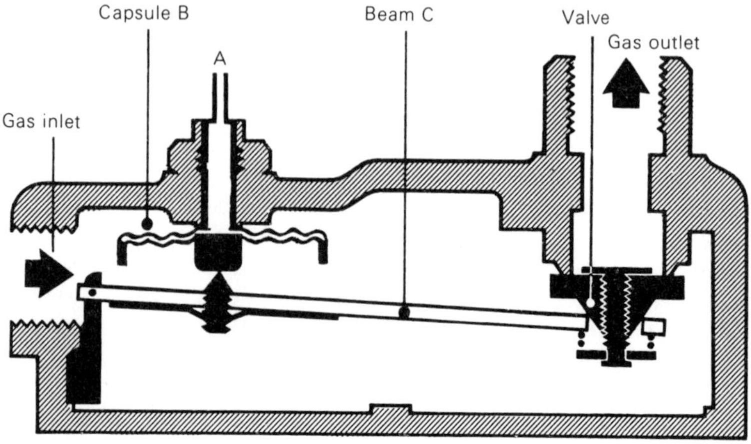

Fig. 25 Flame failure device: mercury vapour valve. To safeguard against failure of burner to light. If pilot light fails main gas supply is sealed off until pilot relit and control returned to open position. Mercury vapour valve works on principle of expansion. When pilot flame causes vapour to expand in sealed tube A, pressure generated causes capsule B to expand, forcing beam C to move downwards which opens valve and gas passes to burner. Should pilot flame go out, tube cools, pressure within it is reduced and valve closes. There are several minor variations to pilot and methods of applying heat to tube

Low-level cut-off valves. These valves are designed to prevent equipment in which water is heated (*e.g.*, boiling pans and water boilers) from boiling dry and being damaged as a result. The valve cuts off the gas supply to the main burner when the water level falls below a certain point. When more water is added the valve operates automatically to allow gas to be supplied to the burner again, which is relighted by the pilot. It will be seen that the pilot light is an essential part of this system.

Selection of gas equipment

The British Gas Corporation maintains a list of approved appliances and manufacturers, and offers an advisory service.

Gas Safety Regulations, 1972

These regulations, which deal with many technical matters, require that only competent people are allowed to work on gas installations. Certain responsibilities are laid upon the user, such as turning off the gas supply and notifying the Regional Gas Authority if a leak is suspected; the user is responsible also for correct operation and maintenance of appliances.

Liquified petroleum gas

Liquified petroleum gas (LPG) is used as a fuel for cooking in circumstances where it is either impossible or impracticable to have a mains supply of natural gas. The two principal types are Propane and Butane, and their approximate heat content is as follows:

Propane: 2500 Btus per cu. ft (94·5 MJ/m^3)
Butane: 3200 Btus per cu. ft (121·0 MJ/m^3)

Both these gases can be changed into their liquid state by the use of moderate pressure at atmospheric temperatures. When they are compressed their volume is greatly reduced: 274 times for Propane, and 233 times for Butane. Hence they can be conveniently stored and transported under pressure in special tanks and cylinders.

LPG is supplied in cylinders when requirements are small. If there is a permanently-piped installation, these cylinders must be stored out of doors for safety reasons. Where the amount used is more than 2000 litres a year (this would yield about 490 therms), bulk tanks are recommended. These are sited out of doors, and away from buildings. Propane is more suitable than Butane for outside storage; it has a higher rate of vaporisation from a liquid state, especially at low temperatures.

When the valve of an LPG container is open, the gas used is constantly replaced by vaporisation from the surface of the liquid in the container. A regulator ensures that gas that has left the container is maintained at a suitable pressure for the purpose for which it is being used.

Because LPG is different in pressure and composition from natural gas, it needs a different type of burner. Several manufacturers fit specially-designed burners to standard items of cooking equipment, and a comprehensive range of appliances is available.

Electricity

At present the kilowatt hour (3·6 MJ) is the electrical unit that is used in Britain. One unit of electricity has the capacity to raise the temperature of 3412 lb of water through 1° Fahrenheit, and this is the heat equivalent of 3412 Btus.

Electricity has the advantage of being energy already generated from an original fuel at the power station. It is clean with no by-products of combustion. Controls on appliances are simple to operate. This is particularly significant in the case of fish fryers and boiling pans, where the source of heat is at a low level. After equipment has been switched off, a considerable amount of residual heat may be left (*e.g.*, in an oven). In the interests of economy this should be used if possible, but it is not always easy to do this.

Routine maintenance of electric cooking equipment is not usually considered necessary, but standing arrangements should be made for repairs to be carried out at short notice. Electrically-operated machinery needs regular servicing. The Electricity Council maintains an approved list of manufacturers and items of equipment.

Solid fuel

Solid fuel is used as a source of heat for cooking purposes in two ways. First, it may be used in a boiler house to raise live steam. Second, it may be fed direct into solid-fuel cooking appliances. Its use for either purpose is fairly rare. Solid fuels are classified in two groups:

(a) bituminous coal;

(b) smokeless fuels.

Examples of the second group are anthracite, which occurs naturally, and coke, which is the product of heating coal in ovens or retorts in a process known as carbonisation. Bituminous coals have a relatively high volatile content and are therefore capable of emitting smoke (which consists of unburnt volatile elements). They have a relatively low heat content, but this varies with the grade of coal. Smokeless fuel has a low volatile content and a high heat content. Values range from 27·85 MJ (26 400 Btus) per kilogram (an average figure for coke) to 33·44 MJ (31 700 Btus) per kilogram (an average figure for Welsh anthracite).

It is exceptional for bituminous coal to be used for catering purposes except for field exercises and civil emergencies. Smokeless fuel is used in boilers for raising steam, and in the type of heat storage cooker shown in Figure 28.

A disadvantage of solid fuel when it is used in the kitchen is the amount of labour involved in refuelling, riddling, etc. Also, even with the most careful attention there is likely to be a problem with dust from fuel and ashes.

Fuel oil

Where live steam is used for cooking, fuel oil may be used in the boiler house for raising steam. In the kitchen, cookers of the heat-storage type may be fired by oil fed into the cooker from a tank outside the building.

Live steam

Cooking systems using live steam raised in a boiler house are comparatively rare, and are usually adopted only when steam is needed for additional purposes to catering, as, for example, in a hospital. However, there are circumstances in which the steam generated may be unsuitable for cooking purposes because it is not clean. This may be the case, for example, when additives are used to prevent scaling. Live steam systems used solely for cooking purposes are very costly to run. Live steam is also raised in the kitchen by generators adjacent to individual high-speed pressure steamers (Figure 38c), and this sort of use is increasing. It is useful at this stage to define some of the terms used in connection with cooking by live steam.

Steam. This is water in the vapour state.

Sensible heat and heat of vaporisation. It is well known that when water is heated in an open vessel the temperature rises until it reaches boiling point (at atmospheric pressure, 100° Celsius), and continued application of heat does not produce a further rise in temperature; instead it produces a change of state—the liquid changes into the vapour, steam. The heat that produces a rise in temperature is known as sensible heat; the heat that produces a change in state to vapour is known as the latent heat of vaporisation. At atmospheric pressure the latent heat of vaporisation is 2257 kJ/kg. When water is boiled in a closed vessel the pressure inside increases, and the temperature rises above 100° Celsius. The amount of sensible heat increases directly with the increase in temperature; latent heat decreases as the pressure increases.

Live steam. This is steam generated under pressure supplied direct from a boiler.

Dry steam. When steam is at the same temperature as that of the water from which it has been formed, it is free from water and is known as dry steam. It is ideal for cooking purposes because it contains the maximum quantity of heat per unit volume. It is known also as dry saturated steam.

Wet steam. This contains a mixture of true vapour and droplets of liquid, and is less efficient as a heating medium.

Superheated steam. This is heated at a constant pressure out of contact with the water from which it was formed—that is, at a higher temperature than saturation.

Latent heat of condensation. When steam condenses it gives up latent heat, and this is known as the latent heat of condensation.

In a live steam system, steam is generated in a pressure boiler at a higher pressure than is used for cooking. Reducing valves are therefore necessary at some stage before the steam enters the equipment in order to reduce the pressure. Steam is transmitted by pipes, which are insulated to minimise heat losses.

Choosing a source of heat energy

When decisions are made as to which fuel to use, in most cases the choice lies between electricity and gas. Other fuels, apart from LPG, are not usually practical propositions. LPG comes into the picture in areas where a mains gas supply is not available, when it may be a worthwhile alternative to electricity. The main considerations in reaching a decision are those of cost and the type of equipment it is proposed to use. In considering costs the total requirements for all activities in a building or on a site are assessed, and it may be that catering needs will form only a small part of the whole. It follows that, while catering managements should be aware of the factors affecting fuel costs and other pros and cons, these will not necessarily be decisive.

Initial cost

Initial costs are made up of the following:

(a) equipment;
(b) laying on services to equipment;
(c) installation;
(d) any ancillary costs related to items such as special ventilation, provision of fuel tanks, etc.

It is the task of catering management to make the necessary comparisons about equipment costs, and this can readily be done by producing priced lists of similar items of equipment for the fuels under consideration. Care must be taken to ensure that comparably powered equipment is being considered. The remaining items are largely the province of the architect and the engineer.

TABLE 3: Amounts of heat energy available from different fuels

Coke	28 MJ per kg
Anthracite	33 MJ per kg
Gas	39·29 MJ/m^3
LPG:	
Propane	94·5 MJ/m^3
Butane	121·0 MJ/m^3

Running costs

1. Comparative cost of fuel. At first sight it may seem simple to determine which fuel is cheapest. Given the heat energy content of a unit of fuel (see Table 3) and its cost, a comparison may be made. In practice, however, it is not easy to arrive at a cost per unit, because charges vary according to the amount needed and certain other considerations. It should be remembered that electricity is energy direct, and not a raw fuel. Electricity tariffs vary not only according to the amounts used, but also according to the time of day at which it is used, cheaper rates being available at off-peak times. It follows that, in order to make an accurate comparison of the cost of a unit of heat energy from different fuels, it is necessary to have working figures for total heat energy needs, and, in the case of electricity, the spread of use over the day.

Information on gas ratings and electrical loadings of appliances may be obtained from the British Gas Corporation, the Electricity Council and manufacturers. With this information, and given the estimated number of hours per day each piece of equipment will be in use, it is possible to calculate a maximum figure for heat energy consumption. But it must be remembered that energy is not consumed at the maximum rate during the whole of a cooking process, and it is difficult to make due allowance for this. Recent tests by the Electricity Council have indicated that the average electrical load factor is 50 per cent, and the average number of hours of use for an electric cooker in a traditional kitchen (for one meal a day) is 4. Using these facts, the following example for estimating the consumption of electricity per day is given:

Item:	electric cooker
Loading:	12 kW
Hours' use per day:	4
load factor:	50 per cent
Typical energy consumption per day:	86·4 MJ (24 kWh)

TABLE 4: Use of equipment: percentage of working week that equipment was in use in a school meals kitchen*

Equipment	*% of working week in use*	*% of working week in which all items of one type were in use simultaneously*
Ovens (4)	21·6	11·8
Vegetable boilers (6)	16·8	2·2
Steamers (6)	16·1	6·2
Pudding boilers (2)	7·9	5·6
Mixers (2)	19·4	7·3
Slicing machines (2)	9·6	6·2

* During a study carried out by the Catering Research Unit, Leeds University

A survey carried out by the Catering Research Unit of Leeds University in school meals kitchens gives an indication of equipment use in the production of a simple two-course midday meal. Figure 26

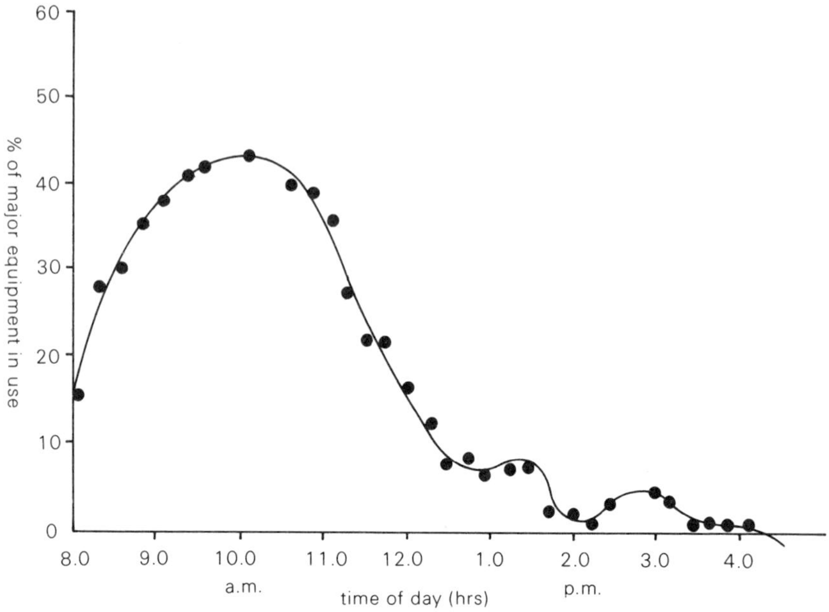

Fig. 26 Graph showing utilisation of equipment, with times, in school meals kitchens studied by Catering Research Unit, Leeds University

shows the distribution of equipment utilisation with times during the working session, and Table 4 shows the percentage of the working week during which equipment was in use. Use of any one type of equipment was less than 25 per cent. A much greater degree of use occurs in the case of cook-freeze kitchens, and account of this should be taken in estimating heat energy needs. Utilisation of equipment is likely to be three times greater. It is convenient to have a rule-of-thumb for heat energy needs; figures of 2·7 to 3·6 MJ per meal are often quoted, but this can be as low as 1·0 MJ in a well organised cook-freeze production unit.

2. Other costs. Other points to be considered with regard to cost are: maintenance, not only of the equipment itself but of any ancillary equipment; insurance; and labour. These are not likely to be of great significance when gas and electricity are compared. Extra insurance costs may arise in the cases of LPG and live steam systems. Labour costs virtually rule out the use of solid fuel, and they may be a major item in live steam systems.

Other factors affecting choice

A caterer sometimes has a marked preference for either gas or electrical equipment, but this is usually subjective and based upon familiarity with the one particular fuel. Usually such considerations are outweighed by questions of economy. A caterer may also prefer a particular fuel for a certain item of equipment. For example, he may want a gas boiling table because of the high degree of control that can be exercised over the boiling rings, or an electric fish fryer because of the simplicity of its controls and the effectiveness of immersed elements. Questions of economy may well override this sort of preference, for almost always it is cheaper to stick to one source of heat energy. However, where electricity is concerned this point may more easily be met, since there will be an electricity supply to the site in any case. A further—and valid—reason for choosing a mixture of gas and electric equipment is to safeguard against times when, through industrial action or for any other reason, there is a breakdown in either gas or electricity supply. The need for this sort of security has to be weighed against the extra cost involved.

Fuel economy and the choice of equipment

It is axiomatic that catering equipment should be designed for the efficient use of heat. During recent years, plentiful sources of cheap fuel have ceased to exist, and equipment designers have become very conscious of the need for fuel economy.

Insulation. It has long been the practice to insulate equipment to prevent the loss of heat to the surrounding atmosphere. Nowadays more items of equipment are being insulated, and more efficient materials are being used.

Temperature and cooking time controls. Thermostats, by means of which the operator may select a temperature that will be automatically maintained throughout the cooking period, were introduced originally to ensure that food was correctly cooked. But they also serve to prevent waste of fuel, and in some pieces of equipment are fitted solely for that purpose. For example, bulk water boilers used for making beverages may be fitted with thermostats that keep the water just below boiling point until it is required for use. Timing devices were also developed to prevent overcooking and for the convenience of the operator; the fact that they also saved fuel was often a secondary consideration. But timers are now being designed specifically to prevent waste of fuel when equipment is carelessly left on. For example, electric grills may be equipped with mechanical time clocks set to switch off the elements at any point up to thirty minutes and gas grills may also be clock-controlled; positive action on the part of the operator is then needed if he is to continue to use the equipment. Another example is the pan-sensing device for gas boiling rings, by means of which the ring remains alight for 30 seconds only after a pan has been removed.

Reference is made in the next two chapters to the efficiency of particular items of equipment.

Chapter 8

Cooking processes and equipment, I: roasting, baking, microwave heating, grilling, frying

Roasting and baking

Roasting is defined as cooking (especially in the case of meat) by exposure to open fire or in an oven; baking is cooking by dry heat in a closed place or on a hot surface (not by direct exposure to fire). Cooking by an open fire is rarely used nowadays, and so the terms roasting and baking are to a certain extent interchangeable. They are both used chiefly to describe cooking in a closed and heated space—that is, an oven. In the oven heat is transferred to the food partly by conduction through the metal runners or sheets on which the food is placed, but mainly through:

a. direct radiation from the oven walls;
b. convection currents of heated air.

The circulation of heated air within the oven may be increased by the use of a fan, which forces air round the oven chamber.

In the days when meat was roasted in front of an open fire a rotating spit was used, and the spit was turned by hand, clockwork mechanism or other means. Nowadays, for obvious reasons of efficiency and cleanliness, the oven has taken the place of the spit in nearly all circumstances. Where spits are used they rotate inside an oven, the heat source is an electric element, and the spit is power-driven. This sort of rotisserie is used on a limited scale for poultry, game and small joints. Usually meat is roasted by standing it in a tin containing hot fat inside an oven, and certain vegetables are cooked in the same way. The term baking applies when the oven is used for cooking bread, cakes, pastry and made-up dishes, and it applies also to the use of bakestones and girdles (chiefly for domestic purposes) to cook scones and other small items. In both baking and roasting an attractive external appearance is given by exposure to dry radiant heat in an enclosed space (or in the case of a girdle by contact with a heated surface), which causes chemical changes to take place on the surface of the food. This is fundamental to the process.

Ovens for roasting and baking

The basic structure

Ovens are usually made of metal, but in special cases they may be brick. The source of heat may be either inside or outside the oven chamber. Examples of the former are ovens with gas burners inside; an example of the latter is a solid-fuel oven where heat is obtained from the fire and from hot gases passing through flues. There are also ovens where the heat source is partly external. For example, in a gas oven the burner or burners may be under a metal plate called a sole. Hot gases then enter the oven round the edges of the sole plate, or through vents in and over the oven's inner wall.

Questions of dimensions and temperature

In the processes of roasting and baking the distribution of temperature within the oven is significant, and convenient automatic or manual control is necessary to ensure suitable temperatures for various kinds of foods and dishes. Uniformity of temperature throughout the oven is important where large numbers of like items are to be cooked, and when products such as bread, tarts and buns are baked a uniform appearance will not be achieved unless the same temperature is maintained throughout the oven during cooking. One way to achieve this is to have a shallow oven, with the minimum clearance between floor and top; another way is to circulate the heated air by means of a fan.

When an oven is used for general purposes, and not just for baking batches of similar articles, different considerations about temperature arise. When several different foods are in the oven together, each may need a different cooking time and temperature. In this case variations in temperature in different parts is an advantage, and the ease with which some items may be removed and replaced while other dishes are left undisturbed is an important consideration. The traditional general-purpose oven with a relatively high chamber and several shelves meets these needs, and it may, because of its greater height, occupy less floor space in relation to its capacity than does the traditional baker's oven, but this will not necessarily be so if the baker's oven has several decks.

Some design considerations

1. Ease in loading and unloading. Except where there are special devices for loading and unloading, the operator must be able to reach easily those dishes that are at the back of the oven, and he will not be able to do this if the oven is too deep. The design of the door must be such as to allow easy access. A hinged drop-down door may cause burns if its dimensions are such that the cook is liable to catch his arm on the open door when he reaches into the oven. Burns may also result if side-hung doors cannot be opened to an angle of more than 90 degrees, because freedom of movement when tins are manipulated will be restricted.

The oven's height from the ground is another point to be considered. The most convenient height for loading and unloading is waist level, and shelves positioned not more than 0·6 m above or below this height are reasonably convenient. If the shelves are lower than this, a great deal of bending and lifting is involved. If they are higher, work becomes difficult and dangerous, especially since hot dishes and liquids are involved. Shelf heights between 440 mm and 1660 mm are usually convenient.

The design of the oven should be such that the shelves may be moved in and out easily, and this is particularly important because it is often necessary to move shelves when the oven is hot.

2. *Efficient performance*. The user of the oven is entitled to expect an even distribution of temperature over each shelf, and in the case of forced-convection ovens the temperature should be even throughout. If this is not so, the matter should be taken up with the manufacturer or other technical expert.

Oven insulation has an important bearing upon efficiency, and this has been discussed in Chapter 7. Ovens are usually built with a double shell, the inner forming the walls and the outer affording protection and good appearance. The space between the two is usually filled with insulating materials such as mineral wool or urethane foam; these materials must also be heat-resistant, since otherwise they would deteriorate.

3. *Hygiene and durability*. An oven should be designed so that it may be cleaned effectively with the minimum of effort, and the materials from which it is built must stand up to working conditions. The high temperatures involved in cooking, and the nature of the materials being cooked, combine to make oven-cleaning difficult. It is therefore essential that the inner surface should be smooth, hard and non-porous, and it must not deteriorate when it is constantly subjected to high temperatures. Stainless steel and vitreous enamel fulfil these requirements, but one disadvantage of the latter is that it is sometimes damaged during transit or installation, and as a result chipping occurs. The inner surface of the oven is not the only part needing careful cleaning. All fittings, including burners in the case of gas ovens, will have to be cleaned often and should be designed with this in mind.

In order to make cleaning easy, some gas catering cookers are designed so that they may be heated to especially high temperatures, at which deposits of soil are burned away. These ovens are known as 'self-cleaning' or 'helping to clean themselves'. Others have drainage holes and plugs in their bases, so that if they are cleaned by high-pressure jets (see Ch. 23) water from these jets may readily drain away.

The range (gas and electric)

This is the most traditional piece of equipment found in kitchens. It consists of an oven (or a unit of two ovens) with a boiling table mounted on top (see Figure 27). The ovens may be general purpose or forced convection. Sometimes they are fitted with upstands, and these serve as splashbacks, and also as supports for eye-level grills. Typical external dimensions for a single-oven range are: 900 mm wide × 778 mm deep × 850 mm high, with an oven capacity of 160 litres. Smaller models are available.

Fig. 27 Traditional cooking range, made up of boiling table and general-purpose oven

There is a considerable variety in the make-up of boiling table tops for ranges. Gas ranges may have either open boiling rings or solid tops with graduated heat (the centre is the hottest part). Electric ranges offer the choice of: a solid top with tapered heat; individual solid boiling plates; and radiant rings. Griddle plates may be substituted for boiling rings or boiling plates.

One disadvantage of the range is that the oven is too low to be ideal for loading and unloading; this is because of the need to have the boiling table at a convenient height. If the boiling table is higher than 910 mm, it becomes difficult to lift pans on and off the range top.

The traditional range is a versatile and compact piece of equipment, by means of which almost all traditional cooking processes may be carried out. A single unit is capable of producing up to 50 meals without ancillary equipment. In practice it loses some of its versatility when, because large numbers are being catered for, there is a division of functions between several members of staff. For example, it is impracticable to have one person using the high-level grill while someone else is tending the oven.

Heat storage cookers

Heat storage cookers have many of the characteristics of ranges, as will be seen from Figure 28. Operating on heat-storage principles, they burn continuously at a low rate. Except for recovery periods after intensive use (and refuelling in the case of solid fuel models), they maintain a constant temperature and are available for instant use. Their use is almost entirely restricted to small residential establishments, and they are not considered suitable for large-scale catering.

Heat storage cookers have fast and slow hotplates with insulating covers to prevent heat loss when the plates are not in use. They have two or more ovens suitable for roasting and baking, slow cooking, and plate-warming. Originally designed for solid fuel, alternative models for oil and gas are now available.

The general purpose oven

These ovens are usually mounted on legs or stands to give a convenient height for use. Sometimes one is placed above another, and, while this has the advantage of being economical in floor space, it means that several shelves are at inconvenient heights. Also, depending upon position, they may block the light or the view across the kitchen. Oven dimensions and capacities are similar to those of ovens forming part of a range. Doors may be either drop-down or side-hinged, and double doors are necessary for wide ovens.

The pastry oven

These shallow ovens with drop-down doors often consist of several decks mounted on a stand. Each tier has its own heating element or burner, so that different temperatures for each oven may be used, or, in the case of some gas ovens, all decks are heated by a single burner system. Gas ovens are externally heated, and this is an additional aid in ensuring the even temperature that is characteristic of this type of oven. Oven heights range from 127 mm to 305 mm. The use of pastry

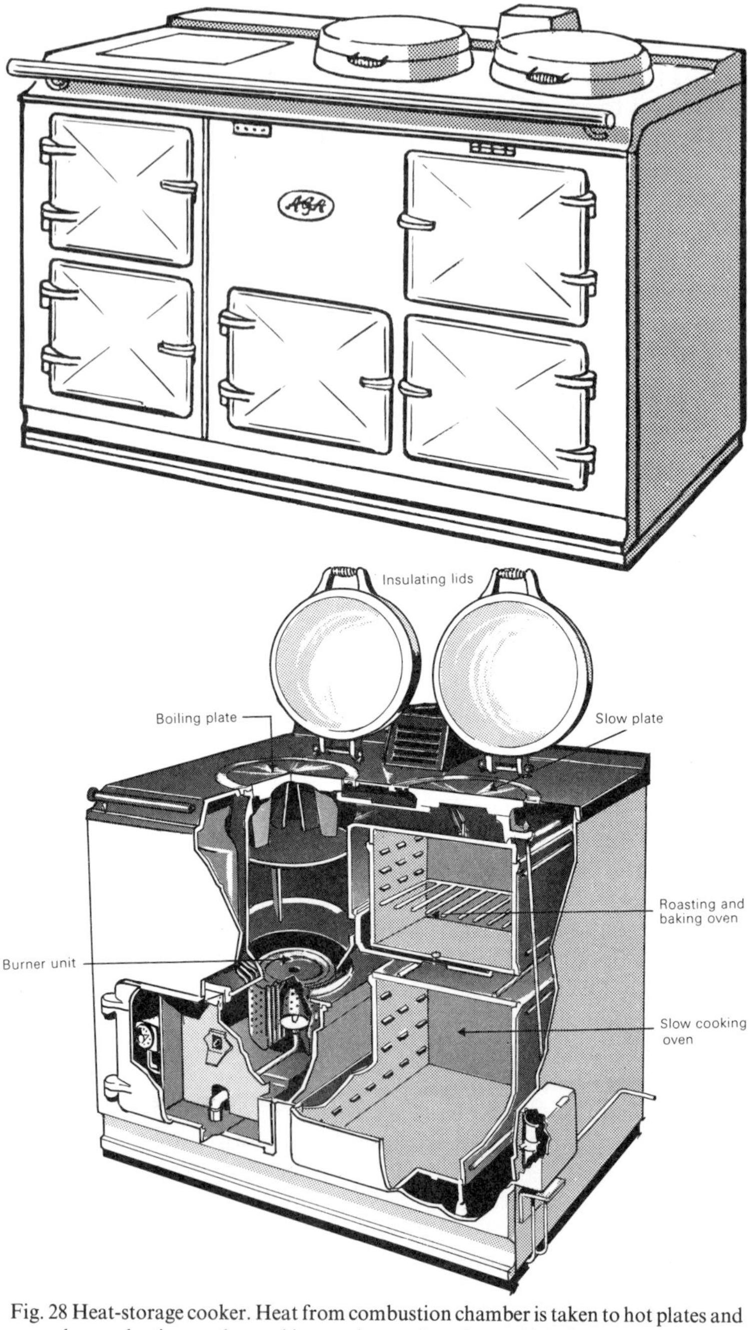

Fig. 28 Heat-storage cooker. Heat from combustion chamber is taken to hot plates and ovens by conduction, and stored in massive castings from which they are made. There are models using solid fuel, oil and gas
(a) external view of four-oven model (b) internal view of smaller model

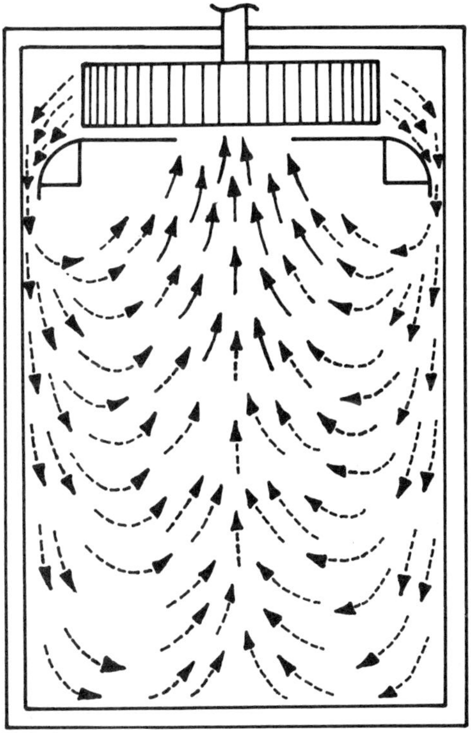

Fig. 29 Forced-convection ovens. Hot air is recirculated by means of electric fan
(a) Typical airflow pattern

ovens is indicated in kitchens where there is a high output of pastry and cakes.

Baker's oven

Ovens for yeast goods are similar in many respects to pastry ovens, but there may be provision for steam injection. Steam is necessary when French bread and rolls with crisp crusts are baked. To obtain this finish the bread when first placed in the oven must be exposed to a steamy atmosphere that cooks the outside but leaves it soft and moist. The process is completed by cooking in a dry atmosphere to give a crisp, brown exterior. Bakers' ovens are not usually found in catering establishments.

The reel oven

In this type of oven, trays swivel between two wheels and the operator stops the mechanism when he wishes to unload. Some models have glass doors. They are designed to give a high output of one commodity at a given time.

The forced-convection oven

The special feature of these ovens is the recirculation of convection currents of heated air by means of an electric fan (see Figure 29a). The fan may be inside the oven, or, in the case of a semi-externally-heated gas oven, below the oven chamber and above the source of heat. The forced-convection oven was originally developed for the regeneration of frozen foods, and it is a standard item of equipment in finishing kitchens. It is, however, suitable for all cooking processes, and it is now widely used for general purposes. A list of points of comparison with general purpose ovens of the traditional type is given below:

(a) less time is needed to heat the oven to the appropriate cooking temperature;

(b) the oven is heated evenly throughout;

(c) food cooks more quickly;

(d) meat shrinks less during cooking;

(e) as pre-heating and cooking times are less, output is greater;

(f) it is generally possible to cook at lower temperatures.

When forced-convection ovens are used for frozen food, the continuous movement of hot air takes away the humid air that develops round frozen food when it is first placed in an oven, and allows heat to penetrate more quickly than would otherwise be possible. The variation in temperature through the oven is not more than 3·5° Celsius, and this means that food is reheated evenly throughout a batch, and cold spots do not occur. It is convenient to load and unload batches of frozen food with like reheating times by means of a trolley. For this purpose, oven shelves are designed as a capsule that can be rolled *en bloc* on to a specially-designed trolley. Forced-convection ovens are available in a very wide range of sizes (oven capacities from 60 litres to 280 litres). There are several counter-top models, which are suitable for use in snack bars and very small kitchens. Figure 29b–c shows two typical ovens.

Microwave heating

When food is heated by microwaves, high-frequency radiation waves penetrate the food and cause water molecules in it to vibrate, and thus generate heat. Microwaves penetrate to a depth of up to 35 mm, and because of the depth of penetration food is heated very rapidly. No surface browning takes place, because the temperature in the oven is lower than that of the food being heated, and the food is not exposed to radiant heat. However, there are special heat-absorbing plates that may be used for browning purposes. Microwave ovens heat food in about one-seventh of the time taken by a conventional oven, and are ready for almost instant use. Microwaves are particularly suitable for reheating chilled food. Where frozen food is concerned, because ice absorbs microwave energy less rapidly than does water, the rate of rise in temperature is slower than for thawed food. If full power is maintained for long enough for frozen food to be reheated, results may be unsatisfactory; by the time that all cold spots have reached a satisfactory temperature, some parts will be overdone. Hence it is

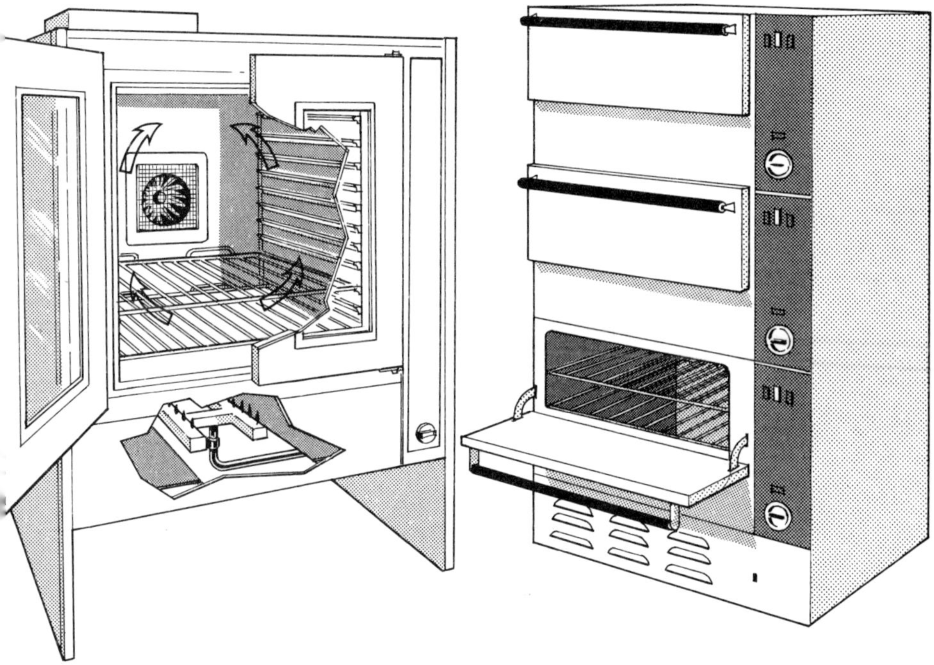

Fig. 29(b) Forced-convection oven heated externally by gas
(c) Electric multi-deck forced-convection oven

common practice to allow food to defrost beforehand. Food is withdrawn from the cold store and placed in the refrigerator for this purpose (see Chapter 6, Example 7). Another method is to heat frozen food in the microwave oven for a limited period, and then to allow it to rest for a similar period, during which time the heat that has been generated will be distributed evenly through the food. This process is then repeated until the required temperature is reached. Some microwave ovens have pulse control, so that ovens are switched on and off automatically for suitable periods to allow frozen foods to be defrosted and heated in this way. Recently, sensing devices have been developed by means of which the cooking cycle is automatically adjusted according to the state of the food during the defrosting and heating processes.

When food is heated by means of microwaves it should not be heaped, as this would cause uneven heating.

Microwaves may be used in conjunction with infra-red heat, in which case there will be surface browning of the finished product. Forced-convection ovens may be microwave-assisted.

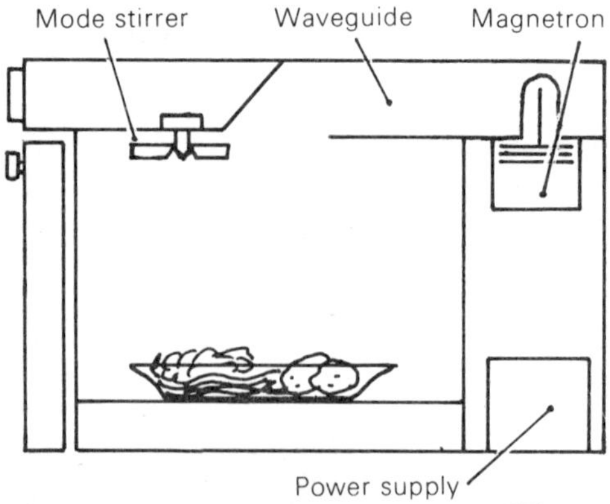

Fig. 30 Microwave oven
(a) Components: Magnetron generates high-frequency microwaves. Waveguide guides microwaves through oven. Mode stirrer distributes energy evenly within oven
(b) Typical design

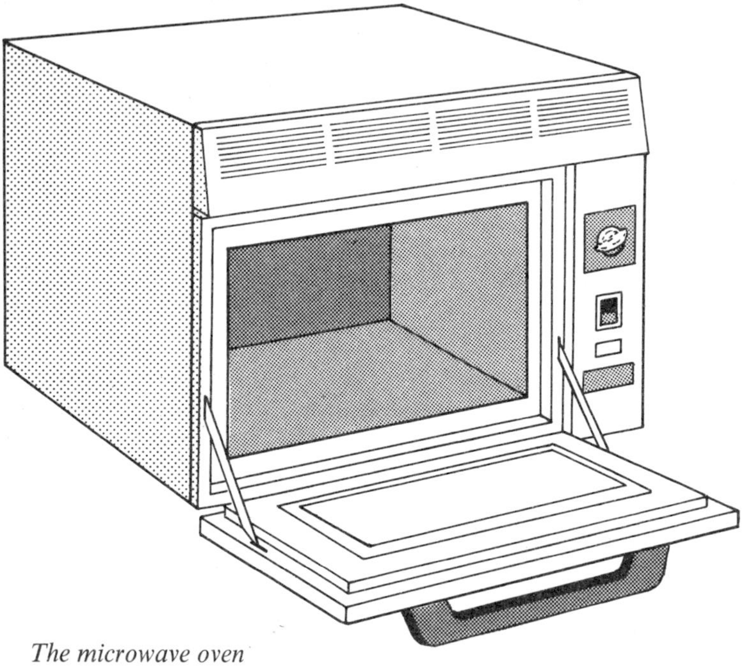

The microwave oven

Figure 30a shows typical components of a microwave oven. Microwaves are generated by means of a magnetron, guided to the oven by means of the waveguide and distributed evenly by means of the mode-stirrer. Oven doors have at least two separate interlock systems to ensure that the supply of microwave energy power is cut off when the door is opened. In some models the oven will not operate if the interlock system fails. British Standard 5175 specifies safety requirements for microwave ovens.

Because they heat foods quickly and convert electricity into heat efficiently, energy costs for microwave ovens in relation to output are low.

Microwave ovens are small, and external dimensions range from 381 mm × 578 mm × 438 mm to 612 mm × 596 mm × 485 mm. A typical oven is shown in Figure 30b. When these ovens are used for large-scale operations, several magnetron units are joined together to form a tunnel, and food passes through them on a moving belt (see Plate 1h).

Except for the tunnel variety, microwave ovens are not suited to heating food for large numbers. Their chief uses are as follows:

(a) As an ancillary in large-scale catering for providing extra items on a small scale, as, for instance, when a few extra portions are needed at short notice;

(b) For regenerating prepared meals (chilled or frozen) for those wanting meals at awkward hours;

(c) For regenerating food for small groups of people (as in a hospital ward);

(d) in snack bars, where chilled dishes are regenerated as called for by customers;

(e) in conjunction with vending units to provide a 24-hour meals service.

In general foil and metal containers should not be used in microwave ovens, because they reflect the microwaves and thereby damage the magnetron. However, in certain cases, by following the manufacturer's recommendations, it is possible to use this type of container.

Grilling

Grilled food is cooked by radiant heat. In the traditional charcoal grill, where food is cooked over an open fire, the source of heat is red-hot fuel. In the cases of gas and electric grills, heat usually comes from red-hot metal or heated refractory bricks. In electric grillers, elements are of either wired or rod type. Some grills combine radiant heat with infra-red heat. Small pieces of meat (chops, steaks, beefburgers, etc.) and fish are the principal foods cooked by grilling. It is fundamental to the process that the finished product is tasty and succulent and of attractive appearance.

Underfired grill (flare grill)

A typical model is shown in Figure 31a. A disadvantage of this type of grill is that melting fat and juices from the meat when they drip below may cause burning smells, and also cleaning difficulties.

Overfired grill or salamander

This type of grill (see Figure 31b) may also be used for making toast, and for browning dishes such as cottage pie. The position of the grilling tray or hearth is adjustable. A channel below the hearth collects any drips of fat and juices.

Dimensions of grills. Typical dimensions for the grill area are 610 mm × 495 mm, with overall dimensions of 710 mm × 690 mm × 610 mm. It is essential that the grilling tray is at a convenient height for the operator—that is, between shoulder and waist level.

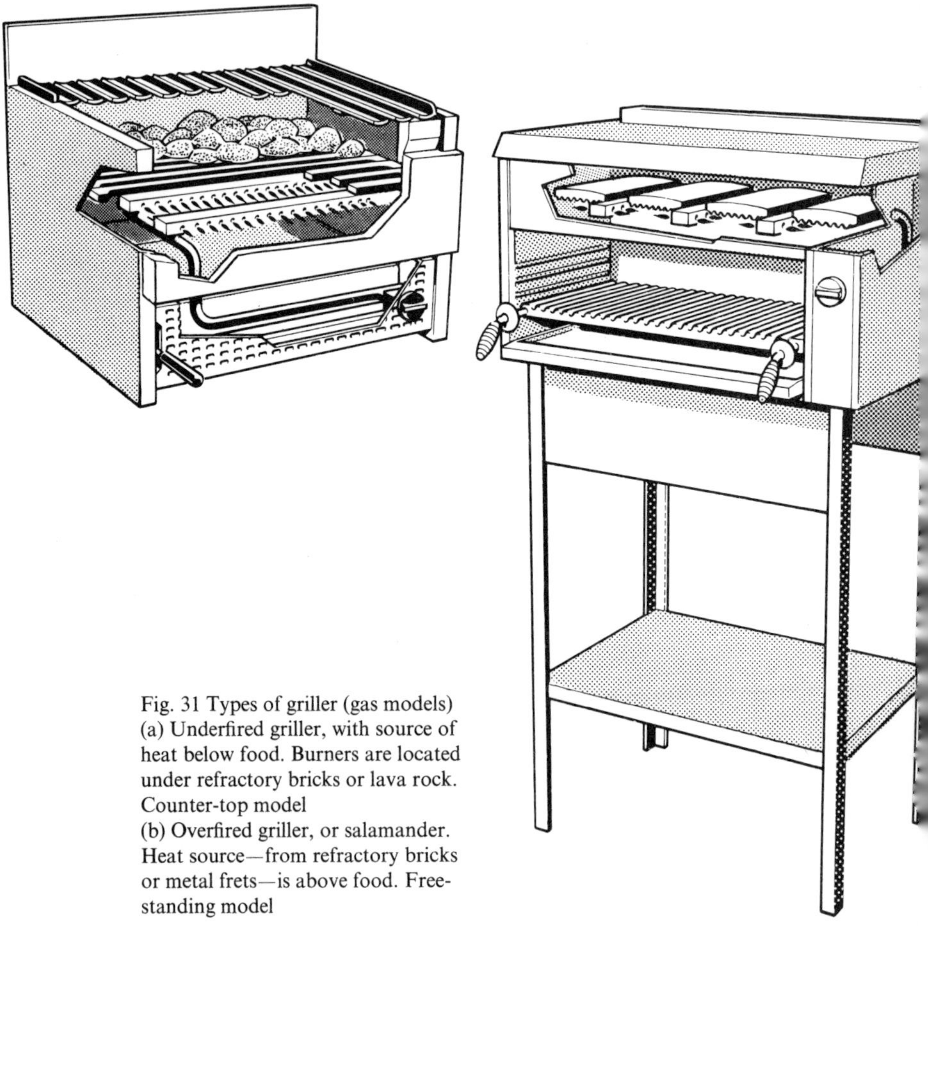

Fig. 31 Types of griller (gas models)
(a) Underfired griller, with source of heat below food. Burners are located under refractory bricks or lava rock. Counter-top model
(b) Overfired griller, or salamander. Heat source—from refractory bricks or metal frets—is above food. Free-standing model

Toasting

There are two types of equipment used solely for toasting bread:

1. Rotary toaster. This is designed for toasting on a large scale. Bread is fed into racks that pass in chain between radiant heating elements that toast both sides of the bread at once. The finished product is delivered into a tray. The colour of the toast may be controlled by varying the speed at which the racks pass between the elements. Output is up to 9 slices a minute.

2. Pop-up toaster. These automatic toasters are similar to domestic models, and are available to take 2, 4 or 6 slices. The degree of browning may be controlled by a built-in time switch. Models are available with a red light and a bell to indicate that toast is ready and the next batch may be inserted.

Frying

When food is fried, heat is conducted to it by means of hot fat or oil, in which it is either partly or totally immersed. Transfer of heat is very rapid, and, although the temperature of the frying medium is much lower than that of the elements used in grilling, the temperature at the surface of the frying food may be as high as that of grilled food. The frying medium is maintained at a temperature ranging from 150° Celsius to 190° Celsius according to the type of food being fried.

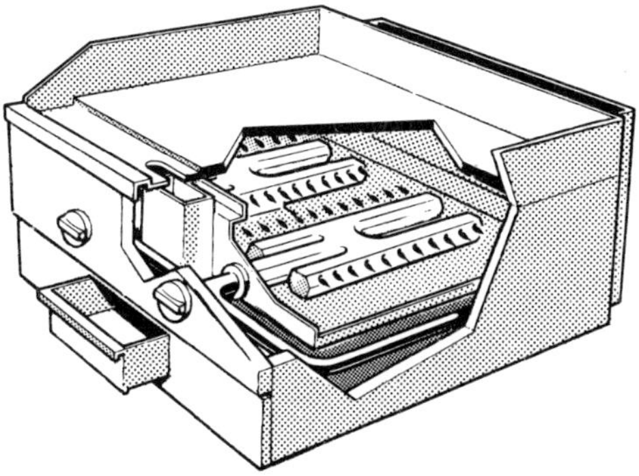

Fig. 32 Gas-fired griddle plate, counter-top model. Solid plate, which has drain channel, is heated from below by gas bar burner

Shallow frying

When food is shallow fried (that is, partly immersed in fat or oil or cooked in its own fat—for example, bacon), a shallow metal pan of stout construction is used. The food rests on the bottom of the pan, and must usually be turned at least once to complete the cooking process. There are several pieces of equipment suitable for shallow frying. Pans similar to, but larger than, the ordinary domestic variety may be used on the top of boiling plates and rings. Very shallow

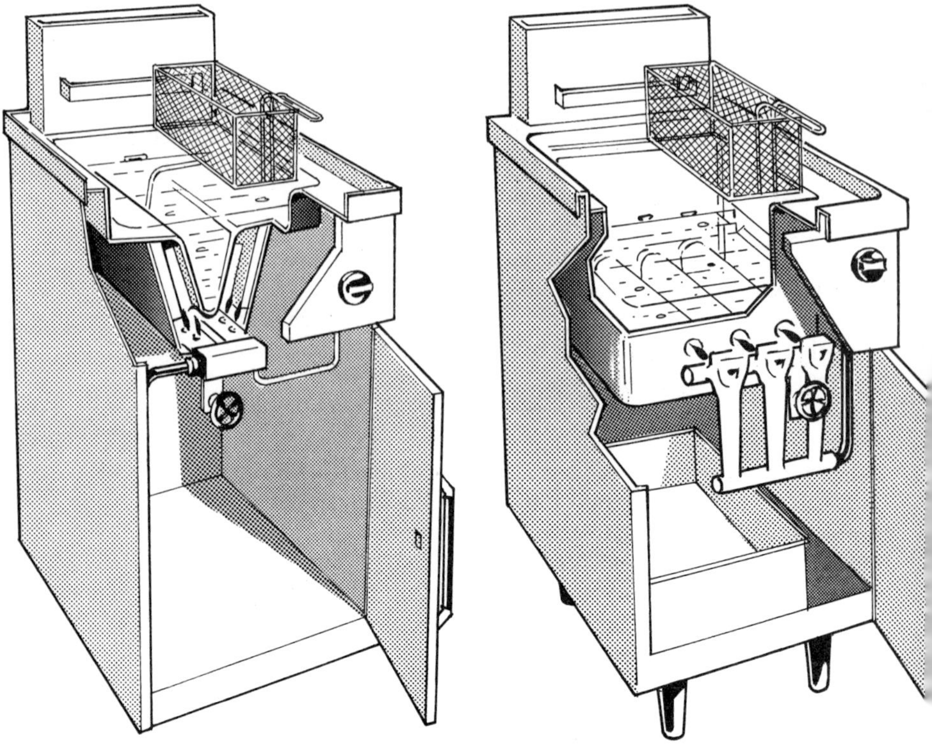

Fig. 33 Types of deep-fat fryer
(a) Gas-heated fryer with V-shaped pan heated above bottom of pan
(b) Gas-heated fryer, immersion-tube type. Burners fire into tubes immersed in frying medium

frying may be done on a griddle, which is a metal plate heated by gas or electricity. Griddles may be separate items of equipment (they are usually counter-top models—see Figure 32), or they may be mounted over a cooker, or they may be included in a boiling table. The bratt pan, a full description of which is given in the next chapter, and which is shown in Figure 37, may also be used for shallow frying.

Deep-fat frying

The simplest form of fryer that can be used for deep-fat frying, where food is totally immersed in the frying medium, is a round or oval pan about 150 mm to 200 mm deep, sufficiently thick and strong to withstand the weight of oil and the high temperatures to which it will

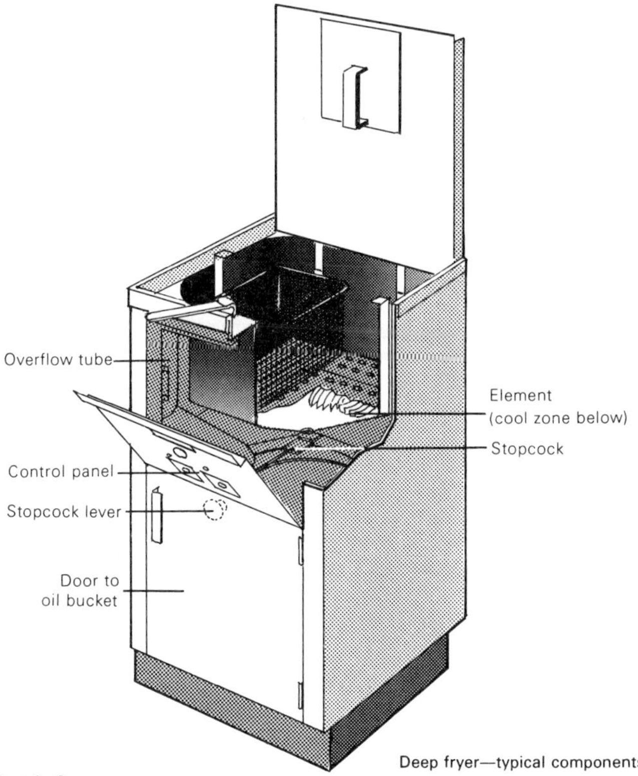

Deep fryer—typical components.

(c) Electric fryer
All these fryers have relatively cool zones below heat source, into which food particles can sink and remain without charring

be subjected. But this sort of equipment is unsuitable for large-scale operations. Large pans of oil are difficult to move, and when the oil is hot they are potential sources of danger. In all large establishments, and in small ones where there is a steady demand for fried food, it is customary to install one or more fryers in fixed positions, with their own sources of heat.

Deep-fat fryers create certain problems in kitchens, in that frying smells are very penetrating, and also oil tends to sublime during the cooking process and as a consequence grease may be deposited on various surfaces in the kitchen. When fryers are installed, special attention is given to ventilation, and extractor fans near fryers usually have grease filter units (see Chapter 3). Splashbacks to fryers help to prevent the dispersal of grease, but only to a limited extent.

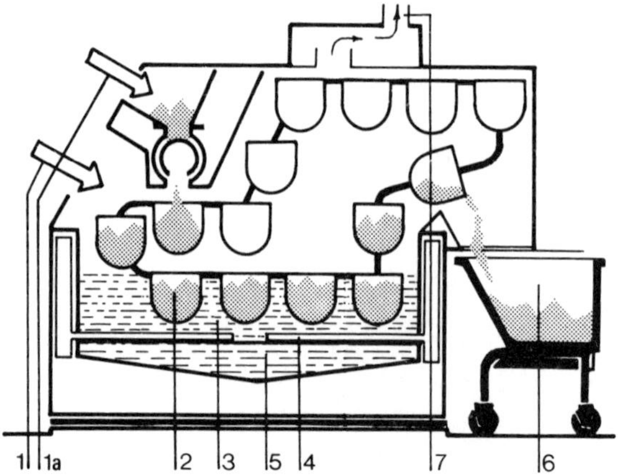

1 Loading by hand
1a Automatic loading
2 Basket
3 Frying oil
4 Immersion type heating elements
5 Draining area
6 Food service pan (may be either mobile or stationary)
7 Vapour hood

Fig. 34 Electric continuou deep-fat fryer

Design of deep-fat fryers

1. Size and dimensions of pan. When a fryer is to be used chiefly for frying chipped potatoes, which are cooked in batches in baskets, a narrow, deep pan is suitable. For items such as fish and doughnuts, which rise to the top when cooked, wider, shallower pans are better. Deep pans maintain the quality of the oil better than shallow ones, because the oil does not oxidise to the same extent. (Oil deteriorates through oxidisation.) Another point to be considered in relation to pan size is the amount of food to be cooked in one batch. Pans should not be too large for the size of the batch, since this again leads to excessive deterioration of the oil. Two small pans are more useful than one large one. This is partly because they are more flexible in use, but also because pre-heating times are shorter; it has to be remembered that oil deteriorates rapidly during any period when it is hot, but frying is not taking place. Fryers are often designed in units of one, two or more pans.

2. Cool zones. Nearly all fryers are of the cool-zone type (see Figure 33). Small particles of food that break away during frying fall into the cool zone, and are thus removed from the main body of the oil where they would carbonise, causing the oil to deteriorate and impairing the appearance of the finished cooked food through the deposition of carbonised particles.

3. Controls. Fryers are fitted with thermostats to control oil temperature; these may be adjusted to a maximum of 190° Celsius. Such control is essential for a good end-product; it is also an important safety factor, since overheated oil is a fire risk. For safety reasons some gas fryers incorporate a second cut-off device which, if the thermostat should fail, comes into operation at a temperature of 215° Celsius. Electric fryers sometimes have a second thermostat bonded to the heating element, which is effective if the main thermostat becomes defective. This prevents damage if the fryer is accidentally switched on when there is no oil in the pan. Cooking timers, usually with bells, are often fitted. When a gas fryer is chosen, the controls should be checked for ease and safety in lighting.

4. Capacity. The capacity of fryers is reckoned in output of chips (raw state, not blanched) per hour.

Continuous deep-fat fryers

Figure 34 shows the way in which these fryers operate. Because items are automatically fed into the fryer in small amounts, incoming food does not perceptibly affect the temperature of the oil; hence a temperature about 10 per cent lower than usual is used, and as a result oxidisation is considerably reduced and the oil's life thereby lengthened.

Oil clarifiers

After each day's use it is necessary to strain frying oil to remove particles of cooked food. This may be done manually, or a mobile oil clarifier with an electric pump may be used (see Figure 35).

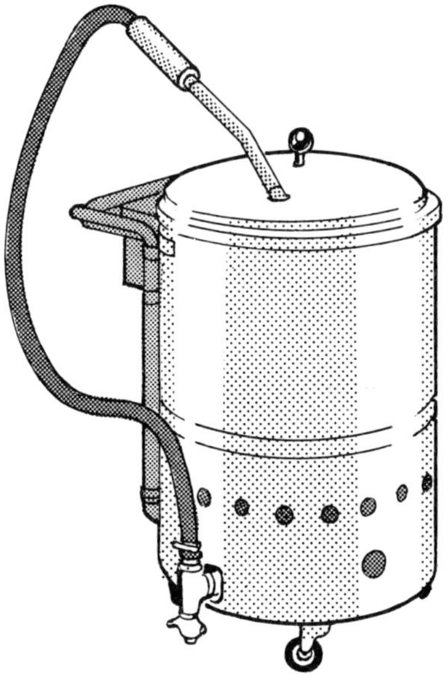

Fig. 35 Mobile oil clarifier. Pumps oil out of fryer and filters it into reservoir at base of cylinder. Clear oil is then pumped back into fryer

Chapter 9

Cooking processes and equipment, II: boiling, stewing, steaming

When the processes of boiling, stewing and steaming are compared with those of roasting and baking, two main differences are found. First, food is cooked under moist conditions rather than in the dry atmosphere described in the previous chapter. Second, cooking temperatures are much lower. In boiling and stewing, and in steaming at atmospheric pressure, temperatures do not rise above boiling point—100° Celsius. But in baking temperatures up to 260° Celsius are common.

Boiling and stewing

When food is boiled it is immersed in water maintained at boiling point, and heat is transferred from water to food by conduction and convection. The outside of the food, which is in contact with the boiling water, quickly reaches a temperature of 100° Celsius, but the cooking is not complete until the required temperature has been reached throughout the mass of the food. This temperature is not necessarily 100° Celsius, for it may be that a lower temperature is enough to cook the food. Boiled potatoes are an example. They are completely cooked when they are soft throughout, and this condition is reached when there is a temperature at their centres of 65° to 71° Celsius, which is sufficient to burst the starch grains and soften the cellulose. But when meat is boiled not only must the temperature throughout be raised to 100° Celsius, but it must be held at that point for some time in order to soften the fibrous insoluble collagen in the meat and convert it into soluble gelatin. The length of time needed for this varies according to the size and quality of the meat being cooked.

The stewing process is similar to boiling, but in this case the liquid in which the food is cooked is maintained at a slightly lower temperature, and the amount of liquid used is kept to a minimum. Because the temperature is lower, the transfer of heat is more gradual, and the movement of the liquid is less violent. These are important points in the cooking of certain foods. For example, fruit needs this sort of cooking if it is not to disintegrate.

Equipment for boiling and stewing

The basic requirements for boiling or stewing small quantities of food are simple. All that is needed is a container that will hold water and withstand heat, and that has a lid to prevent undue loss of steam. It is not practicable, however, to use very large portable containers for this purpose, mainly because of the weight of liquid involved. If it is remembered that 1 litre of water weighs 1 kilogram, it will readily be appreciated that portable pans of more than about 14 litres are unsuitable. Saucepans of this capacity and under can be accommodated on the boiling table of the range, or on free-standing boiling tables. Where food is to be cooked in larger batches than a 14-litre pan will hold, equipment is needed that can be filled and heated without being moved. It is interesting to trace the development of equipment for this purpose.

The Soyer boiler

During the Crimean War, complaints were received about the quality of food served to the troops, both in the field and in the hospitals, and one of the main causes was bad cooking. A chef of that period, Alexis Soyer, whose name became world-famous, had already achieved renown for his exhibits at the Great Exhibition of 1851. Soyer agreed to go to the Crimea to investigate the problem, and he quickly realised that one of the main difficulties in providing well-cooked food for the troops was the lack of suitable equipment in which large quantities of food could be cooked at one time. Very quickly he designed, made and put into use for the first time the boiler that was the forerunner of those used in catering today. An improved design of Soyer's boiler, still bearing his name, is used today in the army for field exercises, and is available for use in civilian emergencies. During the Second World War it proved its worth for emergency feeding of the population in many British cities after heavy aerial bombardment.

The Soyer boiler is a round, open-topped vessel made of iron with a diameter of about 0·76 m, with a rounded base and a capacity of 45 to 90 litres. It is supported on a cylindrical stand, which forms the surround to the firebox beneath. The boiler has a metal chimney, and a metal cover for the pan.

Boiling pans

1. General description. Boiling pans used today are similar in principle to Soyer boilers, but they have many refinements and modifications. Rustless metals and surfaces provide durable, hygienic and easily-cleaned finishes. Stainless steel is usually used for the inner casing of the boiler and for the lid. The outer casing also may be of stainless steel; vitreous enamel is an alternative finish. The lid is usually hinged and counterbalanced to facilitate lifting. Taps with swivel arms are fitted near by so that the boiler may be filled easily with water for cooking or cleaning.

2. Capacity and dimensions. Boiling pans are available in capacities from 45 to 180 litres, but the sizes most often chosen are 45 and 90 litres. Caterers usually prefer to have several smaller boilers rather than one or two very large ones, for three reasons. First, more flexible arrangements are possible with several boilers. Second, because smaller quantities of food need shorter cooking times, vegetables suffer less loss of nutrients. Third, because less weight of water is involved, certain foods, such as potatoes, are less likely to break up during cooking. There is, however, the disadvantage that several small boilers occupy more floor space than a few large ones. Typical dimensions for boilers are: diameter 760 mm for both 45- and 90-litre pans; height 680 mm for 45-litre and 760 mm for 90-litre pans. Modular boiling pans have square or rectangular casings so that they may be fitted *en suite*. The height of the boiling pan is important to the operator, especially when the pan is to be used for dishes such as milk sauces that need frequent stirring. Also, it is difficult to clean the inside of a high pan. Heights greater than 760 mm are inconvenient for most people.

3. Facilities for emptying. Solid foods are lifted out of boilers either before or after liquid has been drained off. It is possible to have mechanical means for doing this, in which case food is cooked in a wire basket with a handle; this is removed from the boiler by means of pulleys. This sort of apparatus is, however, rare. Liquids are usually drained off by means of a draw-off cock, and the outlet is protected by a removable strainer so that it does not become blocked with particles of food. It is usual to provide a waste outlet gulley underneath the outlet, so that waste water may run directly into the drain. Removable anti-splash funnels are hung over the outlet tap while the boiler is being drained. Where apparatus has a tilting mechanism, draw-off taps are not needed and the pan is emptied by pouring.

Types of boiling pan

Single boiling pan. These are heated directly by means of a gas burner or electric element. They are used for cooking vegetables and meat, but are unsuitable for foods such as milk and thick liquids that are liable to burn, because there is a concentration of heat at the bottom of the boiler near the burner or element.

The jacketed boiler. The jacketed boiling pan has an outer jacket of steam or water, which ensures even heat distribution. In kitchens with facilities for live steam, boilers have jackets into which live steam is injected. Another type of boiler has a jacket from which air has been

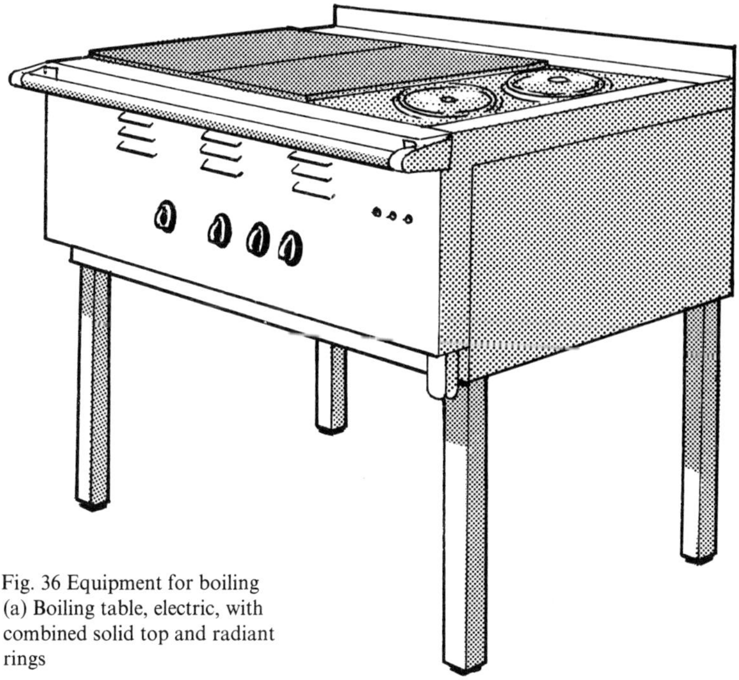

Fig. 36 Equipment for boiling
(a) Boiling table, electric, with combined solid top and radiant rings

evacuated. There is a small sump in the jacket, which, when heated by gas or electricity, produces steam. The sump does not need refilling, and the boiling pan has automatic temperature control. A simpler type of boiling pan is the one with a water jacket. Some water-jacketed pans are dual-purpose, with an inner pan that is removable so that food may be cooked directly in the outer pan. A dual-purpose pan has a funnel-shaped inlet for filling the outer pan, a gauge to show the water level in the outer pan, and a steam outlet. Since there is no automatic filling device, care must be taken to see that it does not boil dry. Two kinds of jacketed boiler are shown in Figures 36c–d.

The tilting boiling pan. This pan is carried on trunnions, and is provided with a large cog wheel that engages with the pinion. Turning a handle on the pinion shaft causes the large wheel, which is rigidly connected with the pan, to rotate, carrying the pan with it. This leverage makes the process of tilting easy to carry out, and the rate of pouring is always under control.

The tilting kettle. This is a small, floor-mounted piece of equipment with a tilting mechanism operated by a lever, and with immersion

Fig. 36(b) Boiling table, gas, with open top and series of ring burners

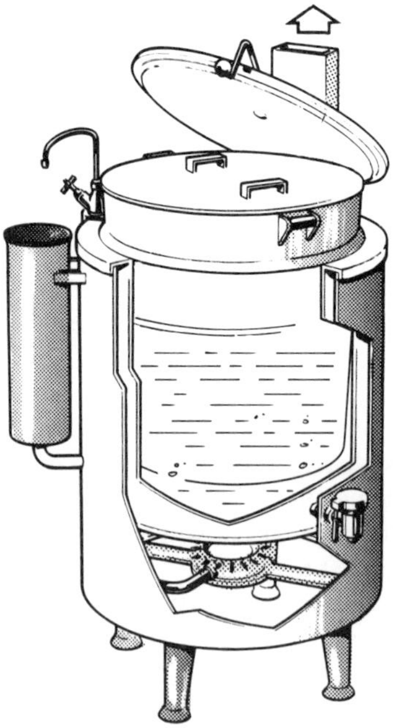

(c) Boiling pan, gas, dual-purpose, with removable inner pan

(d) Boiling pan, gas, jacketed

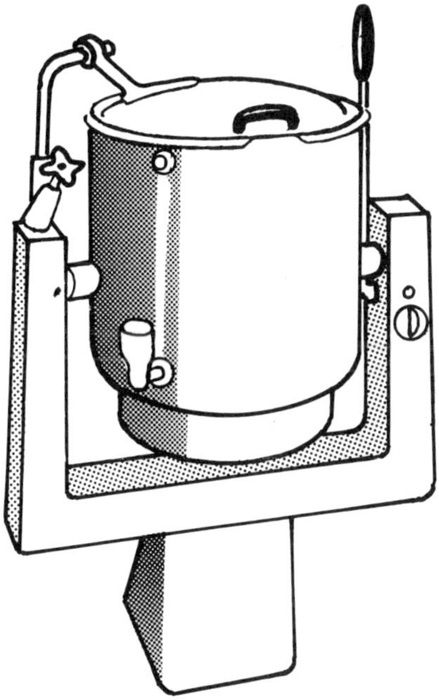

(e) Tilting kettle, electric, with rotating hand wheel

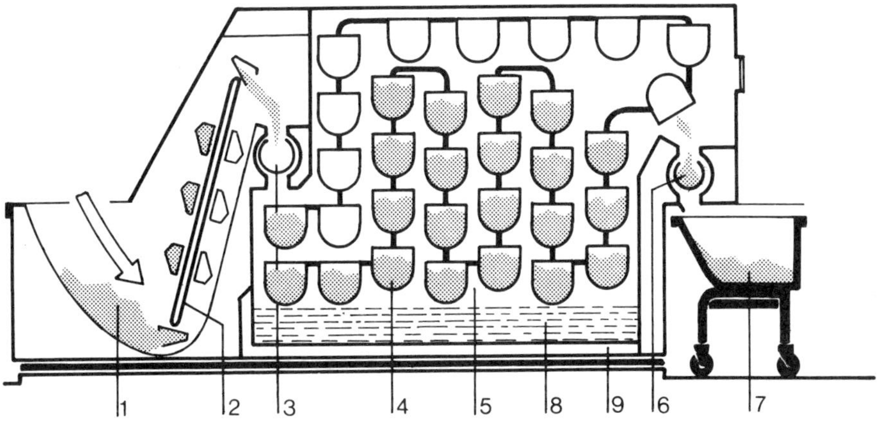

1 Automatic loading
2 Endless hoisting system
3 Loading drum and patented steam seal
4 Stainless steel perforated basket.
5 Steaming chamber
6 Unloading drum and patented steam seal
7 Food service pan (may be either mobile or stationary)
8 Water
9 Steam heating

(f) Continuous multi-purpose cooker

elements as the source of heat. It has a quick heating-up period and a rapid recovery rate. It is particularly suited to batch cooking, and to cooking frozen vegetables. A typical capacity is 40 litres, and typical overall dimensions are 762 mm × 495 mm (back to front) × 1015 mm high. A space of 230 mm is needed for tilting (see Figure 36e).

The bratt pan. The bratt pan (shown in Figure 37) is a shallow pan that may be used for boiling, and also for frying and griddling. It usually has a tilting mechanism similar to that of the tilted boiling pan. Its characteristics are versatility, and a rapid heating and recovery rate. It is particularly useful for those meat and poultry dishes that require meat to be partly cooked or seared by dry heat before it is cooked in a liquid medium, because the whole cooking process may be carried out in the same piece of equipment. The tilting bratt pan is emptied by means of a broad lip to facilitate the flow of liquid and to avoid drips. Non-tilting pans have a specially-designed draining device and a shaped shovel for removing solid food.

Continuous-boiling equipment. In this type of equipment foods such as vegetables or rice are loaded automatically into small containers that pass in chain through a bath of boiling water. Because the amount of food in each container is small, cooking time is short, and hence the quality of the finished product is good. A continuous supply of freshly-cooked food is available, and it is not necessary to keep it warm for any length of time before service. The continuous boiler shown in Figure 36f has a device at the end of the cooking chain for rinsing farinaceous foods, such as rice, to separate the grains. Sophisticated equipment of this type is suitable for large establishments only.

The boiling table. The free-standing boiling table (Figure 36a–b) is similar to the boiling table that forms part of a cooking range, but, because there is no oven below, it is possible to have a more convenient height for lifting heavy pans. A suitable height is 770 mm. There is always a need for some boiling space in a kitchen for cooking miscellaneous items in small quantities. Also, some caterers prefer boiling tables to fixed boiling pans for cooking vegetables, because they obtain superior results by cooking small quantities in batches. Where this is the practice, it is convenient to have a small sink close to the boiling table and at the same height, so that the work of carrying and lifting heavy pans is minimised. Even so, a considerable amount of manhandling is involved, and a better method might be to use tilting kettles or high-speed steamers.

The stockpot stand. This is a boiling table with one ring only, designed specifically to take a stockpot. The stockpot has to be filled from above, and is emptied through a draw-off tap, so the height of

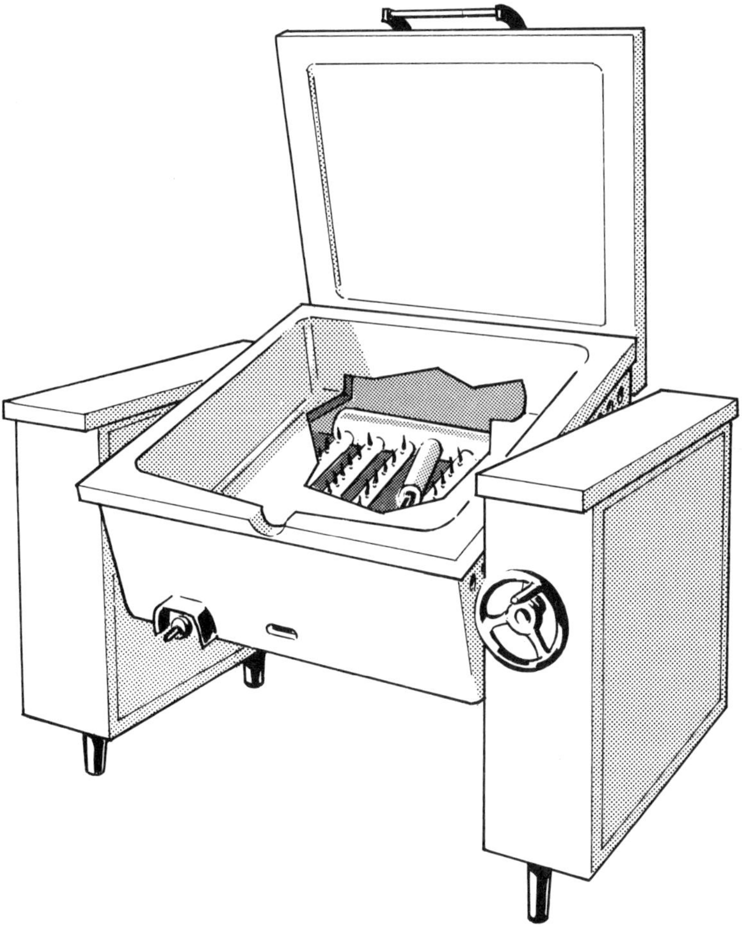

Fig. 37 Bratt pan, gas model. Versatile pan with tilting mechanism, used for boiling, braising and frying

the stand has to be suitable for both purposes; a typical height for the stand is 450 mm. Stockpots have capacities of 45 litres or more.

Steaming

As a cooking method steaming has a great deal in common with boiling and stewing, but the essential difference is that, although boiling water is used, food does not actually touch the water but is cooked in the steam it generates. When the steam used for cooking is generated at atmospheric pressure, temperature conditions are similar to those for boiling. Where steam is generated at a higher pressure temperatures are higher, and in consequence the cooking time is reduced. At a pressure of 103 kN/m^2 the temperature is about 121° Celsius.

When food is steamed there is no weight of water—as there is in boiling—to cause food to disintegrate, and leaching of soluble constituents does not take place, so that two of the disadvantages of boiling, which apply especially when large boilers are used, do not apply to steaming. One disadvantage is that certain foods sometimes discolour; this can happen with potatoes. There is no cooking liquor with this process.

Equipment for steaming

Simple steamers

The essentials of equipment for steaming are: a vessel in which water may be boiled to generate steam; a stand upon which food may be placed so that it is in steam but out of the water; and a lid to ensure that there is no unnecessary loss of steam. Instead of being placed on a stand, food may be put in a container connected with the vessel holding the water, which will serve the same purpose.

In one type of simple steamer water is put into a round or oval pan into the top of which fits a covered vessel, with perforations in its base, for holding food. In another type a vertical pipe connects the two compartments and leads steam from the lower to the upper compartment, delivering it through a hole in the side near the top of the vessel. Additional tiers may be used with both these types of steamer; three is usually regarded as the maximum. Larger steamers are usually oval in shape, up to 500 mm long, and have three tiers.

This type of equipment has disadvantages. The base is heavy to lift, and the top tier difficult to reach. The steamer needs topping up with boiling water from time to time, and there is always the possibility that this will be forgotten, and it will boil dry. These disadvantages have been met in the steaming oven, which also has the advantage of taking a much greater load of food.

Essential features of the steaming oven

The steaming oven consists of a square or rectangular box fitted with shelves. A supply of steam is obtained either by heating a well of water in the oven base, or by admitting steam generated outside the oven by means of a valve.

Types of steaming oven

The atmospheric steaming oven. This is a fixed appliance with a well of water in the oven base heated by either gas or electricity, and with an automatic filling cistern fed from the mains water supply. See Figure 38a.

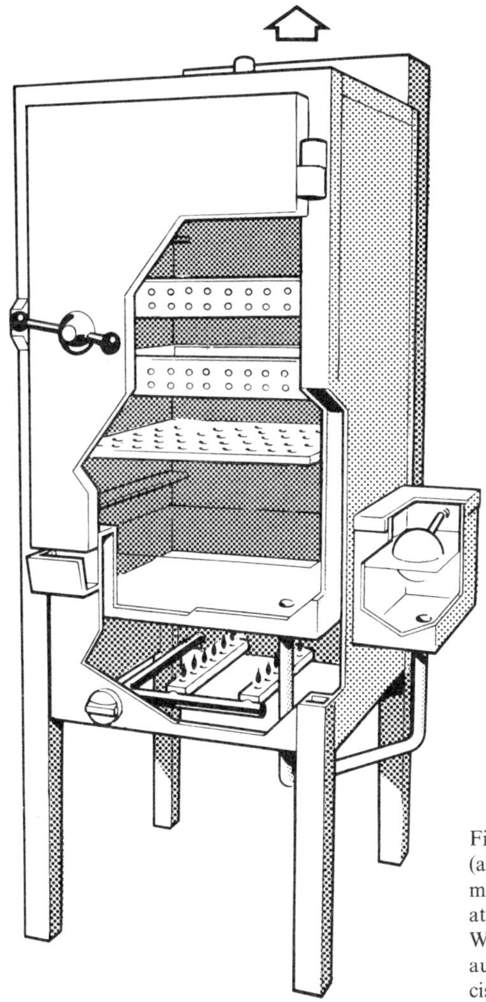

Fig. 38 Kinds of steamer
(a) Steaming oven, gas model. Steam is at atmospheric pressure. Water level is maintained automatically by feed cistern

A ball valve in the cistern controls the supply of water and ensures replenishment as required. Water is kept at the correct level in the oven even though a rapid change into steam is continuously taking place, and, because the amount added at any one time is small, the water does not go off the boil. It is important that the water should not boil more rapidly than is necessary to maintain a temperature throughout the oven of 100° Celsius, since over-rapid boiling would waste fuel and cause excessive emission of steam into the kitchen. The amount of steam necessary to maintain the required temperature is

Fig. 38(b) Rotapan. Variation on usual type of atmospheric steaming oven. 4 circular compartments open separately

not fixed, and will vary with the amount of cold material present in the oven, and also on the external temperature and the insulation of the oven chamber. A thermostat is usually fitted to ensure that the correct temperature is maintained without waste of fuel. A drip tray is provided beneath the oven door to collect the water that condenses from steam when the oven door is opened. A tap at the base allows the oven to be emptied for cleaning. Steaming ovens should be cleaned daily after use, and it is convenient to have a floor gulley nearby for the disposal of waste water and also of condensate from the drip tray.

Atmospheric steaming ovens are used for puddings, vegetables, fruit, rice and pasta foods, and also for meat and poultry when long, slow cooking is needed. Portable steaming ovens for use on top of ranges and boiling tables are available, but are not in common use. They do not have any automatic controls.

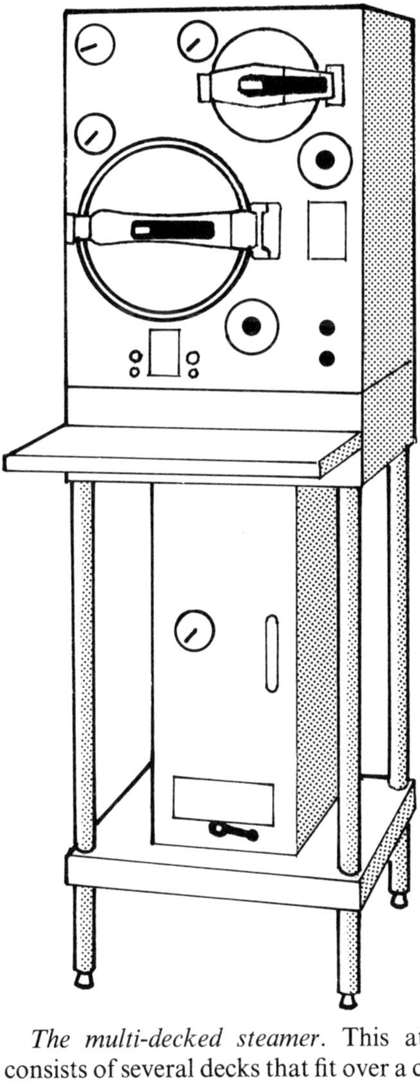

Fig. 38(c) High-pressure steaming oven, electric model, with two oven compartments and steam generator below oven

The multi-decked steamer. This atmospheric type of steamer consists of several decks that fit over a circular water well, which may be swung out sideways for loading and unloading. Each compartment may be attended to separately, and this is a big convenience where foods with different cooking times are being cooked, or where different finishing times are necessary—for example, for first and second sittings of diners. See Figure 38d.

The high-pressure steaming oven. Where there is a facility for live steam, ovens are fed with steam from the boiler house provided clean steam is available. A pressure of 34 kN/m^2 is often used, but pressures

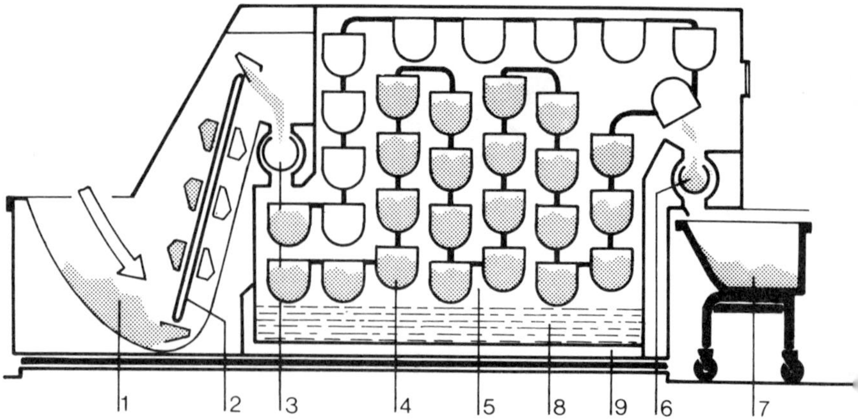

1 Automatic loading
2 Endless hoisting system
3 Loading drum and patented steam seal
4 Stainless steel perforated basket.
5 Steaming chamber
6 Unloading drum and patented steam seal
7 Food service pan (may be either mobile or stationary)
8 Water
9 Steam heating

Fig. 38(d) Continuous steamer for cooking potatoes and other vegetables

may go up to 96 kN/m². Higher pressures are unsuitable for foods such as steamed puddings, because their texture tends to become close. This apart, the range of foods that may be cooked in this type of steamer is similar to that for atmospheric steaming ovens. Modern high-pressure steaming ovens do not obtain their steam from a remote source. They operate at pressures from 83 kN/m² to 97 kN/m², and steam may be generated in various ways:

(a) by an external generator, usually sited immediately below the oven;

(b) from water poured into the base of the oven;

(c) from water supplied direct from the mains, in which case steam is generated in the oven shell.

These ovens, which are extremely compact and efficient, are fitted with timers, pressure gauges and, in some cases, pressure selector switches, so that the operator may choose a lower pressure for cooking certain foods (*e.g.*, sponge pudding). Some cookers have automatic defrost cycles for frozen foods.

Ovens may be free-standing or counter-top, with base areas ranging from 0·16 m² to 0·51 m². The two-oven model shown in Figure 38c has overall oven dimensions of 508 mm (width) × 718 mm (depth) × 679 mm (height); the stand dimensions are 508 mm (width) × 905 mm (depth) × 1556 mm (height). The large oven takes a pan that holds 3·4 kg, and the smaller oven takes a pan that holds 1·13 kg. It will cook 1200 × 100 g portions of fresh peas an hour. Plate 2 shows a single compartment high-pressure steaming oven in use.

This type of steamer is particularly useful for cooking vegetables. Because of the speed at which they cook, they may be used to keep a service counter continually supplied with batches of freshly-cooked vegetables. Speed and immediacy of cooking, together with the fact that there is no leaching, ensure that when green vegetables are cooked quality is very good, and there is little loss of nutrients. Frozen boil-in-the-bag foods may conveniently be regenerated in these cookers.

Low-pressure steaming ovens. These ovens have internal feed cisterns and operate at low pressures—usually at 0·34 kN/m². An advantage of this type of steamer over the atmospheric type is that when different foods are steamed at the same time there is no intermingling of flavours.

Cookers using moist air circulated by fan. In the base of the oven is a trough containing a small amount of water. At the top is a vertically-mounted fan. When the cooker is closed and the heat source (gas, electricity or steam) is switched on, air is circulated from the bottom to the top of the cooker, and it remains in circulation at a selected

Plate 2 High-pressure steamer in use

temperature, picking up heat and humidity as required and transferring them to the food. Temperature, humidity and circulation are automatically controlled. The circulating air has a humidity of 95 per cent. This method of cooking is particularly suitable for meat, as there is little or no shrinkage.

The continuous-steam cooker. The continuous vegetable and potato steamer shown in Figure 38d works in a similar way to the continuous boiler, and has similar advantages with regard to quality of end-product. Containers pass in chain through the steaming chamber.

Chapter 10

Equipment for service areas and for transporting meals

Equipment for keeping food hot

One of the fundamental precepts for good cooking is to serve food at the right temperature. As a rule no difficulty arises about cold food, but every cook is familiar with the problem of trying to serve hot food hot. When large numbers are concerned, the problem becomes even more complicated.

Ideally food that is to be served hot should be sent to the table as soon as it has been cooked, when it will be at the correct temperature for serving. Losses in nutritional value after cooking and loss of aroma and flavour will be minimal. Prompt service after cooking is important for most foods, but especially so in the case of vegetables, which suffer in both eating quality and nutritional value if they are kept for any length of time.

In call-order catering and in systems using continuous-cooking equipment the ideal may be easily achieved, but in most large kitchens some delay between completion of cooking and serving is inevitable. When the kitchen is some distance away from the dining room, delays are likely to be considerable. Let us take the case of a kitchen providing meals over a two-hour period by the cafeteria system of service. It is obvious that, even though relay cooking may be practised for cooking vegetables, all clients cannot be served with food as soon as it has been cooked, and arrangements must be made to prevent heat loss during the serving period. It is usual to provide hot cupboards for this purpose.

Not only must food be hot at the time of service, but so must plates and any serving dishes. A cold plate or dish can quickly cool food, and in large dining rooms, where the distance from service counter to table inevitably causes food to lose heat, it is all the more important that plates and dishes are hot. It follows that the uses of hot cupboards are:

(a) keeping cooked food hot;
(b) heating plates and dishes.

For both these uses the temperature inside the hot cupboard is critical. Too high a temperature may damage the glaze of ceramic ware, or cause it to crack, and plastic plates may become discoloured, or, in extreme cases, melt. Uncovered food in a hot cupboard dries out even at relatively low temperatures; the higher the temperature the more rapidly this happens. For plate-warming, a temperature of about 60° Celsius is suitable, while about 82° Celsius will be adequate for keeping food hot. It should be remembered that the Food Hygiene (General) Regulations, 1970, require that certain foods be kept at temperatures either below 10° Celsius or not less than 62·8° Celsius.

The hot cupboard: general description

Like the oven, the hot cupboard consists of a metal box with shelves into which a source of heat is introduced. The essential difference between the two is the temperature at which they work. Hot cupboards are either mounted on legs or have skirtings that fit flush with the floor. In the latter case, it is essential that there are no gaps or crannies that are difficult to clean, or which might harbour mice. Hot cupboards should be insulated to conserve heat and to provide reasonable working conditions for staff serving meals.

The most common design of hot cupboard has a table top and a cupboard below, the top being used either as a counter or as a hot table on which dishes stand before service. When the hot cupboard forms part of an integrated service counter, dimensions and design will be such that it can be fitted *en suite* with other components of the counter (see Figure 2).

Hot cupboards usually have external surfaces of stainless steel, and internal surfaces of aluminium sheet steel or other rustless metal. Typical dimensions are as follows: height, 840 mm to 915 mm; depth, 610 mm to 760 mm; width, 610 mm to 2·4 m. In choosing a hot cupboard that is to be used as a serving counter, thought should be given to the convenience of the client as well as the staff. Where young children are concerned, the height should be less than for adult clients.

Hot cupboards may be heated by gas or electricity. Where live steam is available, steam is injected into a coil of pipes fixed to a plate in the base of the hot cupboard. Usually the temperature is thermostatically controlled.

Cabinet hot cupboards. These are usually twice the height of the counter type, and have two compartments, one on top of the other. Hence they have a large capacity in relation to floor area, and in some circumstances they form useful screens between kitchen and servery area. Narrow models, about 350 mm deep, are suitable for single stacks of plates.

Hot cupboards with doors on either side. In the standard hot cupboard, doors are provided on one side only. But it is sometimes convenient to have doors on both sides so that food may be put in at one side and taken out from the other. This sort of arrangement is shown in Figure 6. One disadvantage of this type of hot cupboard is that there may be big heat losses. A design that minimises heat losses is described in Chapter 4.

Hot cupboards with roll-away doors. The advantage of roll-away doors is that the whole of the contents of the hot cupboard may be seen at the same time.

Variety of models. A great variety of hot cupboards is available with a wide range of dimensions to meet special needs. These include wall-mounted units.

Heated trolleys. Electrically-heated trolleys are used for carrying food from the kitchen to the service point and keeping it hot during transit and also, in most circumstances, during service. Some have separate compartments, insulated from the heated part, for cold foods. A widely-used model is shown in Figure 40, but many sizes and types are available, including those suitable for short outside journeys. When size of trolley is being considered, the total fully-loaded weight and any gradients on its route must be borne in mind. It may be difficult to push a trolley that is larger than 910 mm high × 610 mm deep × 910 mm long.

The bain-marie. One way of keeping food hot is to immerse the bottom and sides of the food container in hot water. A water bath used for this purpose is called a bain-marie. Open-topped bains-marie are used in the kitchen by the chef to keep items such as sauces hot while he is dishing up. When a bain-marie is used to keep food hot while it is being served the top is closed, but there are cut-outs of various sizes into which food containers fit. The bain-marie may form part of the top of a hot cupboard, as in Figure 39, or it may be mobile (as in Figure 21), but in the latter case the bain-marie is of a slightly different type. It would be inconvenient to have water in the base of a mobile bain-marie, and so the well is heated directly by an electric element. Known as a dry bain-marie, it is also used at times in fixed service units, in which case the source of heat may be either gas or electricity.

A water tap is needed nearby for filling the traditional bain-marie, which must, of course, be emptied after use. An advantage of the dry bain-marie is that no plumbing is needed. Also, where it forms part of a hot cupboard, it does not project so far into the cupboard as does the wet variety. However, the dry type is not always suitable when meals are served over a long period, since it may not keep the food hot enough.

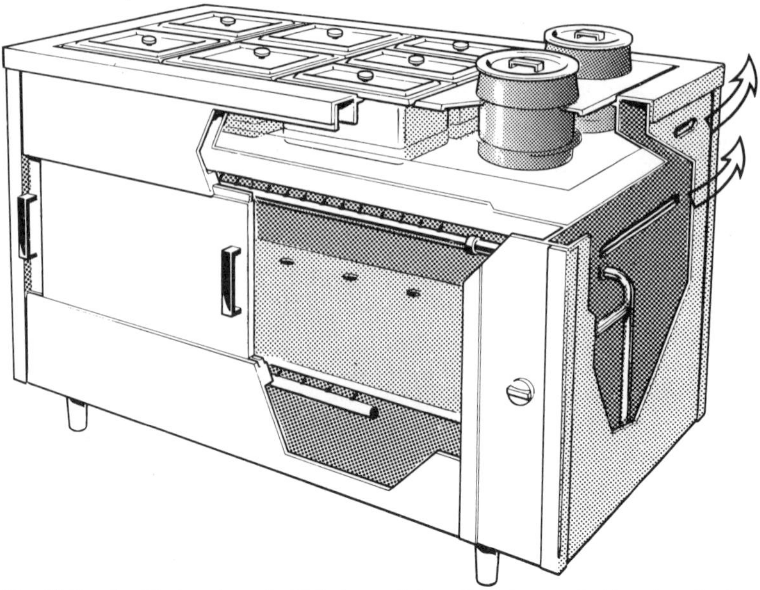

Fig. 39 Gas-fired hot cupboard with bain-marie top. Containers to hold various foods are partly immersed in heated water bath (bain-marie). Food also kept hot on shelf below

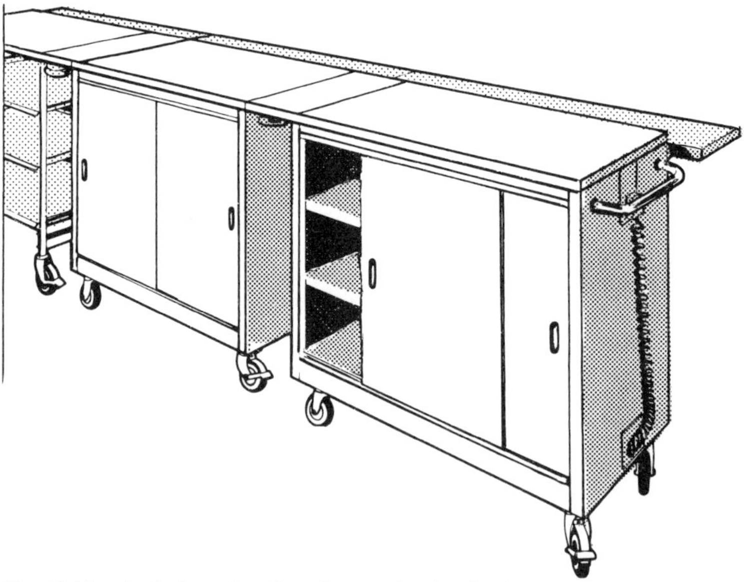

Fig. 40 Electrically-heated trolleys for carrying hot food and plates. May be used individually or linked together by bridging pieces, to form service counter. Folding tray slides available. Unheated trolleys form cold section of counter

Food service counters

Several items as well as hot cupboards may form part of the food service counter, as follows: cold section; refrigerated section; display cabinets; display shelves with 'sneeze' plates (that is, plates to protect food on shelves from clients' sneezes, etc.); beverage section with storage below for cups and saucers and equipment for making beverages and soft drinks dispensers; sections for stacked trays and for cutlery; a turntable from which clients help themselves; and a cashier's desk (see Figure 2). In some cases where clients help themselves to certain items, provision is made for some containers to be raked for ease of access.

Mobile service counters

Where meals are served at a distance from the kitchen, several trolleys may be linked together with bridging pieces to form a service counter, as shown in Figure 40. This arrangement may be used in other circumstances where it is either impossible or undesirable to have a fixed counter. The range of facilities available with a mobile service counter is, of course, limited.

Ancillary items to the service counter

Infra-red lamps. It is sometimes the practice for staff working at cafeteria counters to keep slightly ahead of clients by serving food on to plates and putting them on an overshelf from which the client chooses. To prevent food from cooling while it is on the shelf, infra-red lamps may be fitted above; an alternative is to warm the shelf by means of built-in infra-red heaters.

Plate dispensers. The use of these was described in Chapter 6. Dispensers may be electrically heated or unheated; they may be mobile, or fixed to form part of the service counter. The spring-operated mechanism that releases the plates (see Figure 41) may be adjusted to suit the weight of plate as necessary.

Heated cup-stacking unit. This revolving unit accommodates cups stacked in four columns, and it has an element designed to heat the insides of cups but not the handles.

Tray and cutlery stands and trolleys. Instead of having a space for trays as part of the counter, separate tray stands or tray trolleys may be provided. Stands and trays for cutlery are also available.

Tray slides. These are fitted at the front of the counter for the convenience of the client.

Drinking-water facilities. Various types of equipment are available to dispense water quickly and without drips into individual containers. For example, water is dispensed on pressure from a tumbler, and stops flowing when the tumbler is removed. These facilities are usually sited separately from the service counter.

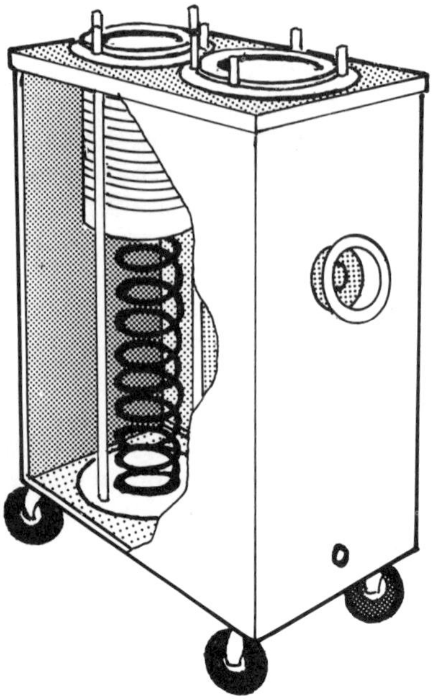

Fig. 41 Mobile plate dispenser. Heated plates are continuously available at height convenient to operator. Dispensing mechanism is spring-operated, and there is electric heating element. Dispenser is refilled with plates in washing-up area

Equipment for maintaining the temperature of food in transit

As well as heated trolleys, which have been mentioned earlier in this chapter, there are several pieces of equipment designed to keep food at a required temperature during transit; some examples are shown in Figure 42. The type of container shown in Figure 42a, which usually has cork as the insulating material, is satisfactory for keeping food hot in bulk, but it is not sufficiently well insulated to be suitable for frozen foods. Equipment using expanded polystyrene as an insulator, which is suitable for frozen foods, is shown in Figure 42b. Insulated stacking trays are shown in Figure 42c, and a plate warmer in Figure 42d.

Another way of keeping individual meals hot is to use a container into which heated charcoal is inserted; in Britain this method is associated with the provision of meals to old people. Other containers are heated electrically and they also store heat so that the container keeps food hot during transit once the storage core has been charged.

Equipment for hot beverages

Almost all catering establishments serve hot drinks—chiefly tea and coffee—and therefore need facilities for the supply of boiling water. It may be that demands have to be met over a very short period, as at breakfast or tea-time at a boarding school; or hot drinks may be wanted over a longer period, as in the case of a snack bar. Whatever

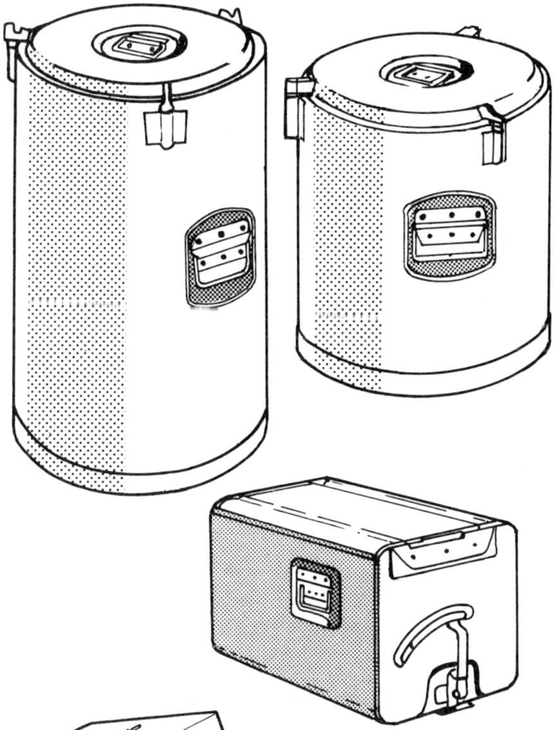

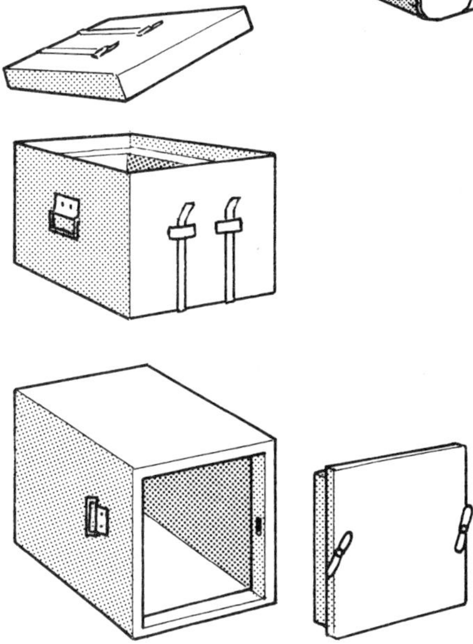

Fig. 42 Insulated equipment to keep food hot or cold during transit
(a) Double-walled metal containers with insulating material between walls. Circular containers of 4·5-litre and 9-litre capacity intended for liquids. Rectangular container, with capacity of 32 litres, for solid food, holds 3 standard baking or steaming tins

(b) Insulated boxes for carrying frozen foods short distances. Boxes and lids have plywood exteriors, inner layer of expanded polystyrene and aluminium linings

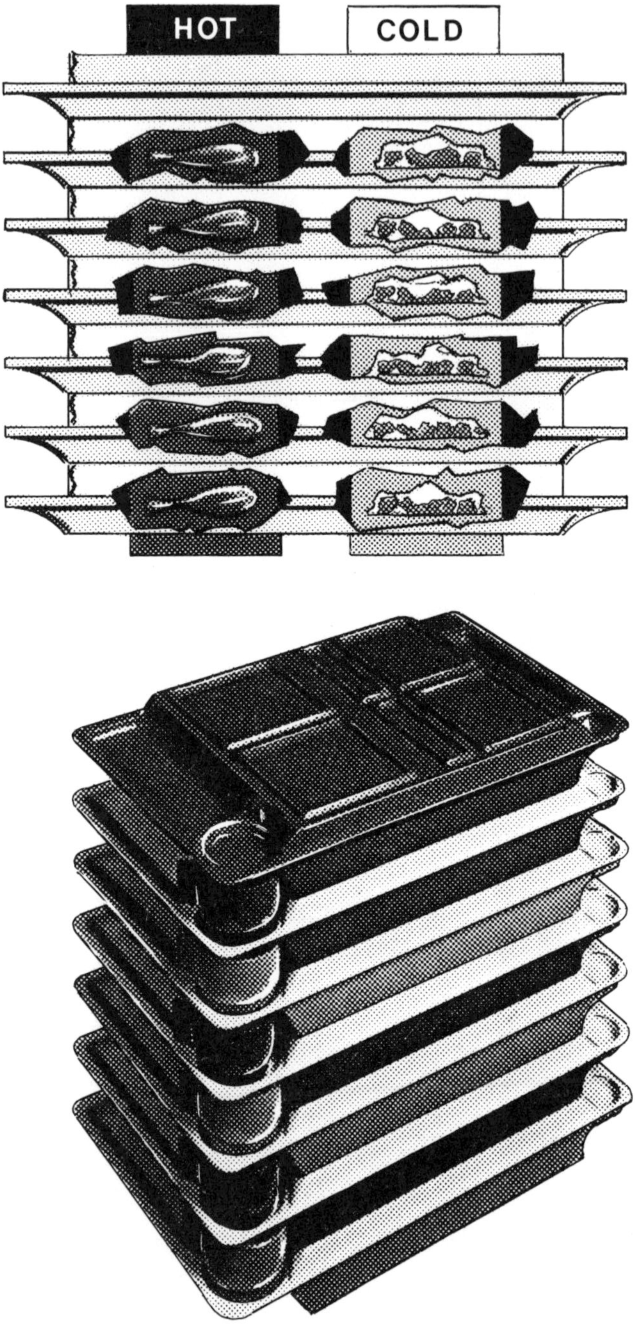

Fig. 42(c) Insulated stacking trays with separate insulation for hot and cold items. Suitable for hospital use and for meals-on-wheels schemes

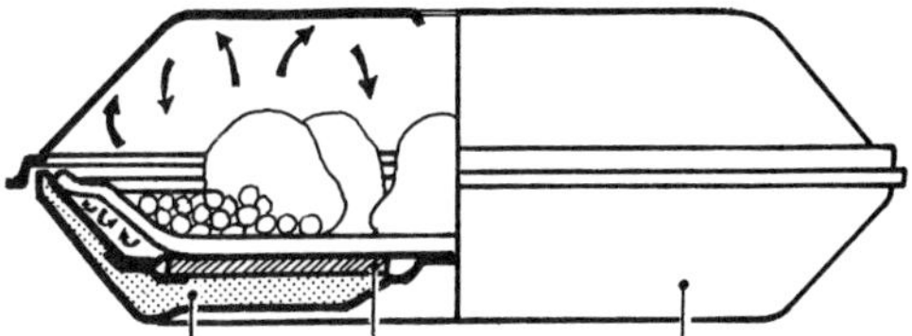

Fig. 42(d) Plate-warmer for plated meal. Heat provided by heat-retaining pellet. Warmer is insulated

the type of service, the facilities provided must be adequate to meet maximum demands without undue delay.

It is obvious that, where large numbers are concerned, it is not practicable to heat water for tea and coffee in kettles. The average quantity of boiling water needed to serve two cups of tea or coffee per head is 400 ml so for breakfast and tea meals, 40 litres are needed for every 100 people. This quantity could be provided by several kettles, but it would be inconvenient to do this regularly, and so facilities for heating water in bulk are necessary.

Bulk water heaters. The simplest piece of equipment is a bulk water heater fixed to a stand or counter, which is heated by gas or electricity (see Figure 43a). Essential features are:

(a) A draw-off tap;

(b) A gauge to show the water level.

Other features available are:

(a) Insulation;

(b) Thermostatic control, whereby the water temperature is maintained at just below boiling point until it is needed;

(c) A thermometer;

(d) Automatic lighting, with a flame-failure device (gas models);

(e) A cut-off device that operates when the water level is low.

When boilers are insulated, the time taken to reach boiling point is reduced because thermal efficiency is increased. Bulk water heaters are available with capacities from 9 to 135 litres.

The bulk water heater is suitable in circumstances where everyone wants his hot drink within a short time, as, for example, during the morning break at a college or factory. But where a continuous supply of boiling water is needed over a long period it is not suitable. Once the initial supply of boiling water has been exhausted, some time elapses before a fresh supply is available. There is also the disadvantage that, if for any reason water is kept at boiling point for a long time, it will become flat and thus unsatisfactory for tea-making. (It is well known that only freshly boiling water should be used.)

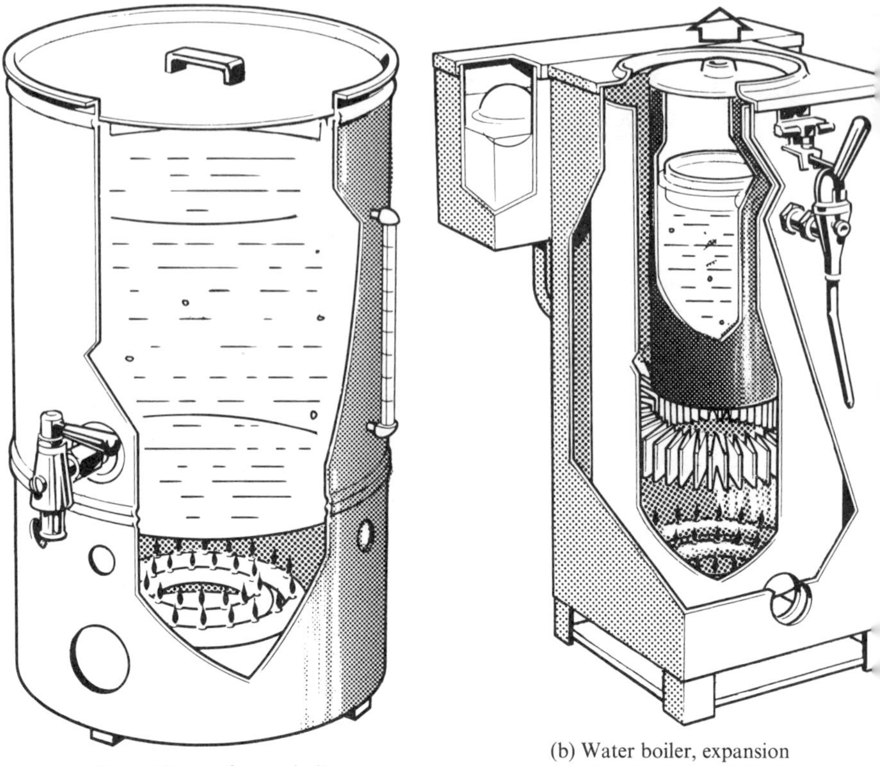

Fig. 43 Types of water boiler for making hot drinks
(a) Bulk water heater (gas-heated model)

(b) Water boiler, expansion type (gas-heated model). Relies on principle that water expands when heated. Supplies boiling water instantly on demand

Unless there is an automatic cut-out, there is always the possibility that this equipment will be allowed to boil dry.

The expansion type of water boiler. This kind of boiler gives an almost continuous supply of boiling water for an indefinite period, but it takes a short time to heat up in the first place. Its operation depends upon the expansion of water when it is heated, and, though design details may differ, the principle is the same in all boilers of this type (see Figure 43b). Rapid heating is achieved by providing a large heating surface for a small amount of water. The boiler is fed with cold water from a tank, which has a ball valve to control automatically the water level in the boiler. When the water reaches boiling point, it expands enough to reach the dispensing chamber to which the draw-off tap is connected.

The pressure-type water boiler. A constant supply of boiling water

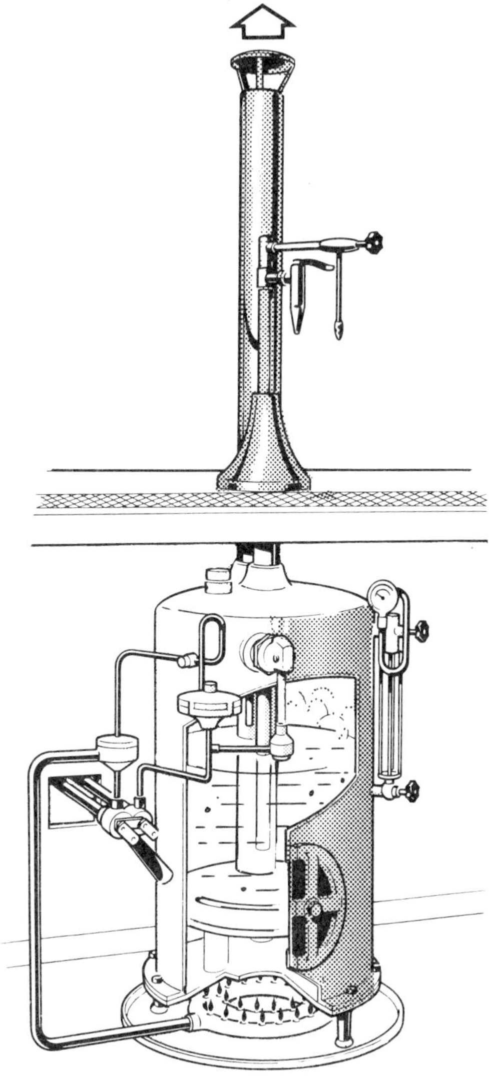

(c) Water boiler, pressure type (gas-heated model). Housed under counter. Heats and stores water at about 105°C at pressure of up to 50 kN/m^2, and supplies boiling water instantly on demand

may also be obtained from the pressure type of boiler. This operates on the following principle: when water is heated in a closed vessel, steam generated on the surface sets up sufficient pressure to force the water through a draw-off column to the outlet pipe. Water is stored at a temperature of about 105° Celsius at a pressure of up to 50 kN/m^2. As will be seen from Figure 43c, the pressure-type boiler is housed under the service counter.

Output of expansion and pressure-type boilers. The output of café boilers (as these two types are known) is expressed in litres per minute. The shorter the period of time over which a given quantity of water is needed, the greater the demand on the capacity of the equipment.

Café boilers are intended to give what is known as a continuous intermittent flow. When tea or coffee is made, containers are filled in turn and the draw-off tap is turned off while the next container is put in place. The boiler's performance fits in with this procedure, for short breaks are essential to allow recovery.

The café set. This consists of a café boiler together with additional items such as side urns for storing hot milk or coffee, or apparatus for making coffee (see Figure 44).

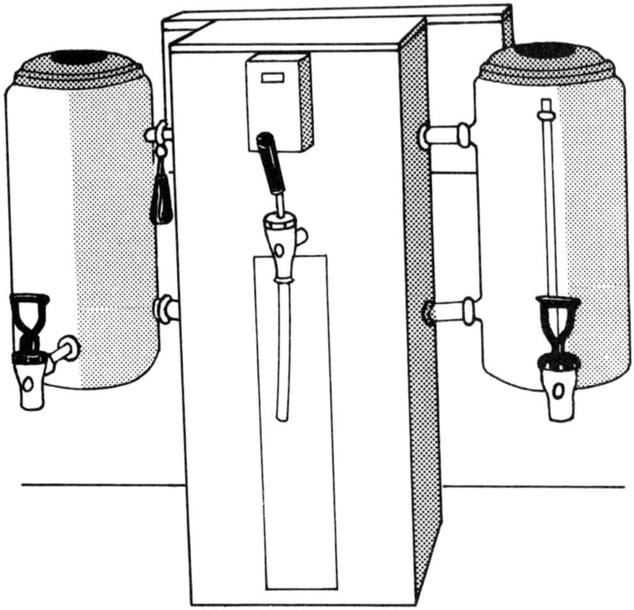

Fig. 44 Café set. Electrically-heated model has water boiler of expansion type and side urns for coffee and milk

The steam injector. The steam injector may be either an ancillary to a pressure café boiler or an independent unit. In addition to heating small quantities of milk, beverages and soup, it may be used to cook scrambled eggs. The steam pressure is about 200 kN/m^2.

The milk heater. When direct heat is applied to a large quantity of milk, the milk is liable to burn. To avoid this, milk needed for coffee and other drinks may be heated in a double pan; but if hot milk is needed regularly it is convenient to use a milk heater. This is a water-jacketed urn with thermostatic controls set at 71° Celsius. An alternative is a sealed vacuum system, which gives fast and economical heating. It is an advantage to have an automatic temperature control, because if overheated milk is used for coffee the quality is impaired.

Coffee-making equipment. A wide variety of equipment is available.

Insulated urns. These urns are used either when hot drinks are served some distance away from beverage-making facilities, or where clients help themselves. They are often seen on the office or factory tea trolley, or in the refectory of a university hall of residence.

Cold beverages. Facilities for serving cold beverages include refrigerated chilled-water dispensers, refrigerated milk dispensers, soft drink dispensers and equipment for aerating soft drinks.

Chapter 11

Refrigeration and freezing: refrigerators, chill stores and freezers

When food deteriorates and becomes unfit for consumption, several agencies may be involved. Food may be contaminated with bacteria associated with food poisoning (*e.g.*, salmonella, staphylococci) or moulds, yeasts, or putrefying and souring bacteria that cause food spoilage. Or there may be biochemical and physical reactions that cause changes in texture and palatability. The chief aim in preserving food is the control of bacteria and moulds, while retaining acceptability.

There are many ways in which food may be preserved. Heat may be applied, as in the process of canning, to destroy organisms. The food's moisture content may be reduced to the stage where growth is inhibited, as in dehydration, or preservatives may be added to inhibit growth. It is possible for food to be irradiated with small doses of gamma rays, though this method is not permitted in the United Kingdom. Finally, we come to the use of low temperatures as a way of inhibiting the growth of bacteria and moulds and preventing food spoilage.

Refrigeration

Refrigeration is the cooling of a space or substance below the environmental temperature, and it has been practised for many centuries. The ancient Egyptians cooled liquids by means of evaporation. Wines were poured into porous earthen jars, which were exposed to the dry night air. The Greeks and Romans and the ancient Chinese used pits for storing natural ice and snow. In Britain in the eighteenth and nineteenth centuries blocks of ice were cut from lakes and ponds in winter, and stored in underground ice-houses. It has long been the practice to use cellars and caves, which are unaffected by outside variations in temperature, as cold stores. Sir Francis Bacon, the famous Elizabethan, was interested in refrigeration, and was indeed carrying out an experiment to preserve a fowl by stuffing it with snow when he caught the chill that was believed to be the cause of his death. But it was not until a mechanical means of refrigeration was developed that preservation of food by chilling had a practical application on a wide scale. The technique of mechanical refrigeration was first applied to the making of artificial ice; it developed rapidly during the twentieth century, and was applied to a wider field.

Mechanical refrigeration

Mechanical refrigeration is achieved by means of a heat pump—that is, a machine or plant in which mechanical, thermal or electrical energy is used to produce and maintain a low temperature through a refrigeration cycle. The pump operates to control the temperature within an enclosed cabinet, and an underlying principle is that of the latent heat properties of refrigerant liquids when they pass from a liquid to a gaseous state. Use is also made of the principle of heat exchange. Heat will flow from a substance with a higher temperature to one that is cooler until both are at the same temperature. It follows that, if the temperature of one part of a cabinet can be maintained at a low temperature, in time the whole cabinet and anything it contains will also be kept at this temperature.

In mechanical refrigeration there is a thermodynamic cycle that takes heat at a low temperature and rejects it at a higher one; the cycle must receive power from an outside source. There are several basic cycles, and that most commonly used in refrigeration is the vapour-compression cycle. In most cycles use is made of the fact that when a liquid changes into vapour it takes up heat. A refrigerant that has a low boiling point when in its liquid state is used. During the cycle the refrigerant changes from liquid to vapour (when it absorbs heat) and from vapour to liquid (when it gives off heat—known as the latent heat of condensation).

Vapour-compression refrigeration cycle

The basic components in the vapour-compression cycle are the compressor (usually operated by an electric motor), the condenser and evaporator. These three components form a sealed unit filled with refrigerant, which alternates between liquid and vapour as it circulates through the system.

The compressor is a pump, which compresses the refrigerant in its vapour state. This compression causes an increase in its temperature (a well-known thermodynamic principle). After compression, the vapour is forced through a delivery valve into the condenser. Here the vapour gives up its heat to the environment, and in consequence returns to its liquid state. (Electric fans may blow on to the condenser coils to help this process.) The liquid now passes through a throttling valve into the evaporator. At this stage, because of the reduction in pressure, the liquid refrigerant returns to vapour, and in so doing absorbs heat from the environment. From the evaporator the refrigerant returns to the compressor, and the cycle is complete. The evaporator consists of a series of coils within the refrigerator cabinet, and it is from the interior of the refrigerator and its contents that the refrigerant absorbs heat.

In many vapour-compression units there is a receiver in which the liquid refrigerant is stored after leaving the condenser before it goes on to the evaporator. A diagram of the vapour-compression cycle is shown in Figure 45.

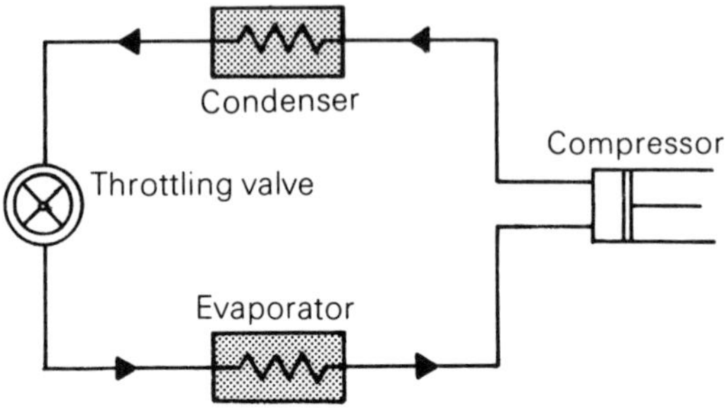

Fig. 45 Vapour compression refrigeration cycle

The following are examples of suitable refrigerants: ammonia; carbon dioxide; sulphur dioxide; methyl chloride. Dichlorodifluoromethane, or Freon as it is commonly called, is widely used. Freon 12 is the trade name for a wide group of hydrogenated hydrocarbons containing one or more fluorine atoms, which are used as refrigerants and propellants.

The temperature of refrigerators is controlled by thermostat. For a general-purpose refrigerator in which perishable foods are to be kept for short periods, 4° Celsius is suitable. Where a refrigerator is used for one type of food only (*e.g.*, meat or fish), the temperature best suited to that particular food is chosen. The following is a useful guide:

Meat and fish	0·6°C
Dairy produce	4°C.
Fresh foods and vegetables	10 – 15°C.
Chilled foods	0 – 4°C.
Frozen foods	–20°C.
Ice cream	–15 to –17°C.

The design of refrigerators

A refrigerator cabinet consists of an inner and an outer casing with thermal insulating material such as expanded polyurethane or expanded polystyrene between. The inner casing is of stainless or sheet steel finished with enamel, plastic or aluminium. It must be so constructed that condensation and drips from food cannot penetrate to the insulating material. The outer casing may be of enamelled steel or stainless steel. A refrigerator is often fitted with a defrosting device that operates by means of a time clock. During the defrosting process, ice that has formed on the evaporator is melted.

Refrigerators may be of the reach-in type or the walk-in kind. Reach-in refrigerators are available in sizes ranging from 0·35 m^3 to 2·8 m^3. Rustless slatted shelves, with supports to allow shelf positions to be varied, are standard fittings.

Walk-in refrigerators are available in sizes starting at 2·8 m^3. Often known as chill stores, they may be built in, but more usually they consist of prefabricated modules. Where it is intended to use the chill room for storing meat in large joints or whole carcases, rails and hooks are fitted so that the meat is surrounded by cold air. Otherwise, shelving comprises the whole of the fitments. The condenser for the chill store may be fitted at some distance away, in a position where its heat may readily be dispersed. The door is designed so that it may readily be opened from the inside, so that it should not be possible for anyone to be trapped inside.

Fish refrigerators. The smell of wet fish is readily absorbed by other foods, and so where large quantities are used a special refrigerator is kept to store it. A fish refrigerator usually has a galvanised lining and galvanised perforated drawers. It is the practice to store wet fish with any ice that was supplied when it was delivered, and this helps to keep it moist.

Roll-in refrigerators. These are designed for use with trolleys, and they are particularly suitable when the catering system calls for large numbers of similar items to be stacked and removed from the refrigerator at one time. Roll-through refrigerators allow trolleys to be taken in and out from opposite sides, as shown in Figure 6. In certain circumstances this gives a convenient workflow.

Ice-cream conservators. These are designed specifically for storing ice-cream, and are often provided on loan by the ice-cream manufacturer.

Freezer storage units. These may be chests, upright reach-in cabinets or walk-in stores.

Upright freezer cabinets are similar to cabinet refrigerators designed to chill foods, the principal difference being that of temperature. Compared with the chest type, the upright model has the advantage that the contents are easier to see, and access is easier. It occupies less floor space than a chest of similar capacity.

Chest-type freezers are usually cheaper than upright models. They have the advantage that cold air is not lost to any extent when the lid is raised, because cold air is heavier than hot air. Their chief use is for storage, but they may be used to freeze small quantities of food provided that the unit is powerful enough to do this and the amount does not exceed 10 per cent of the chest's capacity. This type of freezer is often chosen for a small residential establishment when it is intended to freeze garden produce, or a few cooked items for occasional use.

Dual-temperature refrigerators are available with two compartments, one of which is suitable for storing frozen food. They have two entirely separate refrigeration systems, and their use is indicated where space is limited and needs are small.

Walk-in storage freezers. The freezer store, also known as the cold store in the food industry, is similar in principle to the chill store, but it has a number of special features. Because the temperature is well below freezing (−20° Celsius), it is necessary to have devices to prevent the formation of ice round the doors, since this would cause them to freeze up. Electric heating strips round the doors are used for this purpose. The floor, which in modern modular units consists of factory-built panels, incorporates a heater mat. The mat prevents the ground below the store from freezing, and expanding as a result. (This is known as frost heave.) Evaporators incorporate electric elements, which operate to provide automatic defrosting.

The storage freezer or cold store is usually used for stocks of prepared and packaged frozen foods. In planning the arrangement of these stocks it is necessary:

(a) to use storage space to the best advantage;
(b) to make it easy to rotate stocks correctly;
(c) to minimise the amount of labour involved in storekeeping.

So far as the last two points are concerned, it should be borne in mind that the storeman (even though he will wear special warm clothing) should not spend a long time in a store with a temperature of −20° Celsius. Trolleys and dollies are often used in preference to fixed shelves, chiefly because less manhandling is involved. Other advantages are that a mobile arrangement is more flexible, and less circulation space is needed. In very large systems, roller shelves are used, but these are expensive.

Locating the refrigerator and freezer

The refrigerator's position in relation to convenient workflow has been discussed in Chapter 5, but there is the further point that its position also has a bearing upon the efficiency with which it works. Here the chief consideration is the condenser, whose function it is to disperse the heat of condensation. It should be sited in a position from which heat may readily be discharged—that is, away from the heat of the kitchen and where there is a free flow of air. A position on top of the cabinet and near the wall, although common, is unsuitable. It is also bad practice to site a refrigerator in a small storeroom. The heat from the condenser will be dissipated into the stores, and if the storeroom is shut up for any length of time, for example over the week-end, heat will not be dispersed. As a result the refrigerator's efficiency will be impaired and the temperature of the storeroom may become unsuitable for its contents.

Apart from the question of the condenser, it is undesirable that the refrigerator should be in a warm place; if it is, warm air from the surroundings will be taken in when the door is opened.

Use and performance of the refrigerator

Temperature of food input. When food is put into the refrigerator, heat is taken out of it, as we have seen, until all the contents are at the same temperature, but this process takes time. The difference between food at room temperature and the atmosphere of the cabinet may be as much as 10° to 12° Celsius. If the refrigerator is packed with such food, it may be some hours before the temperature of all the food is reduced to 4° Celsius. If cooked food is placed in the refrigerator before it has cooled to room temperature, the process takes much longer. If food is actually steaming when it is put into the cabinet, condensation on the evaporator is considerably increased, causing it to become heavily frosted and therefore less efficient. The result may be that over a period of 12 hours the temperature of the food has not been reduced to the required degree, and this may constitute a food hygiene hazard. It is an important maxim that food should be cooled to room temperature before it goes into the refrigerator. This does not apply, however, to walk-in chill stores, where the volume of cold air in relation to the amount of stored food is much greater. Some special refrigerated stores are specifically designed for chilling food rapidly as soon as it has left the oven.

Checking the temperature. The temperature of the refrigerator should be checked daily, and refrigerator thermometers are available for this purpose.

Defrosting. A certain amount of drying takes place on the surface of all uncovered food in the refrigerator. This is because the air itself loses water vapour by condensation on to other cold surfaces, and in turn it takes up moisture from any uncovered food. Thus the cold surface of the evaporator gradually collects a coating of frost, which, when it reaches a thickness of 4·0 mm, begins to affect the efficiency of the machine. Except where there is automatic defrosting operated by means of a time clock, the refrigerator should be defrosted regularly by switching off the electricity supply and opening the door to allow the temperature to rise and the frost on the evaporator to melt. Weekly defrosting is often sufficient, but the determining factor is the amount of ice on the evaporator; this should never be allowed to become more than 12 mm thick.

The refrigerator door

The design of the door is a major factor in the efficient operation of a refrigerator, and in the walk-in type safety is involved also. To conserve energy it is vital that opening the door should have a minimal effect upon the internal temperature. The door should be designed so that it may be opened and closed quickly. The closure mechanism should be robust to keep maintenance to a minimum, and the door should be well sealed to prevent any unnecessary loss of cold air. In the case of walk-in refrigerators, for safety reasons the door must be capable of being opened with ease and certainty from the inside. The user should not open the door unnecessarily, and should close it as soon as possible.

Freezing

In most circumstances and for most foods, chilling acts as a preservative for a few days only. For longer-term storage it is necessary to use much lower temperatures, and food is preserved by means of freezing. This is not a new process: the first shipment of meat by refrigerated ship from Australia to England took place in 1880. The meat was not frozen before loading and it was not intended to freeze it, but by the end of the voyage the meat had frozen. The freezing process was slow, and, though it was successful so far as preservation was concerned, the quality of the meat suffered. The structure of the cells was ruptured and as a result the meat's texture was less acceptable and there was a loss of moisture when the meat thawed. In order to overcome problems of maintaining quality when food is frozen, the process of quick freezing was developed.

Quick freezing

When food is frozen slowly there is damage to the structure of the cells probably because of changes in osmotic pressure and salt concentration. When food is frozen quickly the cell structure is not damaged and the quality of the food is not impaired.

In the process of freezing food to preserve it, the temperature is reduced to well below freezing point, down to $-20°$ Celsius or lower. This is considerably below the level at which micro-organisms are active, but this very low temperature is necessary to ensure that biochemical and physical changes are arrested also.

The aims in quick freezing may be summarised as follows:

(a) to freeze food without damaging its texture;

(b) to inhibit completely the growth of micro-organisms;

(c) to inhibit changes in food that would otherwise cause deterioration.

The application of quick freezing to catering

The application is two-fold. First, the caterer can avail himself of commercially-produced quick-frozen foods. Secondly, he can freeze his own products, either on a large scale as described in Chapter 6, Examples 2, 4 and 7, or in a much smaller way. In describing methods of quick freezing, we shall be concerned chiefly with its direct application to the catering kitchen.

Air-blast freezing

In this process refrigerated air at a temperature of –30° to –36° Celsius (or lower) is blown over food to ensure rapid freezing. Generally hot food at a temperature of 80° Celsius can be placed in the air-blast freezer. The freezing process usually averages one-and-a-half to two hours, but this depends upon the nature of the food and its depth (38 mm is often taken as a maximum). Food should be evenly spaced and of even thickness. It is customary for food to be covered to prevent loss of moisture, but this is not essential. After freezing, the product is stored consistently at a temperature not higher than –18° Celsius. Unless this is so, the same sort of damage to cell structure occurs as when food is frozen slowly.

The air-blast freezer

The general construction is similar to that of a refrigerator, the chief differences being:

(a) Fans circulate the cold air to provide the air blast;

(b) The temperature is much lower.

The blast freezer can have sophisticated controls, which include timer, warning lights, thermometer and temperature chart recorder. It should be capable of reducing the temperature of incoming food from 70° to –20° Celsius in not more than 90 minutes. Small freezers are fitted with shelves, and larger ones consist of one or more compartments known as tunnels. Trolleys are used to wheel food into the tunnels, each of which can take several trolleys (see Figure 46).

Cryogenic freezing

Cryogenics is a branch of physics concerned with how materials

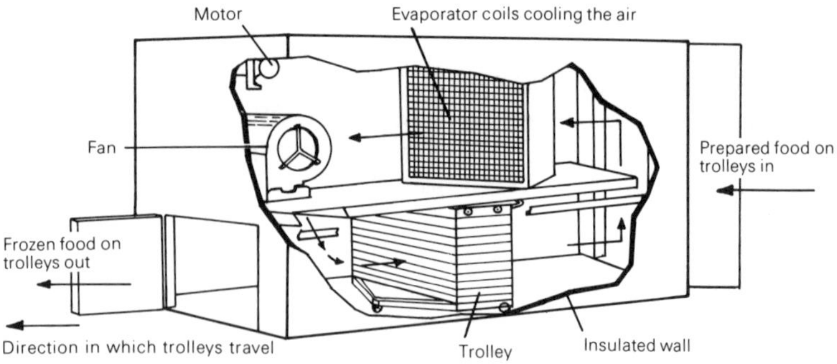

Fig. 46 Air-blast freezer. Prepared food enters freezer tunnel by trolley, and leaves by exit door after 1½ to 2 hours

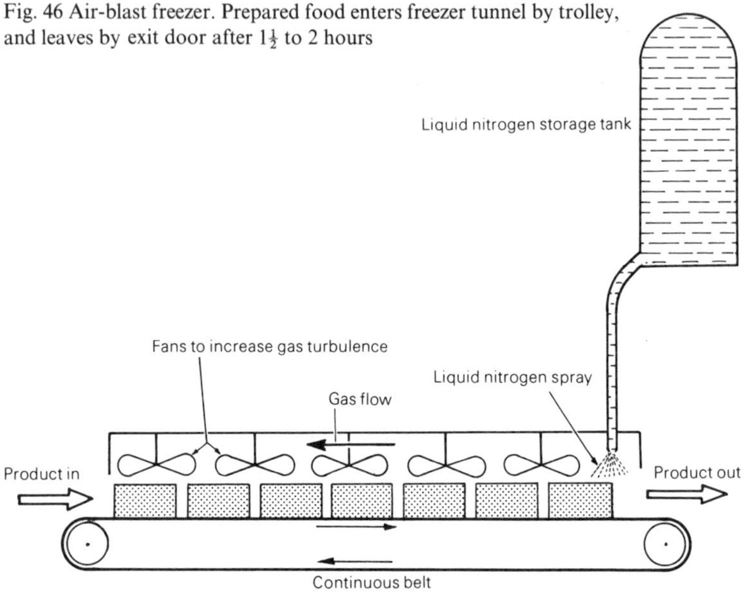

Fig. 47 Example of cryogenic freezer. Food passes through insulated tunnel on moving belt. Liquid nitrogen used for freezing

behave at low temperatures, but the term has come to be applied to the use of gases with very low boiling points for freezing foods. In cryogenic freezing much lower temperatures are used than in the air-blast method, and consequently food freezes more quickly.

Two gases are in general use: liquid nitrogen (which has a temperature of −196° Celsius), and liquid carbon dioxide (which has a temperature of −78° Celsius). Both gases are colourless, tasteless and inert, and so may be sprayed directly on to foods without adverse effects. Liquid nitrogen and carbon dioxide are stored under pressure. When the pressure is released the liquid changes either to gas or to a solid frozen state, and in doing so absorbs heat from the surroundings and from food.

Types of cryogenic freezers

Tunnel freezers. These consist of insulated tunnels with conveyor belts (see Figure 47). Liquid nitrogen is piped to the freezer under pressure and then sprayed through nozzles. Half the capacity to absorb heat is in the liquid—which is sprayed on to the food—and half is in the vapour that forms. When the food first enters the tunnel it meets fairly cold gas travelling in the opposite direction. As it passes down the tunnel the food meets colder and colder gas until finally it passes under the nozzles and is sprayed with liquid nitrogen. This method of cooling by stages reduces thermal shock and prevents food from cracking when sprayed with liquid nitrogen. The speed of the belt and the rate of injection of liquid nitrogen can be varied as necessary to suit the nature and depth of the food to be frozen.

Liquid carbon dioxide is also used in tunnel freezers. When it is sprayed, because of the rapid change in pressure small particles of solid carbon dioxide, known as CO_2 snow, are formed. The vapour formed absorbs a negligible amount of heat and freezing takes place chiefly because of the sublimation of the CO_2 snow.

Tunnel freezers are not likely to be used in cook-freeze catering if the output is less than 3000 to 4000 meals a day.

Snow spiral freezers. The snow spiral is a compact insulated box containing a continuous spiral conveyor that moves food through an ultra-cold atmosphere. Liquid carbon dioxide is sprayed from jets in the roof of the cabinet, and the resulting CO_2 snow and cold CO_2 gas is circulated by specially-designed fans to ensure optimum gas velocities. Freezing times range from 10 to 60 minutes according to the nature and size of the product. Liquid nitrogen is also used for this type of freezer, which is suitable for large-scale operations.

Snow hoods. When food passes under the snow hood, by means of a conveyor belt, it is sprayed directly with carbon dioxide snow to produce either rapid chilling or crust freezing. This method has a commercial application. If the food sprayed is in cartons, some of the snow stays in the carton and keeps the food cold during transit. Chickens in cartons are crust-frozen in this way.

Batch freezers. These are designed for small-scale operations. The batch freezer consists of a cabinet into which liquid carbon dioxide is sprayed. Cold CO_2 gas is circulated by means of fans. Food is taken to the freezer in special two-part trolleys. The freezer is capsule-loaded, and only the upper part of the trolley enters the cabinet. With a temperature range of $+10°$ Celsius to $-70°$ Celsius, this freezer is suitable also for chilling foods in a cook-chill system.

Ancillary equipment for cook-freeze systems

In systems similar to that described in Chapter 6, Example 2, a considerable amount of ancillary equipment is needed. A list is given below.

Item	*Application*
Aluminium foil containers with lids	Where the system calls for disposable containers that will be used through the stages of freezing, storage and regeneration
Lidding machines	For dispensing and fitting lids to aluminium foil containers
Polythene moulds	For use as containers during the freezing process as an alternative to disposable containers
Transparent plastic bags and wrapping	For wrapping various items, such as cakes, bread rolls, etc., before or after freezing
Sealing machine	For sealing plastic bags and wrappings
Automatic dispensers	For portioning and dispensing liquids and sauces into containers before freezing
Insulated containers (see Figure 42b)	For transporting food from the production kitchen to finishing kitchens

Chapter 12

Catering machinery

Most machines are introduced into kitchens with the object of saving labour, though there may be several subsidiary reasons also. Nearly all of them are power-driven, but there are a few worthwhile hand-operated pieces of equipment. Electrical loadings range from 0·2 kW to 25 kW.

Reasons for using kitchen machinery

1. Saving labour

Most food-preparation machines carry out tasks more quickly than they could be performed by hand. Where this is not so, labour may still be saved, as the operator is free to do other work when he is not attending to the machine. Usually it is expected that savings in labour costs will either cover the cost of buying, installing and maintaining the machine, or more than cover it. But the intending purchaser may wish to reduce man hours for particular tasks for reasons other than cost. It may be difficult to attract labour for certain routine, monotonous or physically distasteful tasks such as dishwashing and potato-peeling. In these circumstances the introduction of machines may be an aid in recruiting and retaining staff.

2. Saving on skilled labour

Machines may be introduced to carry out work that would otherwise require skilled craftsmen; a meat-slicing machine is an example. Considerable skill is needed to carve well by hand, whereas little skill is involved in operating a slicing machine. Again the object may be to cut costs—skilled labour is expensive—or to overcome the difficulty of obtaining skilled labour.

3. Standard and consistency of performance

A machine may be expected to operate to a more consistent standard than a man, and in some cases the standard is better. For example, meat cannot be minced satisfactorily by hand, and few operators could match the results produced by electrically-operated slicers and shredders. Consistent results are less easily achieved where skill and judgment are required from the individual operating a machine. For example, when an electric mixer is used for making short-crust pastry, the quality of the end-product depends very much upon the accuracy with which the operator measures the liquid for binding the pastry, and upon his judgment as to when each stage in pastry-making is complete.

4. Speed

Reference has already been made to the speed at which machines operate, and this has connotations in addition to direct savings in labour. It may, for example, affect the time at which it is necessary to open a kitchen in the morning, or the starting and finishing times of a shift may be reduced.

5. Hygiene

Machines may offer advantages over hand operations so far as food hygiene is concerned. Where this is so, it is usually because the product is subject to much less handling. But any advantage derived from this may be negated if the machine does not lend itself to thorough cleaning, or if disinfection through cleaning is not regularly practised. The meat-slicing machine is a good example of this. If it is operated correctly, the meat need scarcely be touched by hand. But, if it is not properly cleaned, the machine itself will harbour possibly-harmful bacteria.

General points concerning the selection of catering machinery

When it has been decided to buy a machine for a particular task or set of tasks, various points should be considered before a particular model is chosen:

1. Cost

This has already been mentioned in relation to possible savings in labour. The prospective buyer will also need to consider the relative cost of similar machines produced by different manufacturers, and of machines with similar functions but varying output and degrees of automation. He must be quite clear as to what items are included in the basic price, and what are charged as extras, with their prices. This applies particularly to electric mixers, which have large numbers of attachments, and to dishwashing machines, which often need considerable lengths of tabling. Maintenance as well as running costs should be compared.

2. Performance

Points to consider here are:

(a) Quality of end-product (*e.g.*, can a slicer produce smooth, even-textured slices over a range of thicknesses?);

(b) Capacity (*e.g.*, how many potatoes will a peeling machine take at a time?);

(c) Output over a given period (*e.g.*, how many racks of crockery will a dishwasher take each hour?);

(d) The amount of manpower needed to operate the machine.

3. Ease and safety in operation

Relevant points are:

(a) Access to controls—no awkward reaching, bending, stretching or stooping should be necessary;

(b) Amount of energy needed from the operator (*e.g.*, how much effort is necessary to use, lift and adjust various parts, and to adjust the mechanism?);

(c) What safety features are incorporated, and does the machine comply with any appropriate regulations and recommendations? (*E.g.*, does a slicing machine have a safety guard to prevent the operator's hand from coming into contact with the blade, and is it impossible to use the machine if the guard is not in place?)

Food preparation machinery

Mixing machines

These are designed to deal with all mixing and beating operations, and the electric mixer is an essential piece of kitchen equipment. Processes such as rubbing in and creaming are not completed at high speed in the conventional type of mixer (shown in Plate 3), but the machine does not need constant attention and the cook is free to carry out other work during intervals of mixing, provided that he is at hand when a critical stage is reached.

A typical mixer is shown in Plate 3a, and the interchangeable tools that fit on to the vertical spindle driven by the motor are shown in b, c, d, e and f. The beater or other tool rotates eccentrically within the bowl; if this were not so, the whole mass of food in the bowl would be carried round and round without any of the relative movement of the different ingredients that is necessary for proper mixing. The spindle also has an epicyclic action, which ensures that the beater operates to within a small fraction of a centimetre from the bowl's surface.

Mixing machines usually have three gears, so that the speed of the mixing tool may be varied. A high speed is necessary to whisk liquids such as eggs and cream, but if this were used for rubbing fat into flour some of the mixture would be thrown out. Unless a low gear is used for mixtures of dense, elastic texture, such as yeast doughs, the machine begins to labour and the motor may be damaged. The operator sets the speed by means of a gear lever (clearly shown in Plate 3a). In some models the machine is automatically switched off when the gear is changed, and the machine then has to be restarted. Examples of running speeds of machines of various capacities are

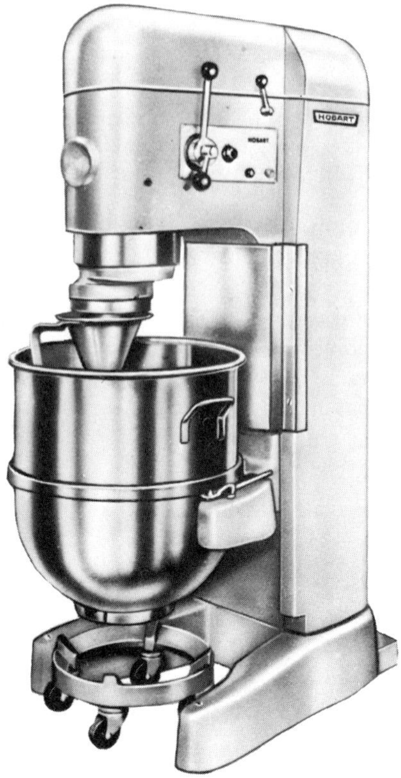

Plate 3 Electric mixer.
This free-standing mixer (a) has range of interchangeable tools:

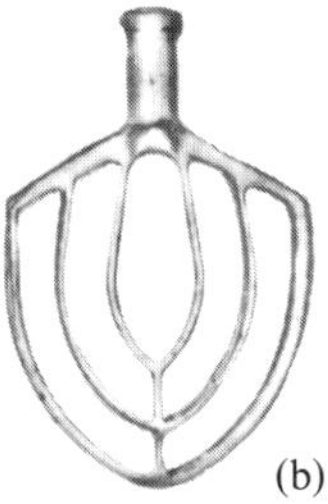

(b) Beater

(c) Whip

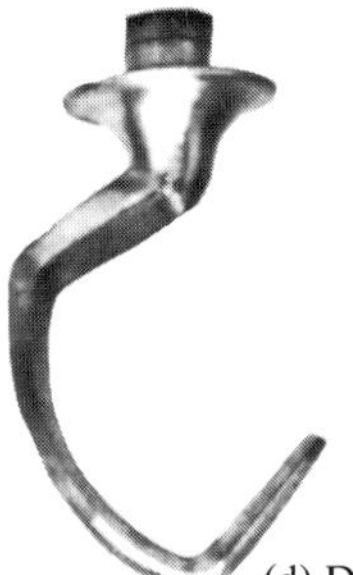

(d) Dough hook

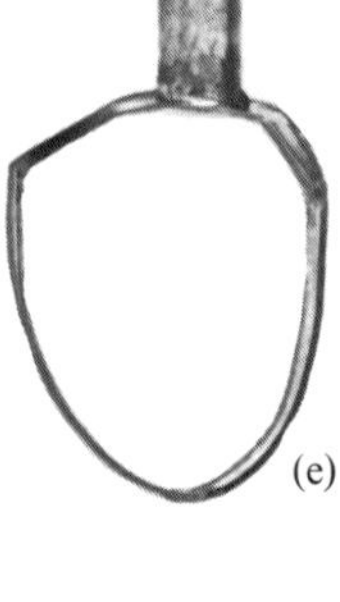

(e) Pastry knife

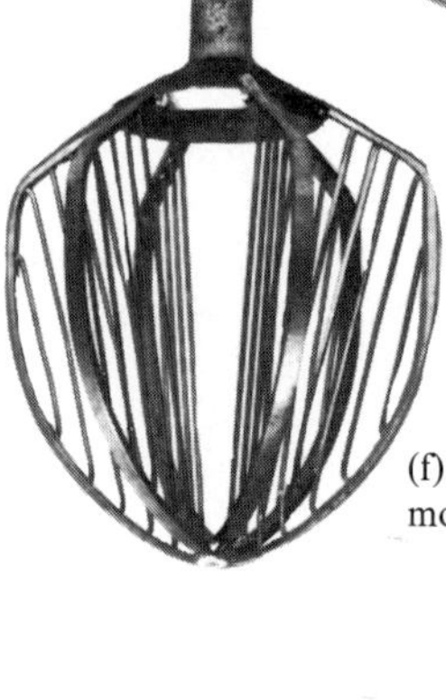

(f) C wing whip (40-litre models and larger)

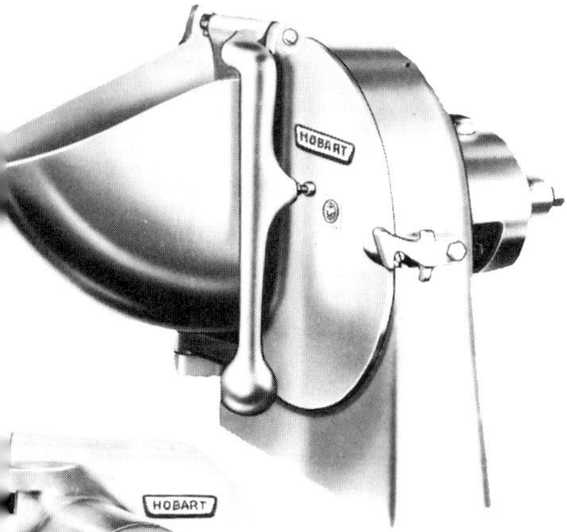

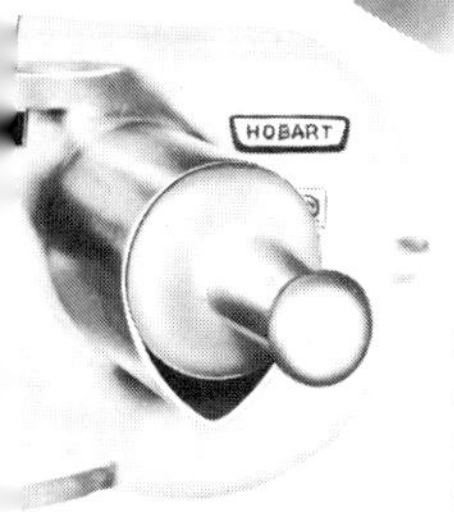

(g) Vegetable-slicer attachment. This has several plates, of which selection is shown

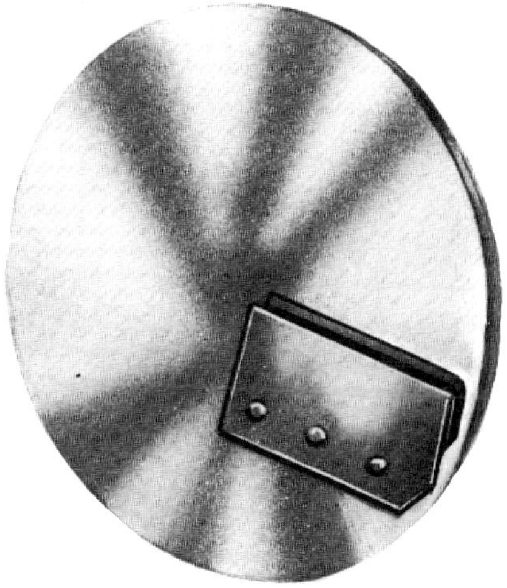

(h) Julienne plate (for julienne strips)

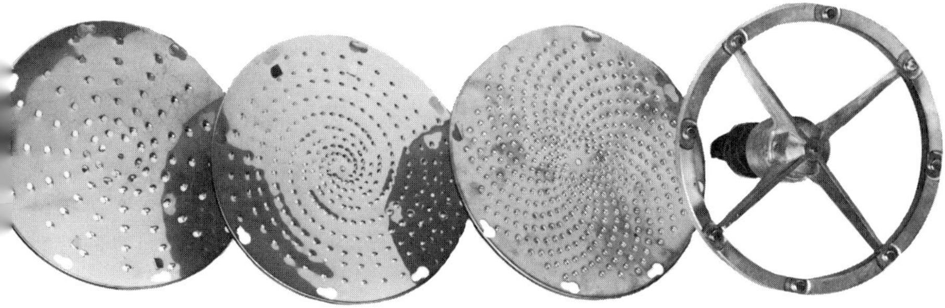

Coarse shredder plate (j) Fine shredder plate (k) Grater plate (l) Plate-holder

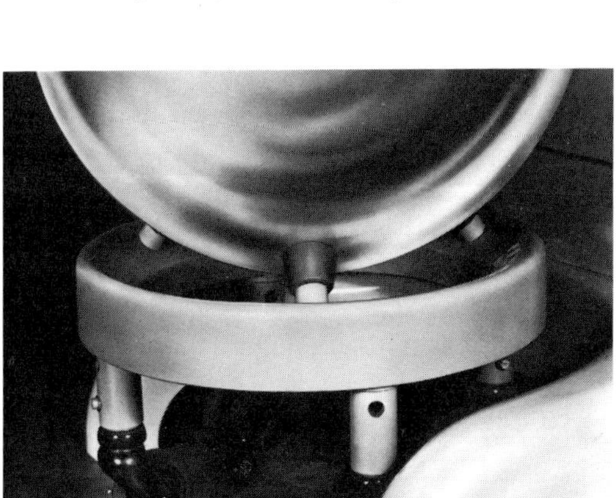

(m) Bowl trolley is useful for large mixers

given in Table 5. (The capacity relates to the maximum volume of food that may be mixed in the mixing bowl.) These vary from make to make, but are affected only slightly by differences in mixes.

The tools of the mixer and their uses are as follows:

Beater: for mixing cakes and puddings, mashing potatoes, etc.;
Whip: for whisking light mixtures such as egg whites, batters and sponges;
Dough hook: for yeast mixtures;
Pastry knife: for pastry-making;
Wing whip: as for whip (supplied for larger mixers).

The machine has a hub at the top to which a range of attachments may be fitted: vegetable slicer and shredder with numerous plates for slicing, shredding, grating, crumbing, etc. (as shown in Plates 3g, h, i, j and k); mincer for meat and other foods; coffee grinder. Of these, the vegetable slicing attachment and the mincer are probably the most widely used, and are highly-valued features of the machine.

Machines may either stand on the floor or be mounted on a stand or bench. They may be fixed to a mobile stand, and this is useful for teaching purposes. Suitable stands at the right height for the operator may be bought from the manufacturer of the machine.

Special features and extra items

Bowls: It is usual to have at least two mixing bowls, so that there need be no delay in mixing while a bowl is being refilled. Large mixers have attachments to allow bowls of different sizes to be used. (This is necessary to allow smaller quantities to be mixed; if the bowl size is too large, ingredients cannot be mixed successfully.)

Extension rims: These may be fitted to the top of the mixing bowl to prevent splashing when light mixtures are whisked, or to prevent powders from being flung about at the start of mixing. They should not be used to increase the load in the bowl of dense commodities, or the machine may be overloaded.

Bowl dollies (see Plate 3m): The mixing bowl may be wheeled to and from the machine by means of a bowl dolly, and thus heavy lifting on and off the machine is avoided. They are not supplied with smaller models.

Power-lifted bowls: In smaller mixers the bowl, after having been placed on the machine, is raised into the operating position by a hand-operated mechanism. In larger models (say 60 litres and over), powered bowl lifts are available, either as optional extras or as standard features.

Timing mechanisms: These are available to help the operator, but he will still need to use his judgment in some operations. For example, the time taken for a given quantity of margarine and sugar to be creamed will depend upon the physical qualities of the fat and sugar and the temperature of the ingredients and implements.

Bowl self-locating units: These patented units operate in conjunction with the bowl trolley. When the bowl is pushed to the machine, the unit automatically locates it into position, so that it may be clamped down and wound up into the correct operating position.

Performance of the mixer. Mixing machines perform all the work for which they are designed as well as it could be done by hand, and for some operations, where considerable power is needed, a better result is achieved. For example, when fat and sugar are creamed by machine, the specific gravity of the resulting mixture is considerably lower than that obtained in the average hand mix, and this demonstrates that the operation is done more efficiently by machine than by hand. In the case of attachments for slicing, etc., not only is the finished standard superior to that usually obtained by hand, but the speed of output is much greater.

Use of the mixer. Mixing machines are comparatively simple to operate, and the skill required relates to measuring ingredients, ensuring that they are in the correct state for mixing and judging when each process is complete, rather than in the operation of the machine itself. There are, however, a few points about care in use that need some emphasis:

1. The bowl needs to be secured firmly and correctly in accordance with the manufacturer's instructions. Usually perforated lugs on each side of the bowl fit over pins in the bowl holder (see Plate 3a), and a lug at the back engages with a spring socket in the middle of the holder. If the bowl is not centred correctly, mixing tools will rub the sides of the bowl and cause wear. As a result, worn metal may be mixed with food, and may be detected by discoloration of the food.

2. The mixer is precision-made, and all parts should be handled and stored with care to prevent accidental damage. A dented bowl may be the cause of friction between tools and bowl, as described in (1) above.

3. To avoid overloading the motor, the machine should always be switched on before the bowl is raised, so that the tool is rotating before it comes into contact with the contents.

4. Too high a gear should not be used for dense mixes.

5. When the machine is switched off the tool continues to rotate, and the heavier the tool the longer rotation continues. The operator should wait until the tool has come to rest before attempting to remove it. If this is not done, injuries such as broken bones and severe bruising may result.

6. The rule of allowing moving parts to come to rest applies also to attachments such as mincers.

TABLE 5: Examples of running speeds of mixing machines of various capacities (Speed is expressed in revolutions per minute and refers to beater speed)

Capacity *Gear*	*10 litre* *rpm*	*20 litre* *rpm*	*30 litre* *rpm*	*39 litre* *rpm*	*58 litre* *rpm*
1	140	107	68	68	68
2	250	198	165	165	165
3	446	361	274	274	274

7. Because an electric mixer does its work so easily, there is a danger that foods may be overmixed, and this may affect the finished product unfavourably. For instance, when fat is rubbed into flour to make short-crust pastry, if mixing is continued for too long the fat and flour will bind together and form a mass that will not take up the necessary amount of water. As a result, the pastry will be difficult to roll out, and when it has been cooked the texture will not be right. Another example occurs when flour is added to mixtures of either creamed butter and sugar plus egg or beaten egg and sugar (as used for sponges). In each case the amount of mixing at this stage should be the minimum necessary to obtain a homogeneous mixture. If mixing is continued beyond this point, the sponge will be tough and maximum volume will not be achieved.

Ultra-high-speed mixers. These mixers, which were developed at the Baking Industries Research Station, Chorley Wood, are also known as Chorleywood mixers. Their speeds are such that bread dough is mixed in from 2 to 4 minutes, and puff pastry in 20 seconds. Special timing devices are incorporated to control each mix.

Vertical-cutter mixers. In the vertical-cutter mixer, blades rotate at high speed within an enclosed bowl to cut and mix ingredients simultaneously. Extremely versatile, the VCM may be used for chopping and mincing meat, mixing puddings and cakes, washing and chopping vegetables at the same time, mixing salads and mixing salad dressings. Most of these operations take less than a minute. The machine is free-standing, and the bowl pivots for emptying. It is an advantage to have a floor gulley near by, so that water used for washing vegetables or for cleaning the machine may be disposed of easily.

Vertical-cutter mixers are available with the following bowl capacities: 15 litres, 25 litres and 40 litres. They have very high outputs, and are suitable for large and busy kitchens and commissaries for the central preparation of food.

Mobile turbo-mixer. Designed to work directly in the boiling pan, the turbo-mixer eliminates the need to take food from machine to boiler and *vice versa*. As well as saving time and labour, heat losses from cooked food are reduced. It may be used for mixing, cutting and emulsifying. The mixing head consists of a three-bladed knife unit that operates with either a fine or a coarse sieve to give various cutting grades. The head is supported by a three-wheeled carriage with a brake and a rear wheel, which swivels for steering (see Plate 4).

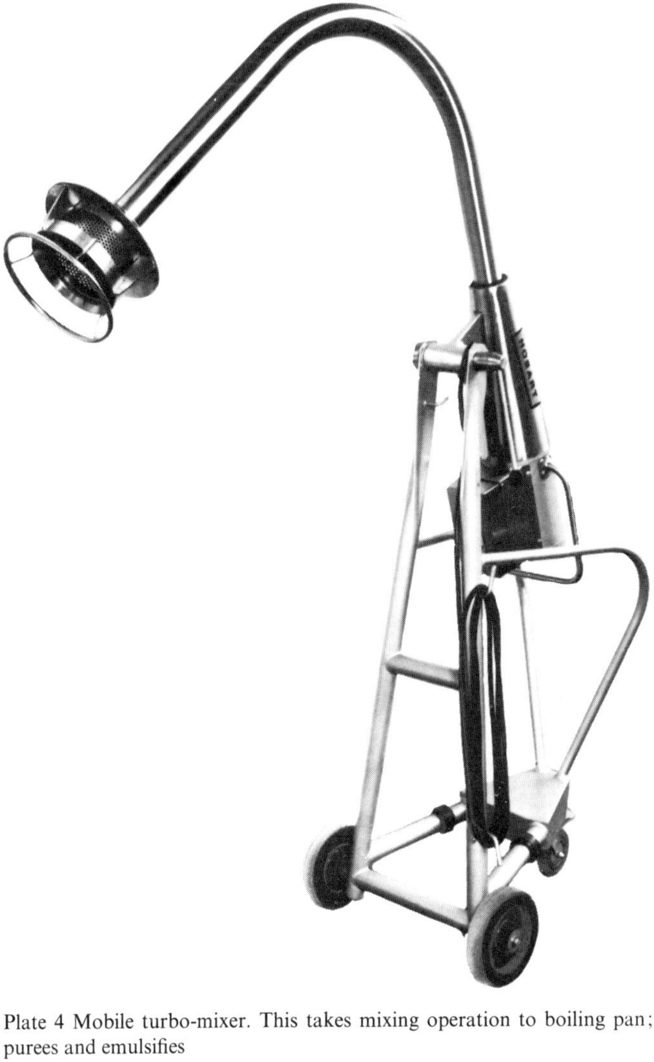

Plate 4 Mobile turbo-mixer. This takes mixing operation to boiling pan; it mixes, purees and emulsifies

General-purpose unit

These units take a range of attachments, similar to those described for the electric mixing machine. If mixers and general-purpose units are of the same manufacture, the attachments are interchangeable.

Vegetable preparation machine

Similar in function to the general-purpose unit, this machine is less versatile because it has fewer attachments. A large food hopper is provided to allow for the bulky nature of vegetables.

Food cutter

In this machine, shown in Plate 5, food is cut in a bowl by means of two stainless steel knives. A knife guard, and a mechanism to prevent

Plate 5 Food cutter. Food is chopped at high speed in bowl. Range of attachments can be fitted to hub. Here power dicer is seen in action

the machine's being used when the guard is not in place, are important features. The machine has a hub to which standard attachments may be fixed.

Chipping machines

Power-operated chippers have outputs of chipped potatoes ranging from 9 to 18 kg a minute. A selection of different cutters allows the size of chip to be varied, and provides for crinkle-cut chips (which are particularly crisp when fried) as well as the standard variety. A typical power-operated machine is shown in Plate 7. Hand-operated chippers of various designs and capacities are available. Power-operated machines are standard items of equipment in

Plate 6 Potato-peeling machine

Plate 7 Potato-chipping machine

establishments where there is a large demand for chipped potatoes.

Slicing machines

The principal task of this machine is to slice meat, though it may be used also for other commodities. Carving meat by hand requires considerable skill. The unskilled carver does not produce slices of good appearance and even thickness; much meat is wasted because it is not presentable, and if the thickness of the slices varies a further problem of quantity control is created. Hence, the slicing machine is one of the basic items of kitchen equipment.

The principal parts of the meat slicer are the power-driven circular knife and the feed hopper, by means of which food is held firmly against the knife. Most machines are of the gravity-feed type with the hopper at a suitable angle to the blade, as shown in Figure 48. The food is moved manually backwards and forwards against the rotating knife. In another type of machine both operations are automatic.

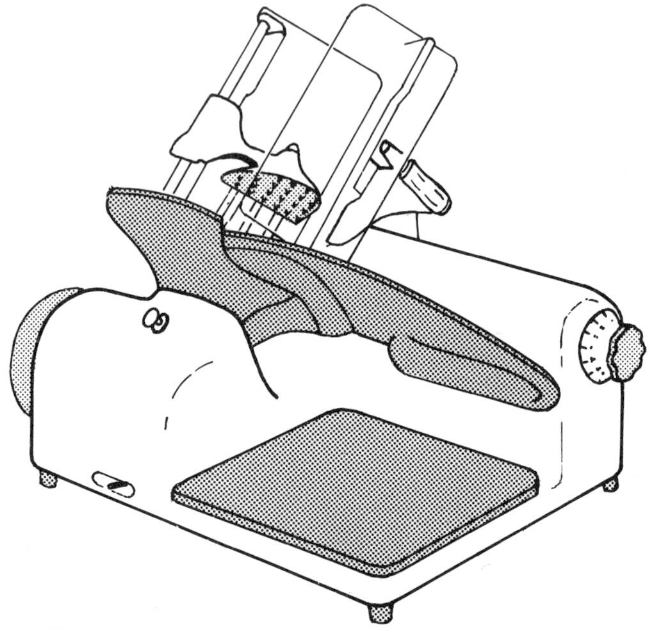

Fig. 48 Electric slicing machine, gravity-fed

As in all slicing and carving, a sharp knife is essential, and a sharpening attachment, consisting of grinding and honing stones, is a standard fitment. When the sharpener is brought into use, the knife passes between the stones and is sharpened after a few revolutions.

The operator chooses the required thickness of slice by means of easily-adjusted controls. In the case of machines with power-driven carriages there are two carriage speeds, from which a choice is made according to the texture of the food to be sliced. A knife guard designed to prevent the operator's hand from coming into contact with the rotating knife is an essential feature, and it should be so designed that it is not possible to use the machine unless the guard is in place.

Bulk feed hoppers for holding items such as fruit (which must be free from stones) and vegetables enable these commodities, if they are of sufficiently firm texture, to be sliced.

Much thought has been given to slicer design to ensure that they are safe to operate and are not a food hygiene hazard. If the machine has an adequate guard the operator will not cut himself while he is using the machine, but he may do so when he is cleaning it. The question arises as to whether the knife should be made to dismantle for cleaning purposes, or whether, to lessen the possibility of accidents, it should be cleaned *in situ*. Where it is intended that the knife should be removed, a guard to cover the whole of the blade's cutting edge should be supplied and used. The general design of the machine should be such that there are no areas where food and grease might be trapped, and cleaning should be safe and easy.

Mincing machines

Essential parts are the worm, the knife and the perforated plate through which meat passes after it has been cut up. The size of the perforations of the plate determines the fineness of the finished product. The smallest electrically-operated mincer has an output of 1·5 kg a minute when a plate of 3·2 mm is used. Hand-operated machines are not usually used. Except where large quantities of minced meat are needed regularly, it is better to choose a more versatile piece of equipment rather than a mincer.

Pie-moulding machines

In some catering concerns, particularly where there is snack-bar-style catering, there is a considerable demand for individual pies, and where these are made on the premises a pie machine, which offers uniformity of size and appearance and saves a great deal of labour, offers considerable advantages.

Meat tenderisers

Meat is tenderised in these machines through the action of an intricate arrangement of knives (see Plate 8a–b). The use of a tenderiser enables cuts of meat which would otherwise be unsuitable for the purpose to be made tender enough for grilling, and also different meats or meat and other ingredients may be combined to produce items suitable for grilling or frying; the various ingredients are knitted together as they go through the machine.

Potato peelers

A potato peeler is an essential item of equipment, except in kitchens where ready-prepared potatoes are always used. The peeler operates to bring potatoes (or other root vegetables) into contact with a rough surface that removes the peel by abrasion. Basic parts of the machine are: the hopper; the peeling chamber, which is a fixed

Plate 8a and b Meat tenderiser

container lined with carborundum or serrated metal; and the base plate of the chamber, which is surfaced with the same abrasive material and which rotates at a moderate speed, thereby throwing the potatoes against the abrasive surfaces. The base plate, or disc, usually has an undulating surface to increase efficiency of operation.

The machine is connected with the cold water supply, and a spray of cold water into the chamber removes dirt from the potatoes and peel scrapings from the chamber. The hopper has a lid to prevent splashing. The peel chamber has a watertight door and a chute for discharging the peeled potatoes. The outlet pipe from the peel chamber usually has a waste-dilution unit (also known as a waste accelerator) leading into it. Its purpose is to flush the parings speedily down the drain to prevent blockages being caused. Where there is no waste-dilution unit, it is necessary to have an interceptor or trap between the machine and the drain, but this is much less satisfactory. The trap consists of a chamber, which has an inner sieve to trap the peel. Emptying the trap is a messy business. It is difficult to dispose of the sludge which collects there, and there is a hygiene hazard if the trap is not cleared regularly and efficiently.

Potato peelers may be either pedestal or bench models. Custom-made benches and stands usually give rise to dirt traps between peeler and bench, and are seldom hygienic. It is therefore much better to mount bench models on the manufacturer's purpose-designed stands. The heights of stands and pedestals may be adapted according to whether the buyer wishes the peeler to discharge at sink height (usually 910 mm) or lower down. Many users prefer to have potatoes discharged directly into the sink, but the disadvantage of this is that the hopper is rather high for loading. The potato peeler shown in Plate 6 gives an idea of the difference between loading and discharge levels.

Machines are rated according to the weight of potatoes that they can take at one loading—for example, 3 kg, 6 kg and 14 kg.

Use of the potato peeler. The operation of the machine is simple, but attention to various details will contribute to efficiency, help to avoid breakdowns and reduce waste.

1. Before potatoes are put into the machine they should be roughly sorted into buckets, and any foreign matter such as stones, straw and excessive soil should be removed. In particular, a watch should be kept for stones, as these damage the peeler's lining.

2. During sorting, any potatoes of abnormal size should be put on one side. This is because if there are considerable differences in size all the potatoes will not be ready at the same time.

3. The machine should be switched on before the potatoes are

loaded; otherwise there would be an excessive initial load on the motor.

4. Potatoes should not be left in the machine for longer than is necessary for the removal of dirt and the greater part of the skin. Usually, because of irregularities in shape, it is not possible to remove all the skin without losing a great deal of the flesh as well. Preparation is completed by hand, when skin from the inner parts of hollows on the surface of the potato and any remaining eyes are removed.

As a rule, two or three minutes is long enough for potatoes to be left in the machine, but this time varies with the type of machine, the condition of the abrasive plates (these become worn in time) and the condition of the potatoes. Some machines have timers to control automatically the length of the peeling process. The operator should adjust the timer to suit the circumstances. In particular, the time should be reduced for new potatoes.

When potatoes are left too long in the machine the efficiency of the peel trap, if there is one, may be impaired because of the presence of a considerable amount of starch in the sludge, which causes foaming. When once the skin has been removed, continued friction rubs away the white flesh underneath, and this creates foam in the interceptor, slows down the filtering process and calls for more frequent emptying of the trap to prevent flooding.

Cleaning and maintenance of potato peelers. The peeling chamber is washed thoroughly after use. If the base plate is removable (it usually is), it is lifted by means of the hooks provided, and any waste matter remaining below is removed. The maker's instructions about lubrication should be followed. Regular servicing of the peeler is particularly important, since a breakdown considerably disrupts work in the kitchen.

Other food-preparation machines

These include:

Bread buttering and slicing machines;
Butter-pat machines;
Cream air whips (cream is aerated to give maximum yield, and there is no risk of overwhipping);
Coffee-grinding mills;
Liquidisers (useful for mixing soups, etc., in small kitchens, and for special diets);
Pastry rollers, hand-operated or power-driven (the pastry passes between an upper and a lower roller).

Dishwashing

Dishwashing is an important operation in catering for several reasons. From the point of view of hygiene, it is essential that a high standard is maintained by operators, and that they have the equipment to enable them to achieve this. Aesthetically, clean, sparkling tableware free from defects adds greatly to the enjoyment of a meal. Finally, there is the point that washing up, if done by hand, can account for a considerable proportion of the total labour costs in catering.

Processes involved in dishwashing

Whether dishwashing is done by machine or by hand, up to five processes are involved, as follows:

1. Scraping or stripping to remove food scraps. This process, which is not necessary for all items, is done by hand.

2. Pre-rinsing. When washing up is done by hand, pre-rinsing is rarely carried out. In many automatic dishwashers there is a pre-rinse section. Where no provision for pre-rinsing is made in the machine, pre-rinsing may be carried out manually. Its object is to remove or loosen gross soil; it is not necessary for lightly soiled items such as tumblers and tea plates.

3. Washing. In this process various types of soil are removed. Soil may be divided into three main groups, as follows:

a, that which is water-soluble, and can therefore be removed easily by immersion in hot water;

b, that which may be removed by hot water containing a suitable detergent;

c, that which requires friction for its removal.

Group (c) includes egg, starchy products (especially reconstituted potato), and any food that has become crusted during cooking, or has been allowed to dry on crockery and cutlery. This is the group that presents the greatest difficulty.

4. Rinsing. Tableware is rinsed to remove dirty dishwater from the surface. When a heated rinsing sink is used, as shown in Figure 7, the temperature is maintained at between 77° and 82° Celsius. In dishwashing machines rinsing is carried out automatically at temperatures between 66° and 82° Celsius.

5. Drying. The rinsing processes described above usually heat tableware to a sufficiently high temperature to ensure quick drying of most items without the aid of cloths (known as air drying). But it is unlikely that glassware will have a sparkling appearance unless it is given a polish with a clean cloth. Cutlery, plastic ware and stainless steel dishes do not always dry completely without the use of a cloth, and cutlery, like glassware, often needs a final polish to give it a good appearance. Some dishwashers incorporate hot-air dryers to accelerate drying, and such dryers are particularly indicated where plastic or stainless steel ware is used, or where a rapid turn-round of dishes is required.

Types of dishwasher

Three types of dishwasher have been developed, each with a different method of applying friction to remove soil.

Dishwasher, turbulent immersion type. This type is rarely seen nowadays. It consists of a sink in which the water is agitated by means of a motor-driven impeller, and the turbulent water so produced provides the friction to remove soil from tableware. Usually there is a second sink for rinsing. A considerable amount of manual labour is needed, and operation is not speedy.

Dishwasher, brush type. Here friction is provided by two cylindrical brushes, fitted to the side of a sink, which rotate on parallel axes so that the tips of the brushes just touch. The operator places plates between the brushes until all soil has been removed. Subsequently the plates are placed in racks and immersed in a rinsing sink of the kind shown in Figure 7, or in some models they are racked and placed in a section of the machine where they are rinsed by means of sprays.

Although a great deal of manual work is involved, the operator usually works at a good rate because he can do so rhythmically. Good results are obtained from these machines, which are simple to install, use and maintain.

Dishwasher, spray type. The spray type of dishwasher is the kind that is in general use. In this machine soil is removed by means of the scrubbing action of high-pressure hot water jets. Machines of this kind bear no resemblance whatever to a sink, and, except for the hooded type, they appear from the outside as large rectangular boxes with an opening at each end with either lift-up doors or splash curtains (see Figure 50). Some small models have hoods that may be tipped to either side as needed (see Figure 49). There are several different kinds of spray dishwasher. Plate 9 gives an inside view of a flight dishwasher, and illustrates the action of spray jets, which is common to all spray-type machines.

Push-through spray-type dishwasher. This is the simplest type of machine, and is semi-automatic. Plates and other articles are stacked in racks, and in some cases pre-rinsed—that is, the rack is pushed over a sink and the contents are rinsed by means of a hand-held spray. The rack is then pushed into the machine, where the plates are sprayed with hot water and detergent for a timed period determined by the operator. At the end of this period the rinsing process operates automatically. After this, the operator pulls out the rack and inserts the next one, and so on. There is a separate tank for the rinsing water, which is maintained at a higher temperature than the washing water.

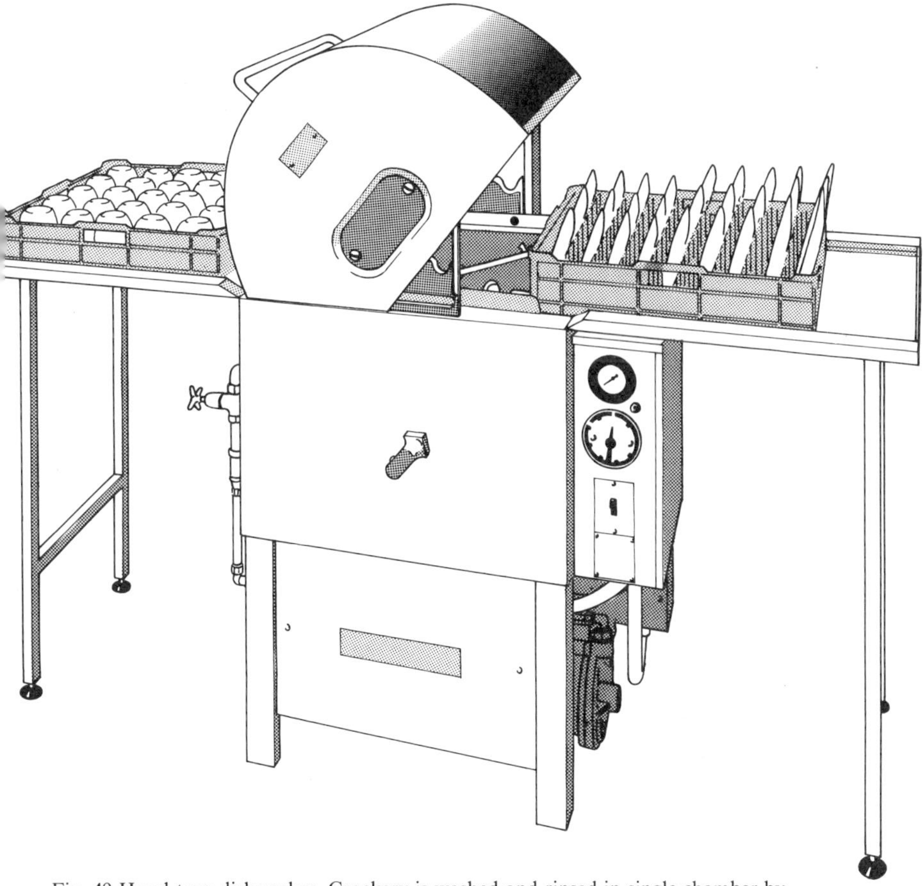

Fig. 49 Hood-type dishwasher. Crockery is washed and rinsed in single chamber by spray jets. Operator selects length of washing period, and rinsing follows automatically

Special racks suitable for cups and tumblers, and containers for cutlery, are provided.

Automatic spray-type dishwasher. Here, instead of the racks being pushed in and out by hand, a conveyor takes them through the machine, and there are separate sections for washing and rinsing. Machines are usually of modular construction, and pre-rinse and hot-air drying sections are included if the client wishes. The output of this type of machine is obviously much greater than for the push-through type, and less labour is needed.

Flight-type dishwasher. This type has a pegged conveyor belt. Dishes are loaded directly on to the belt between the pegs, as shown in Plate 9, and racks are not used except for cutlery, cups and glasses.

Hence much of the work of moving racks into position is eliminated, and the flow is smoother. Plate 9 shows the belt passing underneath the machine to complete its circuit. In the flight-around model, which is a variation of the flight, the belt does not turn over; instead it stays at the same level, and after passing through the machine turns through 180° and returns along the outside of the machine, as in a merry-go-round. This arrangement (shown in Figure 16) saves a great deal of space, and means that the machine may be loaded and unloaded at adjacent points.

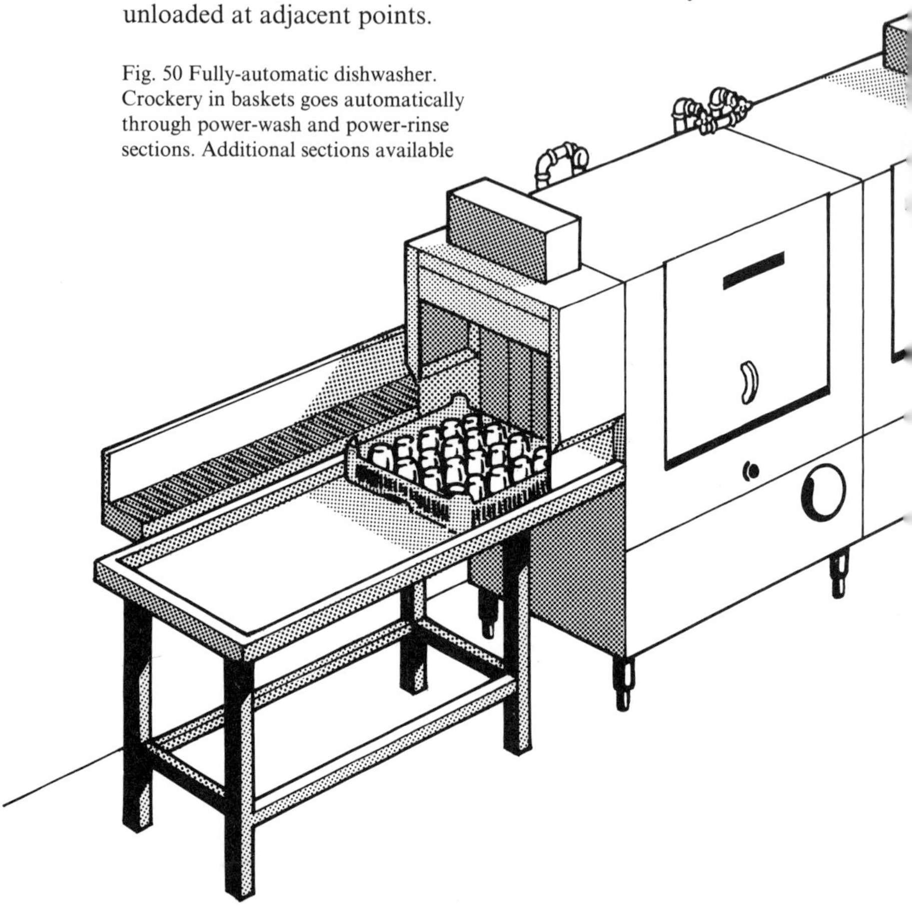

Fig. 50 Fully-automatic dishwasher. Crockery in baskets goes automatically through power-wash and power-rinse sections. Additional sections available

Capacity of dishwashers

For a fully-automatic rack-type machine this is reckoned in the output of racks per hour, which may range from 150 to 200 (508 mm × 508 mm). The push-through type takes one rack of this size at a time, and the average wash/rinse cycle takes one minute.

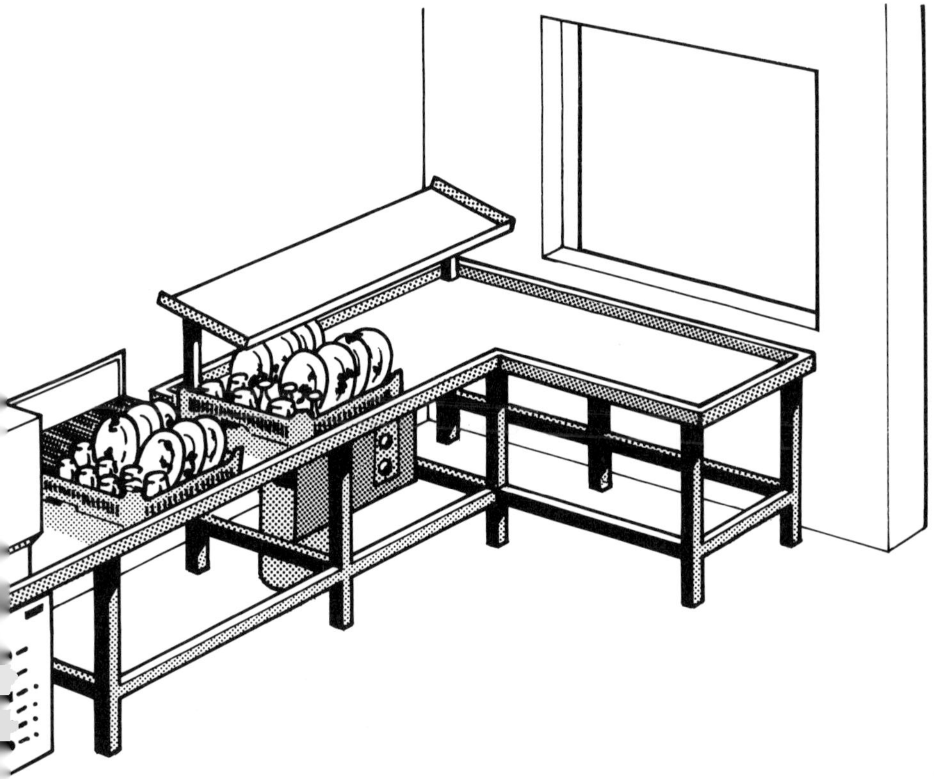

Special features of dishwashers

Hot water supply. It is usual for hot water to come from the domestic supply, and the dishwasher has facilities for boosting the temperature to those needed for (a) washing and (b) rinsing.

Water pressure. Where the required water pressure is not available, a booster pump is fitted.

Energy recovery system. A heat-exchange condenser unit (shown in Plate 9) may be fitted on some models to recover some of the heat input and thus to save on running costs.

Ventilation. Ventilation units integral to the machine are available for some models.

Spray jets. These operate from the top or the bottom of the machine, or from both. In some models they are fitted in boxes, which are easily removable for cleaning purposes.

Strainer baskets. Food particles that fall to the bottom of the machine collect in strainer baskets, which are removed and emptied when washing-up is finished.

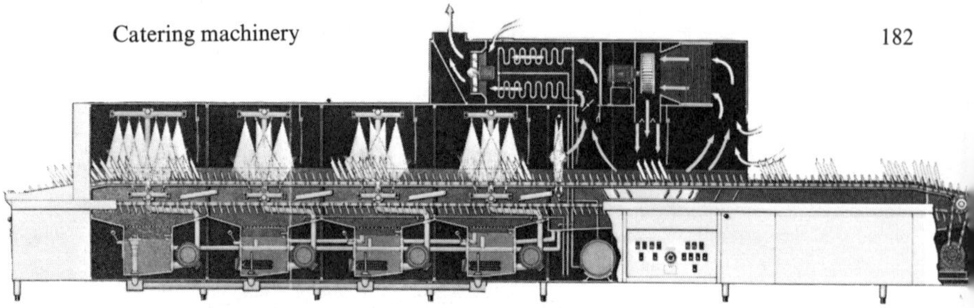

Plate 9 Flight-type dishwasher where crockery is fed directly on to moving belt. Processes of pre-wash rinse, washing, rinsing and final rinsing shown in (a). Other features shown in close-up.

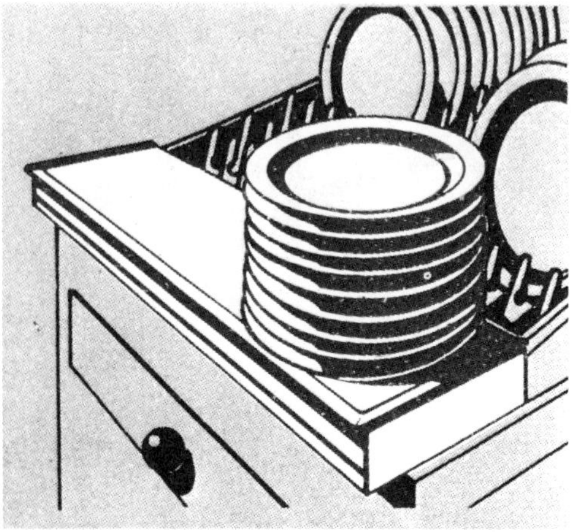

(b) Stacking platform at each end of machine with anti-drip rim

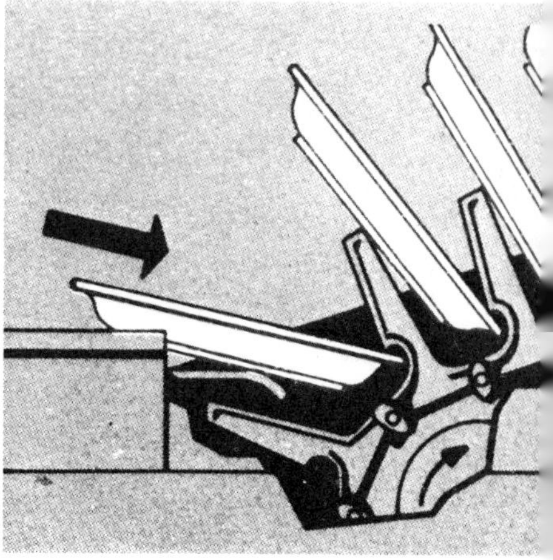

(c) Loading of plates between angled pegs

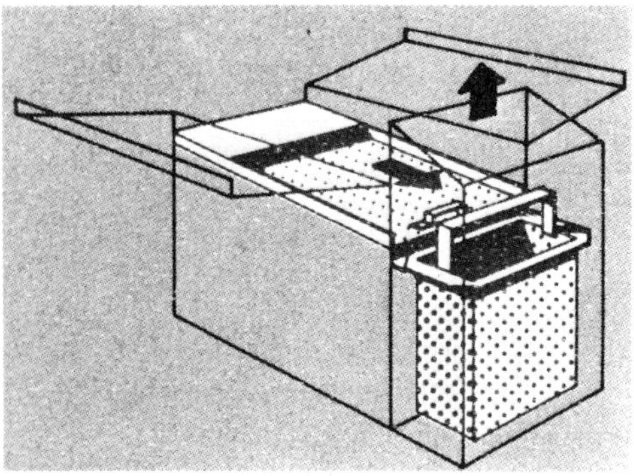

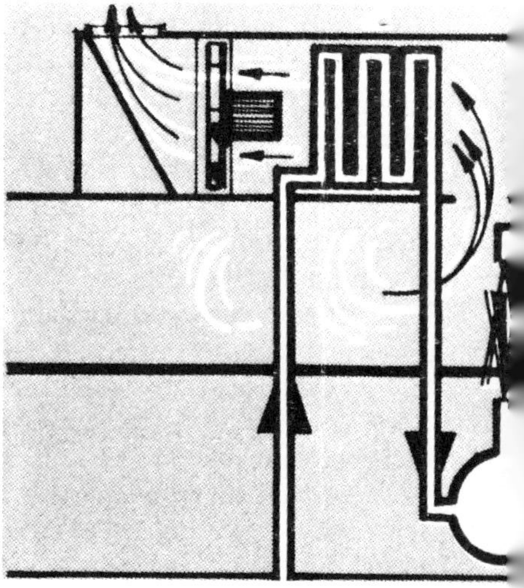

(d) Sloping filter to direct food soil to deep basket for removal from outside machine
(e) Condenser with energy feed-back to save energy

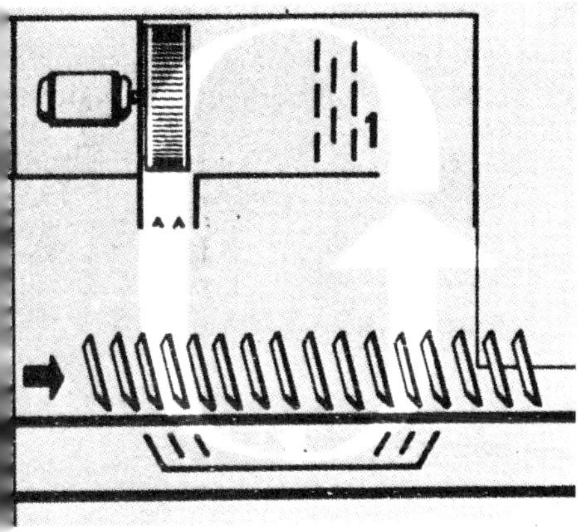

(f) Hot-air dryer to speed up drying

(g) Safety stop: cut-out operated by any item that reaches end of conveyor

Tabling. Except for flight-type machines tabling is needed at the entrance and exit to the machine to accommodate racks. At the entrance, space for three baskets is necessary to maintain a smooth flow of work, and at the exit space for three to four baskets is needed to allow crockery to dry. Insufficient tabling negates some of the advantages of having a machine.

Detergent dispensers. Electronic detergent dispensers are available that automatically dose the washing water with the necessary amount of detergent, and maintain a suitable level of detergent throughout the washing process.

Rinse-injection units. In order to reduce the surface tension of the rinsing water, and thus speed the drying process, rinsing aids are often used, and these are dispensed automatically by means of rinse-injection units attached to the machine.

Ancillary equipment

Water softeners. The effectiveness of dishwashers depends to a large extent upon the force of water from the jets, and efficiency may be greatly impaired if jets are blocked by deposits of hard-water salts. Hence, in hard-water districts a water softener to treat the water before it enters the machine is essential.

Waste-disposal units. The most hygienic way of disposing of food waste is by means of an electrically-operated waste-disposal unit. This reduces waste to fine particles and discharges it into the main drain, but there are some areas where the use of such a unit is not allowed. So far as plate waste is concerned, it is convenient to have the waste-disposal unit sited near the work stations of those who are scraping plates. However, if the rate of return is very fast, and if there is a considerable amount of waste, the ordinary type of waste-disposal unit (as shown in Figure 51) may cause a bottleneck. This difficulty is overcome by the provision of a trough linked with a waste-disposal unit into which waste food is scraped (see Figure 15).

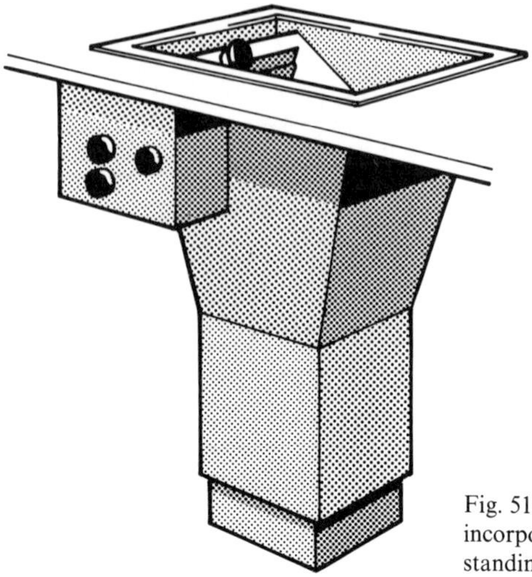

Fig. 51 Waste disposal unit, incorporated in benching; free-standing types also available

Overshelving. Soiled tableware often needs a certain amount of sorting before it goes through the dishwasher. Overshelving, raked at a convenient angle, is provided to accommodate racks and containers into which cups, glasses and cutlery are sorted.

Trolleys. Clean items are returned to the service area or to hot cupboards by means of trolleys or other mobile units, usually purpose-designed. Much of the equipment used is dual-purpose, *e.g.*, mobile plate dispensers, mobile tray stackers, mobile cutlery dispensers. Among the various types of trolleys used for clearing dirty tableware, one with tray slides instead of shelves is worth special mention. When the client has finished his meal he returns his dishes on a tray to the clearing trolley, which is taken to the wash-up area for dismantling. The tray often has a turned-down lip instead of a rim along one side, so that the client finds it convenient to fit the tray on the table while he has his meal.

Conveyor belts. Used crockery and cutlery may be returned to the dishwashing area by means of conveyor belts, and these may take quite long routes and also move to higher or lower floor levels by means of spiral mechanisms. Usually the client has to return his dishes to the conveyor belt on a tray, which is dismantled in the receiving area by staff whose work stations are at right angles to the belt. Cutlery is sometimes removed by means of magnets instead of being manhandled. These installations are expensive, but in large establishments savings in staff costs may justify their use.

Electrically-operated roundabouts. These rotate between the dining room and the wash-up area. The client puts his tray of used dishes on the roundabout, for collection and dismantling by catering staff in the wash-up area.

Pan-washing machines

These are similar to semi-automatic dishwashers, but they are especially designed to remove very heavy soil. They have large wash chambers to accommodate bulky pans. Pan-washing machines are not widely used.

Waste compactors

Figure 52 shows a waste compactor that reduces the volume of waste materials such as empty cans and cartons. This piece of equipment is particularly useful in finishing-kitchens where there is usually a lot of packaging to be disposed of.

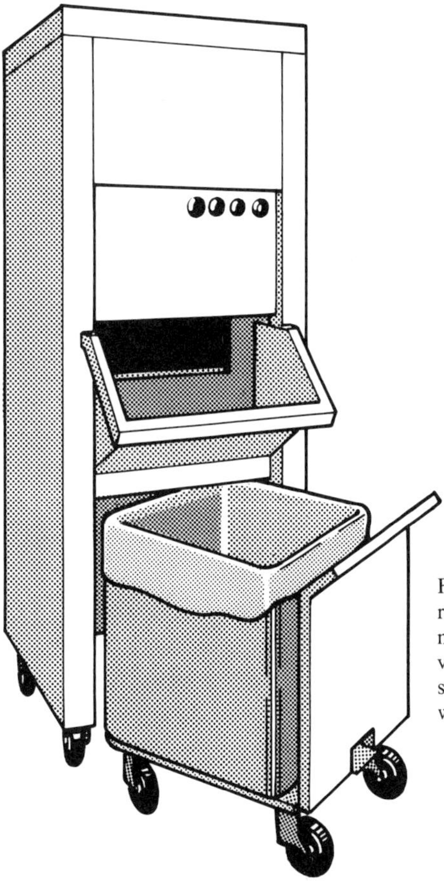

Fig. 52 Waste compactor, can reduce rubbish (packaging materials, cans, etc.) by up to $\frac{1}{12}$ of volume. Here loading hopper and section, lined with plastic bag, in which waste is compacted

Chapter 13

Vending and vending equipment

When the term vending is used in catering, it refers to the automatic dispensing of beverages, food and other items. The means of dispensing is the vending machine, which performs its function when coins or tokens are inserted.

Although vending in catering is of recent origin—it did not make headway in the United Kingdom until the 1950s—the vending machine has a long history. In AD 215 an urn was designed by the Greek mathematician Heron; it had a delicate mechanism which dispensed a tiny quantity of holy water when a coin was dropped on to it (see Figure 53). In more recent times, vending machines for chocolate and cigarettes were familiar sights outside tobacconists' shops and at railway stations in the Britain of the 1920s and 1930s.

Nowadays, vending has developed into much more than a minor sales aid for a limited number of items. The numbers and types of product, and the machines available, are extensive, and vending has

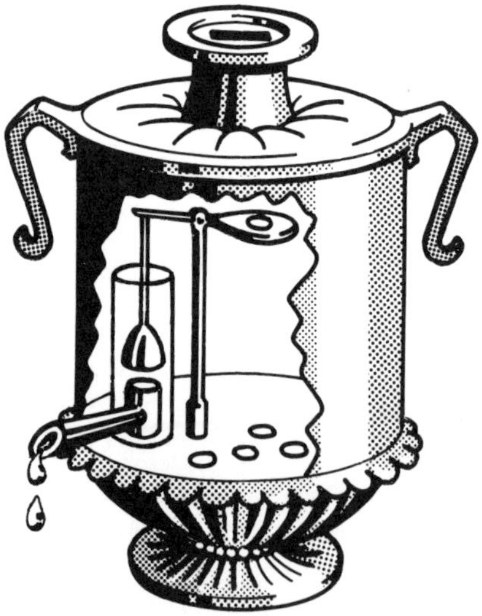

Fig. 53 Heron's holy water dispenser, AD 215

many applications. The increased scope of vending has been made possible by the development of convenience foods—instant coffee and soups, for example—and by the greater sophistication of vending machines and associated equipment in an electronic age. At the same time rising labour costs (especially where plus rates are involved) and increased costs of building accommodation (and sometimes shortage of accommodation) have meant that vending, which makes minimal demands upon labour and floor space, is in certain circumstances economically attractive either as an adjunct to a catering system or as a complete system in itself. The convenience foods and instant beverages that are often (though not invariably) used in vending machines are now widely accepted in the home and elsewhere. The consumer has also come to accept (though he does not always like) the impersonal, undemanding service that vending gives. Also, more and more people expect light refreshments at frequent intervals both at work and at leisure.

Typical instances of the use of vending machines are: the provision of beverages, and possibly snacks, to employees during normal working hours; the provision of beverages and/or some food items at mealtimes as an ancillary to conventional catering; the provision of main meals and snacks at meal breaks for staff working awkward hours—for example, on a night shift.

The provision of vended snacks to employees during normal working hours

This is the vending application that probably springs most readily to mind, because it is widely practised for clearcut reasons. The cost of ingredients for tea and coffee is normally comparatively low, but the cost of labour for making these drinks and serving them at or near the employees' work stations is high. This is particularly so when lay employees carry out this task for a small group of workmates, though the cost here is usually hidden. When staff are employed specifically for the purpose, and a 'tea lady' with her trolley makes the rounds, labour costs are almost certain to be lower—but they are no longer hidden. They are charged either against the employer or against the employee, and usually both parties are reluctant to pay high overheads for the cost of a simple service. On the other hand, employers are not always happy about hidden costs, or the inconvenience caused by employees who disappear to make the tea. Hence vending machines are now widely used. Milk bottles and collections of mugs—some chipped and stained—have disappeared from work benches and the tops of filing cabinets.

How the system works. The vending machine is geared to a steady output of drinks over a long period, rather than a high output concentrated into a few minutes. Hence, instead of members of staff having fixed tea-breaks, the arrangement is that they fetch drinks when they feel they would like them. It is usual to provide cold drinks as well as hot throughout the year. Cold drinks during winter are particularly popular with young people and those doing hot or heavy work. In large factories and office blocks vending machines may occupy sites scattered throughout the building. Where there is a concentration of employees, it is convenient to site machines in banks. One of the main considerations is the distance between the employee's work station and the nearest vending machine. In a typical installation, five 200-cup machines are installed for 500 employees. Machines are cleaned and loaded once daily, and average consumption is two drinks per person. At a factory where workshops are scattered more machines—one for every 50 employees—are installed so that everyone has convenient access to a machine.

The use of vending at mealtimes as an ancillary to conventional catering

In this sort of arrangement clients take part of the meal from the service counter in the usual way, but they supplement this with vended items; or they may take their entire meal from the machines and ignore the service counter. Examples of the sort of vended service provided are:

1. Beverages in the dining room or coffee lounge instead of, or as well as, service over the counter;
2. Hot dishes may be served over the counter, while all other items are vended;
3. Hot snacks may be vended.

This kind of vending may be introduced for the following reasons:

1. Because of lack of space at the service counter;
2. To reduce the number of catering staff employed at mealtimes.

Vending meals and snacks for staff working awkward hours

Staff working night shifts (such as nurses, doctors, members of the police force and factory workers) are entitled to expect the same facilities for meals and refreshments as day workers, but, where such provision involves employing catering staff at overtime rates, the cost of these meals will be much greater. Often the cost is subsidised by the employer, so that his concern is not with making this meals service pay, but with minimising the amount of subsidy. In many circumstances the cheapest and most satisfactory way of catering is to provide vended meals. Food served may be of the manufactured frozen variety, but often it is cooked on the premises. The chef cooks extra amounts of standard menu items during the day and either freezes or chills them under controlled conditions (for the sake of hygiene). Later a selection of these dishes is loaded into a refrigerated vending machine. The client chooses what he wants, and receives with it a key that operates a microwave oven, in which he reheats the food. Cold menu items are vended in the usual way.

Vending has a great many applications, and several other possibilities come to mind when various kinds of vending machine are considered.

Examples of vending machines

Vending machines for hot drinks (cup). The machine dispenses several different hot drinks: tea, coffee; chocolate; and soup or a savoury drink. The dry ingredients for the drinks, which include milk powder and sugar, are kept in separate containers inside the machine; disposable cups are stored in the cup stack. The machine is connected to electricity and water supplies, and it contains a thermostatically-controlled water boiler. Another basic feature is the coin mechanism. When the correct selection of coins is inserted, and the buyer has chosen his drink by pressing the appropriate button, the following sequence is initiated: heating water; throwing measured amounts of ingredients into a cup; ejecting the cup; filling it with heated water. Figure 54 shows a typical vending sequence.

Vending machines for cold drinks (cup). These machines dispense cold drinks made either from syrups or from powders, and they are similar to hot-drink machines. The main difference is that they contain a chilled water system instead of a boiler.

Vending machines for hot and cold drinks (cup). This type of machine (shown in Plate 10) offers fewer varieties of drinks than are provided by separate machines for hot and cold drinks.

Machines vending cold drinks in bottles, cans or cartons. A cooling system, which needs to be connected to a power supply, is incorporated in the machine. Cans are opened by means of a ring-pull, or, if a different type of can is used, a can-opener is attached to the machine.

Bulk milk machines. Milk supplied in special bulk containers is kept at a suitable temperature by refrigeration—electrical connection is necessary—and is measured into the cup by means of a tube and valve. Cups are stacked inside the machine. Simple in design and easy to keep clean, these machines offer a hygienic way of dispensing cold milk.

Some points to note about beverage vending machines. Where no mains water supply is available a machine with a water tank, designed

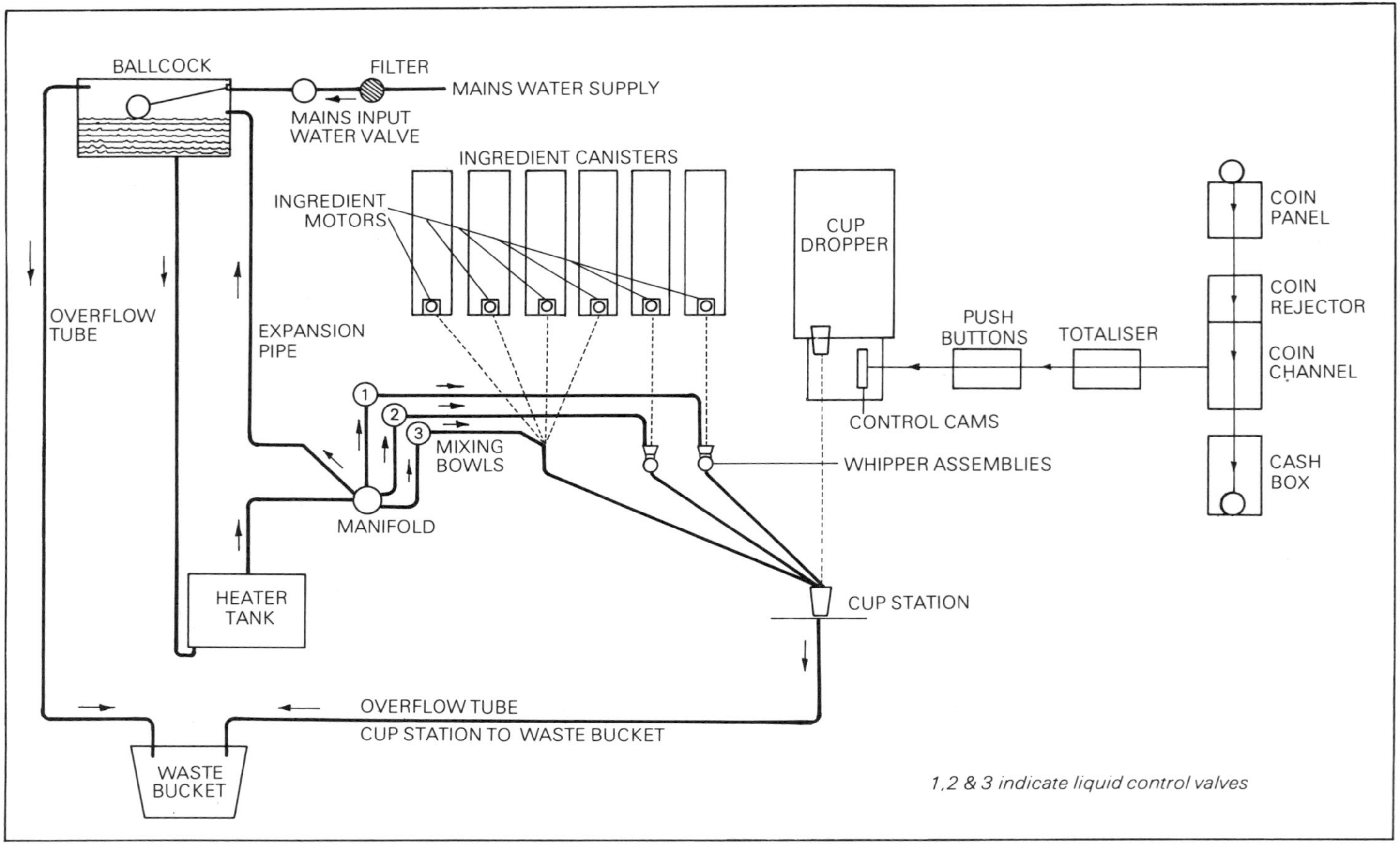

Fig. 54 Typical vending sequence in hot-drinks machine

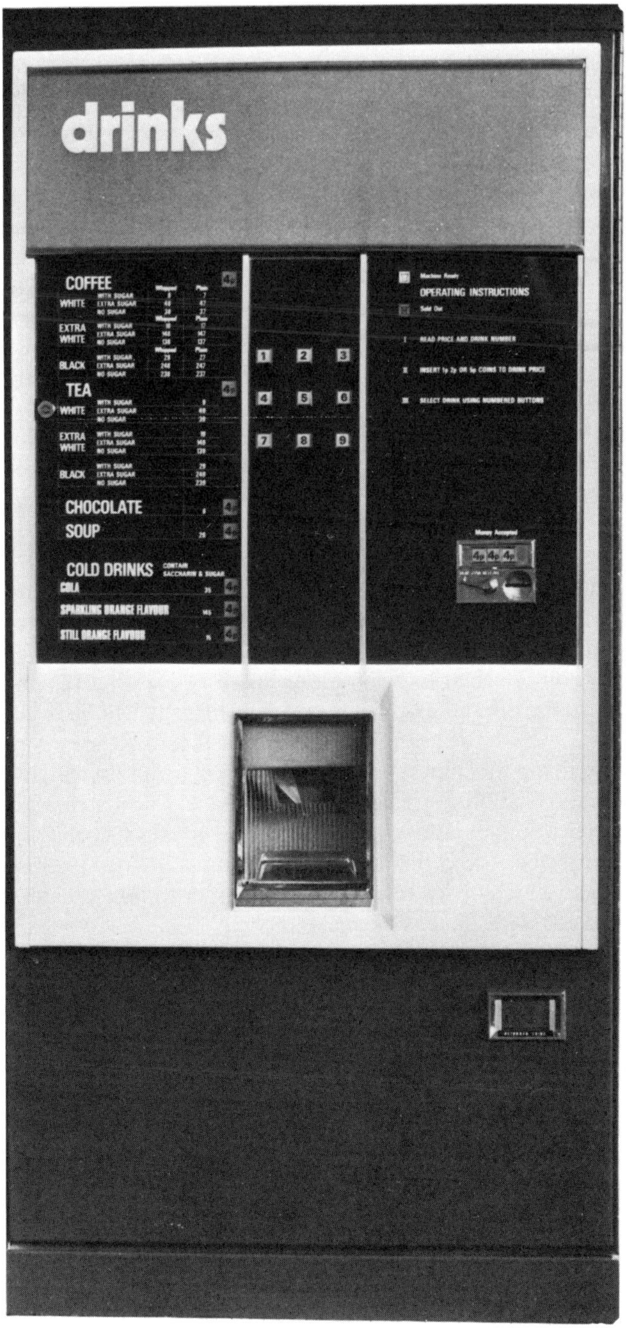

Plate 10 Hot and cold beverage dispensing machine. 32 selections are available from this machine. Drinks are selected by client's reading off number and price on left-hand panel, inserting required coins and tapping out number on push buttons on central panel

to be filled by hand, can be supplied. When it is not intended to charge the client, the coin mechanism may be omitted from the machine. This arrangement is known, rather oddly, as 'free-vend'.

Machines dispensing food items and snacks

The storage compartments of these machines may be designed for a particular type of food—for example, sandwiches, pies, snacks in dishes or canned foods—or they may be suitable for a variety of items. They may be refrigerated or heated, and some are designed especially for dispensing canned soups and other canned savoury snacks. The way in which the customer is given access to the food he has chosen varies; the following are examples:

1. Some machines have separate compartments, each with its own door; when the customer inserts a coin and makes his choice the mechanism allows the appropriate door to open.
2. Endless belt machines have shelves attached to vertical moving belts. After coins have been inserted and a choice made, the belt moves down to allow the contents of the lowest shelf to fall under gravity to the delivery station.
3. 'Lift' machines are fitted with horizontal shelves across the width of the machine. At either end, running vertically, is a lift. When the customer has chosen, each lift moves to that shelf. An empty tray is pushed automatically from one lift on to the shelf; this causes all the other trays on the shelf to move along sideways, so that the end tray is moved to the lift at the opposite end. The lifts then go up to the delivery station, where the customer helps himself to his choice.
4. Rotating drum machines contain a revolving drum on which is mounted circular shelving divided into segments. Food items are loaded into each segment, and when the customer makes his selection after having inserted a coin the drum revolves until the right item is opposite a door, which opens to allow the customer to take the item.

Servicing and maintenance of vending machines

Machines must have daily attention from a trained operator, whose duties include:

(a) Refilling;
(b) Removing any perishable stock whose shelf life has expired;
(c) Rotating stocks of snacks and sweets where appropriate;
(d) Cleaning (meticulous attention is needed here);
(e) Cashing;
(f) Rectifying minor faults, such as a jammed coin, a hung-up cup, or clogged canisters or throw mechanism.

The operator's daily tasks take about 20 minutes, and at the same time any defects should be noted and reported. Maintenance of the machine's working parts may be undertaken by the manufacturer, or by the catering concern's specially-trained technician.

Hygiene

In general, vending machines are capable of providing food and drinks under extremely hygienic conditions, but much depends upon the way in which the operator carries out his duties, and upon the care exercised in observing good hygiene practice, especially where perishable foods, and prepared chilled or frozen cooked foods, are concerned. Caterers should be familiar with:

(a) *The Food Hygiene (General) Regulations*, 1970;
(b) *Food Hygiene Codes of Practice*, No. 7: *Hygiene in the Operation of Coin-operated Food Vending Machines*;
(c) *Food Hygiene Codes of Practice*, No. 9: *Hygiene in Microwave Cooking*.

All are published by H.M.S.O.

Other points to note about vending machines and their use

1. Siting. Machines should be sited in well-lit areas and should not cause obstruction; an alcove is ideal. It is often convenient to site them in banks, but this may sometimes conflict with the need to have machines near their users. (A distance of 27 m is considered reasonable for an employee to walk for his mid-morning beverage; a longer distance wastes time.)

2. The vending machine should be positioned to ensure easy access for cleaning both the machine and its surroundings.

3. Walls and floors near the machine should have easily-cleaned surfaces.

4. Where meals and snacks are provided, there should be an adjacent dining area.

5. One advantage of vending machines is that if circumstances change they are easily moved to new sites.

6. Beverage machines, with their throw mechanisms, represent the ultimate in portion control. Other types of machine, even without automatic control or portioning of foods by the manufacturer, readily lend themselves to strict portioning.

7. Portion control, combined with recorded information on the number of portions dispensed, allows strict stock control to be exercised.

8. If the demand is variable or miscalculated, there may be waste of perishable foods.

Vending contractors

Vending operations may be carried out on behalf of the management by a contractor. Usually management either takes a percentage of profits or pays an agreed level of subsidy.

Ancillary equipment for vending machines

Microwave ovens. These have already been referred to in Chapter 8. When they form part of a vending system, as shown in Figure 55, a plastic key or token may be issued with the pack of food. The client uses this to operate the microwave oven. Keys have slight variations that determine the length of time for which the oven will operate, and they are colour-coded accordingly as well as being stamped with the appropriate time. Thus the operator who packs the food for vending may readily select the correct key. The buyer, after having removed wrapping and key, puts his food in its dish in the oven and uses his key to activate the oven. A red light shows during heating, and a green light indicates that the food is ready for removal. Snacks take from 10 to 30 seconds, and main meals from 40 to 60 seconds to heat. An alternative to keys and tokens is press-button operation.

Disposable containers. Disposable cups may be made of plastic, plastic-coated paper, waxed paper or plain paper. Their design must

Fig. 55 Automatic hot-food vending system, with microwave oven incorporated

be such that they nest in the cup stack and may be easily separated from the stack by the cup-ring mechanism so that they drop down singly to the cup station. They should be sufficiently stable when filled and held, and the consumer's hand should be protected from excessive heat. Typically, the cup has a ring at the top to allow easy separation. For heat insulation they are either ribbed to allow an air flow between fingers and part of the cup wall, or they have double walls to protect the fingers while keeping the contents hot. Cups for cold drinks are similar, and, although insulation is obviously unnecessary, they are often ribbed for greater stability; the alternative is stronger material. Cups are often translucent, which is necessary when filling mechanisms are controlled by light beams, which would be ineffective if cups were opaque.

Disposable plates and dishes. Usually these are of aluminium foil, plastic or paper. They must be rigid enough to allow easy and safe handling, especially when plates are full of hot food. Various shapes and sizes of dish are available to suit the compartments of different kinds and sizes of vending machine.

Containers for microwave ovens. Metal foil containers are not suitable because they affect the penetration of the food by the microwaves, and this screening effect means that the automatic timing allowed will be inappropriate; metal foil may also damage the magnetron. Plastic material must be capable of withstanding distortion in either the refrigerator vending machine or the oven.

Wrapping material. Food is wrapped to protect it from contamination and to retain moisture. Transparent material is usually used, so that the customer may see the food before he buys it.

Beverages. Ingredients for beverages must be able to flow. Flow is defined as the free running of a dehydrated ingredient within the canister or during dispensing. If ingredients are not free-running they will clog in the canister, the throw mechanism will be upset, and the strength of the drinks dispensed may vary. Flowability is affected by damp, and it is therefore essential that the ingredients are kept in moisture-proof packaging. Products manufactured and packed specifically for vending are available.

Food. Food may be bought already portioned and packed for vending; this facility applies to complete one-course frozen meals.

Introducing a catering system based on vending

When it is proposed to introduce a vending system, considerations involved are similar to those involved in the introduction of any new system. However, it is wise for the management to ask a vending expert to assess the feasibility of the operation, as expertise in this field tends to be limited.

TABLE 6: A summary of useful information about vending machines

Vending times	
Cycle for beverages with instant ingredients	10 seconds
Cycle for tea made from the leaf and coffee made from ground beans	15–20 seconds
Refrigerated merchandiser	10 seconds
Plated meal of average size in a microwave oven	1 minute
Output from a hot food dispenser	5–6 a minute
*Safe holding times**	
Cold plattered food in refrigerator merchandiser at a temperature of 4°C.	Up to 48 hours†
Hot plattered food in heated merchandiser at a temperature of 69°C.	Immediate use usual; maximum six hours for extended service§
Sandwiches, rolls, etc., at ambient temperature	maximum two to four hours
Types of beverage machines and their capacities	
Machine for dispensing ingredients	To serve small numbers, say about 10 people
Table-top or wall-mounted machine	To serve about 30 people
Free-standing vending machine	Capacities from 200 to 1000 cups
Capacities of refrigerated merchandisers (as used in connection with microwave ovens)	80–100 main meals 200–300 snacks

* These are taken from *Vending*, published by the Automatic Vending Association of Britain.

† As the quality of the food may deteriorate, and as people do not like to buy yesterday's food, in practice a maximum of twenty-four hours is recommended.

§ Although food may be held with safety for the maximum period, it may not be palatable and its appearance may have deteriorated. In practice this type of machine is best used for a known demand at a known time, so that the holding period is strictly limited.

Chapter 14

The individual kitchen: assessing equipment requirements

The task of assessing how much equipment is needed in a kitchen is a responsible one, and it is by no means easy. It is, of course, essential that there should be enough equipment to allow the right amount of well-cooked food to be served at the required time, and for sufficient variety to be offered. But, if more equipment than necessary is provided, not only is money wasted at the time of purchase and installation, but also the kitchen's running costs are increased. Extra space is needed to house unnecessary equipment, and so more labour is needed to man and clean the kitchen. The extra equipment itself needs to be cleaned and serviced, and it can also be the cause of extravagant use of fuel.

If the kitchen is only slightly over-equipped the effect upon running costs may be negligible, but gross over-equipping results in a kitchen that is both costly and difficult to run.

There is no simple formula for determining equipment needs because circumstances vary, and because the various considerations involved have complex interrelationships. However, there are certain fundamental principles upon which sound decisions about choosing the quantity and type of equipment may be based. There are also various lists of equipment and rules of thumb that may be used as guidelines, but if they are used it is essential that they should be related to individual circumstances, and that they are brought up to date when new equipment comes on to the market, or when new systems, or modifications of systems, are introduced.

Some of the basic questions to be asked when lists of equipment are drawn up are: how many people are to be catered for? What sort of meal, and how much food, are they to be given? At what times, and over what periods of time, are they going to eat? How is the food to be cooked? What types of equipment are on the market, and of what capacities? In the following paragraphs we shall approach these questions in an oblique way, and shall look at some basic considerations.

Basic considerations

Output of the kitchen

Obviously the first point to be considered is the number of meals that the kitchen is intended to produce. It has already been pointed out (in Chapter 4) that for a kitchen producing main meals (other than a cook-freeze unit) the output is related to the production of a specific meal—that is, either the midday or the evening meal. In drawing up a list of equipment, the first consideration is the number of main meals to be served; it should then be decided what extra items will be needed for other meals, such as breakfast and tea.

For cook-freeze kitchens, as has been mentioned in Chapter 4, output is defined in terms of output per day and not per main meal. The output may be expressed as:

(a) the number of meals;
(b) the number of portions;
(c) the weight of food to be frozen.

All these figures are, of course, interrelated, but it should be remembered that the output of a cook-freeze unit on any one day does not usually comprise a day's menu, and the unit does not necessarily produce a full range of menu items. Consider the following example:

Number of meals consumed per day:	3000
Average weight of one meal:	0·454 kg
Percentage (by weight) of food prepared in the cook-freeze unit	70

Total daily requirements of food produced by the cook-freeze unit:

$$\frac{3000 \times 0{\cdot}454 \times 70}{100} = 953{\cdot}4 \text{ kg—say } 950 \text{ kg}$$

Another point arises: the number of days on which meals are needed does not necessarily correspond to the number of days on which the cook-freeze unit is in operation. (In the case of schools and universities it is likely to be fewer.)

Example:

Total weight of food consumed per day:	953·4 kg
Number of days on which food is consumed:	200
Number of days on which the cook-freeze unit is in production:	240

Required daily output of the cook-freeze unit:

$$\frac{953{\cdot}4 \times 200}{240} = 794{\cdot}5 \text{ kg—say } 800 \text{ kg}$$

In kitchens and snack bars where continuous service is maintained, output is related to the number of snacks of various types produced per hour at periods of maximum demand, and the list of equipment is planned to meet this maximum.

Type of meal

It is necessary to know what type of meal is to be provided, and the style of cooking proposed. For example, less equipment will be needed for a simple two-course meal than for a meal with many courses offering complicated and sophisticated dishes where final cooking is done to meet the client's individual requirements. In the first instance boilers and bratt pans are likely to be used for many menu items, whereas in the second (as in a restaurant) a series of small pans used on a boiling table or solid-top range will be more suitable. The question of whether a choice of dishes is to be offered makes a difference whatever the style of the establishment. It is often assumed that where a choice of dishes is offered more equipment is necessary, but this does not always follow, although a greater range of equipment may be needed. Offering a choice often makes it easier to use each piece of equipment regularly to its full capacity. For example, if chipped potatoes are served to a total of five hundred clients at one meal, facilities for frying five hundred portions of chipped potatoes are needed. If, however, the clients have a choice, it may be that on any one occasion no more than two hundred portions of chipped potatoes are served. Take another example. Where a cold table is featured regularly as an alternative to a hot meal, many items will need no cooking (for example, salad plants and bought-in items), while others may be cooked at off-peak periods (for example, cold desserts, cold roast meat). Hence, less equipment is needed.

The menu

It is always helpful when considering what equipment to provide to draw up a specimen menu to cover a period of several weeks, but it is absolutely essential when the menu offers a wide choice of dishes. The specimen menu is used as a general guide, and also as a check when a draft list of equipment has been drawn up, to see that on any one day the equipment covers the demands of the menu, but that equipment is not lying idle to any great extent. (It should be noted that if the check shows that alteration is necessary, it may be that the specimen menu as well as the equipment list needs revision—or alteration to the menu alone may be all that is needed.)

In the case of a cook-freeze kitchen, production is always planned to make full use of the installed equipment, and questions of its lying idle should not arise. The specimen menu is used as a general guide and to help assess total production requirements over a period, and from this a daily production schedule may be drawn up. The daily production programme should harmonise with the proposed equipment list, and, if a check shows that this is not so, one or the other—or both—must be modified.

Length of service period

Sometimes the service of meals is restricted to a very short period, say half an hour; in other circumstances meal breaks are staggered, and there is a service period of two hours or longer. This affects the amount of equipment needed. For example, many more batches of vegetables can be cooked in a high-speed cooker during a two-hour service period than in half an hour, and the same applies to batches of chipped potatoes. Some menu items and pieces of equipment are not affected to the same extent. For example, with an extended service period one might stagger the cooking times of steamed puddings, but, because of the length of cooking time, one would not expect to produce two batches of pudding for the same meal from one steaming oven.

In finishing kitchens most foods have already received their prime cooking, and cooking times are usually short. Batch cooking is generally practised. Hence, the period over which meals are served is particularly significant, and the best use of equipment is achieved when there is a long period of service. This point is illustrated in Chapter 6, Example 5, where the forced-convection ovens in a finishing kitchen serving meals over a two-hour period are used to end-cook four batches of food.

Quantities of food and portion sizes

Reference has already been made to the total weight of food prepared in a cook-freeze kitchen as a measure of output. Total weight is particularly important in that context, because the capacity of a blast freezer is expressed in output of food, by weight, over a given period. In the case of cooking equipment and for food preparation machinery, information about:

(a) quantities of individual foods to be provided for a given number;
(b) the portion size for various dishes is needed.

Basic quantities are discussed in detail in Chapter 21, but some references to typical quantities and portions will be made here also in relation to various items of equipment.

Capacity and output of equipment

Equipment used for boiling

Where liquid food is concerned, it is very easy to assess how many portions boilers and pans will hold. All one needs to know is the capacity of the boiler and the number of portions per unit volume, as the following example shows:

Capacity of boiler:	45 litres
Number of portions of custard sauce per litre:	12
Number of portions of custard sauce per boiler:	$45 \times 12 = 540$

However, if the boiler used is dual-purpose, with a removable inner pan, the capacity of the boiler when used for making custard sauce relates to the inner pan. In the case of a 45-litre boiler, the inner pan capacity is usually about thirty litres, and the number of portions of custard sauce per 45-litre boiler is thus 360.

Where solid foods are concerned, there is not the same direct relationship between the amount of food and the boiler's capacity, because one is expressed in kilograms and the other in litres. However, the amounts of various solid foods that the boiler will hold may be directly observed, and the figures recorded for future use. Also, reference may be made to information published by manufacturers and others. For potatoes and other root vegetables allow five kilograms (weight as purchased) per ten litres. An average portion is 200 g. The following is an example:

Capacity of boiler:	45 litres
Allowance for potatoes (weight as purchased):	10 litres/5 kg
Average portion of potato (weight as purchased):	200 g

Number of portions of potato per 45-litre boiler:

$$\frac{45 \times 5 \times 1000}{10 \times 200} = 112{\cdot}5\text{—say } 100.$$

Green vegetables are much bulkier, and so need more space. The allowance is 10 litres per 2 kg (weight as purchased). For example:

Capacity of boiler:	45 litres
Allowance for green vegetables (weight as purchased)	10 litres/2 kg
Average portion of green vegetables (weight as purchased):	100 g

Number of portions of green vegetables per forty-five-litre boiler:

$$\frac{45 \times 2 \times 1000}{10 \times 100} = 90.$$

It is not usually practicable to cook potatoes or custard sauce in batches in boilers because of the lengths of time involved in cooking, cleaning the boiler and heating it again after it has been refilled. In the case of green vegetables, however, it is usual to cook two or more batches, depending upon the length of the service period, because:

(a) cooking time is short;
(b) since only a small quantity of water is used for cooking, the boiler recovers quickly;
(c) it is unnecessary to clean the boiler between batches;
(d) it is good practice to use the cooking liquor from the first batch for successive batches.

If a tilting kettle is used instead of a boiler, cooking time will be shorter and recovery rate will be faster. All electric boilers are designed to boil a quantity of water equal to their stated capacities in one hour. Thus, a 45-litre boiler will boil that quantity of water in one hour.

When pans are used for boiling, the quantity of vegetables per litre is less because pans may not be filled as near to their brims; ease and safety in lifting and handling have to be considered. Ten litres per 4 kilograms should be allowed for potatoes and root vegetables. This consideration does not apply to green vegetables, since a much smaller quantity of water is used for cooking, and they are not covered with water.

An average figure for boiling space for vegetables is 50 litres per 100 meals.

Roasting and baking ovens

Where most foods are concerned, the number of shelves and their dimensions are critical in determining the amount of food an oven will hold. It is necessary to consider shelf dimensions in relation to the containers used in the oven. Unless dimensions of shelves and containers harmonise, shelf space—and therefore oven capacity—is wasted. Circular or oval containers are obviously unsuitable because they cannot fit flush. For most foods it is usual to use rectangular or square containers of standard dimensions, and three sizes are in general use.

The Gastronorm module. The basic module is 527 mm × 324 mm, and containers are produced in multiples and fractions of the module and in different depths (see Figure 56). Roasting and baking ovens (as well as other items of equipment) designed specifically to accommodate these modules are available. Given the following facts, an oven's output may be calculated:

1. Number of oven shelves;
2. Number of standard containers that each shelf will accommodate;
3. Numbers of portions of various dishes per container.

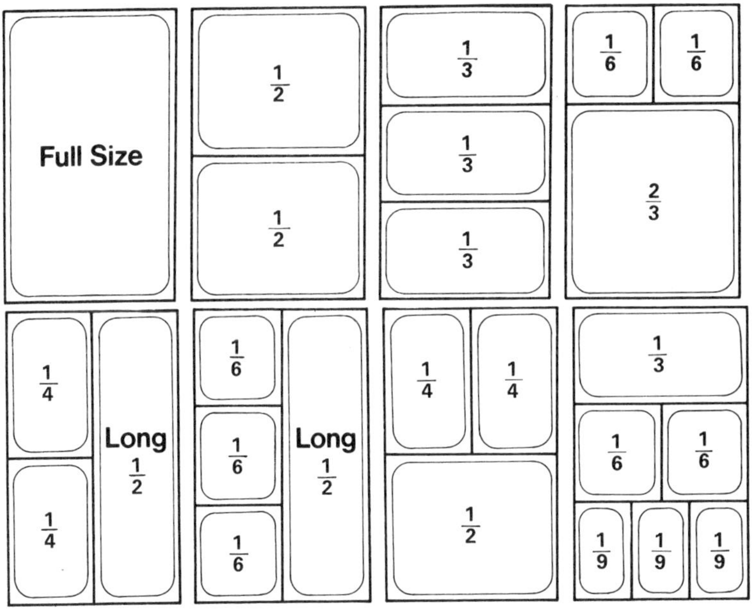

Fig. 56 Gastronorm containers, based on module of 527 × 324 mm, available in many sizes. When used for service, can be arranged in various combinations in standard opening of 510 × 305 mm in service counter. Examples shown

Example

Capacity of oven	234 litres
Number of oven shelves	3
Dimension of shelves	686 × 560 mm
Number of Gastronorm containers (527 mm × 324 mm × 64 mm) per shelf	2
Number of portions per container	30
Number of portions per oven	180

Containers 64 mm deep are suitable for dishes such as casseroles and milk puddings, but this is too deep for pastry and baked sponges, which need containers 32 mm deep, and the number of portions is reduced by half. This means that the output of the oven per load is halved, but, since cooking times are much shorter than for casseroles and milk puddings, it is possible to load the oven at least twice in the average working session.

The school meals service module. A module of 407 mm × 254 mm × 77 mm is widely used for school meals in the United Kingdom, and fractions of this (halves, thirds, etc.) are available. Ovens with capacities of 140 litres usually have shelf dimensions that harmonise with this module, and take six full-sized containers (two per shelf). Allowing twenty-five portions per deep container, and twelve for tins 38 mm deep, the output per oven load is 150 and 72 portions respectively.

Module of 484 mm × 242 mm. The half size of this module, 242 mm × 242 mm, is in general use for foil containers, and, where the depth is 38 mm, it holds eight average portions. Many forced-convection ovens are designed specifically for frozen foods packed in this size of container.

In forced-convection ovens shelves are placed more closely together than in conventional ovens. This is possible because much of the air moves horizontally across the shelves (see Figure 29a). Hence they take a greater load per unit of capacity. For example, one model of forced-convection oven with a capacity of 200 litres holds 6 Gastronorm containers, 527 mm × 324 mm × 64 mm. Its output per load is about 15 per cent greater than that of a conventional oven. Also, cooking takes about 10 to 20 per cent less time, and preheating only about 10 minutes. Thus, for items with short cooking times, more batches can usually be produced during a working session than would be possible with a conventional oven.

Not all food cooked in ovens fits into modular containers; this applies to joints of meat and poultry which have irregular shapes. Here, shelf dimensions are less critical. 100 litres of oven capacity is needed for between 128 and 160 kg of meat, or 96 to 128 kg of poultry.

A useful average figure for calculating the amount of oven space needed for a two-course meal in a conventional kitchen is 130 litres per 100 meals; this may be reduced by from 15 to 25 per cent if forced-convection ovens are used.

Steaming ovens, atmospheric type

Modular containers may be used for steamed puddings and other items, and steaming ovens should have shelf dimensions that harmonise with the chosen module. Steaming ovens take greater loads per unit of capacity than do conventional roasting and baking ovens. Because the temperature is even throughout the oven and there is no radiant heat, the whole of the oven space may be used, and for a given oven capacity the number of shelves is greater.

Example

Oven capacity:	169 litres
Number of shelves:	5
Shelf dimensions:	584 mm × 431 mm
Number of containers, 407 mm × 254 mm × 77 mm, per shelf:	2
Number of portions per container:	25
Number of portions per oven:	250

Woven mesh baskets, 64 mm deep, are used for cooking potatoes and root vegetables. One square metre of basket area takes about 50 kg of potatoes or root vegetables.

Example

Oven capacity:	169 litres
Number of baskets:	5
Area of each basket:	0·25 m^2 (584 × 432 mm)
Total basket area:	1·25 m^2
Quantity of potatoes per m^2:	50 kg
Quantity of potatoes per portion:	200 g
Number of portions of potato per oven:	$\frac{50 \times 1{\cdot}25 \times 1000}{200}$ = 312—say 300

It is not feasible to load the oven more than once in relation to any given meal period. Where considerable use is made of steaming an average allowance for steaming ovens of the atmospheric type is 67 litres per hundred, but for many types of menu this would be too much.

High-speed steamers (self-generating or with their own generators)

These ovens are intended chiefly for foods that can be cooked quickly and produced in several batches during the period of meal service. It follows that the output during a given period, as well as the size of batch it will take, are significant.

Example

Pan capacity:	3·4 kg
Number of loadings of fresh peas per hour:	30
Output per hour of fresh peas:	102 kg
Size of portion of prepared fresh peas:	100 g
Number of portions per hour:	1020

Deep-fat fryers

The output of deep-fat fryers is expressed in weight of chips (raw to finished state) per hour, and depends not only upon the pan's capacity but also upon the heat input. An output of 2·25 kg of chipped potatoes (fried from raw) per kilowatt may be expected. But chips are often given a preliminary cooking, during which they are not allowed to brown; this is known as blanching. When blanched chips are given their final cooking, the output per hour is doubled. In the following example it is assumed that frying takes place over a period of an hour-and-a-half, and that the potatoes have been blanched.

Example

Electrical loading of fryer:	10 kW
Output of chipped potatoes (blanched input) per hour:	4·50 kg per kW
Portion size of cooked chips:	100 g
Length of frying session (blanched input):	1·5 hours
Number of portions of chips (blanched input) per frying session:	$\frac{4{\cdot}50 \times 10 \times 3 \times 10}{2}$
	= 675—say 650

A general guide to the capacities and output of cooking equipment is given in Table 7.

Hot cupboards

Hot cupboards are needed for two purposes: to warm plates and dishes, and to keep cooked food hot.

Plate warming. The amount of hot cupboard space needed for warming plates is easily assessed. The following is a guide:

Allow one third of a metre run of hot cupboard (of counter height) for each 100 plates.

There are, however, a few points to remember:

1. When cold menu items are served regularly at each meal, less plate-warming space is needed.

2. If a bain-marie hot cupboard is included in the reckoning, allowance should be made for its projection into the hot cupboard area. This may mean that only one shelf is available instead of the usual two (see Figure 39).

3. It may be convenient to re-use plates during the service period as they return from the dishwasher, and if the turnround is fast they will be fairly hot when they reach the servery. If necessary they can occupy their former space in the hot cupboard before they are used again. This may mean that the number of plates in use is, say 80 per cent of the number of portions served. This should be allowed for when hot cupboard space is calculated.

Dish warming. If cafeteria service is employed, no separate allowance need be made for warming dishes because space so occupied will almost certainly be reoccupied later by dishes of cooked food that are being kept hot. But, if vegetable dishes, sauceboats and serving platters are provided for either waitress or family-style service, this will not necessarily be so. Dishes, sauceboats, etc., may be taken straight to table as they are filled, or this may be the case with some of the dishes.

To achieve economic use of space, it is wise to choose stacking tableware. Even so, the preferred shapes for tableware—circular and oval—do not harmonise with the dimensions of hot cupboard shelves. The space needed for warming these dishes is unlikely to be less than that needed for plate-warming.

Keeping food hot. Food that has to be kept hot is taken straight from the oven to the hot cupboard, and therefore the dimensions of the hot cupboards, including any bains-marie, should harmonise with standard containers used in the ovens. The amount of space necessary will vary according to the period over which the meal is to be served and the amount of batch cooking involved. If too much hot cupboard space is allowed, staff are sometimes tempted to dish food too early and to keep it hot for an unnecessarily long time. An average allowance is a run of 0·6 m for each hundred meals.

Machinery

Key points about catering machinery have already been discussed in Chapter 12: output over a given period; the amount of labour saved; the versatility of some machines; and the costs involved. All these points are relevant when it comes to choosing machines for a particular establishment. The following examples illustrate the sorts of reasons that govern choice.

Example: Choice of potato peeler for a kitchen with an output of two hundred meals a day

Quantity of potatoes used each day: 40 kg

Q. Whether to choose a peeler of 6·5 kg or 13 kg capacity?

A. The smaller peeler would need to be loaded seven times, and the larger peeler three times. Bearing in mind that the timing for each load is between two and three minutes, the expense of the larger model is not easily justifiable, and a peeler with a capacity of 6·5 kg would be suitable.

Example: Choice of either a power unit or an electric mincing machine for a kitchen producing five hundred meals a day, and regularly featuring home-made hamburgers on the menu

Q. Whether a power unit or a mincer would be more suitable?

A. The kitchen already has a mixing machine with a vegetable slicing and shredding attachment and a mincer, but the main part of the mixer is in heavy use, and it is not possible to produce the required amount of minced meat from the mincing attachment.

In these circumstances either would be suitable, but a power unit of the same manufacture as the machine would probably be better. The attachments now used with the mixer could be used also on a new power unit. This would give greater flexibility in the use of both machines.

Example: Choice of a dishwashing machine for a kitchen with a daily output of 600 meals

Q. Whether to choose a machine of the brush type, or a fully-automatic spray-type machine?

A. The brush-type machine involves a considerable amount of manual labour for its operation, and, because each plate has to be manhandled through the brushes, the process tends to be slow. For this number of meals a fully-automatic machine is indicated.

Refrigerators

Requirements for refrigerator space vary, and the following are some of the factors involved:

1. Frequency of deliveries for perishable foods;
2. The number of meals served each day;
3. Whether the establishment is open on seven days a week. At week-ends, deliveries of perishable foods are unlikely.
4. The number of cold menu items (desserts, meats, etc.). Such items make greater demands upon refrigerator space.
5. The amounts of frozen foods that are to be used.
6. Whether facilities are needed for the controlled thawing of frozen foods.

The amount of refrigerator space allowed often falls between $0{\cdot}42\ m^3$ and $0{\cdot}9\ m^3$ per 100 main meals served.

Interchangeability and versatility of cooking equipment

So far we have not looked at inter-relationships and alternative methods of cooking foods. Again, a specimen menu may be used to check a draft list of equipment from this point of view. Has allowance been made for the fact that potatoes might be boiled on certain days and steamed on others, when the steaming ovens would not otherwise be in use? And so on. Would it be better to substitute a bratt pan for a boiler because it is more versatile? Should the specimen menu be revised in order to allow for the interchangeability of some cooking methods? The list of equipment shown in Figure 19, which relates to Chapter 6, Example 2, is an example of good use being made of versatile equipment.

Standard lists of equipment

Large catering concerns responsible for the management of establishments with similar styles and objectives draw up lists of equipment to ensure that catering units attain a given standard, and also to save the work of preparing individual lists. Bodies such as the Department of Education and Science and the Scottish Education Department produce lists to be used as guidelines for school catering. These are of general interest, but they should be seen against the background of the type of catering to which they relate. They are often used as a base, and when they are used in different circumstances they should be modified accordingly. The Scottish Education Department's *Schedule of Recommended Equipment, Storage and Accommodation*, published in *Educational Building Note 14*, appears in Appendix 1. A list of equipment used in finishing kitchens appears in Appendix 2.

A check-list

It is helpful to have a check-list of information needed and decisions to be made before equipment is bought for individual catering establishments:

(a) Estimated number of meals and refreshments to be supplied.
(b) Period over which meals and refreshments will be served.
(c) Estimated demand at peak periods.
(d) Style of meal.
(e) A typical menu covering a period of several weeks.
(f) Quantities of basic foods to be used, expressed by weight or volume, in the state in which they are delivered to the premises (*e.g.*, fresh, frozen, etc.), for a given number of meals.
(g) Dimensions of containers in which food will be cooked and served, and the average number of portions in each container.
(h) Range of suitable equipment that is available.
(i) Output of each item of equipment.
(j) Cost of equipment, both initial and running.

Equipment for finishing kitchens

The following is a list of cooking equipment suitable for installation in a finishing kitchen:

Boiling table	For miscellaneous use, sauce-making, regenerating frozen vegetables, and frozen boil-in-the-bag dishes.
Deep-fat fryer	For items to be fried, especially frozen or ready-prepared chipped potatoes.
Forced-convection oven	For regenerating a miscellaneous range of foods.
High-pressure steam cooker	For regenerating frozen foods in batches, especially vegetables and boil-in-the-bag frozen foods.
Jacketed boiler or dual-purpose boiler	For making sauces in large quantities.

Microwave oven	For regenerating small quantities of frozen foods.
Microwave oven with extra facilities:	
(a) infra-red	Where browning facilities are needed.
(b) forced-convection	Where particularly fast regeneration of food in bulk is needed.
Microwave oven, tunnel	For regenerating small quantities of frozen foods in a continuous sequence (large establishments only).
Steaming oven, atmospheric pressure	For regeneration of frozen vegetables, heating steamed puddings, and miscellaneous purposes.
Tilting kettle	For regenerating frozen vegetables, and heating milk and soups.

Equipment for snack bars

Modular equipment is often used in snack bars, a popular module being 610 mm × 610 mm. Many pieces of equipment are designed for counter tops. Figure 1a shows how a counter-top module may be fitted on to a base, which may be an unheated cupboard, a hot cupboard or an oven. Back-bar equipment, as it is often called, is extremely compact.

The following is a list of equipment suitable for back bars. All are available as counter-top items and as modules, unless otherwise stated.

Bain-marie
Boiling plate unit
Fryer
Griddle
Grill, salamander type
Grill boiler (griller/toaster with boiling plates above)
Heated display cabinets (not usually modular)
Hot cupboards (not counter-top)
Microwave oven (not modular)
Oven (not counter-top)
Equipment for beverages (obviously not modular)

TABLE 7: A guide to the capacity of cooking equipment and refrigerators

Item	*Food*	*Capacity*
Boiling pan	green vegetables	2 kg/10 litres
	potatoes and root vegetables	5 kg/10 litres
Bratt pan of typical dimensions (662 × 610 × 178 mm)	bacon rashers	400 portions an hour
	chops	250 an hour (average output 200 portions an hour)
	eggs, fried	30 per batch 600 an hour
	eggs, poached	800 an hour
	fish, poached	200 portions an hour
	stews and braised dishes, pot roasting meat joints	27–32 litres
Fryer, deep-fat	chipped potatoes (from raw)	2·25 kg/kWh
Griddle of typical dimensions, 610 mm × 457 mm (0·28 m²)	bacon (35 × 20 g slices)	280 slices an hour
	beefburgers (90 mm diameter, 70 g)	32 per batch 500 an hour
	eggs, fried	30 per batch 450 an hour
	sausages, 35 g	80 per batch 400 an hour
	steaks, 115 g	12 per batch 150 an hour
Oven, roasting and baking	cakes, small	250/m² shelf area
	pies and dishes cooked in trays	19·5 kg/m² shelf area
	poultry, roast	96–128 kg/100 litres
	meat, roast	128–160 kg/100 litres
Oven, steaming	fish	72 kg/100 litres
	potatoes and root vegetables	384 kg/100 litres (58 kg/m² shelf area)
	puddings in individual moulds, 76 mm diameter	160/m² shelf area
	puddings in cylindrical moulds	300 kg/100 litres
Grill, underfired	steaks, 115 g (cooking time 3–6 mins)	65–86 per m²
Griller/toaster	steaks, 115 g (cooking time 2–4 mins)	65–86 per m²
	toast, 125 mm × 100 mm	65 slices per m²

Item	*Food*	*Capacity*
Refrigerators	meat	1 tonne/3·4 m^3
	fish, wet	1 tonne/4·25 m^3
	mixed dairy produce	1 tonne/7·1 m^3
Freezer refrigerator (range of average storage densities)		
reach-in type		160–217 kg/m^3
walk-in type		128 kg/m^3

Note: In reach-in freezer refrigerators a higher figure for storage density is achieved when standardised packaging is used. The figure for the walk-in type assumes its use.

Chapter 15

Staffing

Of the many factors that contribute to the successful operation of a catering establishment some of the most important concern the staff—their quality, their efficiency, their ability and their willingness to work together. No matter how good facilities may be, good results will not be obtained unless the staff are of suitable calibre; conversely, good staff are capable of overcoming adverse conditions and circumstances—but this should not be taken as an excuse for bad conditions. As in most types of organisation where a group of people with assorted skills and responsibilities works as a team under the direction of a supervisor, it is the person in charge who is the key figure. He, more than anyone else, determines by his personality, attitudes, organising ability and expertise whether staff realise their full potential and work efficiently as a group to achieve the known aims and objectives of the concern. At the same time, each member of staff contributes an essential part to the whole, and it is therefore necessary to examine the factors affecting their work to make successful operation possible.

Scope of catering work

The set-up of a large kitchen is extremely complex—much more so than is often appreciated. Also, the range of duties and skills involved is considerable; this depends not only upon the size of the establishment but upon the type of catering involved. At one end of the scale is an unskilled employee working at the fairly simple job of eyeing potatoes; at the other end is the head cook or chef—a craftsman producing dishes requiring high degrees of skill and culinary knowledge, which are the result of training and experience linked with natural gifts. In between there are jobs for which varying degrees of skill and experience are needed. But neither routine tasks of preparing vegetables nor high standards of craft skill are needed in finishing kitchens where prepared frozen and other convenience foods are extensively used. Nor is the highest level of craft skill necessary in establishments where very simple meals are provided, for example in a nursery school. But it would be a mistake to believe that there is any establishment where no cooking expertise is needed.

In addition to work associated with cooking, there are jobs that require clerical ability and skills concerned with finance, book-keeping and the buying of food. In large concerns, especially those with a number of catering units, or where sophisticated plant is in use, there may be jobs demanding a knowledge of maintenance engineering. Training, specialised knowledge and skill are called for from the first moment when the menu is planned, and an understanding of nutrition is valuable throughout the range of processes. After the menu has been planned, the ordering of stores calls for sound knowledge of buying methods and commodities. When the goods are delivered, careful checking before storage and issue demand ability in the storekeeper—including that of assessing quality—and from that stage onwards varying degrees of skill are necessary for preparation and cooking. Again, however, the level of skill and knowledge varies with the system of catering used. For example, it is much simpler to order and check convenience foods than those in their raw state.

When food reaches the service area it must be dealt with quickly, deftly and carefully. A certain amount of tact and social skill is called for when clients are being dealt with.

And then, beyond all this, there is the work of the supervisor, who must understand all these various operations and be capable of organising and arranging the routine so that work flows smoothly to a successful end. At the same time, he may need the ability to deal with the financial side of the work.

Grades of staff and responsibility

In general, four main groups are employed in catering establishments, and within each group are various grades corresponding to the nature of the work to be done, and calling for different levels of skill and experience. It is the practice to set out the responsibilities of a post in writing, and to define the nature of the job.

Management staff

In this group several different designations are used to describe the person in charge: director, food services manager, catering manager, domestic bursar, supervisor or superintendent. Where only a part of the work is managerial and supervisory, titles such as cook-supervisor or cook-in-charge are used. Management functions may relate to a single establishment or to a group of several units, but we are not concerned here with the sort of management exercised from a head office.

Director. This title usually implies a high level of responsibility in a large and complex undertaking, such as a cook-freeze unit or the catering on a university campus.

Food services or catering manager. The holder of either of these posts is usually required to undertake more responsibility on the finance and policy sides than would be expected of a supervisor. In consequence, it may be that much of the direct supervision of staff is delegated, but this is by no means always the case.

Domestic bursar. As the term implies, responsibilities here cover the management of an institutional household as well as the catering. The post is usually associated with a residential establishment.

Supervisor or superintendent. The postholder is directly responsible for the supervision of staff, and as a rule has other management duties. Usually there is little or no responsibility for the financial side.

Cook-supervisor or cook-in-charge. The term cook-supervisor is self-explanatory. A cook-in-charge sometimes carries out similar duties but on a smaller scale, or he may have a more limited function relating mainly to cooking and a certain amount of staff supervision.

Duties. The duties of management staff may include any or all of the following:

1. Determining the system of catering, the style of meal and the quantities of food to be allowed in consultation with others as appropriate, or advising on these matters.
2. Preparing a catering budget or part of it in consultation with others, or advising on the budget.
3. Determining the prices to be charged for meals and refreshments in consultation with others as appropriate, or advising on charges.
4. Keeping expenditure within an approved budget.
5. Making arrangements for the supply of food and other items.
6. Buying food and other items.
7. Menu planning.
8. The control of food stocks and equipment.
9. General responsibility for the organisation of the work of preparing, cooking and serving food.
10. General responsibility for the care, cleaning and maintenance of equipment and premises.
11. Keeping records as necessary.
12. Checking and certifying accounts for payment.
13. The appointment, promotion, supervision, welfare and on-the-job training of staff.

In practice it is rare for management at unit level to undertake all these responsibilities. Catering is often undertaken by large concerns, and in such cases most policy matters are decided at head or regional office level. This might apply to matters such as style of meal and size of portions. A multiple firm with catering facilities at each of its branches expects to maintain uniform standards. In the case of meals provided at maintained schools in Britain, recommendations on nutritional standards and food usage are laid down by the Department of Education and Science (for England and Wales) and the Scottish Education Department, and these are reinforced by local education authority policy decisions. Large organisations, whether public or private, usually negotiate their purchasing arrangements at national or regional level.

Generally speaking, if the caterer in charge of a unit has a wide range of duties and responsibilities, he is employed in an autonomous or semi-autonomous establishment, but not all such establishments employ a caterer. In a small private school or nursing home, for example, it would be wasteful to employ someone with a full range of management skills to control a small catering operation; hence a cook-in-charge might well be appointed, and be supported by lay management.

Again, it is not uncommon for various management tasks to be allocated to group managers, organisers and advisers, in which case the emphasis at unit level is on supervisory rather than management duties. It is with the manager as a supervisor that we are directly concerned in this chapter.

Staff responsible for cooking

The head cook or chef, with his assistants, is responsible for cooking the meal. The work may be divided into sections, but in non-commercial catering there are not usually more than three:

1. Meat, fish, poultry and other main-dish items;
2. Puddings and pastry;
3. Vegetables and salads.

It sometimes happens that the third section is left to unskilled staff, but this is not good practice. Vegetables and salads form an important part of the meal, and, although much of the work is unskilled, preparation and cooking should be under the immediate supervision of a skilled member of staff.

In addition to cooking, the duties of the head cook or chef may include: writing stores requisitions and planning menus in conjunction with the supervisor or manager; organising the work of the cooking staff, or in some cases the work of all members of the kitchen staff. If he has numerous additional duties, he may be able to devote very little time to actual cooking, and, if he is a highly-skilled craftsman, this may be an unfortunate loss. There is also the point that a good cook does not necessarily possess the ability to manage staff or to organise their work.

Assistant cooks may often be in charge of a section of a kitchen, or of a shift at times when the head cook is off duty.

It is axiomatic that all staff who have cooking duties must have some knowledge of their craft, but in finishing kitchens and snack bars only limited skills are needed. Hence staff are often given a limited amount of training designed specifically for this work, since it would be wasteful to employ highly-skilled staff.

Staff concerned with general duties and the service of meals

This third group of employees includes all those who do such jobs as vegetable preparation, cleaning, washing up, serving meals and miscellaneous tasks. Although this work is often described as unskilled, some training—though it need not be extensive—is necessary to ensure the correct handling of tools and equipment, and efficient working methods. Such training is often given on the job, and after further training promotion to a post as cook may follow. Manual dexterity is necessary for many duties, and those engaged in serving food should also have good appearance, pleasing personalities, social skills, a good eye for quantities and the ability to do simple calculations. Waiters and waitresses need a considerable amount of skill, and personal qualities are particularly important. However, the number of waiting staff employed in the non-profit sector is comparatively small.

In large serveries, or in establishments where light refreshments are provided at times when senior staff are off duty, a member of the serving staff may be designated as foreman.

Staff concerned with clerical and semi-clerical work

The kind of work undertaken by staff in this group includes the following:

1. Ordering or requisitioning supplies;
2. Receiving, checking and controlling stores;
3. Checking accounts and certifying them for payment;
4. Taking bookings for meals, including special requirements, *e.g.* for visitors, conferences, etc.;
5. Keeping records of meals and refreshments served, and other miscellaneous records;
6. Collecting and banking cash;
7. Routine work in connection with budget control and the analysis of expenditure.

These duties are not always assigned to staff employed specifically to do clerical work; some may be undertaken by the catering manager or supervisor, or his assistants. Alternatively, some tasks may be undertaken outside the catering establishment. For example, accounts may be checked at the head office or in the institution's general office.

The storekeeper. The post most usually associated with catering clerical work is that of storekeeper. In addition to Item 2, and possibly 1 listed above, he is responsible for the issue of stores and the care of storerooms, and he undertakes the routine work of regular stocktaking, so that much of his work is manual. No catering experience is needed for this job, but it is necessary to have a knowledge of commodities. The storekeeper should be able to assess the quality of incoming food and to check that it accords with its specification, so that he can draw the manager's attention to any defects. He should also possess a basic knowledge of suitable storage conditions for different kinds of food. He should be trustworthy, methodical and good at simple arithmetic. The post of storekeeper is a responsible one.

Few establishments employ full-time storekeepers, and the duties are often combined with those of cook. Alternatively, all or part of the work is done by the catering manager or his assistant. In small establishments a lay member of staff, such as a warden or house-parent, sometimes undertakes storekeeping duties.

The cashier. Where payment for meals is collected by means of a cash register, a cashier is employed; his duties often include cashing up and banking the money received. Many cashiers work part-time, while others combine cash-register work with general clerical or storekeeping duties. Qualities needed are: powers of observation (to spot all food items on a client's tray); nimble fingers; quickness at simple arithmetic (though this depends upon the type of cash register used); good appearance; social skills; and trustworthiness.

Clerical staff, general. Staff employed on general clerical duties work in the catering manager's office.

Hours of work

In residential establishments, and those providing full meals facilities, full-time staff usually work a forty-hour week, but hours are often much shorter where only one meal daily is provided, when a working week of thirty to thirty-five hours is common. A five-day week or its equivalent is usually worked—for example, ten days in two weeks. This latter arrangement is common in residential establishments where staff must be available on seven days a week. Wage-earning staff who work on Saturdays, Sundays or public holidays are paid at higher rates.

As a rule senior and skilled staff are full-time employees, but in residential establishments part-time cooks are sometimes employed for evening and week-end work. Many unskilled staff are part-time employees working at peak periods on duties connected with the service of meals and clearing up. Married women with domestic responsibilities often come forward for this kind of work. An alternative to employing part-timers at peak periods is to have multi-duty staff who do other work, such as cleaning and housekeeping, at off-peak times.

When a manager works out hours of duty he is, of course, concerned with manning the establishment adequately and offering suitable hours to his staff, but he is also responsible for keeping costs to a minimum. Hence work schedules and menus are planned to keep hours of work at times when plus rates are payable down to the lowest reasonable level. Overheads on employing staff, which include insurance and administration, are considerable, and this means that extra expense is incurred when part-timers are employed. One advantage of employing multi-duty staff is that this reduces the total number of staff needed, and thus helps to keep down overheads.

Breaks for meals and refreshments

Full-time staff need breaks for their midday and evening meals. It is usual for these meals to be taken on the premises, and staff often prefer a short break only, because this means that their working day finishes earlier. It is often difficult to decide on the timing of staff meals, because the service to clients must have priority. In general it is bad practice for staff to have their break before the main service of meals, because this would mean that they were not available for dishing up immediately beforehand. Hence the quality of the food would suffer, through having to be kept too long in the hot cupboard. From the point of view of kitchen routine it is often important to keep the washing-up facilities, particularly the dishwasher, in continuous use, and so it may be better for the staff concerned to have their meals in two sittings.

Tasks of laying the staff table, reserving food for staff meals, and cooking fresh batches of such items as chipped potatoes, should be specifically allocated to ensure that staff are adequately looked after.

It is usual for full-time staff to take a short mid-session break or—in the case of very early starts—to have a breakfast break. Light refreshments are normally provided by the employer.

Rates of pay and conditions of employment

Minimum rates of pay and conditions of employment for certain groups of catering workers are laid down by the appropriate wages council. In other cases pay and conditions are governed by national negotiating machinery, on which employers' associations and the recognised employees' unions are represented. Employees' rights are set out in the Employment Protection Act, 1975, and other legislation.

The Unlicensed Place of Refreshment Wages Council

Industrial canteens are covered by Orders made by the Council under the Wages Council Act, 1959, and the Employment Protection Act, 1975, but certain categories of worker, including those employed in hospitals, children's homes, old people's homes, universities, colleges and schools, are specifically excluded. The Council issues Orders laying down statutory minimum remuneration for various grades of staff, including managers.

Hourly rates are specified for time worked—other than on a Sunday or rest day—between 7.00 a.m. and 7.00 p.m. Higher rates apply for time worked outside these hours, and for time in excess of nine hours. There are special rates for work on a Sunday or rest day. Various grades of staff, with their rates of pay, are defined. Conditions laid down by the Council include entitlement to annual holidays and sickness benefit.

The Licensed Residential Establishment and Licensed Restaurant Wages Council

Orders made by this Council, which cover minimum rates of pay and conditions of service, apply to staff employed at licensed residential establishments, licensed works hostels and other such establishments. Hospitals, homes for children and old people, schools, colleges and universities are specifically excluded.

The National Joint Council for Local Authorities' Services (Manual Workers)

This is one of several national joint councils concerned with rates of pay and conditions of employment for staff employed by local authorities in England and Wales. (There is a Scottish Council associated with the N.J.C.) It lays down general conditions and rates of pay for manual workers, and designates grades of staff employed in the school meals service and residential establishments. Rates of pay for the various grades are agreed, and some special conditions of service—chiefly concerned with the position of staff during school holidays—are laid down. Cook-supervisors and cooks-in-charge are designated as manual workers. Local authorities often use the rates of pay and conditions of service agreed for the school meals service for all catering staff employed in non-residential establishments.

The National Joint Council for Administrative, Professional, Technical and Clerical Services

The function of this Council is similar to that of the manual workers' Council. It agrees salary scales for school meals supervisors; these are related to the capacity of the kitchen expressed in output of meals. For other catering supervisors and managers at unit level, the employing authority, at its discretion, selects a suitable scale (not specifically designed for catering) from those published by the Council.

The Whitley Councils

The national negotiating machinery for the Health Service consists of the Whitley Councils. The General Council covers general conditions of service, and functional councils cover pay and particular conditions of service for various groups.

The National Joint Industrial Council for Civil Air Transport

This negotiates rates for its catering workers.

Legislation covering employees' rights and industrial relations

A feature of modern industrialised societies is the mass of legislation—some extremely complicated—that governs relations between employers and employees and their trades unions, and gives rights to employees. Those responsible for the appointment and supervision of staff need to have some basic knowledge of employees' rights, and of the various government agencies that exist to deal with disputes and to enforce rights. Large concerns usually employ personnel officers whose duties include advising supervisors on these matters. The Department of Employment issues information and explanatory leaflets, as does the Hotel and Catering Industry Training Board.

The principal current legislation governing industrial relations in Britain is as follows:

The Trade Union and Labour Relations Act, 1974;
The Employment Protection Act, 1975;
Health and Safety at Work, etc., Act, 1974;
Sex Discrimination Act, 1975;
Equal Pay Act, 1970;
Trade Union and Labour Relations (Amendment) Act, 1976;
Contracts of Employment Act, 1972.

The rights given to employees by this legislation include:

Contract of employment. The employer must give to the employee at the start of his employment a written statement giving the main terms of employment, including details of pay, holidays, holiday pay, sickness and sick pay.

Equal pay for women. Men and women carrying out like work, or work graded as similar, must receive equal rates of pay.

Guarantee payments. Employees who are not provided with work because of short-time working or lay-offs are entitled to guarantee payments for limited periods.

Maternity rights. The expectant mother has the right not to lose her job because of her pregnancy, to return to her job after the baby is born, and to receive maternity pay.

Medical suspension. An employee suspended from work under statutory regulations following examination by an employment medical adviser or an appointed doctor is entitled to be paid normal wages for a maximum of twenty-six weeks.

Minimum period of notice. An employee is entitled to the following periods of notice:

After four weeks' service: one week;

Between and two and twelve years' continuous employment: one week for every complete year;

After twelve or more years of continuous employment: twelve weeks.

Redundancy. An employer must consult the appropriate trade union about proposed redundancies.

Redundancy payments. Employers are required to make lump sum compensation payments to employees dismissed because of redundancy. The amount is determined by the employee's pay, length of service with the employer and his age. The payments are financed in part by a redundancy fund established by the Redundancy Payments Act, 1965.

Sex discrimination. An employee may not be discriminated against on grounds of sex or marriage in matters such as pay, selection for a post, transfer, appointment and dismissal. An employee has the right of appeal to an industrial tribunal if he or she considers he has been discriminated against because of his sex.

Trade union membership and activity. An employee is protected against discrimination because he belongs to a trade union. If the employer recognises a trade union, officials are entitled to paid time off work for duties concerned with industrial relations between union and employer and for training purposes.

Unfair dismissal. An employee may not be dismissed unfairly. An employee who considers that he has been unfairly dismissed may appeal to an industrial tribunal, which can award reinstatement or re-engagement or cash compensation.

Safe and healthy working conditions. The employer must provide and maintain safe plant and systems of work, and a safe and healthy working environment.

Written statement of dismissal. If they ask for them, employees are entitled to written statements of dismissal.

Certain employees are excepted from some of the provisions

detailed above. Those with contracts for fewer than twelve weeks' employment are excluded from guaranteed pay, medical suspension payments, procedure for handling redundancy and notice of dismissal provisions unless they actually work for more than twelve weeks. There are several other exceptions, and qualifying conditions attach to most of the provisions.

Discipline and grievance procedures

Legislation on unfair dismissal and the system of appeal by employees to industrial tribunals has focused attention on disciplinary rules and grievance procedures, since these are material considerations when cases of alleged unfair dismissal are considered. The Employment Protection Act requires that written particulars of employment, which must be given to each employee, specify the disciplinary rules applicable to him, and the person to whom he may apply if he is dissatisfied with any disciplinary decision that refers to him, or if he has a grievance. It follows that employers need to have a code of disciplinary practice and procedure, and that supervisors should be aware of the procedure and follow it. Failure to do so may cause problems and embarrassment to both employer and employee. Disciplinary codes usually define the circumstances that warrant instant dismissal—this would apply to very serious offences only—the procedure for giving warnings about unsatisfactory conduct, and normally provide for at least one warning to be written. It is usual for the individual to be given an opportunity to state his case before action against him is taken, when he may be accompanied by a representative of his choice. Generally speaking, hasty and ill-considered actions about disciplinary procedures—and above all about dismissal—are to be avoided.

A code of practice on disciplinary rules and procedures is published by HMSO, *Code of Practice, 1: Disciplinary Practice and Procedures in Employment*. This code was prepared by the Advisory, Conciliation and Arbitration Service, a statutory body, and came into effect in June 1977. Employers are not bound to follow the guidance given in this code, but industrial tribunals may take into account whether it has been complied with.

Appointment of staff

Appointing kitchen staff, or recommending whom to appoint, is often one of the duties of the catering supervisor. In making appointments there are other factors to consider besides those of qualifications and experience. It is, of course, impossible to ensure that every appointment is in every way successful, but certain points help in reaching good decisions. Appearance is the easiest to assess.

High standards of personal hygiene and neatness in appearance and dress are very important, and so the candidate's appearance should be carefully observed. Hands, fingernails and hairstyle are key points. Work in a kitchen makes considerable physical demands and staff need to be strong, healthy, and, for the most part, quick and dextrous in movement; to a certain extent these qualities can be assessed during the course of an interview. The interviewer should aim to find out whether the applicant has any of the following qualities: a genuine interest in food and catering; concern for people and their welfare and comfort; a spirit of enquiry about new methods and equipment; a wish to gain promotion. Traits such as reliability, honesty, good humour, tolerance and the ability to mix with others cannot easily be assessed at an interview, though a skilled interviewer can often discern such traits as aggressiveness, shyness, over-confidence and touchiness. It is always advisable to take up references as to capability and experience from previous employers, or, where there has been no previous work experience, a character reference. A medical history and certificate, particularly as regards fitness to handle food, may also be required. The duties of the post and the conditions—especially hours of work and holiday allowances—should be clearly explained, and it should be checked that the applicant's personal and domestic circumstances are not likely to prevent him from fulfilling requirements. It should be constantly borne in mind that it is much easier to appoint staff than it is to terminate the employment of unsuitable staff. Procedures for disciplining and—in the extreme case—dismissing, are complicated, time-consuming and costly, and the outcome may well be uncertain.

Training and promotion

Some training is necessary for all types of catering work, but of course its extent varies according to the scope of the work and the degree of skill and knowledge required. Training provided by an employer (or other agency) for employees is known as in-service training. Employees may be trained on the job or away from the workplace. Off-the-job training may take place at the employer's staff training centre, at a college of further education or elsewhere. Training may be classified as follows:

Induction training. Given to an employee when he first takes up his job to familiarise him with the organisation's policies and practices. All staff need some induction, but those with management responsibilities need a considerable amount because they will be concerned with implementing the organisation's policies.

Training in manual and craft skills. This applies particularly to general assistants who need to acquire the necessary manual skills, and to those seeking to qualify as cooks or to be promoted to a higher grade of cook.

Management training. This applies chiefly to those seeking promotion to a supervisory or management level. There is often a good deal of training offered in management subjects to those already in management posts.

Training in theoretical subjects (for example, nutrition)

Briefing. Instruction of this kind is necessary in a number of circumstances—for example, when there is a change of company policy, when new legislation affects employees at various levels, or when new products or equipment are introduced.

We shall now look at the sort of in-service training provided for different groups of employees.

General assistants. Practical training is usually given on the job by a senior member of staff, who may himself have been given some training on the best way to do this. When a new kitchen is opened staff are often trained as a team; the training starts a few days before the date when clients' meals are first to be served. Off-the-job instruction is usually given to groups of staff on such subjects as food hygiene, safety, washing-up routines and the use of machinery. It is possible for courses on these subjects to be arranged at colleges of further education, but large organisations usually make their own arrangements, and gear training precisely to their own needs. Training is usually given at slack times and near to the employees' place of work, but this is not always possible when a college of further education is involved.

Chefs, cooks and assistant cooks. Both on-the-job and off-the-job training is usual, and the two methods are combined. Ideally, the on-the-job work experience during training should harmonise with the programme of formal instruction, so that the learner is able to practice what he has learned at training sessions. Employers with good training facilities often run their own courses covering cooking craft and associated subjects. Also, many employers release selected staff to attend classes at colleges of further education. Most of these courses lead to recognised qualifications such as the City and Guilds of London Institute's series of certificates, 706, Cookery for the Catering Industry: 706/1, Basic Cookery; 706/2, Cookery; 706/3, Advanced Cookery.

Craft trainees. Employees—usually young people—who are recruited as craft trainees follow a graded programme that combines on-the-job training with day release to attend courses leading to recognised qualifications.

Waiting staff and food service supervisors. May be released to study for the City and Guilds 707 series, Food Service Subjects: 707/1, Food Service and 707/2, Advanced Serving Techniques.

Supervisory and management grades of staff. Staff in these grades are often recruited from those already holding professional qualifications. Once they have received induction training their further needs relate chiefly to briefing and refresher courses, and courses designed to develop their potential. Good training opportunities at this level are vital if an organisation is to be progressive, and if it is to make the most of its senior staff. However, many of the less senior supervisory and management posts are held by people who have been promoted within the organisation—possibly from posts as cooks. In choosing staff for this kind of promotion, management potential and qualities of leadership are looked for: a good cook is not necessarily a good manager or supervisor. For staff in this category, training in management subjects is often given by means of graded experience under supervision, coaching sessions with senior members of staff, and, in large organisations, through attendance at formal courses arranged by the employer. Alternatively, staff may attend day-release courses at a college of further education—for example, a course leading to City and Guilds Certificate 771, Organisational Studies.

Management trainees. Some employers offer posts as management trainees to young professionally-qualified people. The training offered relates largely to graded experience and to coaching from senior members of staff.

Employers' training schemes and facilities

Large organisations often employ their own training officers, who are responsible for identifying training needs and planning training programmes; and instructors, who are responsible for off-the-job training. The instructor may operate from a centre with a training kitchen, a lecture room and other facilities.

The Hotel and Catering Industry Training Board

The HCITB was set up under the Industrial Training Act, 1974. Its purpose is to encourage and promote training. The Board makes a levy on employers (except those who are exempt), and pays grants to employers for training and associated activities, provided that they come within the Board's requirements. It follows that those who come within the scope of the Board should plan their training to take advantage of its various grants.

Those outside the scope of the Board include the school meals service and welfare catering undertaken by local authorities, and the hospital service.

The Local Government Training Board

Whereas the HCITB is a statutory body, the LGTB is not, but it has a similar purpose and function within the sphere of local government.

Staffing ratios and conditions affecting them

The number of staff employed in relation to the number of main meals produced is known as the staffing ratio. This is clearly important, not only as regards the efficiency of the kitchen, but also from the point of view of overhead costs. The number of staff is not the only factor to be considered; there is also the question of their grades. It is useful to have in mind a general figure as a guide when assessing numbers of staff before going on to a more detailed consideration of the subject. For a catering establishment using conventional methods and serving one main meal a day, the ratio may range from one member of staff per thirty meals to one per fifty or more meals. In the case of residential establishments more staff in total are employed, but their duties are staggered so that the number on duty at any one time is not likely to be greater than in a non-residential establishment. The range quoted is rather wide, giving a difference of four staff in the case of a kitchen producing 300 meals, but it is difficult to be more exact because of the number of variables. In the first place, the number of staff employed per meal decreases as the output of the kitchen increases because there are economies of scale. Secondly, the amount of labour-saving equipment installed varies. Thirdly, general conditions in the catering premises affect the amount of work to be done, and consequently the number of staff employed. In a well-planned kitchen the work can be done with less effort, and therefore usually in a shorter time, because work circuits are efficiently arranged and transport distances are reduced to a minimum. Fourth, the type of meal served will vary; a three-course meal will take slightly more labour to prepare than will a two-course meal, and it will involve considerably more labour for service and washing up.

The staffing ratio can be expressed also as the number of hours of work per number of meals served, and this gives a rather more precise estimate. Often the two ratios are worked in conjunction. The caterer has in mind how many members of staff will be needed in the kitchen during a working session, or any part of it, to complete the tasks in hand, and also the total number of hours to be worked. Whenever both full- and part-time staff are employed a ratio relating to numbers of hours worked rather than numbers of people must be used.

Most large catering organisations use staffing scales that have proved suitable over the years for their style of catering. The use of these scales enables them to achieve parity between establishments and to forecast and control labour costs. Some scales have an allowance for absenteeism through sickness and other causes built in; others are very tight, and overtime has to be worked or temporary help employed when the staff is below strength. Standard scales of this kind have to be modified to suit circumstances, and this may be done through an approved set of allowances or deductions from the basic scale, or the unit manager may be allowed to exercise a degree of discretion.

Two examples of circumstances where major modifications of standard staffing scales are necessary are the finishing kitchen and the cook-freeze unit. In the former case it is usual to reduce the basic staffing ratio in terms of hours of work by 40 to 50 per cent. In the latter case, it is reckoned that, because of greater rationalisation, staffing requirements in terms of hours of work by kitchen staff may be reduced by one-third.

A more fundamental approach to the calculation of staffing hours than using rules of thumb or prescribed scales is to analyse the tasks involved in the preparation and serving of meals and associated activities, and to note the time taken to carry them out by an average worker. The caterer makes this sort of analysis for various reasons, one of which is to help in calculating what hours of work to allow. But when an exercise of this sort is mounted on a large scale it is usually the province of the work-study expert, and we shall be studying this field in the following chapter. Here we shall look at the results of a work-study project in so far as they concern staffing levels. Figure 57 gives a staffing ratio graph published in *Study of Work in Hospital Kitchens to Determine Staffing Ratios*, Management Services (NHS), DHSS, HMSO, 1973. The report says that meals to be included when using the graph as a means of calculating staffing needs are: breakfasts, lunches, suppers and other meals that involve the kitchen staff in a significant amount of work. Light refreshments, such as coffee and biscuits, should not be included. The following instructions are given for its use:

> By reference to the vertical scale of the graph, the appropriate 'numbers of meals' point should be projected horizontally to the graph line, and at the point of intersection a vertical projection should be made down to the horizontal scale, which will indicate the 'hours per 100 meals' of staff time required to undertake the workload. The total hours can then be calculated by multiplying the ratio (*i.e.*, hours per 100 meals) by the appropriate 'number of meals', and dividing the product by 100.

The report suggests that, to equate the total hours of work with the

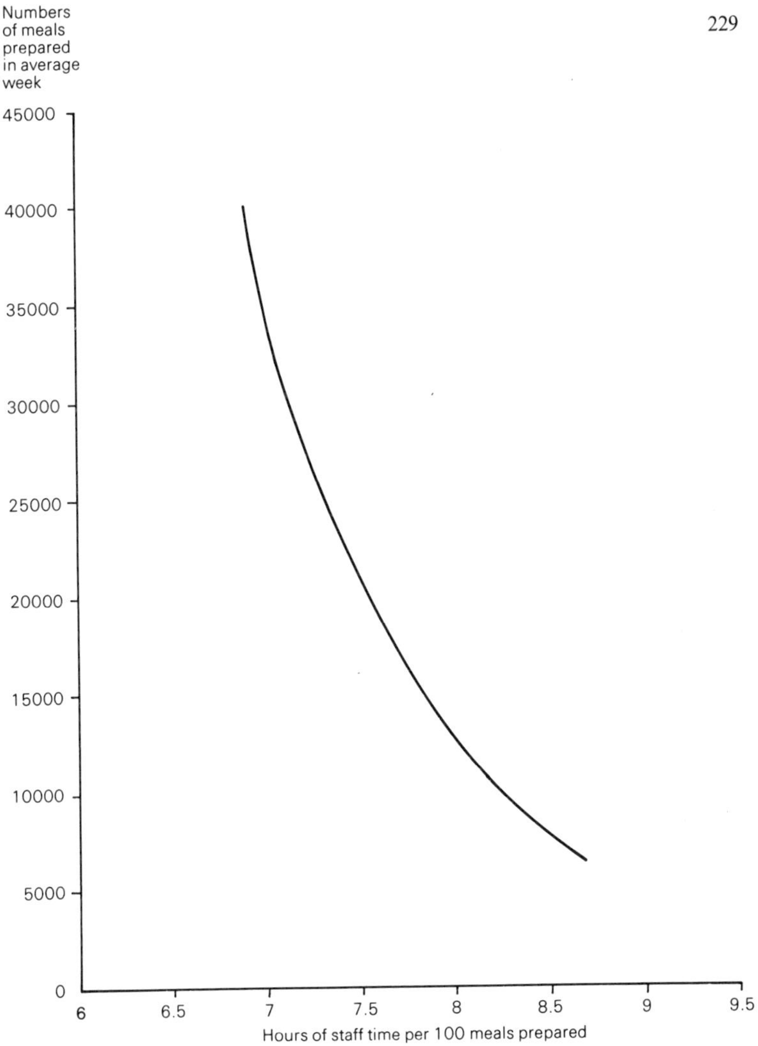

Fig. 57 Staffing ratio graph for hospitals

total hours of staff time needed to undertake this work, provision must be made for annual and sick leave, and to do this twelve-and-a-half per cent should be added. The following formula expresses this:

$$H=\frac{MR}{100}+12\tfrac{1}{2}\%\text{ of }\frac{MR}{100}\text{ or }\frac{9MR}{800},$$

where H = total hours of staff time required; M = the average number of meals produced each week (vertical scale of graph); and R = hours of staff time per 100 meals (horizontal scale).

The time spent by the kitchen staff on non-kitchen work (for example, service in the dining room) is not included in the total number of hours.

Figure 58 shows a typical scale of allowed hours used by local authorities in connection with school meals.

Table 8 gives minimum staffing standards prescribed by the Department of Health and Social Security for certain kinds of hospital.

The importance of good conditions

Amenities that should be available for all kitchen staff are:

Cloakrooms with individual lockers;

W.C. and washing facilities within easy reach of the kitchen and close to the staff entrance.

In some circumstances, especially where staff are engaged in frying chips, etc., since frying odours cling to the person, the provision of showers is an advantage.

The provision of a staffroom is usually desirable, but its importance depends upon the number of staff employed and the amount of off-duty time they will be able to spend there. Sometimes a staff alcove serves instead of a separate room. Facilities should be available for staff who feel unwell.

Another important amenity—which should present no problem—is the provision and service of well-cooked meals with good table appointments to kitchen staff. The appreciation of good food is one of the prime concerns of all those involved with catering, and meals for staff should be as good in quality and as well served as those in the dining room. At the same time, it should not be the practice to appropriate more than a fair allocation for staff meals.

The effects of physical conditions in the kitchen on the health and convenience of staff have already been mentioned, and they are dealt with at greater length in Chapter 16. There is another type of atmosphere, however, that is not physical, and this affects working conditions perhaps more than anything. The atmosphere created by a happy and contented staff is quickly felt by any reasonably sensitive visitor, and usually a happy kitchen is also efficient. A happy atmosphere depends upon many things, but what influences it more than anything else is the character, personality and attitude of the supervisor.

The supervisor as a leader

The supervisor is in a unique position to determine the success or otherwise of the establishment for which he is responsible. His technical expertise is, of course, extremely important, but it is very

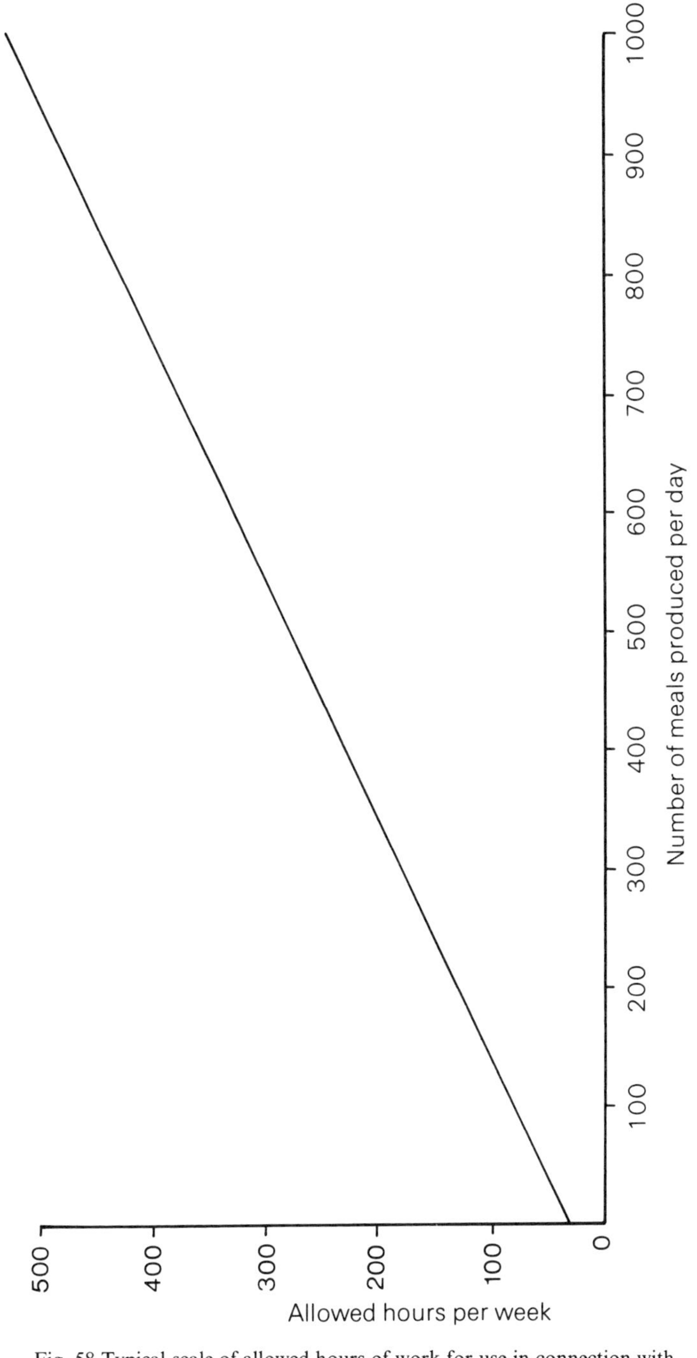

Fig. 58 Typical scale of allowed hours of work for use in connection with school meals. Graph shows scale used in local education authority for estimating allowed hours of work in kitchens producing conventional 2-course meals for schoolchildren. Extra allowances or deductions are made for conditions that vary from standard

much easier to acquire than is the less tangible knowledge of human behaviour. Yet this is of vital importance. The young person first shouldering the responsibilities of management usually finds staff management the most burdensome aspect—particularly when his staff are much older and more mature emotionally, and have a wider experience of life than he has. He may well have studied behavioural science and man management: now he is in a situation where he must show leadership qualities in order to get others to co-operate in the performance of a task.

There is no doubt that some people are better leaders than others, and this gives rise to the idea of the born leader, but in fact people can develop leadership qualities through formal study and by other means. Men and women who earn the title 'born leader' are those who study human nature and have a sensitive understanding of human relations. The supervisor should make an effort to enter into the interests of his staff, share information about everyday happenings and special events, and show concern and understanding about domestic and personal problems. The supervisor who is able to do this will find himself amply repaid.

Another essential quality in a leader is the maintenance of high personal standards. Any rules and regulations that are imposed upon the staff, either by him or by senior management, should be followed without fail by the supervisor. This applies, for example, to timekeeping, and to regulations about safety, personal appearance and hygiene. For example, kitchen staff are required to wear protective clothing, and whenever the supervisor is in the kitchen he also should always wear it. The supervisor leads by example, and in doing so he must accept a very severe self-discipline.

The staff's respect for and loyalty to the supervisor are indications of sound leadership, and they are essential to success. But, important though they are, they are by-products of right action rather than the result of a definite aim. Giving praise where it is due may earn respect (as well as being constructive), but not more so than criticism—provided that it is constructive and reasonable—and both should be offered in an unemotional way. Some find it easier to do the former, and some the latter, but each has its place. Consistency in requirements, standards and attitudes is, of course, essential, and any impression of favouritism must be avoided. Also, respect is earned by the supervisor who is active and competent about the kitchen, sharing in work problems and difficulties, and listening to the advice and opinions of those performing any particular task—and accepting good advice. In addition, it is well to offer staff opportunities to make suggestions and discuss problems and grievances informally.

Another quality of a successful supervisor is the ability to reach a decision without undue delay, and then to ensure that it is carried out. Dilatoriness and wavering are bad qualities in anyone who leads a team.

However well a kitchen may be organised, difficulties, problems and major or minor crises will arise from time to time—for example, defects and breakdowns in equipment, power cuts, unexpected changes in the demand for meals because of weather conditions, etc. These happenings are usually outside the supervisor's control, but he must deal with the situation and adapt his arrangements to keep production going if at all possible. The ability to remain calm and unruffled throughout, and to maintain a sense of humour, is essential to successful management. The supervisor who can remain detached will handle difficulties and problems when they arise with comparative ease, whereas one who allows his emotions to become involved will not.

Another important quality is the ability to delegate responsibility. Delegation is necessary wherever the amount of work for which the supervisor is responsible exceeds what is reasonable for him to perform entirely by himself—but there is another reason for delegation. Junior members of staff need to have adequate experience to develop their supervisory and management potential to fit them for more senior posts. In many small establishments the supervisor has very little opportunity or occasion to delegate. Hence, when he is promoted to a more senior post, he may find it difficult to do so. Apart from this, reasons for not delegating may be a fear of loss of control or prestige, or a feeling (quite wrong) that in doing so he is not properly shouldering his responsibilities. Sometimes he finds it easier to do a job himself than to instruct others how to do it. The ultimate responsibility for delegated work lies with the supervisor. It is not easy to delegate, and yet to maintain unobtrusive control.

TABLE 8: Minimum staffing standards for kitchen staff in long-stay hospitals

Minimum standard
Kitchen staff (excluding Catering Manager or other person in administrative control):

Hospitals under 100 beds	1 per 15 persons fed
Hospitals with 100–300 beds	1 per 25 persons fed
Hospitals with 300–700 beds	1 per 35 persons fed
Hospitals with 700–1000 beds	1 per 40 persons fed
Hospitals over 1000 beds	1 per 45 persons fed

Of these, approximately 40 % should be in the Cook and Assistant Cook grades, and 20 % in supervisory grades (Assistant Head Cook and above).

Provided that there are satisfactory kitchen facilities, this staffing standard should make it possible to provide cooked dishes for breakfast, dinner and supper.

This table is published in *Health Service Catering, Catering for Long Stay Hospitals*, DHSS, Catering and Dietetic Branch.

Chapter 16

Ergonomics and work study

Work study and ergonomics have been developed and formalised in industrial societies in a technological age, but neither is new in concept. Each is concerned with efficiency, but the approach is different.

Ergonomics

Ergonomics is the study of efficiency of persons in their working environment. The approach is always through the study of the human being, and seeks to establish his capabilities and his limitations. The aim of ergonomics is to ensure that tools, equipment and the working environment are suited to people and their physical needs. In the preceding chapter reference has often been made to the comfort and convenience of staff. Now we shall look at this subject in a slightly different way, and shall consider briefly some aspects of ergonomics that have a bearing on people who work in catering. We shall consider the working environment, posture at work, problems of lifting, and the design of tools and equipment controls.

Lighting

The question of lighting requirements is approached through a study of the eye, its structure and how it performs. The eye receives light over a wide angle, but the angle of sharp vision, when objects are seen in clear focus, is small. The eye moves continually and the area of retina outside the angle of sharp vision acts as a monitor, so that if something different happens the eye tends to move so that the object of attraction is in focus. One factor that determines how well we can see is the amount of light present. For most tasks, efficiency is increased if the worker can see well, and various tasks need different levels of illumination if they are to be accomplished at maximum efficiency. The lumen is the unit used to measure light energy, and the lux relates to the number of lumens to the square metre. The levels of light needed to perform various tasks at one hundred per cent efficiency have been studied, and the results tabled. In practice it is reckoned that the lighting level should be such as will allow ninety per cent efficiency, on the grounds that the extra cost of providing the much higher level of lighting needed to give complete efficiency is not justified.

The following recommendations apply to catering activities:

Food preparation areas:	150–200 lux
Dining tables:	100 lux
Office work and accounts:	300 lux

The recommendations refer to the illumination at approximately table-top level.

It is interesting to compare the figures given above with daylight values. On a cloudy day a typical value is 1000 lux, and on a clear day 10 000.

Although the eye can adapt to a certain extent to different levels of illumination, if the range is too great it cannot do so. Discomfort is then caused, and the ability to see may be decreased. In kitchens glare from large windows and reflected light from stainless steel working surfaces may cause discomfort. The kind of lighting is important also. Lighting in dining rooms, and especially in service areas, should be chosen to enhance the appearance of the food, and should not produce unappetising colours. For psychological reasons working areas should if possible have some windows—preferably with a view of the outside—so that staff may enjoy the variety provided by natural changes in daylight, and do not feel shut off from the world outside.

Heat

It is well known that the body needs to maintain a reasonably constant temperature, and that its mechanism is upset when the temperature varies significantly from normal. It is also well known that the basic metabolic processes produce heat, and that when work is being done there is more activity and in consequence more heat is generated. The heat output from the basic metabolic process is about 60 watts; during light work it increases to 200–300 watts; and for heavy work the figure is one kilowatt or more. This heat must be dissipated if body temperature is to be maintained at a normal level, and this may be accomplished by several means:

Convection, where heat is lost to surrounding air currents;
Evaporation through perspiration;
Conduction, for example through feet or hands on cold surfaces.

Most heat is lost by convection, but perspiration also is important, especially where temperatures are high. Several other factors affect the loss of body heat, such as the temperature of the air, its humidity and the speed at which it moves.

In a kitchen, attention must be given to the following:

1. Minimising the amount of water vapour released into the atmosphere by carefully controlling the processes of steaming and boiling;
2. The extraction of hot, humid air that would inhibit perspiration;
3. The maintenance of air currents through adequate ventilation;
4. Keeping down the amount of radiant heat by using well-insulated cooking equipment;
5. Siting work stations that are likely to be used for long periods away from cooking equipment with high heat outputs.

Staff should be advised to wear loose clothing to allow air to circulate and perspiration to evaporate. Cotton is preferable to man-made fibres because of its absorbent properties. Work involving bending and stooping, such as loading and unloading low-level shelves, is particularly stressful when there is excessive heat, and from this point of view there is a great deal to be said in favour of trolley-loaded ovens and eye-level ovens.

Excessive heat results in a greater load being placed upon the heart, and involves a significant drop in efficiency; the capacity to work is reduced, and longer-than-normal rest periods are needed for recovery from working in such conditions. People begin to suffer from stress caused by too much heat when the temperature rises to about 30° Celsius, but the onset will be earlier where humidity is high.

Little has been said of the effect of low temperatures, because excessive heat and steam at peak periods are the major environmental problems in kitchens, but efficiency is impaired at low temperatures also; hands and feet are particularly affected.

Noise

Sound is the sensation caused in the ear by vibrations of surrounding air. Fluctuations in air pressure are originated by a vibrating body, and they are transmitted as pressure waves. The frequencies of sound waves are measured in Hertz, one Hz being equal to one cycle of sound per second. The intensity of sound depends upon the magnitude of the pressure variation within the sound wave. The decibel (dB) is the unit used in comparing intensities of sound; the decibel scale is complex, and involves the logarithm of the ratio of two pressure variations. One decibel is about the smallest change in intensity that the ear can detect.

Several questions arise about noise, the most important of which is the level at which hearing is likely to be permanently damaged. This varies with the frequency of the sound waves. It appears that at high frequencies—1200 Hz or more—continuous exposure to intensities of 80 dB or more can produce deafness, whereas at lower frequencies intensities can be higher without causing damage. For example, 90 dB is the critical figure at 300 Hz. A rule of thumb is that noise is likely to be at a dangerous level if it is necessary to shout in order to be understood by someone standing about a metre away. Noise at this level is not likely to occur continuously in a catering establishment.

Another question that needs to be answered is whether high noise levels detract from efficient performance. The indications are that noise is not likely to slow down the rate of work, but it is possible that more mistakes may be made when surroundings are very noisy. On the other hand, staff engaged in monotonous work may perform better when there is background noise. However, those who are engaged upon work that requires great concentration may find it very difficult to concentrate in noisy surroundings. This often presents problems for the supervisor, who needs to have his office near the kitchen so that he may readily supervise operations, but finds it difficult to do clerical and administrative work at certain noisy times of the day. And, of course, there are many tasks in the kitchen that demand great concentration.

Another point is the question of communication by speech against a background of noise. People can communicate reasonably effectively even if their every word is not heard, for if the listener hears most words correctly he can usually fill in the rest, and it is reckoned that communication is satisfactory if three-quarters of the words spoken are heard accurately. For this to happen, the sound of the speaker's voice must be at a level of at least 6 dB above the background noise. As people's intensity of speech varies—ranging from 55 dB to 75 dB at a listening distance of about a metre—some find it much more difficult to make themselves understood against background noise than others. An average intensity of speech at a listening distance of one metre is about 65 dB.

Difficulties in communicating by speech arise occasionally in kitchens, but they are more generally associated with people in dining rooms. Some practical measures for alleviating noise problems were discussed in Chapter 3.

Posture in kitchen and dining room

Work benches, desks, tables and chairs should be designed to enable people to maintain natural postures without strain or unnecessary fatigue. In the kitchen most work involves standing, though it is good practice to sit down for suitable tasks, such as polishing cutlery. When work is carried out on a bench or table top, the posture causing least strain is one where the trunk is balanced over the legs, the arms above the elbows hang freely, and the forearms are at right angles to the body, which should not be in a stooping position. This posture is suitable for many kitchen tasks—for example, preparing salads and serving food—but it is not suitable for jobs where pressure has to be exerted, or where the food to be dealt with is in fairly deep vessels. Where pressure has to be exerted, as in rolling pastry, the working surface should be about 80 mm to 100 mm below the elbows. Very precise processes, such as putting finishing touches to small cocktail savouries, require the work to be much nearer eye level than this, even though the posture that has to be adopted creates more strain.

Although people need to work at different heights according to their own height, individual variations cannot usually be allowed for because fixed standardised equipment cannot readily be adapted, and it is preferable to cater for shorter-than-average people so that all may work with their upper arms relaxed, even though this means that taller people may have to stoop. A suitable working height for activities such as serving food and light preparation work is 900 mm, but where all the staff are male a height of one metre is better. For pastry benches and heavy preparation work a suitable height is 800 mm (900 mm in the case of all-male staff). Kitchen stools (kept for the purpose) or other low stands may be used for very deep mixing vessels.

The height of a chair for sitting should be such that the weight of the legs may be supported on the feet and not by the seat of the chair; otherwise blood circulation in the legs will be restricted and there may be painful pressure on the nerves in the thighs. Ideally, the sitter should be able to place his feet squarely on the floor; at worst he should be able to touch the floor (or foot-rest) with his toes. There should be a gap of 200–230 mm between underside of table and top of chair seat to allow the thighs to be clear of the table. Horizontal dimensions also must be considered, for the sitter needs to have his chair close to the table and his knees well under it. He also needs space for his feet, although it is possible for him to sit with them tucked back. Horizontal clearances of 300 mm from the edge of the table and 450 mm at floor level for the feet are necessary.

The height of dining tables should allow the diner to have his elbows slightly below table level, as most people prefer this position. Obviously everyone will not be suited by standard chairs and tables, but experiment has shown that a table height of 700 mm and a chair height of 430 mm will suit the optimum number of people. Lower heights should be chosen where furniture is to be used exclusively by children.

Design of tools

In almost all craftwork the tool best suited to job and worker has gradually evolved through trial and error over the years, but this does not always apply to kitchen tools, and sometimes, because of mass-production methods, slight alterations are made that do not improve the design from the functional point of view. When tools are to be bought in large quantities, it is wise to arrange for samples to be tried by experienced craftsmen, who should observe and report on such points as whether a tool is easy to grip and hold, comfortable to use and of the right weight.

Controls

Some items of kitchen equipment are fitted with a number of controls. Cooking ranges and dishwashing machines are among these, and it is obvious that they should be designed so that it is as easy as possible for the operator to locate the controls, recognise their function, and use them. It follows that in assessing equipment one looks for:

(a) Completely clear and obvious on and off controls, and open or closed controls for valves;
(b) Easy access to controls;
(c) Clear labelling of controls wherever necessary;
(d) A logical arrangement of controls and switches to avoid confusion;
(e) Gauges at or near eye level.

Lifting

Studies that have been made on people's lifting capacity indicate that women should not be asked to carry more than 5–7 kg in the case of continuous working, or more than about 15 kg for loads that are carried infrequently. Men have greater lifting strength, and therefore they, rather than women, should be employed for heavy lifting. However, where weights exceed 30 kg male staff should be especially chosen for their strength and fitness for such work, and they should be given special training. Many kitchens are staffed almost entirely by women, and this should be remembered when premises are being equipped.

Heavy kitchen tables, dining tables and chairs, all of which have to be moved frequently for cleaning purposes, should be avoided. Lifting from high or low levels is particularly difficult and awkward, and this should be borne in mind when shelves and racks are designed, fitted and loaded. It is usual to instruct staff that heavy or awkward items should be lifted by two people sharing the load.

Work study

Work study is concerned with increasing productivity, and it seeks to achieve this through improving planning and methods of operation and control, and increasing the operating effectiveness of all employees. It will be seen that the study of ergonomics has an application to the improvement of methods and the operating effectiveness of workers. Work study is defined as: 'A term used to embrace the techniques of method study and work measurement, which are employed to ensure that the best possible use of human and material resources is made in carrying out a specified task.'

It is interesting to consider that formal work study has not been developed until quite recent times. Frank and Lilian Gilbreth were pioneers in the field in the United States of America at the end of the nineteenth century and the beginning of the twentieth century. They carried out scientific investigations into the individual motions and movements of a man performing a particular task, and studied ways of adjusting movements in order to reduce fatigue. They developed a technique that they called motion study. They looked at all matters relating to the physical performance of a job, and also at psychological factors. They studied the tools used and layouts. In the early twentieth century Charles Bedaux studied the time taken to perform tasks, and assessed the speed and effectiveness of operators. He used his system of rating assessment in a premium bonus scheme known as the Bedaux Point Premium System. In recent years there has been a wide development of the use of work study, which incorporates method study, motion study (which is now seen as a part of method study) and work measurement. Its application has spread from the factory where it originated to other spheres. It is common practice for large industrial firms to employ work-study officers, also known as work-study practitioners.

There seem to be three main reasons for the comparatively recent development of work study, and they are interrelated. The first is the wish to save time in almost all activities—a wish that has been accentuated by the possibility of doing so. This is evident in many fields, but in none is it more striking than in travel and communications, where the last half-century has produced phenomenal changes—air travel, radio and television have become commonplace. The second is the change in conditions of employment and social conditions. Demands for shorter working hours and higher rates of pay exert great pressure, and involve a continuous search for greater efficiency in production. The third reason is connected with the rising standard of living, which creates a demand for complex products at low prices in large quantities. The manufacturer must focus attention on efficiency and productivity, and the introduction of work study is an effective means of achieving improvements.

So far as the catering industry is concerned, work-study techniques are less easily applied than they are in the factory, but modern food technology has made it easier to introduce standard methods, and rising staff costs in a labour-intensive industry have focused attention on the possibility of increasing productivity through the application of work-study techniques. Work study has been used as a means of developing staffing ratios and introducing incentive schemes.

Since work study is intended to be a means of increasing productivity it is essentially a tool of management, and it follows that managers should appreciate work study and what it has to offer. The supervisor of an establishment also needs basic information, because he may be required to co-operate with work-study practitioners in their studies, to apply the methods they introduce, and to supervise bonus schemes they instigate. But there is rather more to it than this. Although the catering manager and supervisor do not employ the specialised techniques of the work-study expert, many of their aims are much the same and they may be defined as follows:

(a) the most effective use of plant;
(b) the most effective use of human effort;
(c) the proper performance of those employed.

Moreover, the analytical approach adopted by the work-study practitioner is equally well suited to many aspects of kitchen organisation and management. Hence an appreciation of work study methods may help the caterer in his approach to his own work, and influence his mode of thought.

Work study may be thought of as a short-term way of improving productivity, because it is concerned not with research and development (which fall within the field of process study) but with existing practice. There are eight basic steps, as follows:

1. Select. This refers to the field of study, and involves decisions on priority and judgments on the areas in which the most significant improvements in productivity are likely to be made.

2. Record. The recorder observes directly exactly what is being done.

3. Examine. What has been recorded is critically examined with the object of eliminating any unnecessary elements in processes and procedures such as manual movements, transport and delays.

4. Develop. The best possible methods in the existing situation are developed.

5. Measure. The amount of work involved in using the new method is measured, and a standard time for its performance is calculated.

6. Maintain. Suitable methods of control are introduced to ensure that the new standard is maintained.

Two techniques are involved in carrying out work-study procedures—method study and work measurement. Method study is concerned with the development and application of an easier and more effective way of doing a job, and so reducing cost. The term work measurement is self-explanatory: several different methods are used.

The work study practitioner uses performance rating as a means of establishing correct time standards for a task. Performance rating is defined as: 'The observer's assessment of the speed and effectiveness at which the element or elements of work were performed by the operator under observation, relative to the observer's concept of standard rating.' The British Standard Rating scale of 0 to 100 is normally used, and the rating of 100 is defined as: 'The average rate at which a qualified worker will naturally work at a job, provided he knows and adheres to the specified method, and provided he is motivated and applies himself to his work.'

When a time study is carried out basic times are compiled for each activity, and the following formula is used:

$$\frac{\text{observed time} \times \text{observed rating}}{\text{standard rating}} = \text{basic time}$$

Basic time is used to calculate standard times, but, since it relates only to work performed and not to time spent in other ways, additional allowances are made. About ten per cent is usually added for rest and personal allowances, and allowances may be made also for various contingencies that might interrupt work. Some examples of basic times for various catering tasks, expressed in minute values, are given in Table 9. These times relate to a study of the school meals service undertaken by the Local Authorities Management Services and Computer Committee in connection with a work-study-based incentive scheme.

Catering staff perform many different tasks during the day. In the LAMSAC study weekly standard hours tables for preparing a given number of meals were built up from basic times for various food-preparation operations related to a specimen menu cycle, and of course other activities, such as cleaning, were included.

Activity-sampling techniques were used by Management Services (National Health Service) in their project described in *Study of Work in Hospital Kitchens to Determine Staffing Ratios*. Rated activity sampling was supported by method study. The data collected during the study, which was conducted at several hospitals, were analysed, and performance tables were produced for each hospital. After a critical examination of activities to decide to what extent they had been influenced by inefficient methods of work and other non-standard factors, the data were adjusted to provide an analysis of kitchen work as it would have been had it been carried out efficiently and under good conditions. Provisional staffing ratios were then developed and tested for validity, at other hospitals. A great deal of information of interest to caterers in general is contained in the report of this piece of work study. A clear and concise account of work study, designed to be of use to supervisors and managers, is given in *ABC of Work Study* by Stan Oakley (Pitman Publishing, 1973).

TABLE 9: Time allowances for various food-preparation tasks (expressed in basic minute values per 100 meals)

Food	*B.M.V.*
Batter (other than frying)	14·70
Fried fish	31·50
Grated cheese	5·84
Salad	37·40
Potatoes:	
Peel by machine and eye by hand	22·00
Chip by machine	10·40
Wash and slice cabbage or other greens	10·40
Wash and peel sprouts	56·90

Chapter 17

Safety

It is axiomatic that a good employer and a good supervisor have the safety and welfare of staff in mind, but, since the Health and Safety at Work Act, 1974, came into effect, much more attention has been focused on safety. The Act places considerable responsibilities upon employers, who are also required to have a written statement of safety policy. The employee is, of course, as much involved as the employer with safety at work, and a considerable part of management's responsibility lies in establishing good working procedures, seeking the co-operation of staff, and providing any necessary training. Under the Act the employer's responsibilities are not confined to workpeople; he has duties to others also whose health or safety may be affected by his activities. Where catering is concerned one thinks particularly about the duty to provide clients with safe food, and this aspect of safety will be dealt with in Chapter 23. References to safety appear throughout the book, since it is not a matter that can be considered in isolation. Here we are concerned with general considerations, and some miscellaneous items that have not been touched upon previously.

Safety and the individual

Safety, so far as the individual engaged in catering work is concerned, starts with the person and his clothing, and it is important that good standards are established and maintained, and the reasons for them explained. Wearing jewellery at work is inappropriate, because rings and bangles may catch in equipment and earrings, stones in jewellery and suchlike may drop into food and escape notice. Hair should not be so long that it could become entangled with equipment or brush against food or working surfaces. These points are usually readily appreciated by staff.

So far as clothing is concerned, footwear is probably the most significant item, since most kitchen accidents are caused by falls. The faller may well be carrying hot food or crockery or glass, and hence, in addition to any injury caused by the fall itself, he may suffer burns, scalds or cuts. Even in the best-regulated kitchens floors are sometimes wet or greasy, and pieces of dropped food may be slippery.

There are also risks to the feet from falling objects and spilt hot food and liquids. Footwear should have non-slip soles, should not have high heels and should not expose the toes, and should in general be designed to protect the feet from injury.

Protective clothing should fasten neatly, and should not have tie strings that are long enough to become entangled with equipment or machinery. Those engaged on work at the sink should wear waterproof aprons.

The working environment

Since falls figure so prominently in kitchen accidents, it follows that floors need special consideration. Kitchen floors are by their nature inclined to be slippery, especially when they are wet or greasy, so there should be a drill for mopping up spills as soon as they have occurred, and the floor should be kept free from residual grease by regular and thorough washing and rinsing. Non-slip surfaces may be provided in particularly hazardous areas, but their all-over use is not always recommended because they are more difficult to keep clean. Mats and floor racking, such as duckboards, in front of the sink are undesirable because people may trip over them. If mats are used at the kitchen entrance they should be set in matwells, but mats that do not fit properly into the well are a particular hazard.

Obstruction such as pipes and taps near floor level and projecting corners of equipment may also be causes of falls and injuries, as may unexpected obstructions in the shape of tools or equipment left in the wrong place on the floor.

Accidents are always more likely to happen where there is insufficient space for staff to move around. Often premises are designed with adequate circulation space, but later on extra equipment is brought in either because it is necessary to increase output or because new items come on to the market. Then insufficient thought may be given to safety implications when it is installed; awkward corners or bottlenecks may be created, or the operator of a new machine may not be allowed enough working space.

The importance of good lighting has already been discussed. When staff are working with potentially dangerous machines and tools this factor becomes particularly significant. Environmental conditions such as temperature and humidity are also important, because if they are such as to cause stress staff are likely to be more accident-prone, especially when they are particularly busy.

Equipment and tools

In Chapter 12 reference was made to the need to consider safety when buying catering machinery, and this applies equally to all equipment and tools. When machinery and other heavy items are installed they should be fixed securely so that there is no danger of their toppling off a stand or bench. The isolating switch of power-operated machinery should be within easy reach of the operator. It is often the practice to display notices concerning the safe use, or the authorised use, of machines. For example: 'This machine should be used only by trained and authorised operators.' Such a notice should be permanently fixed on or near the machine. The maintenance of equipment, especially machinery, is important from the point of view of safety, and a maintenance record should be kept so that the employer may readily establish that he has taken reasonable care over maintenance.

Training in safety

The safe use of tools, equipment and machinery is part of the basic training for all cooks, but the fact that general assistants also need this sort of training is sometimes overlooked. Responsibility for the training of general assistants usually rests with the kitchen supervisor. It is sometimes taken for granted that staff will understand the basic points about using gas and electric equipment, but this is not always so, and many people understand the use of either gas or electric cooking equipment, but not both. When untrained staff are appointed, the supervisor should check that they understand basic safety points and the use of controls.

Kitchen organisation and routine

The appreciation of safety hazards, careful training in safety and the posting of safety notices are not in themselves sufficient to secure safe methods of working. Good routines and working methods should be established in consultation with staff so that there is general agreement that certain procedures are correct and sensible, and that the staff as a group will follow them. Order, tidiness and method are essential to safety, and it is the supervisor's responsibility to plan and establish good work routines.

Procedures in case of emergency or accident

General instructions to and discussions with staff should include such matters as what to do in the event of fire, how to use fire-fighting appliances, and knowing who is responsible for first aid. It is helpful to have a list of telephone numbers for use in case of emergency, accident or illness prominently displayed, and there should be ready access to the first-aid box. The positions of stop-taps and main switches should be generally known.

Good housekeeping

It is a good plan to make regular checks on the condition of the building, fitments and equipment, and then any repairs necessary for safety can be organised. Staff should understand that it is their duty to report to their supervisor any defects they may notice.

Accident records

It is necessary to keep a record of all accidents, and it is often convenient to keep an accident book for this purpose, or there may be a prescribed form. An analysis of accident records may be useful in establishing what the main hazards are, and accident statistics are useful in assessing the success or otherwise of a particular safety policy.

Legislation

The supervisor should be aware of the provisions of the Health and Safety at Work, etc., Act, any regulations made under the Act, and any other legislation that may be relevant. For example, under the Offices, Shops and Railway Premises Act, 1963, and the Prescribed Dangerous Machines Order, S.I. 1964, No. 971, certain machines are prescribed as 'dangerous'. Young people under the age of eighteen may not be set to clean any specified dangerous machine (the Factories Act, 1961, and the Dangerous Machines (Training of Young Persons) Order, S.I. 1954, No. 921, refer to this), and only fully-trained staff or those under adequate supervision may use them. 'Dangerous machines' include the following: circular-knife food-slicing machines, potato chipping machines, and the following when they are power-operated: worm-type mincers, rotary-knife bowl choppers, vegetable preparation machines, and food mixers when attachments involving cutting operations are used.

Chapter 18

Stores accommodation and control

The amount of storage accommodation needed for various types and sizes of catering establishment has already been discussed in Chapter 4. It is now proposed to look in detail at storage arrangements and the control of stocks.

Categories of goods stored

Storage accommodation is required for the following groups of foods: perishables, semi-perishables, dry goods and vegetables; and for the following categories of non-food goods: tableware, kitchen utensils, and cleaning equipment and materials. Stocks of wines, spirits, soft drinks and confectionery may also be held. The storage of perishable foods in refrigerators has, for the most part, been dealt with in Chapter 11.

Temperature as it affects food storage

Vegetables and salad plants. Extremes of either heat or cold cause deterioration in vegetables and salad plants; suitable temperatures in a vegetable store are between 5° Celsius and 10° Celsius. At freezing point or below, considerable damage is caused. Potatoes affected by frost have a characteristic sweet taste and their texture softens, while the delicate textures of green vegetables and salad plants are also damaged by freezing. If the temperature rises to 20° Celsius or more all vegetables start to dry out, and green vegetables quickly wilt and become yellow. (Storage of green vegetables and salad plants should in any circumstances be minimal.)

Dry goods. These are less affected by variations in temperature, but nevertheless they are better stored in a cool place.

Dried fruit and preserves. These may tend to ferment in warm rooms, and a temperature of not more than 15° Celsius is to be preferred.

Dairy produce (other than milk) and non-dairy fats. It is not necessary to store these foods in a refrigerator, but they must be kept cool. Hence, in periods of hot weather, if the stores cannot be kept cool it is necessary to transfer such foods to the refrigerator.

Canned goods. All canned goods are best kept in a cool stores, but pasteurised canned meats need special treatment and should be kept in the refrigerator. These products have not been subjected to the usual sterilising processes associated with canning, and should be labelled: 'Perishable: keep in a cool place', or 'Perishable: keep under refrigeration'.

Wines. Temperatures around 9° Celsius to 14° Celsius (*i.e.*, those found in an unheated cellar) are suitable for storing wines, but temperature, provided that it is even, is not the most critical of the required conditions.

Humidity and ventilation as factors affecting storage

Vegetables and salad plants. A humid atmosphere is suitable for vegetables, especially green vegetables and salad plants. In the United Kingdom atmospheric humidity is such that there is usually no difficulty in providing suitable conditions in the vegetable store. If vegetables are stored for any reason in the refrigerator or cold room, they should be placed in containers or wrapped in plastic film or other suitable material to prevent drying. Vegetables, especially green vegetables, need air circulation to keep them cool. This applies particularly to those that generate heat (known as respiration) during storage. It follows that attention must be paid to the ventilation of the stores, and that green vegetables and salad plants should not be allowed to remain tightly packed together for long periods.

Dry goods and canned foods. These are best kept in a dry atmosphere but it is not always easy to achieve this, especially in premises where steam generated during cooking may readily enter the storerooms. In damp conditions the growth of mould is encouraged, tins go rusty, and deliquescent goods such as salt deteriorate rapidly. Account should be taken at design stage of the need for a dry atmosphere in the dry goods store, but the way in which the storeroom is managed is important also. Doors should be kept shut and the room well ventilated by means of opening roof lights, windows and ventilators. Where it is difficult to keep a dry atmosphere in a storeroom next to the kitchen, reserve stores and canned goods are sometimes kept in a more remote storeroom.

Stores other than foods. In general these are best kept in dry, well-ventilated cupboards or stores. Otherwise, packing materials such as cardboard become damp, mould growths are encouraged and some items rust.

Light as it affects storage

Potatoes should be kept away from sunlight, and strong light which will cause them to turn green. On the other hand, during the spring darkness encourages them, and other root vegetables, to sprout, especially in a warm atmosphere. When green vegetables are exposed to light, the loss of vitamin C that always occurs during storage is accelerated. Wine is best stored away from the light.

Protecting food from contamination
With the exception of canned goods, it is possible for almost all foods to be contaminated by rodents if they are stored incorrectly, but dry goods need particular care; they may be contaminated also by insect pests such as grain moths, flour mites and weevils.

Rodents and flies. The windows and any ventilators of all food stores should be screened, when open, to prevent the entrance of rats, mice, insects or birds. There should be no holes in walls or ceilings, or gaps under doors, that could allow rats or mice to enter. Dry goods should be kept in rodent-proof containers. Any 'open food' should be kept covered with muslin during the day to protect it from flies, and also from dust. No 'open food' should be left out overnight.

Insect pests associated with cereals and cereal products. Walls, shelves, floors and storage bins should be cleaned regularly, both to discourage insect development and in the interests of general hygiene. The most opportune time to clean out a bin is before new stocks are added; areas needing special attention are corners and rims. It is bad practice to keep on adding new supplies to old, because this allows time for pests to develop in the old stock at the bottom of the bin, and also spreads any contamination. If there is serious infestation the local authority's Environmental Health Inspector should be consulted; it may be necessary to fumigate the stores.

Contamination by dust and dirt. Dry goods should always be kept covered. It is good practice to keep food stores exclusively for food and ancillary items connected with their storage, receipt and issue. In particular, items such as brooms and brushes, which are associated with dirt and dust, should not be kept in food stores. Fresh vegetables, with their associated dust, should not be kept in stores used for other foods. But this does not apply to canned or dehydrated vegetables; these clean goods are best housed with other like foods.

Accidental contamination with noxious (inorganic) substances. If cleaning materials or any other chemicals are kept in food stores, there is always the possibility that harmful substances may be mistaken for foods, or that food may be contaminated through carelessness. This is another reason why food stores should be used only for food. Another important point is the correct use of containers and labels. Where cleaning materials are bought in bulk and issued in smaller quantities, it is sometimes a temptation to use empty food containers for the purpose. This should never be done, because of the danger of making a mistake. Also, when bulk is broken the containers or packages into which the commodity is dispensed should be clearly labelled.

Using stocks in rotation

Goods that have been longest in stock should be used first. Date-stamping (or coding by date) of goods entering the store is sometimes practised, and in cook-freeze systems, where the rotation of stocks is particularly important, it is usually done. (Where cook-freeze is concerned there is a second reason for this—namely the need to identify the batch in case any queries about quality should arise.) Some goods arrive in the kitchen either date-stamped or carrying a code number that indicates the date. But date-stamping is time-consuming, and most caterers prefer to rely upon a regular system of arranging goods on the shelves so that they are automatically brought forward in the order in which they came in. As we have seen, where goods are stored in bulk stocks will not be rotated properly if new stocks are added to old. To guard against this, it is often convenient, where the size of pack is suitable, to keep goods in their original wrappings inside the storage bin.

Storeroom fittings

Dry goods, catering equipment and tableware

Although food and equipment are stored separately, fittings needed for their storage may be considered together, for there are several common requirements.

Ready access to goods in constant demand. Most goods with a high turnover that are kept on shelves should be on shelves that are not higher than 1·9 m nor lower than 0·77 m. But very heavy or bulky goods are more conveniently stored just a little above ground level. High shelves are best occupied by goods that are used less often, and especially lightweight items. Steps should be provided as necessary to give access to high-level shelves. In the dry goods store it is often convenient to use the space below the lowest shelf for storage bins fitted with castors, so that they may be drawn out easily for use and for cleaning purposes. Where this is so, a suitable height for the first shelf is 900 mm.

Fitments should be designed to make the best use of the space available. In many storerooms it is obvious at a glance that space is being wasted in two ways. First, there is more than necessary between shelves, and second, the shelves themselves are deeper than the containers or goods being stored. Of course, there is a great deal to be said for erring on the safe side, for if shelves are too close together and not deep enough to fit containers they are useless. What is wanted is harmony between shelving and containers, and, because many containers and packs have standard dimensions, the task of harmonising is not so difficult as might at first appear. If the first shelf is 900 mm high, in many cases the following heights will be suitable for further shelving: second shelf, 1·375 m; third shelf, 1·8 m; fourth shelf, 2·175 m. Ready-made shelving systems are often used, and these have the advantage of flexibility in that shelf heights are adjustable. Various depths of shelves are available, and it is also possible to have adjustable custom-made shelving.

Where there are long spans of shelves, they may be supported by vertical props at intervals. If these supports are too close together, or if the intervals do not harmonise with the dimensions of the containers, a great deal of space is wasted. It can happen that the legs supporting the bottom shelf are so placed that it is impossible to use the space below for bins.

Shelves can be designed and used to take either single rows of goods or more than one row. In the latter case it saves time, and stock control is easier, if like goods are kept behind like. It is convenient to keep items such as flavourings, herbs and spices on narrow shelves, and it is often possible to use wall areas unsuitable for deeper shelves for them. Shelves may be needed with depths up to 600 mm, most of them probably being between 230 mm and 305 mm deep. The total length of each type of shelving is calculated according to the number and type of items to be stored.

Where containers are concerned, the best use of space is made if they are square or rectangular rather than circular; this point was made in Chapter 14 in relation to ovens. Hence it is usual to use square or rectangular bins. But, when it comes to removing containers from shelves, circular shapes are more easily handled, and these are commonly used. There is also the point that they have no awkward corners to be cleaned.

Load-bearing capacity. Storeroom shelves often bear very heavy loads, and this is particularly so where canned foods, liquids and stacks of plates are concerned. An estimate of the weight that a fully-loaded shelf will have to bear is needed by the designer of the shelves, so that he may choose suitable materials and provide any necessary supports. When ready-made shelving is bought, the buyer should check that the load-bearing capacity is suited to his purpose.

Considerations of hygiene. The shelves themselves and any of their fittings should be easy to keep clean, and they should not be fitted in a way that prevents or impedes the cleaning of surrounding areas. In food stores it is considered essential that shelves should be made of impervious material. Laminated plastic, when it is in good condition, meets hygiene requirements, but it can easily be damaged. Rustless metal is more suitable. Often this is meshed, which has the additional advantage of allowing better air circulation. There should be no cracks or crevices that could harbour dirt or insect pests. Where shelves are not free-standing, it is an advantage if they are designed to be easily removable when necessary for the washing or redecoration of walls.

It is not necessary to use impervious materials for shelves in stores not used for food, and such shelves are usually made from wood, which is cheaper.

Mobility. Reasons for having mobile shelves in freezer stores were given in Chapter 11, and these reasons apply also to the storage of dry goods and equipment. In a reserve equipment store stacks of like items, for example plates, may be kept on mobile storage units banked close together with no circulation space in between.

The arrangement of shelves in relation to the storeroom's dimensions. A storeroom's dimensions should be such that a minimum amount of space is necessary for circulation. A long, narrow room offers the maximum amount of wall space for shelving. In larger stores the best arrangement may be to have islands or peninsulas of shelves as well as wall shelving. Rooflights or high-level windows are preferable, since they do not occupy valuable wall space. In the dry goods store provision should be made for a weighing-up bench and trolley parking space.

Vegetable stores

The type of fitting needed in vegetable stores is different in several ways from those in other stores because of the nature of the goods, the type of packaging and the way in which vegetables have to be stored.

Potatoes and other root vegetables are delivered in paper sacks, and if they are to be kept for any length of time they need to be turned out of their sacks so that any bad ones may be seen and removed, and also to allow better air circulation. In practice the turnover of these vegetables is usually fast enough to make turning out unnecessary. Sacks of potatoes and other root vegetables are kept on slatted racks raised sufficiently above floor level (50 to 80 mm) to allow free air circulation, to protect them from any dampness on the floor, and to keep them away from the floor's cold surface. The racks should be made of impervious material, such as plastic or rustless metal, so that they may be kept clean easily, and since they are not fixtures they can be moved when the floor needs cleaning.

In the few cases where potatoes are removed from their sacks before storing a galvanised bin, similar to a coal bin, may be used. The bin is loaded from the top, and has an outlet at the bottom.

Most green vegetables are supplied in units of about 14 kg. Other salad items and fruits are often in trays, and many items will remain in them for the short time that they are in store. Nets of greens and trays of fruit, etc., are bulky, and fairly low shelving is convenient. No shelves at a high level should be provided because they would be unsuitable for fruit and vegetables, but they might be used—incorrectly—for other goods. Shelves should allow free air circulation, and should be of impervious material. Sometimes a raised edge to shelves is provided to prevent round articles from rolling off. Suitable shelf heights are as follows: first shelf, 700 mm; second shelf, 1·175 m; third shelf, 1·6 m. A depth of 600 mm is often appropriate.

Mobile racks may be used in vegetable stores, especially for bulky salad items and greeens. The racks are trundled to the goods entrance for incoming supplies and into the vegetable preparation area as required.

Rough preparation of vegetables sometimes takes place in the vegetable store, and if so benching should be provided for the purpose.

Storage of wines and spirits

The wine store should be free from vibration, and, as we have seen, wine should be kept away from light and at an even temperature around 9° Celsius to 14° Celsius, an unheated cellar being the ideal place. The bottles should be laid on their sides in racks, so that the corks are kept damp. (If the corks dry out they lose their elasticity and cease to keep the bottles sealed.) The label on the bottle should be uppermost so that it can be read without undue disturbance of the wine. Also, if this practice is followed consistently, it will be known that any deposit that there may be in older red wines is lying on the opposite side of the bottle to the label. This is important because the deposit tastes bitter, and care is necessary in pouring to ensure that none gets into the glass. (Before service the wine should be decanted carefully from the bottle into a flask or other container so that the deposit is left in the bottle.) Bottles containing spirits should be stored upright.

Cupboards and stores for brooms, other cleaning utensils and cleaning materials

Clips or dowels for hanging brooms and hooks for hanging such articles as dustpans and banister brushes are needed. Manufacturers often supply liquid detergent and other cleaning aids in stacking containers, and so an area free from shelves should be available for their storage.

Security

It is usually held that it is good practice to keep the main storerooms under lock and key, and to allow access to authorised persons only. One person is responsible for security, but there must be arrangements for others to have access in an emergency. The person in charge of stores cannot be expected to take responsibility for safe keeping unless security arrangements are adequate.

The possibility of burglary has also to be considered, especially in non-residential establishments. It should not be easy to break in through a window, and it is better if windows do not allow a clear view of the storeroom's contents; obscure glass may be advisable.

Stock levels

Experienced catering managers carry in their heads—and often commit to paper—information on how much stock to carry of various commodities and items of equipment in given sets of circumstances; experienced storekeepers do the same. Also, many companies and other organisations have specific policies about the stock levels that should be held. It is common practice to prescribe for each commodity a minimum level below which the stock should not fall, and a maximum amount of stock that may be held. Orders and requisitions are placed accordingly.

Reasons for limiting the amounts of stock held are governed by any of the following considerations:

1. The amount of money that may be tied up if large stocks are held;
2. The amount of suitable storage space available;
3. The extra work involved in checking and handling large stocks;
4. The possible deterioration of certain foods, especially if they are stored unsuitably or if stock is not rotated correctly;
5. The possibility that prices may fall, with the consequent reduction in the cash value of the stock held;
6. Large stocks may be a greater security risk.

Reasons for holding stocks above the minimum necessary for day-to-day needs may include any of the following:

1. Less favourable terms offered by suppliers for more frequent deliveries;
2. Extra charges made by suppliers for breaking bulk;
3. Purchases made direct from the manufacturer, who stipulates a

minimum quantity per delivery;

4. Favourable terms given for a bulk purchase, or a special offer;

5. The purchase of stocks in anticipation of price rises or shortages;

6. Stocks of food (especially convenience foods) held for emergencies such as severe staff shortage, bad weather conditions or a breakdown in essential services.

From the foregoing it will be seen that it is necessary to review regularly any policy about minimum and maximum stock levels and to adapt it to circumstances. It is very important that stock levels should not be so high that food is kept until it is past its best, and reference is made to the shelf life of various commodities in Chapter 19.

Ordering, receipt and issue of stores

There are several reasons why it is necessary to have a clearly-defined system concerning stores, some of which are common to all establishments.

1. There must be a record of what goods have been ordered and received, so that invoices may be checked and cleared for payment.

2. Records are necessary so that any queries that arise at a later date (*e.g.*, over an account, or when an audit takes place) may be cleared.

3. If there is a record of stock in hand, suitable quantities of new stocks may be ordered without the necessity for a physical stock check.

4. It is necessary to control the amounts and quality of goods ordered, received and issued.

5. Records of receipts and issues are often needed for costing purposes.

6. Records of receipts and issues may be used in connection with checks that the meals served over a period conform to a prescribed standard.

7. Records are needed for general audit purposes.

8. A sound system of stores control provides a check on pilfering. If no stock records are kept, pilfering may go undetected or its extent may be unknown. It should be said, however, that not all organisations subscribe to the view that this sort of check is necessary; at least one well-known firm in Britain keeps no records of issues, and allows staff free access to stores.

Some characteristics of an efficient system of controlling stores

1. The system should be comprehensive, designed to cover not only routine procedures but also any queries that may arise.

2. The system should provide the information needed by management and no more; inessentials should be pruned away.

3. The system should be as simple as possible. The more complicated the system the greater the possibility of error, and the greater the amount of work involved in tracing errors; this is especially so if a great deal of copying and transferring of figures is involved. A complicated system is very expensive to run because of the manpower involved, and it makes unnecessary demands upon those responsible for it. It should be remembered that responsibility often falls upon those whose prime interest is not record-keeping. One of the advantages of centralised catering systems is that the amount of clerical work in relation to meals production is low. This is seen in Chapter 5, example 4.

The use of the computer and calculator in stores control

The methods described in this chapter relate to manual systems, but records may be computerised. A small electronic calculator is a basic tool for those concerned with record-keeping.

The scope of stock control

Incoming goods consist of food, cleaning materials, equipment and other miscellaneous items. Procedures are similar for all categories, but there are special features relating to food, and it is with food that we shall be chiefly concerned. The following steps apply to all groups:

1. Ordering;
2. Requisitioning (not applicable in all circumstances);
3. Receipt;
4. Issuing;
5. Returning of empties (if any);
6. Maintaining a consolidated record linking receipts, issues and stock in hand.

Ordering

Goods are ordered by an authorised person, usually the manager or supervisor, who takes account of criteria concerning stock levels, prescribed allowances of food, and buying policies and arrangements. Orders are usually made out in an order book in duplicate or triplicate. The top copy goes to the supplier. In some systems a copy is attached to the invoice when it is cleared for payment as an indication that the account has not previously been paid, or it may be intended for the storekeeper's use. One copy remains in the book. The copy order is used to check incoming goods, and it is annotated where necessary to show changes to the order made by telephone, or discrepancies between goods ordered and goods received. Orders should bear a serial number so that they may readily be identified. A specimen page of an order book is shown in Figure 59. Suppliers sometimes provide their own printed order lists to customers, and one copy of the list serves also as a delivery note or invoice. This arrangement saves clerical work, and makes the procedure of checking incoming supplies very easy. Where several establishments are under the same management, by agreement the supplier may print special lists that cover only those items approved for purchase by the head office of the customer. This provides a ready means of controlling the types of purchase made, since non-approved items are handwritten, and so readily identifiable.

Perishable goods are often ordered by telephone, especially when there are daily fluctuations in requirements. Some suppliers make a point of offering a telephone ordering system, while others provide what is virtually a travelling shop for commodities such as pies and sausages. Although telephone ordering is convenient and saves work, unless orders are properly recorded at the time they are made there may be confusion and difficulty later in checking and clearing accounts. In some systems telephoned orders are confirmed by written orders.

Orders should specify requirements precisely, and this point is dealt with in detail in Chapter 19.

Requisitioning

Central stores are maintained by some organisations. For example, certain County Councils operate stores from which are issued food and other goods to all establishments under their control. Supplies are requisitioned from the stores by the management of the various units. The procedure is similar to ordering, but requisitioning sometimes denotes a greater degree of control from headquarters than when orders are placed direct with a firm. Occasionally requisitions are sent to a head office, where they are checked and collated before being sent on to a commercial supplier.

Receipt of stores

Incoming goods are received by an authorised person who checks them against the order, weighs them where appropriate, and judges whether the quality is satisfactory. This usually takes place immediately on delivery, but where large orders covering several items are concerned an arrangement is often made with the supplier that they shall be accepted unexamined, so that the driver is not delayed. The delivery note or invoice is then endorsed 'unexamined' above the signature, and any complaints are taken up afterwards. A similar arrangement operates for off-peak deliveries, which were mentioned in Chapter 2. An example of the sort of check made is given for meat. Check for: weight, grade (where applicable), cut and

Date 1.12.78 Official Order No. 12300 A

Supplier: Mr JAMES GREEN
Address 6, The High Street, BRIDGETOWN

Quantity	Full Description	Price per Unit
6 x 3kg	"BLUE BRAND" apricot pulp	
6 x 5kg	"RED BRAND" rhubarb in syrup	
6 x 3kg	"RED BRAND" solid pack blackcurrants	

Goods to be delivered to:	Delivery to be made by:
St Mary's Hall, Church Lane, BRIDGETOWN	11. 12. 78

Signed Joan Smith
Manageress

For Conditions see Overleaf

CONDITIONS OF ORDER

1 A delivery note should be forwarded with each delivery of goods
2 The number of this order and the name of the establishment must be quoted in any correspondence relating to it and on all delivery notes and invoices.
3 Invoices should be rendered immediately that goods are supplied.
4 A monthly statement showing date, order number and amount of each invoice should be submitted, otherwise delay may be occasioned in the settlement of accounts.
5 Invoices and statements should be forwarded direct to the establishment concerned.

REVERSE SIDE

Fig. 59 Example of official order form

country of origin, as specified on the order and stated on the delivery note. Check the price against any agreed terms.

When goods have been checked against the order their receipt is noted in the consolidated record that was mentioned earlier, and it is entered in a goods-received book if there is one. It is not often necessary to keep a goods-received book, but it is needed if a storekeeper is responsible for issues to more than one unit. The details to be recorded in the goods-received book are:

(a) Date;
(b) Name of supplier;
(c) Serial number of delivery note or invoice;
(d) Quantity and description of goods;
(e) Price (where this is needed for costing and for valuing stocks).

Goods may be entered in the book on a purely chronological basis, or entries may be classified. The goods-received book is used for checking invoices and clearing accounts for payment, but where such a book is not kept the annotated copy order form is used for the purpose.

A separate goods-received book is kept for equipment because these goods are received at much less frequent intervals. Hence the checking of invoices against entries is easier when separate books are kept.

Issuing stores

It is usual to issue food items daily against a list or lists of goods needed. The manager, supervisor or head cook prepares the daily issues list, or the section heads (meat cook, pastry cook, etc.) may each prepare his own list. In the latter case the lists are often known as requisitions. It is not usual to include on the daily issues list perishable items that are to be used straight away and go direct into the kitchen.

Return of empties

Most containers are non-returnable, but where return is necessary a book should be kept for noting receipts and returns. This enables a check to be made that the appropriate credits for chargeable returned containers are made.

Consolidated records

The records described so far contain all the information that is likely to be needed except about stock in hand, but the information is not consolidated; several sets of documents have to be consulted in order to trace receipts and issues. Consolidated records are compiled from the record of goods received—as shown in the annotated order book or goods-received book—and the record of goods issued as shown in the daily issues sheets, and they also show the stock in hand—that is, the up-to-date figure for stocks held, corrected for all issues and receipts. In principle it is simple to keep such a record, but in practice the records tend to become complicated, for two reasons. First, large numbers of items have to be recorded, not only because of the range of commodities used but also because of different pack sizes. For example, there may be three or four different sizes of can for one variety of canned fruit. Secondly some items require many entries for receipts and issues.

There are two basic methods of keeping consolidated records, and many adaptations of these methods.

The perpetual inventory system

In this system a separate commodity stock sheet or card (also known as a perpetual inventory card) is used for each commodity. Items recorded are: date, order number (if any), quantity received, price per unit, quantity used, stock remaining. Examples of entries are given on the specimen commodity sheet shown in Figure 60. In addition, maximum and minimum stock levels may be shown as a guide to ordering. This helps to ensure consistency of stock levels even when there is a change of manager or storekeeper. Spaces may be provided on the sheet for entries showing the dates when physical stock checks were made, and what adjustment (if any) to the figure for book stock was necessary. In some organisations it is not the practice to record issues, and the balance of stock shown on the commodity sheet is arrived at by checking stocks physically at regular intervals—say once a week. Sheets and cards are filed alphabetically. A good system is that shown in Figure 61, where the name of the commodity is visible and each sheet overlaps the next. Alternatively, the file may be indexed.

System using stock sheets that relate to a given period of time

A complete record of receipts and issues for a given period—usually either a week or a month—is kept on one or more especially-printed sheets, and the stock-in-hand at the end of the period is shown also. The sheets are in either pad or book form. Commodities are listed vertically, and details of quantities received and issued are entered horizontally, or *vice versa*. Usually several sheets are necessary to cover all the items in use. When one organisation controls a number of establishments, a list of commodities is printed on the sheets, though some spare lines for additional items are essential.

The entries for receipts are made up from the annotated order book (or from invoices and delivery notes), or from the goods-received book where one is kept. Entries may be made daily, or—as is usually the case where sheets cover a period of a month—weekly. Entries for issues are made up from the daily issues sheet either daily or weekly.

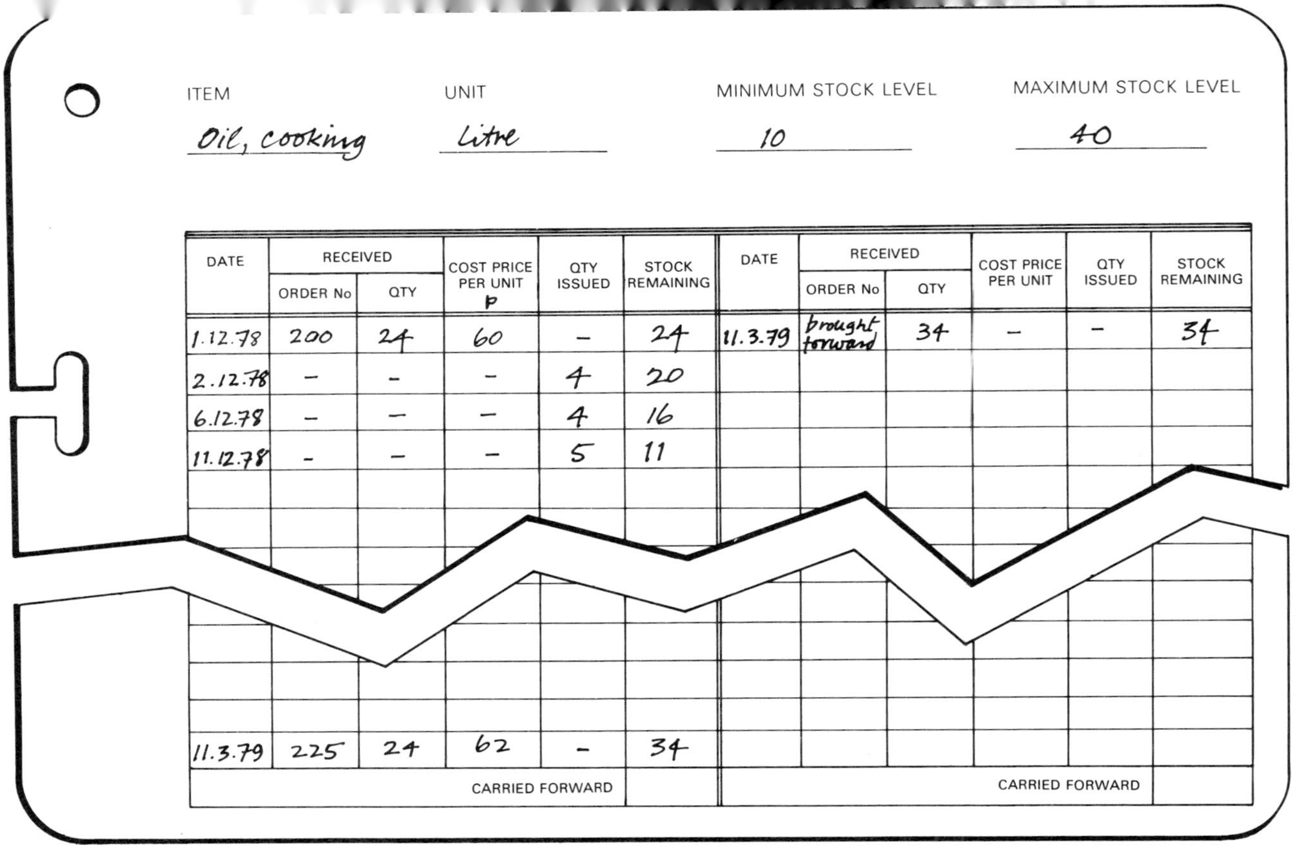

ITEM: Oil, cooking
UNIT: Litre
MINIMUM STOCK LEVEL: 10
MAXIMUM STOCK LEVEL: 40

DATE	RECEIVED		COST PRICE PER UNIT p	QTY ISSUED	STOCK REMAINING	DATE	RECEIVED		COST PRICE PER UNIT	QTY ISSUED	STOCK REMAINING
	ORDER No	QTY					ORDER No	QTY			
1.12.78	200	24	60	–	24	11.3.79	brought forward	34	–	–	34
2.12.78	–	–	–	4	20						
6.12.78	–	–	–	4	16						
11.12.78	–	–	–	5	11						
11.3.79	225	24	62	–	34						
CARRIED FORWARD						CARRIED FORWARD					

Fig. 60 Example of commodity stock sheet

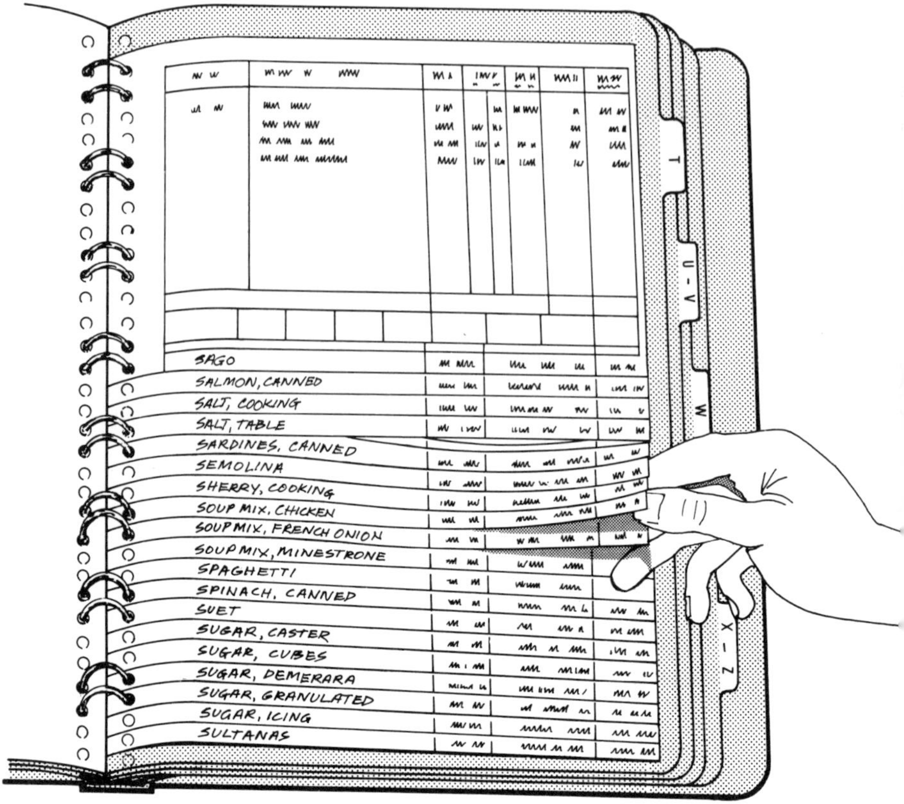

Fig. 61 Visible filing system for records

A specimen stock sheet of this type is shown in Figure 62. Perishable items that do not go into store but direct to the kitchen are not always included. This sort of sheet is sometimes used for costing purposes, in which case extra columns for entering prices are needed. There are several pros and cons about using this method.

1. When there is a printed list of commodities there is very little handwriting to be done.

2. It is particularly suited to systems where information about stores receipts and usages are required at a head office, either for the information of management or because further work (such as costing, or the calculation of nutritional standards and levels of food usage) is to be carried out. If the sheets are kept in duplicate, one copy can easily be sent to head office.

3. Information about stocks may readily be scrutinised without

FOOD STOCK RECORD NO. 5000

NAME OF ESTABLISHMENT CLIFFSIDE SCHOOL		1st WEEK BEGINNING 5/3/79						2nd WEEK BEGINN				
		1	2	3	4	5	6	1	2	3	4	5
Commodity	Unit	Stock Bt. fwd.	Stock Rec'd.	Total	Stock used	Book stock	Stock check	Stock Bt. fwd	Stock Rec'd	Total	Stock used	Boo stoc
1 Bacon, fores	kg	–	–	–	–	–		–	20	20	–	
2 Bacon, sliced	kg	–	27	27	27	–		–	30	30	15	
3 Baking powder	kg	2	3	5	1	4	✓	4	–	4	1	
4 Beans, butter	kg											
5 Beans, haricot	kg											
6 Bicarbonate of soda	kg											
7 Butter	kg	4	8	12	7	5	✓	8	13	8		
8 Cheese	kg											
9 Cocoa	kg											
10 Cooking fat	kg											
11 Cornflakes	kg											
12 Cornflour	kg											
13 Cream of tartar	kg											
14 Currants	kg											
15 Custard powder	kg											
16 Dates	kg											
	kg											

Fig. 62 Example of stock sheet, with printed list of commodities. Sheet covers period of 4 weeks, and is made up at end of each week

the necessity to handle large numbers of single-commodity cards.

4. It has the disadvantage that, in order to bring information forward to the next sheet, entries have to be made for each item each period, whether it has been used or not.

5. It is unsuitable where a very extensive range of commodities is stocked and frequency of use varies considerably. For this reason it is not generally used in residential establishments, or those offering a wide range of catering facilities. It is fairly generally used in Britain for school meals records.

Stocktaking

The system of stock control should provide for regular physical stocktaking. One convenient way of taking stock of food is to check items in rotation, so that all commodities are checked over a period of, say, four to six weeks. Also, it is usual to have a full check made at the end of the financial year and at other suitable times. Full physical checks are often related to accounting periods. For example, if food costs are calculated every three months, full stock checks are carried out at the same interval, so that the value of closing and opening stocks for the accounting period may be calculated accurately.

It is part of the duties of the person responsible for the stores to do routine physical stocktaking, but in addition a senior member of staff or an auditor should carry out spot checks to find out whether the system is working efficiently.

Suitable forms for records: advice on systems

Clear, well-designed forms are essential for any system. Large organisations often design their own forms and have them specially printed, but this is not essential. There are well-known firms that specialise in this sort of work; they also offer advice on suitable systems and suggest ways of keeping the labour involved in record-keeping to a minimum.

A manual of catering records

Once a system has been devised, it is essential that the way in which it operates be described in detail to all those concerned, and instructions on how forms should be filled in are also needed. Otherwise there will be misunderstandings and lack of uniformity, and when staff change the method is likely to be changed. Hence a manual on record-keeping is needed. It is also helpful if instructions on form-filling are printed either on the form itself or on the cover of the book or pad.

CODE No	RECIPE FOR 100 PORTIONS	QUANTITY	COST £	COST p	PER unit	TOTAL COST £	TOTAL COST p	QUANTITY/ 100 PORTIONS
S5	APPLES	10 kg	0	10	1 kg	1	00	
	SUGAR, GRANULATED	2 kg	6	70	25 kg		54	
	FLOUR	2 kg	5	00	32 kg		31	
	MARGARINE	0.5 kg	6	50	12½ kg		26	
	LARD	0.5 kg	6	00	12½ kg		24	
	WATER	200 ml	–	–				
		TOTAL COST OF RECIPE				2	35	2 35

PER 100 PORTIONS		
	DATE	1. 12. 78
	COST	£2.35
	PRICE	£8.00

TITLE BELOW THIS LINE

DESCRIPTION	PRICE	QUANTITY/PORTION	COST/PRICE%
APPLE PIE	8p	25 per dish	30

REVERSE SIDE

GENERAL NOTES & METHOD OF PREPARATION
1. Use fresh fruit (see separate card for canned apples).
2. Make short crust pastry, single crust.
3. Bake in a hot oven, 204° C

DIRECT WORK CONTENT STANDARD MINUTES	DATE	PER RECIPE	PER 100 PORTIONS
CHEFS & COOKS			
pastry	1.12.78	18	18
PREPARATION			
Fruit	1.12.78	16	16
PAN WASH		5	5
MISC.		5	5

Fig. 63 Costed recipe card

Chapter 19

Buying

It is sometimes said that the financial success or otherwise of a catering establishment depends to a very great extent upon the system adopted for buying the goods needed in the kitchen. This is something of an overstatement, since there are other equally important contributory factors, such as a suitable and flexible pricing structure, the standard of cooking and presentation, efficient and economical staffing, and the avoidance of any form of waste. Nevertheless, the statement serves to draw attention to the importance of good buying.

Aims in good buying

The aims in good buying are threefold. The first is obviously to obtain the best possible value for money spent. Thus the catering manager must keep himself informed of current market prices, must be able to assess quality in relation to price, and must ensure that he obtains the best possible terms of supply. Different methods of buying will be dealt with in more detail later, but it cannot be emphasised too strongly at this stage that, although keen prices should be sought, this must not be at the expense of quality—which can happen when prices are cut too closely—and a careful check should be kept on all incoming goods. In the case of non-perishable branded goods, tests for quality and acceptability to the consumer should be made before a commitment to buy is entered into.

The second aim is to obtain supplies that are fresh, sound and in good condition. With some commodities and under certain buying conditions goods may be examined at the time of purchase. This applies to fruit and vegetables when they are bought in the market, and to supplies bought from a warehouse on cash-and-carry terms. But buying direct from the wholesale market is fairly rare, and cash-and-carry buying is unsuitable for most establishments. It follows that in most cases goods are supplied against a written or telephoned order, and are not seen by the caterer until they arrive at the kitchen. Careful examination upon receipt and in use is therefore essential to ensure that quality is up to standard. Any complaints about quality or quantity should be taken up with the supplier immediately, and if necessary the goods should be returned.

It is only in smaller establishments that the caterer will be able to examine all incoming supplies himself, and so it is important that whoever is responsible for the acceptance and use of goods should be reliable in this sector of the work, and should know the procedures to be adopted. For some commodities, such as meat, fish and poultry, the person responsible will probably be the cook, and he should be able to recognise cuts of meat and quality factors for fish, poultry and meat. For provisions and dry goods the storekeeper will be responsible, and he should look for blown or damaged cans, insect infestation of cereals, brands of goods not as specified and so forth, as well as checking for quantity. It is advisable for the manager to examine all goods from time to time, not only as a part of his general duties of staff supervision, but also to keep a watch on the standard of goods supplied. Where there is repeated difficulty or a dispute with a supplier, the services of officers of the local authority should be sought. The Trading Standards Officer (known in some areas as the Consumer Protection Officer) deals with questions of short weight or short measure and complaints about quality. The Environmental Health Officer is concerned with food hygiene. Where there is a complaint that may be a matter of public health, it is the caterer's duty to call in the Environmental Health Officer immediately.

The third aim is to obtain a satisfactory service. This includes continuity, delivery arrangements, communications and the method of submitting accounts.

Buying policy

When an organisation is responsible for a number of catering units, there is likely to be a clearly-defined policy on buying, and it is probable that arrangements for the supply of a large number of commodities will be made either centrally or at area level. In independent establishments the buying policy may be determined solely by the catering manager, or he may be required to consult the board or management committee or the finance director.

Buying methods

Contract buying

One method of buying is through the exchange of contracts, when each side enters into a commitment concerning the supply of goods for a period that may vary from, say, three months to three years. In the first case, prices may be fixed for the contract period; in the second this is unlikely to be so, though prices may be fixed for an initial period, after which they are reviewed. Contract buying is often adopted by public bodies such as local authorities. The procedure adopted is usually as follows: offers to supply are invited through the press, including trade papers. A closing date is fixed, after which offers are scrutinised and compared. References from other customers may be taken up, and samples of the products offered may be tested. The contract is given to the firm that is judged to have made the best offer, price, quality and an estimation of the standard of service being taken into account. Price is, of course, a major consideration.

In theory this system appears to be satisfactory, and it often works extremely well, but sometimes difficulties arise. Where fixed prices are not offered—and they are rare in times of inflation—it is necessary to devise a way of checking that prices are favourable, not only at the time the quotation is made, but subsequently through the period of the contract. This may be done by using market prices, as published in trade papers, as a yardstick. Very often a tender offers to supply goods at market prices minus a discount or plus a percentage on cost. Where this is the case, it is necessary for the buyer to scrutinise market prices and the supplier's accounts regularly to see that the terms of supply are being kept. Another arrangement is that the buyer agrees to pay the price that the supplier, usually a wholesaler, has himself paid, plus a percentage.

Procedures for terminating a contract before the end of its term may be cumbersome, which may cause difficulties if a supplier turns out to be unsatisfactory. On the other hand, a contract gives security of supply, and long-term contracts often prove to be an advantage to both parties. Where a system of contract buying is used, it does not necessarily cover all classes of goods. Fruit and vegetables, for example, are often excluded because there is such a wide range of quality and price.

Buying for delivery to a central store

Some groups of establishments are serviced by a central store, in which case all the buying arrangements are under the direction of a central purchasing officer. Some or all of the goods bought are delivered to the central store, at which there may be facilities for the following: breaking bulk and repacking some items into smaller units; storing frozen foods; butchering. The advantages of this system are that very favourable financial terms can be obtained, reserve stocks can be held against times of shortage, and it is possible to make regular deliveries to all establishments, large or small, remote or near by. However, the services of skilled staff are needed to run the stores, and their wages and salaries and the cost of premises and transport must be carefully assessed against the savings made in food purchases before such a scheme is adopted. In particular, where most of the establishments to be serviced are schools or colleges, it may be difficult to run a central stores economically because of the long periods during the year when the output of the stores will be small compared with its overheads.

Consortium buying

This method is used by some groups of local authorities. Several authorities combine to make common buying arrangements with the object of obtaining very favourable terms of supply because of their collective buying power. The arrangement is under the direction of a central purchasing officer who has responsibility to all members of the consortium. As in the case of a central store, it is necessary to assess the costs of administering such arrangements (which may be considerable) against its benefits.

Negotiated arrangements

Where contracts are not placed, terms of supply are negotiated before a commitment to place an order is made. Offers from several firms have to be compared, and high degrees of skill and experience are needed if the best terms are to be obtained. Where a wholesaler is concerned, for a large account the buyer expects to be offered a discount on his published price list. Accounts may also be opened direct with manufacturers for some commodities. Certain manufacturers of specialised products make a point of dealing direct with caterers.

Cash-and-carry

The cash-and-carry method of buying from a wholesaler gives no detailed statement of account, and for this reason it is unsuitable for most establishments; it is also open to abuse by the buyer. It may be convenient for a small, privately-owned establishment or an owner-caterer because no paper-work is involved.

Meat

Of all commodities, meat is the one that demands the greatest skill in judging quality and determining cut. It takes long experience to become expert in this field, and even specialists would agree that it is extremely difficult to define what exactly is meant by the term 'quality'. The final test rests with the consumer and his palate, but this test can be applied only at a time when redress is virtually impossible. There are, however, certain indicators that help the caterer to assess quality in meat, but careful observation is necessary. He must be able to recognise the cut of meat, and this is not always easy, though experience and application bring the necessary skills. The practice of buying ready-boned joints makes recognition much more difficult. In the case of a bone-in joint, recognition of the bone helps to identify the cut.

Buying meat

Most caterers buy meat by the piece, but in some organisations it is the practice to buy carcase meat—that is, forequarter or hindquarter of beef and sides (half carcases) of pork, mutton and lamb. When joints of meat are bought they may be bone-in or boneless, and obviously a higher price is paid for the same cut if it is boneless. When meat is supplied boned the price is as for bone-in joints, plus any charge for boning, and the bones belonging to the joint are supplied with the meat. Some firms specialise in supplying meat to the caterer boned out, fully trimmed, and ready for oven or pot. Items such as steaks are cut to standard sizes, and chops are carefully graded for size and weight. This virtually eliminates any labour in the kitchen, much of which is skilled, in preparing before cooking, it makes portion control easier, and the cost per portion may be predicted more easily. When carcase meat is bought the price is much lower, but account has to be taken of the yield of edible meat, the cost of employing staff skilled in butchering, and the cost of providing and maintaining facilities for chilling. Usually this method of buying is an economic proposition only for a very large establishment, or where a butchery department serves a number of units under the same management.

Some important steps in securing satisfactory meat supplies are:

1. When specifications are prepared for a contract or other agreement, grade (where appropriate), country of origin and cuts should be specified precisely.

2. A reliable and trustworthy supplier who employs staff who are good judges of meat should be chosen.

3. An order for meat should specify the cut, country of origin and, where appropriate, the grade. If there is a contract, the order should accord with its specifications.

4. When the meat arrives, it should be inspected, the cut identified and its quality assessed. A well-informed and critical customer is likely to get better meat than one who displays neither knowledge nor interest. Where there is a contract to supply, possibly at very keen prices, it is particularly important to exercise good judgment—even more so where contract prices are fixed and the market moves against the supplier. When the caterer is in doubt about quality or cut, he may seek advice from the Trading Standards Officer.

5. Do not order meat ready-minced, because once it has been minced it is virtually impossible to identify the cut, and difficult to

judge the quality. Similarly, it is difficult to establish the cut when meat is supplied ready-diced for the pot.

6. Order a cut of meat appropriate to the method of cooking to be used. Figures 64, 65 and 66, which show the cuts of meat for beef, mutton and pork, also indicate suitable methods of cooking for various cuts.

Classification of meat

We shall shortly give information about the more obvious distinguishing features of various categories of meat, but first it is interesting to note how meat is classified, and why variations in quality occur. Several factors are concerned: breed, condition, contours and the deposition of fat, age and sex. Breed and condition are important, but are of little practical concern to the caterer. Age and sex are of more interest, as they are the controlling factors determining the broad divisions into which beef, mutton, lamb and pork are placed.

CATTLE. Beef is divided into four categories according to sex and age: bull (entire male); cow (female after calving); steer (castrated male); heifer (young female before calving). Old bull beef is usually lean, dark in colour and coarse in texture, and is used chiefly for manufacturing. Young bull beef is now bred specially for the meat market: it is valued for its leanness and is of good conformation and colour. Cow beef also has little fat, and what there is is usually yellow; the flesh is not juicy. It is not usually acceptable for catering, but young cows that have had only one calf may yield quite good quality meat. After the third calf the deterioration in the quality of the meat becomes very apparent. Beef from a heifer is generally considered to be better than that from a steer; the deposition of fat is better, the flesh is not so muscular and the proportion of flesh to bone is higher. The Meat and Livestock Commission has a voluntary system of classification, which came into effect in 1972. Carcases are classified according to five key factors: weight, fatness, conformation, sex and age group.

Fatness: There are five classes, numbered from one to five in ascending order of fatness. Very fat carcases in class 5 are classed Z.

Conformation: Here again there are five classes. Class 5 indicates very good (carcases with thick, lean meat), and Class 1 indicates poor conformation (thin flesh).

Sex: This is indicated by H (heifer); S (steer); C (cow); B (bull).

Age group: Carcases from animals with calf teeth, or in which two permanent teeth have erupted, are classified Y (young). Those in which four or more permanent teeth have erupted are classified T (teeth).

Fig. 64 Cuts of beef

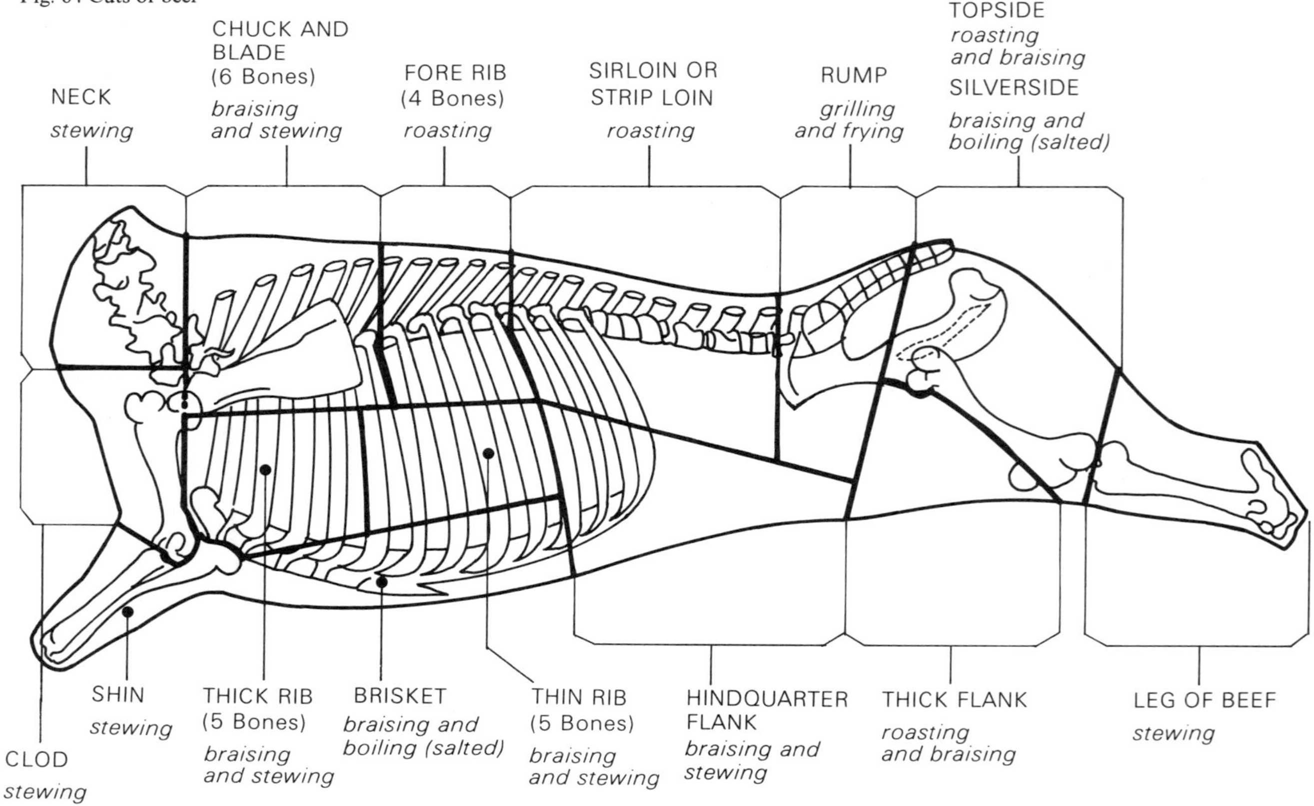

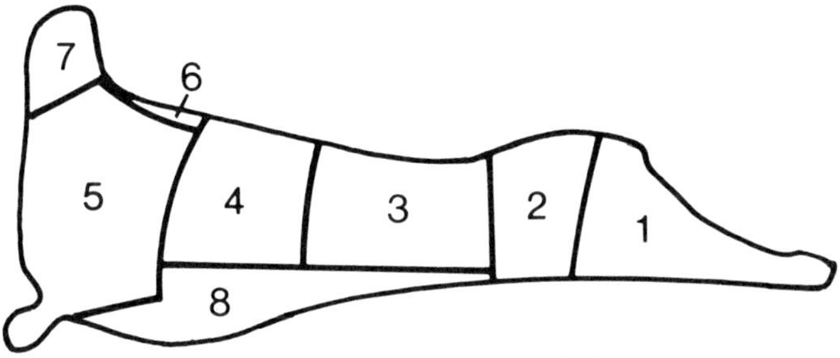

1 LEG
roasting

2 CHUMP
grilling (in chops)

3 LOIN
roasting
and grilling (in chops)

4 BEST END NECK
roasting, grilling (in chops)
and braising (in chops)

5 SHOULDER
roasting

6 MIDDLE NECK
braising and stewing

7 SCRAG
stewing

8 BREAST
roasting or grilling
(minced in lamburgers etc.)

Fig. 65 Cuts of lamb and mutton

As an example of carcase classification, YS 24 describes a side from a young steer (YS) of below-average fatness (2) and above-average conformation (4).

SHEEP. Sheep are divided into the following categories according to sex and age: ram (entire male); tup (entire young male); wether (castrated male); ewe (female after she has had her first lamb); gimmer (female before she has had her first lamb); ewe lamb (young female); teg (young sheep of either sex, entire or not). Meat from the ram or ewe is of poorer quality than that from other groups. For full-flavoured meat the animal must be mature; a three-year-old wether yields full-flavoured mutton. Yearlings (lambs) provide flesh of good quality, lacking toughness and having a good flavour. Good conformation and fat deposition are quality factors.

In practice, sheepmeat carcases may be grouped according to age at the date of slaughter:

Up to twelve months:	lamb
Over twelve and up to twenty-four months:	mutton (or sheep)
Over two years:	hogget.

Most New Zealand lambs are between four and six months old when

Fig. 66 Cuts of pork

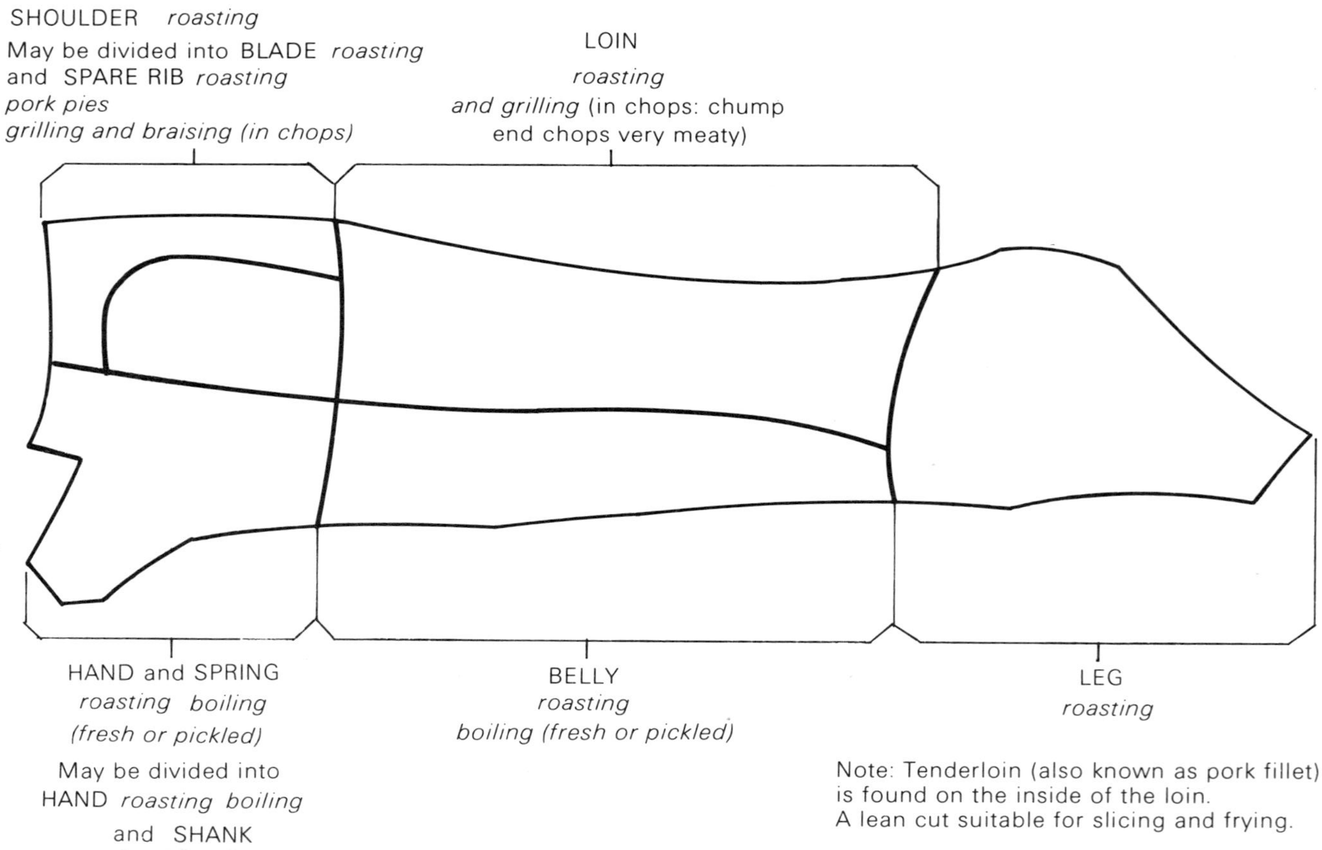

Note: Tenderloin (also known as pork fillet) is found on the inside of the loin. A lean cut suitable for slicing and frying.

they are slaughtered.

The Meat and Livestock Commission classifies sheep carcases by four factors: weight, category, fatness and conformation.

Category: L is used for lambs, Hgt for hoggets and Shp for sheep on an approximate age basis. At the time of writing rams and ewes have not been classified.

Fatness: The classification runs from 1 (very lean) to 5 (very fat).

Conformation: There are four classes: extra, average, poor and very poor. Most carcases fall into fat classes 2, 3 and 4. In these classes carcases of average conformation are identified by the fat class number only, and carcases of very good conformation are identified by the letter E (extra), following the fat class number. Any carcase of poor or very poor conformation, regardless of fat level, is classed as C or Z respectively, and there is no subdivision between average and extra in fat classes 1 and 5.

The New Zealand Meat Producers' Board operates a grading system related to weight range and quality factors. Details are as follows:

New Zealand Lamb Grades

Symbol	*Weight Range (kg)*	*Colour Code*
PL	8·0–12·5	Blue
PM	13·0–16·0	Blue
PH	16·5–25·5	Blue
YL	8·0–12·5	Red
YM	13·0–16·0	Red
YH	16·5–25·5	Red
OL	8·0–12·5	Brown
OM	13·0–16·0	Brown

Note: The first symbol in the table (*e.g.*, the 'Y' in 'YM') indicates the grade, and the second symbol represents the weight range. For example, YM is a Y grade lamb whose carcase weight is in the M (medium) weight range—13·0–16·0 kg. OL is an O grade lamb whose carcase weight is in the L (light) weight range.

The New Zealand Meat Producers' Board defines its export lamb carcase grades as follows:

P Grade: A carcase well muscled in the legs, loin and forequarters. Fat cover is adequate, but not excessive.

Y Grade: A moderately-fleshed carcase with a light, but not deficient, fat cover.

O Grade: A lamb similar to the P grade, except that the legs tend to be elongated and the crutch V-shaped.

New Zealand lamb carcases are graded for these features:

Age: All lamb is under twelve months old at the time of slaughter.

Sex: Carcases may be of either sex, but excluded are those lambs that show strong male characteristics.

Weight: Weight range of dressed carcases.

Conformation: The shape and muscling of the carcase is taken into account in assessing a particular grade.

Fat covering: No carcase may be exported that has excess fat.

Colour: Carcases that have excessively dark lean meat or yellow fat will not be included in any grade.

PIGS. The following classifications, according to sex and age, apply: boar (entire male); hog (castrated male); sow (female that has had a litter); gilt or gelt (female that has not had a litter); porker (young pig of either sex, entire or not). Young boars are now being bred for the meat market but old boars are used only for manufacturing.

The Meat and Livestock Commission classifies pig carcases according to five factors: cold carcase weight, backfat thickness, visual assessment applied to certain carcases, length (at the trader's option) and conformation (also at the trader's option).

Backfat thickness: Backfat measurements are taken in millimetres at two fixed points over the loin, P_1 and P_3. (P_2 is used for bacon carcases.) The two measurements are added together and recorded in a triangle marked on a trotter. For example:

Visual assessment applied to certain carcases: scraggy, deformed, blemished, pigmented, coarse-skinned, soft fat, pale muscle, partially condemned. These are classified Z.

Conformation: Carcases with poor conformation (particularly of the leg, but not poor enough to be scraggy) are classed C.

Examination of meat for quality

When the quality of a joint of meat is estimated, the three main substances of which it is composed are inspected: muscle fibre, fat and connective tissue.

Muscle consists of a number of fibres held together by connective tissues, which form small sacs in which the meat proteins, myosin and myogen, are held. In young animals, and in those parts of older ones that are not subject to much muscular activity (as, for example, in the fillet of beef), the amount of connective tissue present is not great, and in consequence the meat is tender. This type of meat is smooth to the touch when it is cut across the grain, whereas the coarser cuts feel harsher, and when they are cut with the grain the fibres are seen to be noticeably longer. The colour of the muscle varies according to the species and age of the animal. In beef, it is bright red, firm to the touch and shiny when cut. In veal it is pale grey or greyish-red, moderately firm to the touch, and the surface is dry when it is cut. In lamb and mutton the colour is dark red, the flesh is firm and it glistens when cut. Young pork is whitish-grey or pale red in colour, soft to the touch and dull on section. In older animals the flesh is darker.

When judging fat in meat one must notice the amount, distribution and quality. In prime cuts to be used for grilling, roasting and frying a certain amount of fat is essential; some of this should be distributed through the flesh in small quantities—a condition known as marbling. The fat so distributed adds flavour to the meat, and has a basting effect upon the muscle fibres during cooking. Fat other than that distributed through the muscle is often known as 'visible fat'; a certain amount is an indication of good quality, but a large amount is not generally acceptable, as taste nowadays is for lean meat. Beef fat is soft in texture and creamy in colour, while cow beef fat has a characteristic yellow colour. Mutton and lamb fat is white and firm in texture, while pork fat is soft and creamy-white in colour.

Animal connective tissue is of two types: elastin, which is yellow, tough and inedible; and collagen, which is white and, when it is cooked in liquid, is converted into water-soluble gelatine. The presence of connective tissue in muscle fibre has already been mentioned. The amount varies according to the age of the animal and the part of the body. The higher the proportion of connective tissue the tougher the meat, and elastin, unlike collagen, is unaffected by any cooking process. It follows that tough meat cannot become tender as a result of roasting, frying and grilling, but it may do so when it is braised or stewed.

Hanging as a factor influencing quality

One other factor affecting quality remains to be mentioned, and that is the treatment of the carcase after slaughter. Shortly after killing *rigor mortis* sets in, and the muscles become hard and stiff. In time this process is gradually reversed, and the muscles become more tender. Carcases are hung under controlled conditions, temperature being particularly significant to allow the post-*rigor* conditioning to take place. The minimum time for beef is from three to four days, but longer times give improved quality and flavour. However, the process of hanging is costly because of the storage space involved, and it is less important, from the point of view of tenderness, in the case of young animals, and hence the tendency is to hang for minimum periods. An equivalent technique to hanging, known as natural aging, has been developed in Australia. Joints of meat are placed in vacuum-pack bags, which are then sealed and transported at chilled, but not frozen, temperatures. While the meat is in transit, tenderness is improved.

Poultry

The term poultry includes fowls, ducks, geese, turkeys, pigeons and guineafowl, but the caterer is concerned mainly with fowls and turkeys, and to a lesser extent with ducks and geese. Purchases may be made from a poulterer, a butcher, or, where frozen poultry is concerned, from firms specialising in frozen foods. Frozen poultry is used extensively; it is usually cheaper than fresh birds, weight and size are consistent, and, where branded products are concerned, so is quality. As a general rule, however, it is inferior in flavour and texture to fresh poultry.

Classification of fowls

Broilers. These are young, intensively-reared birds that are killed at nine to twelve weeks old at a live weight of between 1·36 and 1·8 kg, and they are the principal type of poultry used in Britain. The birds are killed, plucked and prepared for the table at packing stations.

Boiling fowls. These are hens that have been laying eggs, and they are usually more than two years old; they are often very good value.

Capons. These are male de-sexed birds, and they are killed at eleven to thirteen weeks old. They are usually of very good quality, and weigh about 1·8 to 2·27 kg.

Roasting chickens. This category includes year-old cockerels, pullets and young hens about three to six months old and weighing about 1·36 to 1·8 kg.

Spring chickens. These are about three months old, and weigh about 0·9 to 1·0 kg.

Petit poussin. These are young chickens that are killed at eight to ten weeks old, when they weigh between 226 and 453 g.

Turkeys

The range of weights in turkeys is extensive. Larger birds are excellent for carving purposes, and the ratio of flesh to bone is high, but they may create problems with regard to oven accommodation and cooking times.

Poultry may be bought ready jointed for use in made-up dishes, and this may be convenient, but there is always the possibility that the joints have come from damaged or partly diseased birds. Poultry is sold either oven-ready (dressing includes evisceration) or, more rarely, New York dressed (uneviscerated).

As soon as it is delivered poultry should be checked against the delivery note for description and weight, and the quality also should be checked. Birds should be plump, and the flesh firm and elastic to the touch. The skin should be unbroken. In young birds the breastbone is pliable and the legs and feet are smooth; rough legs and horny feet are signs of an old bird. When poultry is stale the feet become hard and stiff, and later the carcase becomes green round the vent; this is followed by greening of the abdomen, back, ribs and neck. There is an offensive odour. In the case of frozen poultry, signs of deformity or injury should be looked for, and any such birds rejected.

Game

Game includes hares, partridges, pheasants, grouse, blackgame, ptarmigan, wild duck, bustard and venison. It may be bought only from a licensed dealer, and, in the case of home game, only during the permitted shooting season for the species. Game is hung before it is sold so that the muscle fibre becomes more tender; hanging also enhances the flavour.

Fish

Ways of buying fish

Fish may be bought from a local wholesaler or direct from a fish merchant at one of the ports. Another possibility is to buy at the local fish market, in which case the buyer has to arrange his own transport for any fish bought. When fish comes from a merchant special attention has to be given to delivery arrangements, since it is often the practice in the fish trade, unless there is an agreement to the contrary, to deliver at off-peak times.

In Britain the White Fish Authority, in conjunction with the Torry Research Station, provides information and recommendations on buying fish to institutional caterers, and gives model specifications for use in connection with contracts.

Species of fish

Figure 67 shows species of British fish, their average marketed length, and the grounds where they are fished. From time to time certain species become scarce, and less well-known fish take their place. The caterer needs to keep in touch with such market changes.

State in which fish comes to market

Fish may be unfrozen, when it is known as wet fish, or frozen. Frozen fish is not inferior to wet fish, and, because it is often frozen at sea, it may be superior in quality to some wet fish. Fish may also be smoked, and some of this is frozen after smoking.

Smoked fish

A considerable amount of smoked fish is eaten in Britain as a breakfast dish, as hors d'oeuvres, and in made-up dishes such as fish

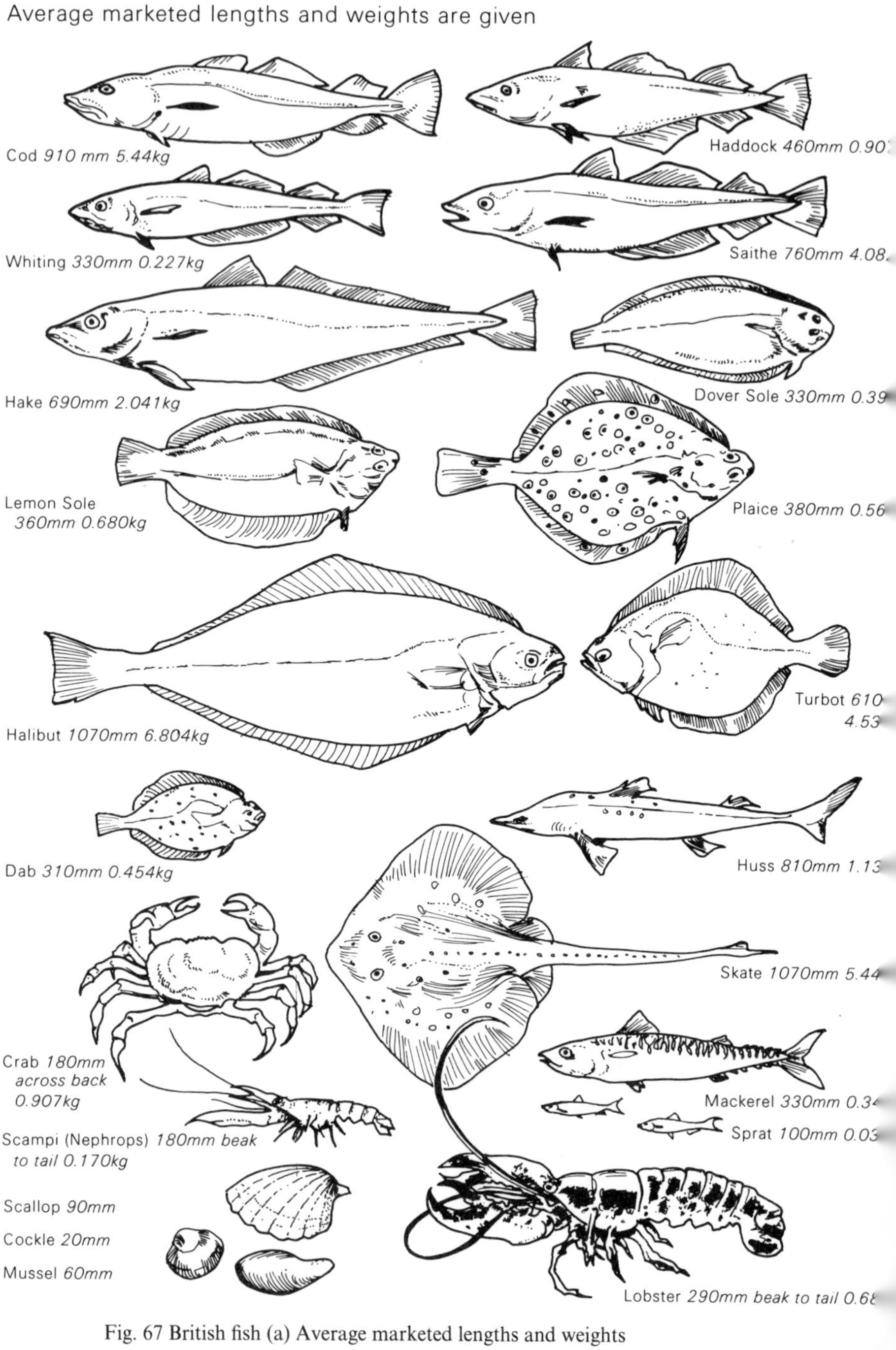

Fig. 67 British fish (a) Average marketed lengths and weights

cakes and fish pies. There are two reasons for curing fish by smoking:

(a) To increase the keeping quality—this was very important before the advent of commercial freezing;

(b) To impart an attractive, characteristic flavour.

The process consists of pickling the fish for a short time in brine and then smoke-curing it over wood chips. During the process the fish takes on a golden-brown colour and loses some of its water content. A good quality product that keeps well should lose about 12 to 14 per cent of its original weight.

The species of fish most commonly cured whole are haddock, mackerel, codling, whiting, herring, trout, eel and salmon. Cured fillets are prepared from haddock, cod, whiting and ling. Herring are cured to produce a variety of products, as follows:

Kippers (fish split and lightly brined before smoking; they may be bought boned or filleted);

Buckling (smoked whole unsplit fish smoked at a higher temperature than is used for kippers; they are lightly cooked during the curing process);

Bloaters (whole fish, dry-salted and lightly smoked).

Smoked fish keep for short periods only. Some kinds are canned.

Quality of fish

Quality varies during the year; it is best just before spawning, and poorest immediately after spawning has taken place. Table 10 shows the best times of the year for buying various species—but it does not, of course, apply to frozen fish.

The size of a fish affects its quality. The flesh of a very large specimen may be old and coarse, while in small fish the proportion of skin and bone to flesh is high. Quality, however, depends chiefly upon freshness, and the following are signs that fish is fresh:

Smell: there should be no unpleasant smell.

General appearance: this should be clean and bright. Abdominal walls should not be discoloured, and the area near the head should not be soft and red.

Eyes: these should be clear and bright, and not shrunken.

Scales: these should be bright, shiny and tight to the skin. (Easily-removed scales are a sign of staleness.)

Flesh: this should be firm and elastic, and should adhere firmly to the bone. (When fish is stale the flesh becomes flabby, and, because the blood decomposes, it reddens above and below the backbone.)

In practice, not a great deal of whole fish is bought, and filleted fish must be judged for freshness on smell and texture only. Frozen fish cannot be assessed until it has been thawed. Where smoked fish is concerned, heavy smoking can partially disguise staleness, but

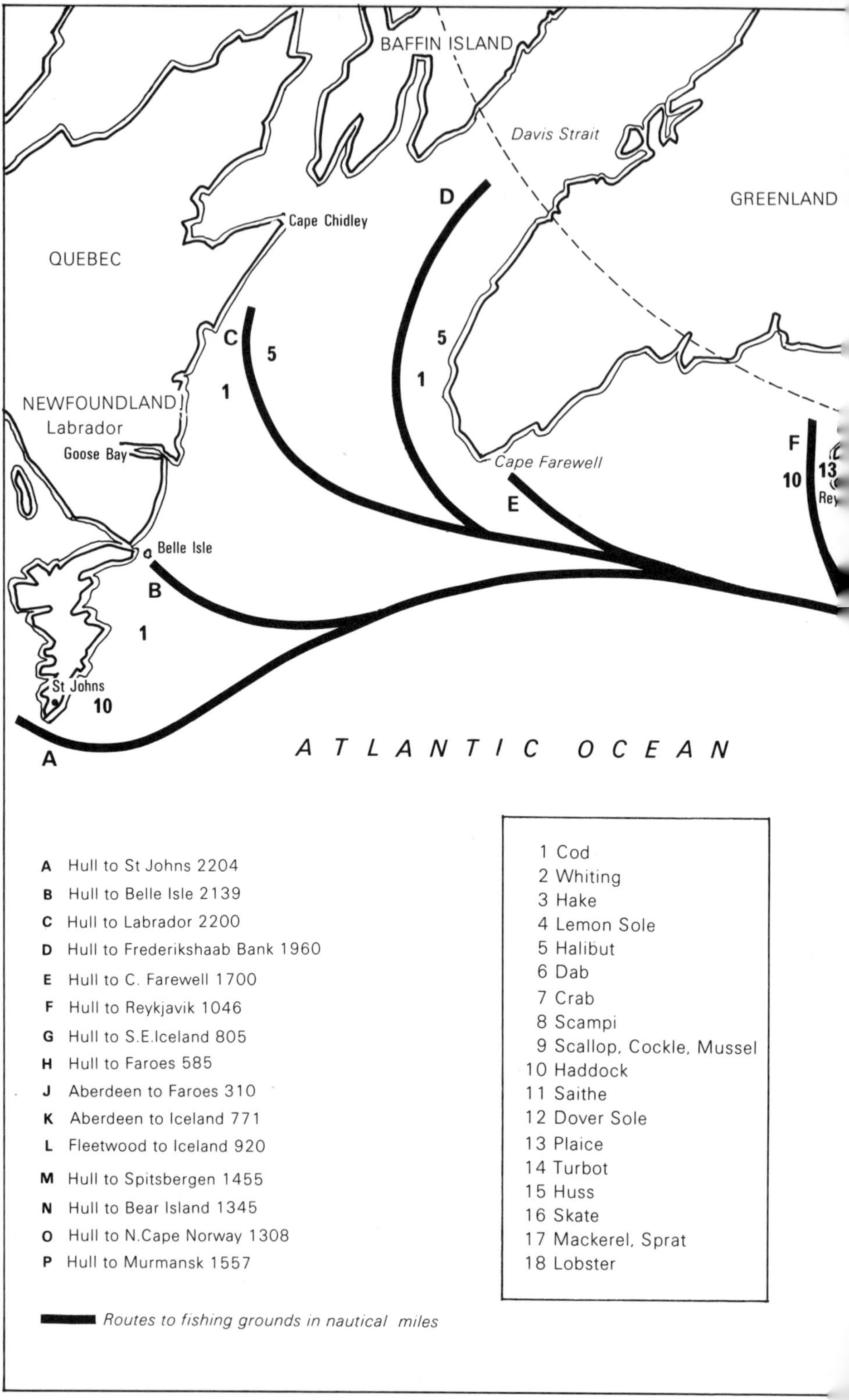

Fig. 67 British fish (b) Where caught

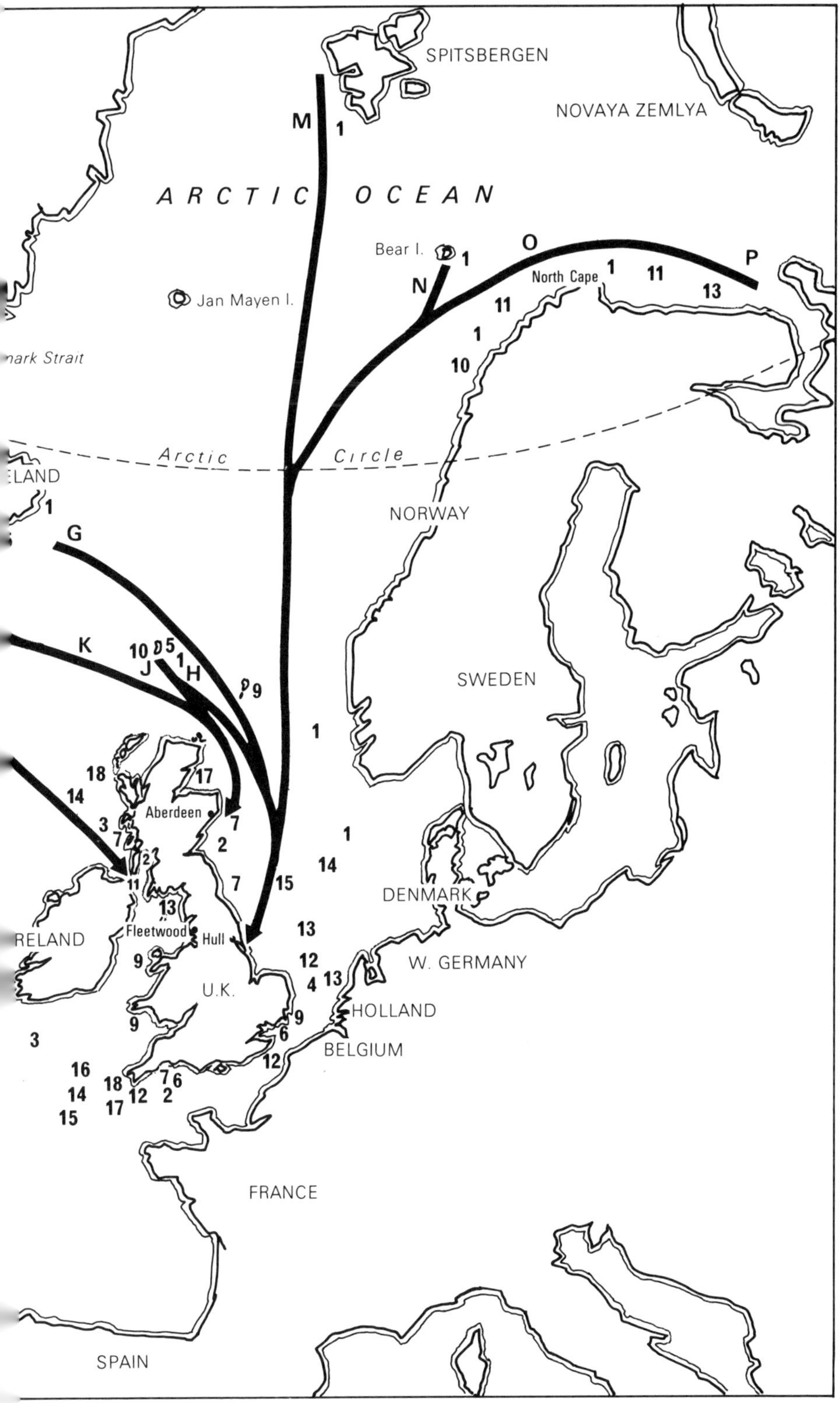

SPITSBERGEN
NOVAYA ZEMLYA
ARCTIC OCEAN
Bear I.
North Cape
Jan Mayen I.
Arctic Circle
NORWAY
SWEDEN
Aberdeen
DENMARK
Fleetwood
Hull
W. GERMANY
U.K.
HOLLAND
BELGIUM
FRANCE
SPAIN
M
N
O
P
G
K
J
H

nevertheless it will be betrayed by pronounced discoloration of the belly flaps, or by an objectionable odour coming from underneath the backbone.

A caterer who is dissatisfied with the freshness of fish supplied may ask the White Fish Authority to make an assessment of a future delivery. They test fish by taste and by various chemical means, and give a score for freshness according to the Torry Taste Panel system, so that an objective assessment is given.

Parasites are sometimes present in fish, chiefly nematode worms, which are slender, unsegmented and cylindrical. They are not harmful, but it is usual to reject infested fish. The White Fish Authority suggests a tolerance of three nematode worms per pack of 3·2 kg of fish.

Fish sometimes have abnormal odours or flavours, such as the 'weedy' or 'diesel' flavours that are common in fish from certain grounds at certain times of year, and such fish are not acceptable.

Range of products available

A considerable range of manufactured fish products and pan-ready items is on sale, including fish cakes, fish fingers, frozen portions of white fish cut from laminated blocks of skinless, boneless fillets, and battered and crumbed frozen portions. Standard-weight fillet portions cut from single fillets may be bought, and fillets may be supplied ready-skinned.

Some points to be considered when fish is bought

1. In the case of round fish, such as cod and haddock, it may be advisable to specify a maximum weight of 1·5 kg and a minimum of 350 g. Fillets within this range will not be too small to give suitable portions; nor will there be large fillets containing large pin bones.

2. Fish fillets bought ready-skinned tend to be more profitable than unskinned fillets. Although the price is slightly higher, there is less waste than when fish is skinned in the kitchen (less than 10 per cent as against up to 16 per cent). Nevertheless, skin-on fillets are sometimes preferred because the skin makes it easier to recognise the species.

3. Buying ready-portioned fish may be an advantage because it ensures good portion control, and the buyer is sure that he will get exactly the required yield of portions. But, where children of widely different ages are being catered for, standard portions are not always suitable because of the big differences in individual requirements. Ready-portioned fish is slightly higher in price, but saves labour.

4. When made-up items such as fish fingers and fish cakes are compared, an important point is their fish content. Usually there is more fish for the money in fillet than in made-up products, but

convenience and relative popularity have also to be taken into account.

Shellfish

A wide range of shellfish is not normally used in institutional catering, and what is used is more likely to be frozen and ready-prepared than fresh. The chief characteristic of a shellfish is that it has no internal skeleton, but instead is protected by an external shell.

Kinds of shellfish. Crustaceans: these have outer skeletons that are jointed or segmented. The group includes the crab, lobster, Dublin Bay prawn, prawn, shrimp and crayfish.

Molluscs: these include the oyster, cockle, mussel and escallop, all of which are bivalves—they have two separate shells hinged together by a powerful muscle. Molluscs such as whelks and periwinkles are univalves, and have single shells.

Tests for freshness. Crustaceans: In the lobster, elasticity of the limbs and tail is the best sign of freshness; if it is stale these are limp, and there is an objectionable smell when the flesh is exposed. This limpness, together with a bleached appearance, is a sign of staleness in crabs also. Prawns and shrimps should have no unpleasant smell, and should feel dry and crisp. When stale they are moist and clammy, and have an objectionable smell; stale shrimps smell of ammonia.

Molluscs: Appearance and smell are of first importance. Fresh bivalves either have their shells tightly closed, or the shells close when they are touched; open or gaping shells are signs of staleness. Fresh univalves have firm bodies that recede into the shells when touched. If they are moist, shrunken and soft, with an offensive smell, they must be considered stale and unwholesome.

Purity of shellfish. Oysters and mussels are often bred or fattened in the tidal waters of an estuary, which may be polluted by sewage. In different parts of Britain various regulations cover the cleaning of shellfish. Imported shellfish should be accompanied by a certificate of purity.

Vegetables and fruit

Buying arrangements

Vegetables and fruit may be bought in various ways. In large towns there are markets to which growers send their produce daily, and caterers may buy at those markets. The buyer visits the market early in the morning, chooses his fruit and vegetables, and has them packed in his own transport for delivery to his establishment. The advantages are that the buyer is able to use his own expertise in choosing, goods are fresh, and market prices are paid. On the other hand, the method takes time and also demands expert knowledge and skill. It may be suitable for a very large concern with a number of nearby outlets. More often, goods are bought from a wholesaler.

Another method is to buy direct from the grower, who transports the goods direct to the buyer. The chief advantage here is that the produce is likely to be fresher because it has not gone to the market. Also, prices may be a little lower because there is no middleman, but this does not necessarily follow. Potatoes, seasonal fruits and market-garden produce are often bought in this way. Another regular supplier apart from the grower is usually needed for items not produced by the grower. Also, when a homegrown crop is scarce or expensive the buyer may have to look for a temporary additional supplier, and at times of shortage this is not always easy.

The buyer should make himself familiar with any grading system that is in operation, and should use it in specifying his requirements. In making arrangements for supply, times of delivery are important. Salad and green vegetables are best delivered early enough to allow for their use the same day, but if they arrive before staff come on duty sacks and nets of vegetables may be left out of doors and are liable to be fouled by animals, or otherwise tampered with.

Points concerned with the buying of fruit and vegetables

European Economic Community standards. The EEC market organisation for fresh fruit and vegetables has as one of its features the application of common quality standards to a wide range of items. EEC standards now apply to many fruits and vegetables, including apples, pears, cherries, plums, tomatoes, cucumbers and cauliflowers. Products are graded in classes according to quality. Typically there are three main classes: Extra, Class I and Class II. There is also a Class III, but this is suspended from time to time when there is enough of a product in higher classes to meet consumer demand. Minimum requirements for all classes are prescribed. Other requirements for each class relate to quality and weight or size.

Potatoes

British maincrop potatoes are available from September, and by the following May the crop is usually finished—or the remaining stock has deteriorated. Early potatoes are usually available from late May until August. Potatoes are imported when home-grown maincrop supplies are scarce and in the early spring, when they help to bridge the gap between seasons. British potatoes should conform to size and other standards laid down by the Potato Marketing Board. Stipulations on size vary from season to season. Potatoes should be examined for damage, disease and size, and the batch should be rejected if more than five per cent are below standard, or if there is an excessive amount of soil. The variety of potato should suit the cooking method to be used. Shallow-eyed potatoes are preferable, because there is less waste in preparation and less labour in eyeing. Any tendency to discolour after cooking is undesirable. Some varieties are more prone to this than others, but the kind of soil in which they are grown, and the type of fertiliser used, are also relevant. When potatoes are to be mashed a white, floury texture is looked for but when they are to be fried a firmer, slightly waxy, texture is to be preferred. Some well-known British varieties are listed below:

MAIN CROP. *King Edward:* oval with red markings; shallow eyes; cream flesh; rarely blackens when cooked; slightly floury, but retains shape well. An all-round potato that is suitable for most kinds of cooking.

Majestic: a thick, kidney-shaped potato with a whitish skin, white flesh and shallow eyes; remains fairly whole in cooking until the end of the year; has a slight tendency to discolour after cooking. Very suitable for chipped or sauté potatoes.

Kerr's Pink (available mainly in Scotland): roundish, with pink skin and medium-deep red eyes; creamy-white flesh; some surface sloughing when boiled; floury. Good for mashing.

Maris Piper: Creamy-white flesh of floury texture; rarely discolours after cooking. An increasingly popular all-round potato, good when baked in its jacket or chipped.

EARLY VARIETIES. *Home Guard:* Creamy-white flesh; rarely discolours after cooking. Very good in June, July and August for boiling and salads.

Ulster Sceptre: a white-fleshed variety, and one of the earliest available; average cooking quality. Good for boiling, chips and salad.

Red Craig's Royal: pale cream flesh; close texture; rarely discolours after cooking. Very good from July onwards, and excellent for boiling.

In general, early potatoes have a waxy texture that makes them good for use in salads but unsuitable for mashing.

Potatoes are usually supplied in disposable paper sacks. The Potato Marketing Board requires that all containers shall carry either an identification number or a registered brand name. Advice on buying and help in taking up complaints may be obtained from the Board.

Potatoes may be bought ready-peeled and also ready-chipped. They are treated with preservative to prevent discoloration, and thus need to be rinsed well before use. They should not be stored for more than a day or so. Ready-prepared potatoes are more expensive, but the extra cost has to be weighed against savings in labour and equipment. One disadvantage is that their vitamin C content is likely to be lower than that of freshly-prepared potatoes. Washed potatoes are also available.

Root vegetables

Carrots, turnips and swedes may be obtained either washed or unwashed, and also ready-prepared for the pot. Washed vegetables should always be used within two or three days, since, once the soil has been washed off, most root crops deteriorate fairly rapidly.

Carrots should be well formed and graded (free from forks, chumps and cuts) and of a good orange colour (poor colour indicates poor quality). They should feel firm and crisp, and should break easily and crisply. Towards the end of the season—from March onwards—carrots tend to go woody in the centre.

Turnips should be of medium size; large ones may be coarse and tough, and strong in flavour. They should be heavy in relation to their size; otherwise they are likely to be coarse and woolly.

Swedes are judged in the same way as turnips, and are good between November and March.

Parsnips should be of good size and shape, with no false roots and without excessive rootlets. Texture should be fairly firm, and softness may indicate decay. The head should be examined for canker. Towards the end of the season (say after March) parsnips may become strong and stringy, with an extremely woody centre core. They tend to grow in inconvenient shapes, which may mean a lot of waste in preparation.

Beetroot are available in two varieties—long and round. They should be firm and of a good colour, and should have no legs. They are often bought ready-cooked for immediate use.

Onions are included in the category of root crops in the trade, though botanically they are bulbs. They grow very successfully abroad in hot, dry climates, and these are often preferred to English onions. Spanish onions are of a distinctive type—large and of good quality, with golden-brown skins and a milder flavour than English onions. They are particularly good for salads. Firm, dry onions should always be chosen. Onions showing green tops or root growths, and those that are soft and damp, have lost their skins or have developed more than one bulb should be rejected.

Green vegetables

In this category come cabbage of various kinds, spring greens, broccoli, Brussels sprouts, spinach, runner beans, broad beans and peas. Their first test relates to freshness and colour. They should be a good green, and anything showing signs of yellowing or wilting should be rejected. Cabbages should have firm, hard heads and should be heavy in relation to their size, though this varies with the variety: Dutch cabbage, for example, is heavier for its size than Savoy, and it is also paler in colour. Brussels sprouts should be small, tight and green and should not have blown heads (which, though edible, are poorer in quality and flavour). The curd of cauliflower and broccoli should be close, firm and white, and the surrounding green should be fresh. Spring greens and Brussels sprouts should not be coarse (this is a sign of age), and should not have too many outside leaves.

Runner and French beans should be long, crisp and clean; they should snap easily and crisply. The bean seeds should be immature. Where the seeds are mature or half grown, the pods are likely to be tough and stringy.

Broad beans should be young, since when they are old the outside of the bean is extremely tough. Pods should be long, firm, and well-filled, and free from any sign of the disease black-eye. Broad beans are not always a good buy. If pods are not well filled, the yield of beans in relation to pods is extremely poor.

Peas should be in pods that are green, tender and well filled. Peas should have clear green shells, and should squash easily when they are pinched between the fingers; division into two halves is an indication of age. It is difficult to buy peas at their point of perfection—young, fresh-picked and with nicely-filled pods—but it is worth going to some trouble in an effort to achieve this.

Salad plants and vegetables

Freshness, crispness and a good green colour are the first and most important points to look for in relation to salad plants, and several others should be taken into account in relation to individual species:

Lettuce: the round type is the most common, and is available all the year round, much being grown under glass, and with good supplies coming from Holland. Cos lettuce, in season during the summer, has a long leaf and is very much crisper and more fully-flavoured than round lettuce, but also it can be tough. There are one or two other varieties that are known for their crisp leaves. Lettuce that has bolted, or is near to bolting, should be rejected.

Cucumbers should be dark green, firm and crisp, and should have a dewy look when cut; if they are limp they are stale. Any with a bitter flavour should be the subject of complaint.

Tomatoes: home-grown varieties, together with those from Jersey and Holland, are available during the summer months and early autumn, and tomatoes imported from various countries are on sale all the year round. Firmness of texture is essential in those to be used for salads, but softer tomatoes (which may be either overripe or not fresh) are suitable for cooking and are usually much cheaper. Likewise, those of irregular shape or with slight blemishes may satisfactorily be used for cooking. Small end-of-crop tomatoes are particularly sweet, and are usually cheap.

Fruit

The fruits bought by the caterer may be divided into three groups—apples and pears, citrus fruits and soft fruits.

Apples. The buyer should know the best varieties available at different times of the year for both eating and cooking, and should choose these whenever possible. He should also note when crops have been good, and take advantage by buying more heavily. Some varieties of British apples are:

Bramley's Seedling, the best-known of English cooking apples, and ideal for stewing and, especially, baking. It has a deep green waxy skin, often with an orange-red flush, and it is available from October until June.

Grenadier, an early season cooking apple, round, flattish and with a yellowish-green smooth skin. It is available in August and September.

Cox's Orange Pippin, the finest-flavoured dessert apple. Its colour is variable, but is usually a palish green with an orange to red flush.

Discovery, a popular new apple. It is firm and juicy, and has a bright red skin with yellow streaks.

Worcester Permain, a juicy and sweet early apple. It has a rich red colour with some pale green steaks, and it should be eaten soon after purchase.

Crispin, a recently-introduced variety. It is a large, yellowy-green apple and has a very good flavour.

Laxton's Superb, of Cox parentage but larger and sweeter. It is a later variety.

Tydeman's Early, similar to the Worcester Permain, but redder, rounder and less conical in shape. It is juicy and sweet-scented.

In addition there is a wide variety of imported dessert apples, of which well-known varieties are Golden Delicious and Granny Smith. Apples should have clear skins of good colour and without blemish, and should be of even shape and size. Those that have been kept in cold store sometimes deteriorate inside, and develop conditions known as bitter pit (small areas of soft brown tissue just below the skin), brown heart (patches of soft brown tissue in the centre) and internal breakdown (similar to brown heart, but usually visible on the surface of the apple).

Immaturity in apples is judged by the shade of green in the skin; the darker and deeper the green, the more immature the apple. Immature apples have a poor, undeveloped flavour, and are too hard and starchy for pleasant eating. Over-ripeness in red and green apples may be judged from the ground colour; if it has a yellowish tinge and lacks lustre the fruit will probably have a poor flavour and a soft, mealy texture.

Large apples are better for cooking because less time and waste are involved in their preparation. Dessert apples should be of medium size (about 100 g), since these usually have better texture and flavour than very large ones.

Pears. Well-known varieties of English pears are:

Comice, which has a superb flavour, and sweet, juicy flesh that melts in the mouth.

Conference, which is a good eating pear and is suitable for cooking also.

There are many imported varieties, among which the William, with its soft, juicy flesh, is very popular. The condition of the fruit at the time it is bought is critical, because it is fully ripe for a short time only, and soon begins to decay. When it is fully ripe, a pear is slightly soft around its stem. Over-ripe pears should never be bought, and fully-ripe pears should be bought for immediate consumption only.

Citrus fruits. The main points to note in the judging of citrus fruits are that they should, in general, have thin, smooth skins (though some grapefruit of very good quality have thick skins), and that they should be heavy in relation to their size, which indicates that they contain plenty of juice.

Soft fruits. These should be dry, sound and of good colour, and the berries should be large. Because these delicate fruits are easily squashed by their own weight, they are packed in punnets and baskets in small quantities. Soft fruit should always be bought for immediate use. Since the season is short, the caterer should watch for the time when fruit is at its best and most plentiful, and the price is lowest; his supplier will advise him. A list of fruit and vegetables and the times when they are out of season is given in Table 11.

Groceries and provisions

It is impossible to deal with these commodities in detail here, but some basic facts about the principal commodities are given.

Flour and other farinaceous foods

Flour. Flour may be obtained from the wholesaler or direct from the miller. Most of the flour used in catering is white. When wheat is milled to produce white flour, the bran and germ are sieved out to give a refined product. The bran and wheatgerm contain most of the B vitamins and iron, and so white flours are fortified by the addition of B vitamins and iron. Calcium is also added. The two main classifications of white flour are strong and soft.

Strong flour has a high gluten content. Gluten has the capacity to stretch and to absorb moisture, and to set when it is subjected to a high temperature. Hence, strong flour used for bread-making gives a big yield, a big volume and a light texture. Strong flour is suitable also for batters, for flaky and puff pastry, and for rich fruit cakes, where the gluten web helps to support the fruit throughout the mixture.

Soft flour, which has a high capacity to absorb fat, is suitable for short-crust pastry, biscuits and rich light cakes, where it gives a soft, light texture. Self-raising flour has had a raising agent (*e.g.*, sodium bicarbonate plus a suitable acidic substance such as calcium acid phosphate) added to and thoroughly mixed with it. Some caterers prefer to use plain flour and to add baking powder.

Wholemeal flour contains between 95 and 100 per cent of the wheat grain. Wheatmeal flours are mixtures of white flour, bran and germ in varying amounts, and they contain between 80 and 95 per cent of the wheat grain according to grade. The flavour of brown flour, especially wholemeal, is good, but it does not produce a good rise or an open texture because of the effect of the bran and germ. In cooking, brown flour is often mixed with white to improve the flavour without spoiling the rise.

High-ratio flour is a special kind of cake flour that gives a good yield and a soft texture that melts in the mouth. It is used chiefly in prepared cake mixes.

Unless the caterer is producing a very limited range of goods he should use at least two types of flour, strong and soft (both of which are available in different grades).

Other wheat products. These include semolina and the different pastas (macaroni, spaghetti, vermicelli, lasagne, noodles and others in various shapes).

Semolina is produced during the preliminary stages in the milling process, when the endosperm of the wheat is broken up into smooth nodules before it is ground.

Pasta is made from semolina especially milled for these products, the most suitable wheat being *Tricitum durum*, which has a high protein content and gives a yellow semolina. This, when mixed with the small quantity of water necessary to form a stiff mixture, gives a dough that lacks stretching power. Good pasta products should have a rich yellow colour, and should be hard and translucent, and glassy when broken. When it is boiled in water pasta should swell to twice its size, it should keep its shape and firmness, and it should not become pasty nor disintegrate in the water.

Oats. These are available as either oatmeal or rolled oats. Oatmeal is produced in several grades—coarse, medium, fine and patent. Rolled oats are heat-treated, and in consequence they are more easily and quickly cooked than is oatmeal. The best oats come from Scotland; they have more flavour than do those grown in England. Oats are liable to go rancid or musty if they are kept too long, and they are sometimes infested by the flour moth, *Ephestia kühniella*; the presence of web-like material indicates infestation.

Rice. Most rice sold in this country is polished. This entails the removal of the husk and outer bran layers, and the process involves a considerable loss of vitamin B_{12}, but it is possible to obtain unpolished rice from firms that deal in so-called health foods. Rice is either long-grained (Patna is the best known) or short-grained (as produced in Italy and Carolina). Long-grained rice is suitable for all dishes where each rice-grain should be separate from the rest, as when boiled rice is served with curry or various chicken and lamb dishes. Short-grained rice, which is blunter and more absorbent, is suitable for recipes where it is intended to produce a homogeneous dish—for example, risotto or rice pudding. Parboiled long-grain rice has been steeped in warm water and then boiled for a short time before it is milled. This product keeps well and absorbs more water than does the ordinary variety (the ratio by volume is rice 1, water 2·5, compared with rice 1 and water 2), and the nutrient content is higher because during the heat treatment soluble vitamins of the B complex are transferred from the outer covering of the grain to the endosperm, and thus are not lost when the grain is milled.

Cornflour, custard powder and custard mixes. Cornflour is prepared from maize, a crop originally grown in America, but now cultivated also in Africa, India and Australia, and parts of Europe that have suitably warm climates.

Custard powders consist almost entirely of cornflour, suitably flavoured and coloured. Custard mixes have sugar and milk powder added, so that the only other ingredient needed to make custard is water.

Arrowroot, tapioca and sago. All these foods come from tropical countries. Arrowroot is obtained from the underground stem of the West Indian plant *Maranta arundinacea*. Sago comes from the pith of the sago palm, *Metroxylon sago*, and tapioca from the underground stem of cassava. Both sago and tapioca are heat-treated during manufacture to make them easier to cook.

Pulses, and products derived from them

This group includes peas, beans and lentils, and also the soya bean. Soya beans as such are rarely used, and other pulses in their dried form are much less used than they used to be. However, they are major items in the diets of many Asians and vegetarians.

Dried peas. There are two main types, marrowfat and split. The former is used as a second vegetable, and in soups and stews, while the latter is mainly used in soups and stews. Marrowfats should be square and wrinkled, and of a good, regular shape. Very good marrowfats are grown in this country and in Holland. Peas known as blue, or imperial, are of inferior type.

Beans. These are chiefly of two kinds, butter and haricot, and both are imported.

Lentils. They may be either red or brown, the former being superior, and again both are imported.

All dried pulses deteriorate with age, and become more difficult to soften. Hence there should be a good turnover of stock, so that a new season's produce may be bought as soon as it is available.

Soya flour. This has high food value, and may be used for thickening soups and gravies, and in small proportions mixed with flour for pastries and puddings. It is a useful adjunct to vegetarian diets, but its starch content is low and thus it is not a substitute for wheat flour.

Textured vegetable protein foods

Most of these are derived from the soya bean, although other protein sources could be used. These foods are designed either to extend protein foods, or to take their place as main dishes. In the manufacturing process defatted soya flour, which normally has a protein content of just over 50 per cent, is texturised. The first step is to make the flour into a dough. This is then forced through fine nozzles, and the extruded product is cut into lengths and dried. An alternative method is to use spinning instead of extruding; this gives a superior product that is suitable for use either as a substitute for meat or poultry or as an extender. TVP food may be left unflavoured, or various flavours may be added. The size and texture can be varied according to the nature of the food that it is designed to simulate. Usually associated with savoury dishes, TVP food is being developed also as an extender for fruit.

Manufactured products such as sausages and beefburgers often contain a proportion of TVP food. In catering its use as an extender of meat, poultry or fish in made-up dishes is widespread. The aim is usually to reduce costs while maintaining portion sizes and the nutritional content of the meal.

The Food Standards Committee, in its *Report on Novel Protein Foods*, HMSO, 1974, recommends that the level of substitution for meals in institutions such as hospitals, schools, etc., should not on average exceed 10 parts by weight per 90 parts of meat over a reasonable period, and suggests that various other institutions should follow the same guidelines. The Committee also made recommendations on the nutritional value of novel protein foods based on field beans and soya when they are used as substitutes for meat. The buyer should check whether products comply with these recommendations, which are contained in paragraph 17 of the summary of recommendations.

Canned foods

The kinds of food available in cans include fruit and vegetables, meat, poultry, fish, soups and milk. We shall refer to some of the main points that concern the caterer.

Canning processes. The canning processes used for most foods involve processing times and temperatures that ensure that the foods are sterile. Corned beef, stewed steak and similar items are processed in this way. Some canned meats, however, such as jellied veal and tongue, are not processed at such high temperatures because this would reduce the quality of the product, and there would be considerable shrinkage. Thus the contents may not be sterile, and their shelf life is limited. Other canned meats, such as shoulders and hams of pork, are pasteurised and are perishable. Aseptic canning is a process that has been developed recently; it is designed to give improved quality. In aseptic canning the food and everything connected with the operation is sterile before the start of the process. It is suitable for liquid or semi-liquid foods. Custard, for example, is canned by this method.

Can sizes and contents. For fruit and vegetables size A10 is common in catering; it holds about 4·5 litres, or 2·7 kg, and is packed in cases of six. The drained weight of the contents (as shown on the can, or checked physically) is important when value comparisons are being made. Corned beef is packed in 2·7 kg cans and other sizes. For other meat products 1·8 kg cans are often used. Most cans of such products as stewed steak, casseroles and hamburgers hold about 1·4 kg.

Brand. Canned goods are labelled with the brand name, the manufacturer and other identification marks. In choosing his brands the buyer should make certain that the quality is suitable, sampling as necessary before buying.

Some points to note about canned fruit and vegetables. When canned peas are bought, it should be remembered that those labelled 'garden' are superior to processed peas; the term 'processed' indicates that dried peas have been used. Solid-pack apples are suitable for pies, and irregular fruit pieces (which are sold as such) and fruit crushes (*e.g.*, pineapple crush) are good buys for certain dishes.

Condition of cans. Blown, rusty or damaged cans should not be accepted, and any that become blown during storage, or start to leak, should be rejected.

Shelf life of canned goods. Under ideal conditions canned foods will keep perfectly satisfactorily for very long periods, but in some foods slow chemical changes may take place. Milk may be stored for up to a year; vegetables for two years; canned fish in oil for five years; and sterilised packs of meat for five years. However, in practice a regular yearly turnover is advisable, and this means that any reserve stocks of canned food should be brought forward and replaced at not more than yearly intervals.

Dried and candied fruit

There are the following kinds of dried fruit: currants, sultanas, raisins, dates, figs, peaches, pears, apricots, apple rings and prunes. Size is important in choosing these fruits, particularly in the case of currants, raisins, apricots and prunes, which should not be too small. Prunes are graded according to size, as indicated by the number of pieces of fruit to the kilogram—for example, sixty-six for large fruit and 154 for small. Dates used for cooking are pitted (stoned), and may be bought ready chopped. Pitted prunes are obtainable, but they are not widely used. Raisins may be either stoneless or stoned, the latter being larger and of a particularly good flavour. Occasionally dried fruits, particularly apricots, are found to be infested with insects; such fruit should be rejected, as should any that are affected by mould or fermentation. Candied fruit is preserved by successive immersions in sugar syrup. Those most commonly used by caterers are glacé cherries and the candied peel of citrus fruits.

Tea

The caterer is able to choose from many different blends and varieties of tea, and it is necessary to find one that is suited to the local water, his clients' taste and the method of making. We shall consider mainly the relationship between the kind of pack, the type of tea and the method of making tea. Individual tea bags are used for convenience when individual pots or cups of tea are to be served; this helps to give good stock and portion control and a standard strength of brew. It also makes for easy disposal of tea leaves. However, this is the most expensive way of buying, and the quality of tea used in these bags does not appeal to the connoisseur. Where tea is to be brewed in bulk in large pots or urns, a fine-leaf tea that will give a quick brew is needed. This may be bought either in bulk or in packs containing enough to brew 4·5 litres. The pre-packed tea is dearer than bulk (though cheaper than individual tea bags), but has the advantages mentioned previously. When loose tea is brewed in small pots the buyer should choose a type with a larger leaf, such as Broken Orange Pekoe. The prices of different qualities of tea do not vary enough to affect materially the cost per cup, and the caterer may well consider it worth his while to buy at the higher end of the market. Several blends should be sampled before any decision is made. Tea will readily pick up flavours from other commodities, and so large stocks should not be held unless storage facilities are suitable. It should not be stored for longer than a year even under the best conditions, or the flavour will deteriorate.

Coffee

Coffee may be bought as beans (roasted or unroasted), ground (usually vacuum-packed to preserve flavour and aroma), or instant (made from liquid coffee that has been reduced to powder or granules by dehydration or freeze-drying). The flavour and aroma of coffee varies according to the country of origin and the degree of roasting. Kenya coffee, for example, has a sharp flavour and good aroma, and Mysore coffee has a very mellow flavour. Coffee with a high roast—which darkens its colour—is used for after-dinner, while coffee with a light roast—which gives a milder flavour—is suitable for breakfast. Since the flavour and aroma of coffee are extremely volatile, the best coffee is produced when the bean is freshly roasted and ground, and ideally it should be ground immediately before use. But the average caterer, if he uses ground coffee, is more likely to buy vacuum-packed coffee for its convenience. This should not be held in store for longer than sixteen weeks, after which, even though it be vacuum-packed, the flavour will start to deteriorate and become bitter.

A mixture of coffee and chicory (known as French coffee) is more economical than pure coffee, not only because the price is lower but also because a smaller amount is needed. It is unsuitable for black coffee, and needs more milk than does pure coffee, and the chicory flavour is not acceptable to everyone.

Coffee may be bought in small bags for individual cups; the contents of the bags may be ground coffee, or a mixture of ground and instant. Instant coffee is very widely used by caterers, partly for convenience and partly because as a rule it is much cheaper. Individual sachets of instant coffee are often bought, especially when clients are issued with ingredients and provided with facilities for making it themselves. Where it is necessary to serve large numbers in a short time and using the minimum amount of labour, packs of disposable cups each containing a suitable quantity of instant coffee may be the most suitable method. Instant coffee is sold in airtight tins or jars, and should not be held in store for longer than a year, since after this the flavour begins to deteriorate.

Sugar, preserves and syrup

Sugar. Kinds of sugar are as follows: granulated, caster (for certain cooking purposes and for table use), cube (for table use for tea), demerara (brown sugar suitable for coffee), soft brown (for cooking), icing, preserving, and coffee crystals (for serving with coffee). Individual packs of granulated and demerara sugar are available, and individually-wrapped cube sugar is often used for reasons of hygiene.

Preserves. In jams and marmalades both the percentage and the quality of fruit are significant. Buyers should check specifications for fruit content and sample as necessary before choosing a brand. A higher-quality product is needed for table use than for cooking.

Golden syrup and treacle. The quality of these is usually consistent.

Fats and oils

Butter. Points to be considered are: flavour, texture, country of origin, nutritional value and salt content. Butters from different countries have particular characteristics. For example, New Zealand butter has a distinctive flavour, a firm texture, is usually well salted and has a high vitamin A content. Danish butter is known for its mild flavour, has a fairly soft texture and is lightly salted. A texture that allows easy spreading may be important; for other purposes a harder texture that can be portioned easily may be preferable. Individually-wrapped portions of butter are available.

Margarine. The grade and type bought depends upon whether margarine is for table use, when good flavour and a soft, creamy texture are important, or for cooking, when texture requirements will vary. A hard margarine is needed for flaky and puff pastry, and a softer one for cakes and puddings. Although all margarine sold on the retail market is fortified with vitamins A and D, unfortified margarine is available to the caterer, but on nutritional grounds the buyer should always choose fortified margarine.

Lard and cooking fat. The major consideration in choosing between lard and cooking fat for pastry-making and shallow frying, or for other cooking purposes, is likely to be price.

Cooking oil. This is used chiefly for deep-fat frying, and samples should be tested for this purpose before a choice is made. An important point to be taken into account when comparing the prices of various products is the amount of oil lost during a standard cooking process, such as frying a given weight of chipped potatoes. Frying oils should have a good resistance to the breakdown that inevitably occurs to some extent during repeated frying processes.

Bacon

Two types are available, smoked and green (unsmoked). Smoked bacon is more expensive than green, and is used for breakfasts rather than for general cooking. Bacon may be bought by the side, the piece or sliced, though buying by the side is not common. Apart from sides, bacon is often vacuum-packed in film to keep it in good condition. Danish and Irish bacon are widely sold in this country as well as British, and country of origin should be specified when orders are placed. A great deal of expertise is needed in the marketing of bacon, and the supplier should be carefully chosen. On delivery, bacon should be examined to check that it is not slimy or out of condition, and also that it is not excessively fat.

Cheese

Many types are available today, both British and European, and Canada, New Zealand and Ireland are particularly well known for their Cheddar-style cheese. Cheddar is most generally used for cooking, but Lancashire is especially good for toasting because it melts quickly. Where a cheese course appears regularly on the menu a selection should be bought, ranging in flavour from mild (for example, Caerphilly) to strong (for example, Stilton or Danish Blue). Most cheeses are cured by being left to mature with salt, and during this time they develop their characteristic flavours. But this does not apply to cream cheese, or cottage cheese (a low-fat variety). Both are perishable, and should be kept in a refrigerator for a few days only.

Cheese is produced in rindless blocks as well as in traditional form. When whole cheeses are bought they should be examined to see that they are without cracks, not greasy and of a good shape. A swollen crown indicates the development of gases within.

Eggs

The quality of eggs is determined chiefly by their freshness, and one way of judging this is to measure the size of the air cell within the egg. This is done by candling; the egg is examined against a light, and a device for measuring the air cell is used. Under EEC regulations eggs are graded for quality in three classes, A, B and C, and, if they meet fairly stringent conditions, some Class A eggs may be described as 'Extra'. For Class A the air cell must not exceed 6 mm in depth, the shell and membrane must be normal, clean and intact, the white must be clear, translucent and of a gelatinous consistency, and there are other stipulations. For Class B the shell and membrane must be normal and intact, the air cell must not exceed 9 mm in depth, the white must be clear and translucent and there are other stipulations. Class C includes all eggs that do not qualify for Classes A or B, but are suitable for the manufacture of foods for human consumption. They may be visibly cracked. Eggs in Classes A and B are also graded into seven weight ranges, as follows:

Grade 1: 70g or over
Grade 2: 65 g and under 70 g
Grade 3: 60 g and under 65g
Grade 4: 55 g and under 60 g
Grade 5: 50 g and under 55 g
Grade 6: 45 g and under 50 g
Grade 7: under 45 g.

Class C eggs need not be weight-graded. All eggs that do not fall into Classes A, B or C are classed as 'industrial eggs', and may not be used for human consumption in any form.

Milk powders, other milk products and non-dairy products

Milk powder is widely used by caterers as an alternative to liquid milk, and it is usually cheaper. The following types are available: full-cream milk powder (containing not less than twenty-six per cent of milk fat); filled milk powder (butterfat removed, and replaced with vegetable fat); skimmed milk powder. Skimmed milk powder has a long shelf life, but milk products containing fat should not be kept for longer than three months, after which the fat may go rancid.

Other milk products include: yogurt (obtainable in large catering packs); ice-cream; instant desserts with milk powder bases; and topping mixes.

Non-dairy products intended to take the place of milk or cream include: whiteners and creamers intended for tea or coffee, and available either in bulk or in individual portions; and non-dairy topping mixes.

Dehydrated vegetables

These are prepared by freeze-drying, and are used by the caterer either for convenience or when fresh vegetables are scarce, of poor quality or expensive. Potato powder and dehydrated onions are widely used, but a whole range of root vegetables, peas, runner beans and cabbage is on the market, and used in many manufactured dishes. The buyer should look for the following:

1. Flavour. This is particularly important with potatoes, where the consumer will notice quite subtle differences.
2. Yield when rehydrated, which should be considered in relation to price.
3. Colour when cooked.
4. Qualities of toughness or tenderness. This applies especially to carrots and runner beans.

Catering mixes and composite packs

Mixes for pastries, puddings, cakes and bread are standard commodities used by caterers. Where an electric mixer is available, the time and labour saved may be associated as much with weighing and storekeeping as with actual mixing. The principal reasons for using them are:

(a) Minimal cooking skills are needed.
(b) The resultant product is standard.
(c) The yield is standard.

The following are some of the packaged desserts available: caramel crême, trifles and instant dessert powders. Many of them have quick-setting properties, which means that they may be served very soon after they have been mixed. This may be a great convenience, and a minimum amount of labour and skill is needed. Instant desserts often have a special appeal to children. Before they are bought, the ingredients and nutritional values of similar products should be compared, and they should also be compared with traditional recipes.

Manufactured prepared frozen foods

These may be bought either direct from a manufacturer or from wholesale firms that have suitable facilities for handling them. The buyer is well advised to sample at least some of a manufacturer's products before he agrees to buy them. In addition to testing for taste, appearance and texture, he should look at such aspects as meat or fruit content and food value. (The supplier will provide information.) In the case of chipped potatoes the cooked yield and the amount of oil they absorb during cooking are important. All such foods should be in a completely frozen state when they are delivered.

Some general points about buying

As well as watching market trends, the buyer must study changes in catering methods and consumer tastes, which may suggest changes in his buying pattern. When the market moves against a particular product, he should consider whether there is a cheaper acceptable alternative. It is essential to maintain good personal relationships with suppliers, and a lot is to be learned from the suppliers' expertise. Considerable shrewdness and negotiating skills are needed.

The buyer should keep himself informed about tariffs, levies and subsidies as they affect food prices, and also about grading and classification systems for various foods, for example, meat, fruit and vegetables.

TABLE 10: When to buy fish

Bass	January–March; June–December
Bloater	September–December
Bream	January–March; June–December
Brill	All the year
Buckling	April–November
Cockles	June
Cod	January–May, July, August, November and December
Coley	All the year
Conger Eel	March–October
Crab	January–October
Crawfish	May–September
Crayfish	January and February; May–August
Dab	September–December
Eel	All the year
Flounder	All the year
Grayling	September–December
Gudgeon	July–November
Gurnet	October–July
Haddock	All the year
Hake	November–August
Halibut	All the year
Herring	April–November
Huss	As for cod
Kipper	All the year
Ling	May–July; September–December
Lobster	March–October
Mackerel	December–July
Mullet	All the year
Mussels	April and May; July–September
Oysters	January–April; September–December
Pilchards	As for herring
Plaice	All the year

TABLE 10 continued

Prawns	All the year
Redfish	June–December
Salmon	March–September
Salmon, smoked	All the year
Salmon trout	February–August
Sardines	As for herring
Scallops	October–April
Scampi	All the year
Skate	August–April
Smelts	October–May
Sole, Dover	All the year
Sole, lemon	All the year
Sole, Torbay	All the year
Sprats	February and March; October–December
Sturgeon	January–March; July–September
Tench	October
Trout	March–September
Turbot	All the year
Whelks	April and May
Whitebait	January–September
Whiting	All the year

TABLE 11: Fruit and vegetables: times when they are out of season

Apples, dessert	Never
cooking	June and July
Pears	Never
Oranges	Never
Lemons	Never
Grapefruit	Never
Peaches	March, April, May and November
Plums (English)	October to June
Soft fruit	October to April
Bananas	Never
Rhubarb	September to December
Tomatoes	Never
Melons	November to March
Tangerines, etc.	February to September
Grapes	Never
Cucumbers	Never
Cress	Never
Lettuce	Never
Radishes	November to March
Mushrooms	Never
New potatoes	September to January
Old potatoes	June and July
Cabbages	Never
Brussels sprouts	March to July

TABLE 11 continued

Carrots	Never
Onions	Never
Leeks	April to June
Beans, French and runner	November to May
Celery	March to June
Peas	October to April
Cauliflower and broccoli	Never

TABLE 12: A guide to some typical pack sizes for groceries, dairy foods, etc.

Bacon, pre-packed sliced	1 × 2 kg
	2 × 2 kg
	10 × 2 kg
	4 × 1·3 kg
Butter	12·5 kg
	25·0 kg
Canned goods:	
corned beef	6 × 1·4 kg
	6 × 2·5 kg
	6 × 2·7 kg
fruits, vegetables	6 × A10
	6 × A6
	6 × 3·0 kg
fruit pie fillings	6 × A10
beans, baked	6 × 2·7 kg
meat products and pie fillings	6 × 1·3 kg
	12 × 1·3 kg
	4 × 1·5 kg
	6 × 2·5 kg
pork luncheon meat	6 × 900 g
	12 × 900 g
	6 × 1·8 kg
Cereals (ground rice, barley, rice, etc.)	12·5 kg
Cheeses:	
whole	27·0 kg, 18·0 kg, etc.
rindless blocks	20·0 kg
	18·0 kg
pre-packed rindless	2·25 kg
	4·5 kg
Coffee:	
ground, in tins	3·0 kg
instant	2 × 700 g
	4 × 700 g
Cornflakes	7·0 kg
Cornflour, custard powder	4 × 3·5 kg
	7·0 kg

TABLE 12 continued

Cooking oil	4 × 4 litres
	4 × 5 litres
	20 litres
Dehydrated vegetables	2·3 kg
Dessert mixes, mousses, trifles, etc.	25-portion yield per pack
Eggs	180
	360
Flour	32·0 kg
Fruit:	
dried, small	3·0 kg
prunes	12·5 kg
Lard, cooking fat	12·5 kg
Margarine	6 × 1·8 kg
	24 × 225 g
	28 × 225 g
	12·5 kg
Milk powder	4 × 3·0 kg
	12·5 kg
	25·0 kg
Pasta products	3·5 kg
	12·5 kg
Preserves	3·0 kg
	12·5 kg
Pudding and pastry mixes	4 × 3·0 kg
	12·5 kg
Pulses, dried	3·0 kg
Sugar	2 × 3·0 kg
	25·0 kg
Soups, packet	2·5 kg
	3·0 kg
	6 × 5-litre yield
	8 × 5-litre yield
Syrup, treacle	4 × 7·25 kg
Tea	2 × 1·4 kg
	4 × 1·4 kg
	13·5 kg
Tea bags:	
individual	400
to brew 2·25 litres	100
Textured vegetable protein food (TVP)	5 × 1·0 kg
	8 × 1·0 kg
	4 × 3·5 kg
Fruit and vegetables	
apples	13·5 kg
bananas	12·0 kg
beetroot	12·0 kg
cabbage	13·5 kg
carrots	12·0 kg
onions	20·0 kg
	23·5 kg

TABLE 12 continued

oranges	88 to 138 per box, depending upon size of fruit
parsnips	12·0 kg
potatoes	25·0 kg
potatoes, peeled or peeled and chipped	13·0 kg
salads, prepared	2·25 kg
tomatoes	6·0 or 5·5 kg
Frozen foods	
chipped potatoes	13·0 kg
desserts	4 trays per pack (weights in trays range from 560 g to 1·4 kg, according to product)
	6 trays per pack (weights range from 567 g to 1·05 kg according to product)
entrées	4 trays per pack (weights in trays range from 850 g to 1·7 kg, according to product)
	6 trays per pack (weights around 935 g)
vegetables	12 × 1·0 kg
	4 × 2·25 kg
	9·0 kg

Note: Some weights in this table have been converted and rounded off from Imperial weights.

Chapter 20

Planning meals

It is difficult to say which is more important to the production of top-quality meals—good cooking or careful planning. The two are closely linked: good planning enables a cook to exhibit his skills, but no amount of careful planning will redeem bad cooking. On the other hand, it is possible for a meal that is not well planned to be tolerable if it is well cooked. Cooking is a craft that cannot be learned from textbooks alone, for a considerable amount of practice is needed before the necessary manipulative skills can be acquired. Also, aptitude and the possession of certain innate qualities—including artistic ability—are needed.

Planning meals is almost entirely a mental exercise, involving both nutritional and psychological elements as well as practical considerations. A good knowledge of cooking is necessary, as are flair and imagination. But sound planning decisions must be based upon a wide appreciation of many contributory factors.

In the home it is usual for meals to be planned ahead in detail for not more than two or three days. The needs of a particular household are well known, so that planning is not complicated and it is not often committed to paper. In a catering establishment, however, formal forward planning is essential. Orders must be sent to suppliers in good time to ensure that adequate supplies are delivered when they are needed. The larger the catering concern the more important this is, because supplies in large quantities—particularly of some items—are not always available at short notice, and suppliers work to delivery programmes that cannot easily be altered. Although meals must be planned ahead and orders placed in advance, they should be adjusted from day to day if necessary. In some organisations, where demand fluctuates considerably, daily adjustment is essential. But the main requirements should be ordered several days in advance. It is usually found to be best, for both convenience and the balance of menus as a whole, to plan not less than one week's menu at one time, and caterers often plan for several weeks ahead, making any day-to-day alterations as needed. For example, when the prices of seasonal fruits such as strawberries or raspberries suddenly drop, the caterer will adapt his menu to include them, or he may take advantage of a supplier's special offer.

Planning a menu for an establishment serving one meal a day and offering no choice is comparatively simple, and very different from the complicated plans necessary in an establishment such as a large hospital, which caters not only for patients but also for nurses by day and night, doctors and other staff. The intricacies of the system make it even more important to plan ahead, and to accept that minor day-to-day adjustments according to circumstance will be necessary. Where menus offer a choice of several dishes for two or more courses, planning is not always so complicated as it might appear at first sight. The caterer usually works to a standard pattern, offering 'dishes of the day', which are varied daily, with a number of standard items that are not varied to any great extent. When an experienced caterer plans a menu, he takes into account all the various factors involved without conscious effort, because they form part of his background knowledge. But newcomers to the business need to study them carefully.

Nutritional considerations

In deciding whether meals are satisfactory from a nutritional point of view, not only individual meals but also all meals to be served during the day, and over a longer period (say a week or a month), must be considered. In Britain most people have either two or three main meals a day, plus other light refreshments, and the aim in planning main meals is to ensure that they contain the necessary nutrients and meet the energy requirements of the consumers. Also, account should be taken of the meal's fibre content. There are several guidelines that may be used in planning menus. The simplest consists of lists of basic foods containing the essential nutrients for a day or a longer period, which are then worked into the menu. Basic foods listed for the day are sometimes known as 'tray foods', because they are easily assembled on a tray to demonstrate to students daily nutritional needs. The Department of Health and Social Security provides lists of basic foods and quantities to cover a period of a week as guidelines for those responsible for catering in homes for the elderly and community homes for children. A list of tray foods taken from the *Second Book of Food and Nutrition*, Mathews & Wells, 1976, is given in Appendix 3.1, and DHSS suggested quantities appear in Appendix 3.2 and Appendix 3.3.

When a catering establishment provides only one meal a day, it is still appropriate to use a basic list of foods, but the principle of providing a certain proportion of the client's daily nutritional needs is usually borne in mind. The principle is very familiar so far as school catering is concerned, and it has been followed for many years by the Department of Education and Science. For example, in 1966 DES Circular 3/66 gave a list of basic foods and quantities intended to give balanced meals and to provide about one-third of the day's requirements for energy and nutrients (see Appendix 3.4). A report entitled *Nutrition in Schools, Report of the Working Party on the Nutritional Aspects of School Meals* (HMSO, 1975) gives an unquantified list of 'some good sources of essential minerals and vitamins' and a suggested pattern of main dishes showing size of portion and frequency of serving (see Appendix 3.5 and Appendix 3.6). The Working Party (whose principal recommendations were accepted by the Secretary of State for Education and Science at a much later date) said that: 'the 1965 standards for energy and protein content of the school dinner should remain unchanged; the edible portion of the food purchased should provide as before 880 kilocalories (3·68 MJ) of energy and 29 grams of protein for the average meal . . . The average school dinner on the plate should aim to provide at minimum one third of the recommended daily intake of energy and between one third and one half of the recommended daily intake of protein.'

The 'daily intakes' to which the report refers are those given in *Recommended Intakes of Nutrients for the United Kingdom, Reports on Public Health and Medical Subjects*, No. 120, HMSO, 1969. Table 1 of this report is reproduced in Appendix 3.7. These recommendations may be used as guides for caterers and dietitians when planning meals for groups of healthy individuals. With these recommendations as a guide and using tables of food values (as published in McCance & Widdowson, *The Composition of Foods*, HMSO, 1978) the caterer can draw up his own list of basic foods, with quantities, for use in planning meals. He might, for example, produce a suitable list of basic foods for vegetarians.

In the case of main meals, the provision of protein is usually the first consideration, and the rest of the meal is planned round that. Traditionally meat, poultry, fish, and to a lesser extent cheese and eggs, have constituted the main protein dish, but emphasis is now being placed upon vegetable protein either as an extender for animal protein or as a dish in its own right. Pulses and nuts are well known as good sources of protein and are suitable for use in main dishes. The energy value of a meal depends partly upon quantity but also upon the nature of the foods included in the menu, as is seen when one looks at the following two meals.

Meal 1 Grilled fish, tomatoes, new potatoes.

Fresh fruit, yogurt.

Meal 2 Roast beef, Yorkshire pudding, peas, baked potatoes.
Fruit pie, cream.

The energy value of the second meal is likely to be at least double that of the first if normal amounts of each are eaten because of:

(a) the amount of fat present in the meat, the Yorkshire pudding, the baked potatoes, the pastry of the pie and the cream;
(b) the higher energy value of peas compared with tomatoes;
(c) the flour present in the pastry.

It is useful to bear in mind that fat has rather more than twice the energy value of protein or carbohydrate.

As well as nutrients and energy value, fibre is needed in the diet. Fibrous foods include fruit, vegetables, wholemeal bread and bran. Drinking water should be freely available. Reference should also be made to the need to avoid excesses of certain foods for health reasons. There is a widely-held medical opinion that fat in the diet should not contribute more than 35 per cent of total energy, and excessive sugar consumption should be avoided on the grounds that sugar provides only 'empty kiloJoules'.

The extent of the caterer's responsibility for meeting his clients' nutritional needs varies with the circumstances. In establishments with permanent residents—for example, children's and old people's homes—the residents depend almost entirely upon the caterer for their food, and hence his responsibility is greater than if he were catering for a factory canteen providing just five meals a week. When a choice is offered, it is up to the client in either residential or non-residential establishments to choose a well-balanced meal that suits him, and it is up to the caterer to see that the selection available enables him to do this.

Variety

A varied diet is important both psychologically and nutritionally, and it is not difficult to understand the psychological reasons. A constant diet of even a person's favourite food would eventually lose its attraction. In the home, where meals are planned to please a few people only, variety is less important than it is in an institution, where it is unlikely that everything served will always be liked by everyone. As wide a variety as possible is important to ensure that even the most difficult individual will from time to time find something he really likes on the menu. However, this point is rather less important when a choice of dishes is offered.

From the nutritional aspect, a varied diet helps to ensure that all constituents necessary for health and growth are present. Where children are concerned, variety is of long-term nutritional significance also. Unless they acquire a wide knowledge of different foods at an early age, their diets in later life may be unduly restricted, and hence detrimental to adequate nutrition.

Variety should be applied to the planning of menus in its broadest sense. It covers cooking methods, choice of dishes and their accompaniments, textures, and the make-up of meals for a day, a week and a month. For example, the same food should not be repeated in the same meal: tomatoes should not be served as soup and then as vegetables; if pastry is served as a *vol au vent* in one course, it should not appear again later in the meal as fruit pie. In the case of a *table d'hôte* menu, no main dish or dessert should be repeated during the same week. Obviously it is not possible or desirable to extend this principle indefinitely, but little if any repetition need occur over a period of a month. When menus and dishes are eventually repeated, it should not be on the same day of the week.

Another point to be considered is variety in the types of food chosen. In the case of meat one may choose between various cuts of beef, mutton, lamb, pork, bacon and ham, and also there are manufactured products such as sausage and salami, and different kinds of offal including liver, kidney, trip, tongue, heart and sweetbreads. Where fresh fruit and vegetables are concerned, variety may be provided even in winter by the use of imported foods, and, of course, canned, dehydrated and frozen fruit and vegetables are always available. Even so, one of the most pleasing ways of achieving variety is to see that menus reflect the season of the year by serving various foods often when they are at the height of their seasons.

Methods of cooking and recipes are other means by which variety may be achieved. In order to use these ways effectively, the manager must have a wide knowledge of cookery, and it helps to have a reference system rather than to rely entirely upon memory. The system may take the form of an indexed recipe book giving quantities of ingredients needed for specific numbers such as 10, 50 and 100. Alternatively a recipe card system may be used. A specimen recipe card is shown in Figure 63. Some nutritional details may well be added to the recipe—for example, energy content per portion. This system is very flexible, since cards are easily added or withdrawn, and moreover it is easily made accessible for use by cooking staff.

Colour

It is well known that food appeals to the senses of smell, taste and sight, and in doing so stimulates the flow of saliva, which in turn aids swallowing and promotes the initial flow of gastric juice that prepares the stomach to receive food. The effect on the organs of smell and taste depends upon the type of food chosen, the recipe and the cooking method. The appeal to the eye is associated with the finish of the dish and the method of service; colour too plays an important part. A wealth of natural colour is available in food, and it can be used effectively to make meals attractive through contrast. Meals and courses all of one colour are to be avoided, as in the following example: steamed fish, white sauce, mashed potatoes and artichokes. Garnishes may be used to add colour; the vivid green of parsley is one of the simplest and most commonly used, either chopped or in sprigs. It is interesting to note, however, that parsley is not popular abroad. In Sweden, for instance, dill is used to garnish potatoes in place of the parsley that would be used in Britain. Tomatoes, lemons, mushrooms, green peas, paprika and red or green peppers are other easily-handled and effective garnishes, while vegetables cut into fancy shapes, truffles, pickled walnuts and shrimps are examples of more elaborate or more expensive garnishes. Decorations added to sweet dishes to give colour include cherries, crystallised flowers (violets, rose petals and primroses), grated chocolate and nuts. It is usually held that in planning a complete meal the colours throughout should be taken into account, but, since the client does not see a formal meal as a whole, it is the make-up of each course that is really important. Colours should be bright and fresh and appropriate to the dish, which they generally are if natural ingredients are used. It is only with artificial ingredients that distaste may be aroused because the food may appear unnatural, and consequently unattractive. To avoid garishness, artificial colouring for desserts and icings should be used sparingly. Colours should contrast or blend, and not clash with each other. Natural colours rarely clash, but in a few cases they do, as with tomatoes and beetroot. Garnishes to be used should be specified when meals are planned, and supplies ordered accordingly.

Season

Reference has already been made to the use of foods in season to give variety, and there are other reasons for doing this. When they are cheapest, they are also at their best. And some foods, such as game, may only be bought when they are in season. One of the disadvantages of menus based mainly on frozen and convenience foods is that they are not readily adaptable to the use of foods in season.

Menus should be seasonable in other senses. During the summer one expects to eat lighter meals, with more salads and generally lighter dishes, and during the winter months one expects rather heavier dishes, with more hot items. Traditional times for serving special dishes, such as pancake day, should not be overlooked, especially when the clients are children.

Delivery arrangements

Frequent deliveries of perishable goods are usual for most catering establishments, except where they are remote from the main delivery routes, but these deliveries fit into a carefully-planned pattern. Deliveries at weekends, except in the case of milk, are rare. The capacity of refrigerators is usually limited to the amounts of perishable foods needed for two or three days at most, so that when menus are planned account must be taken of delivery arrangements for perishable foods. Problems may easily arise at weekends and on Mondays unless the menu planner takes care.

Preparation and skill involved

The time needed to prepare dishes varies considerably. Consider, for example, the preparation of vegetables and fruit. Cabbage, if shredded by machine, is probably one of the quickest to prepare, while runner beans—if prepared by hand—and green peas take longest. Sweets containing fresh fruit also take a great deal of time to prepare. The topping and tailing of gooseberries and the stringing of currants are especially lengthy operations, and, even when a machine is used, the peeling of apples takes a considerable time, too. On the other hand, plums and dried fruit take practically no time at all to prepare.

The work described so far affects the general helpers; the time taken by cooking staff to prepare and cook different dishes varies widely also. To make a rice pudding takes very little time or skill, compared, for instance, with the preparation and cooking of pancakes, or meat or fruit pies. The caterer must appreciate these points when he plans menus to ensure that preparation work is evenly balanced from day to day according to the number and skills of staff available for duty. Periods of overwork and underactivity are both to be avoided, and this applies also to the use of chef skills. Because the number of staff on duty is usually the minimum on Sundays, it is often the practice to simplify to allow for this. Where student residents are concerned a more radical approach is to require them to provide some meals for themselves; in some cases the necessary ingredients are issued to them.

It helps the caterer to appreciate relative workloads if he keeps notes of times taken to perform various tasks for given numbers of portions, such as the preparation of potatoes or the making of pastry.

Information of this kind for different dishes may be recorded on recipe cards.

When considering the amount of preparation work involved in a given menu, it is important to realise that, except for items that are to be served cold, all foods should be cooked on the day on which they are to be eaten, and as near to the mealtime as possible. Meat and poultry in particular, for food hygiene reasons, should not be cooked in advance (see Chapter 23). Generally speaking, the quality of food is better when it has been freshly cooked. Also, vegetables should be freshly prepared in order to conserve their nutrients—especially the vitamin C in green vegetables and potatoes.

Use of equipment

In the planning of menus to make the most effective use of available equipment, the practice for large-scale cooking is the opposite to that for home cooking. In the latter it is sensible to cook as many different dishes as possible in the oven when it is on, or, if it does not have to be used, to cook everything on top and thus to save fuel. In catering kitchens, however, as we saw in Chapter 14, it would be extravagant to install equipment on the assumption that the steaming, boiling and baking facilities should each be adequate for a complete meal. Thus it is necessary to ensure that the chosen meal does not overload any one type of equipment. The following menus illustrate the point.

Example 1: All food cooked in boilers:
Stew, boiled potatoes, boiled carrots;
Milk pudding or custard and stewed fruit.

Example 2: All food cooked in ovens:
Roast beef, Yorkshire pudding, roast potatoes, roast parsnips;
Baked egg custard.

Example 3: All foods, except gravy and sauce, cooked in steamers:
Steamed meat roll, steamed potatoes, steamed carrots;
Steamed fruit pudding.

Texture of foods

Meals should be planned to provide a variety of textures, including crisp and chewy foods. These are necessary to exercise the teeth and jaws, and they help to keep the mouth in a healthy condition. Children have a special need for such foods at a time when their teeth and jaws are developing, though they sometimes show a marked disinclination to chew pieces of meat. Nevertheless, it is a part of their education to learn to do this. Young children often enjoy crisp foods that are easy to handle, such as pieces of apple or raw carrot. Adults usually expect some chewing exercise in their meals, an exception being the very old, who may find mastication difficult, and also the successful manipulation of crisp or chewy foods. In such cases it may be necessary to provide finely-divided food to ensure adequate nourishment. (However, the possibility that teeth or dentures may need attention should be considered, and where appropriate tactful advice should be given.)

Suitability of meals to groups of consumers and people with special needs

Age, sex and occupation are the main factors affecting the choice of suitable foods for groups of consumers. Children should be encouraged to develop catholic palates at an early age by the introduction of a very wide range of foods, and if this can be done successfully there are not necessarily any great differences between menus for children and those for adults. However, there are a few special points to be considered. First, as a rule very young children prefer simple dishes that are not highly seasoned. Second, children's needs for nutrients and energy are high in proportion to their body weight compared with those of adults, but their stomachs are comparatively small. It follows that their meals should not be too bulky. Bread, milk, cheese, meat, fish, liver, eggs, fruit, green vegetables and potatoes are good foods to include in their diet.

At adolescence the need for nutrients is particularly great, and appetites are often very large. It is important that the meals provided should be big enough to satisfy appetites, and that they should have a high nutritional value. Adolescents are great followers of fashion in food as in other matters, so the caterer must take account of current food fashions if meals are to be acceptable to this group. Apart from any question of fashion, it is well known that certain types of dish appeal especially to younger people—fish fingers, sausages and baked beans are good examples.

Meals for old people need especial care. Old people lead less active lives, and their metabolic rates are lower than those of younger people; it follows that their energy needs are considerably smaller. Meals should be easy to digest, and should provide adequate amounts of protein, vitamins and minerals without containing too much fat and carbohydrate.

When he considers the sex of the person to be fed in relation to the suitability of the menu, the manager should realise that personal preferences and energy needs are often associated. Hence women will often choose lighter types of meal and show a preference for salads and fruit, while men, whose calorie needs are significantly greater than those of women, often choose foods with high energy values—pies, crumbles and the like. However, this is not always so, especially where the middle-aged are concerned. Men of this age are often conscious that they need less energy-giving food than they did when they were younger, and are well aware of the health risks of obesity. In consequence, a fair proportion of middle-aged men tend to choose lighter meals.

With regard to occupation, it is mainly a question of meeting the different energy needs for different levels of activity, but one other point must be borne in mind—digestive tolerance. The agricultural worker, who lives a healthy outdoor life, has the proverbial appetite that makes him say, 'I could eat a horse', whereas the city dweller who leads a physically inactive life at a desk and does work that may involve nervous strain, may need food that is not only designed to stimulate his appetite, but is also easily digested.

It is very easy for the caterer to assume that with his specialised knowledge he knows best how to plan his menus, and from many points of view this is true. Nevertheless, it is fundamental that he should take into account the tastes and wishes of those for whom he is catering. The usual means of communication between caterer and client is a representative committee of workpeople, students, pupils or residents as appropriate, through which community views are expressed. So far as new dishes are concerned, reactions may be obtained from tasting panels before they are featured on the menu.

As well as studying his clients' tastes, the dedicated caterer will wish to influence them. He hopes to extend their knowledge of food, and to offer them opportunities to appreciate new foods and dishes as they come on to the market or into the caterer's repertoire. He may achieve this by personal influence and recommendation, or by advance notices designed to arouse interest. In schools he may seek the co-operation of teaching staff, who will often talk encouragingly to young pupils about new dishes on the menu..

Among any sizable group to be catered for there will be some with special needs. Some may have medical conditions—diabetes, coeliac disease or obesity. Others may have dietary needs associated with religion, conscience or a particular way of life. In addition to vegetarians (who do not eat flesh foods) it may be necessary to cater for vegans, who eat no food of animal origin. People with special needs are more easily catered for where the menu offers choice, provided the caterer keeps them in mind when he is planning the menu. Diabetics are usually taught from an early age how to choose suitable meals and judge the right quantities. Where no choice is offered, provision should be made as unobtrusively as possible.

The physically-handicapped also need to be considered, since their food may require special treatment so that it is easily transferred from plate to mouth. Specially-designed crockery and cutlery are available to help the physically-handicapped. Residents in old people's homes may suffer handicap through the infirmities of age. For example, those with failing eyesight or trembling hands may be unable to cope with fish bones or chop bones.

Popular local dishes

Recipes and methods of cooking various foods have in the past grown up mainly by a process of trial and error, and so it is not surprising that, although some methods were fairly common throughout the country, others were practised only in special parts. With improvements in communications many of these special local recipes have become more generally adopted, but even so they enjoy greater popularity in their original districts, and traditional methods handed down through generations still exist. Thus Cornwall claims its pasty, Yorkshire its pudding, Lancashire its hotpot and Norfolk its dumpling. Some local dishes are linked with local foods that are—or were at one time—particularly plentiful or cheap in the area. Examples are the Welsh laverbread (made from seaweed) and the East End of London's eel pie. The caterer is well advised to study local practice carefully with regard to these special dishes, and they should appear on the menu—made to the approved local standard—more often than would be normal in other parts of the country.

Dishes from abroad

There are several reasons for including in the menu from time to time dishes from other countries. Apart from the variety and interest they contribute, they may be particularly welcome to foreign nationals who are studying or working in this country. Also it is noticeable that, with increased foreign travel and the presence of more imported foods in the shops, tastes grow for dishes different in style from traditional English cuisine, and using ingredients not formerly associated with this country. In time, these dishes become accepted, and regarded as standard.

In the United Kingdom, food habits have for many years past been influenced by those of Europe and Asia. The service of foods such as pasta, Vienna sausage, French bread, risotto and curry is commonplace. American cuisine also exerts a strong influence, especially through franchised restaurants, and hamburgers, hot dogs, and fried and toasted sandwiches have become familiar. These American-style foods are particularly suitable for service in snack bars. The custom of offering a large choice of salads is one that might well be adopted from the United States, especially now that the salad bar has become a standard feature of British catering.

The idea of having a special week to feature dishes from a particular country is sometimes used to add interest to meals, and to relieve menu fatigue. This gives an opportunity to make changes in presentation and decor, and in schools may make an educational contribution.

Cost

When he is planning meals the caterer is constantly asking himself: 'How can I achieve all my objectives at minimum cost?' and: 'Should any objectives be sacrificed or modified in order to minimise cost?' These are some of the most important aspects of meal planning, and they will be discussed in the next chapter.

Planning meals in cook-freeze production units

As we have seen, one of the principal aims of cook-freeze is to establish an even workflow throughout the day, thus ensuring the most effective use of staff, machinery, cooking equipment and freezing equipment. Although in the long term the production manager is concerned with the planning of meals, since the dishes produced must be capable of combining over a given period into the planned menu, in terms of daily output the manager is concerned not with menus but with producing dishes that will give maximum output. To achieve this he may plan long production runs, producing three or four times the amount of any one dish than will be needed for any one day. Many of the points made in relation to menu planning obviously do not apply to cook-freeze production units.

Monitoring standards

Where there is a prescription about what quantities of basic foods are to be used, or where there is a target for certain nutrients and energy values, there may also be a monitoring system to check that the targets have been met over a given period. The use of basic foods may easily be checked by reference to:

(a) A consolidated stock record covering a given period, as described in Chapter 18 and shown in Figure 62;
(b) Records of the number of meals served.

Food values also may be checked by reference to these records, using appropriate tables. This kind of monitoring is often carried out by local education authorities in connection with school meals; calculations may be done by computer.

Monitoring may also take the form of spot checks, when the food actually served to a given number of clients is weighed, and food values are calculated. Alternatively, specimen plates of food may be sent for analysis, though this method is not often used because of its expense.

Chapter 21

Basic quantities and costs

Basic quantities

One of the first difficulties facing a student who is given the responsibility of cooking a meal for a considerable number of people is knowing what quantities of food and drink should be provided. The fear of not having enough is well justified, for the prospect of being faced by a group of hungry clients when there is no food left to offer them is not pleasant. On the other hand, the need to dispose of large amounts of left-over cooked food, and the waste of both food and money involved, can cause just as much worry. These problems sort themselves out in time as the caterer becomes familiar with the demand in his particular establishment, but, unless there is some basis on which to reckon amounts, they will recur when special catering has to be undertaken, or when demand changes significantly; and they may be encountered again when the caterer transfers to a new establishment.

Of course it is often possible to refer to previous records, and it is always wise to consult them if they are available. Also, as we saw in Chapter 20, large organisations have their own standard instructions and recommendations about quantities. But a caterer should not have to be dependent upon the availability of this sort of information, and it is essential to acquire early in one's catering career data that can be used as bases for calculating the ingredients needed for a specific meal. Table 13 gives some typical allowances for basic foods and dishes, and for beverages, and these are easily adapted to the needs of different establishments. Quantities to suit the needs of a specific group—children—are given in Appendix 3.8. It is sometimes said that smaller quantities per head are needed when large numbers are being catered for—say one or two thousand—than for smaller numbers—say 50 to 100—but any reduction in quantity is marginal. There may be smaller losses during preparation through the use of machinery or for other reasons (though by no means always), and some marginal savings may be made through rounding down to the nearest unit of purchase (for example, a bag of potatoes) or of weight. On the other hand, when one is catering for very small units rounding up is sometimes necessary. For example, it may be cheaper to use a large can of fruit or meat and to give slightly larger portions than to use several small cans and serve standard portions. It is certainly not true that people will eat less because they are being catered for on a large scale. Confusion often arises here simply because food usually costs less when it is bought in large quantities. This aspect is dealt with in Chapter 19.

A list of basic quantities is only part of the information needed to work out the amounts of ingredients for producing a meal; appropriate recipes must also be consulted. Some recipes, such as those for pastries, sponges, foundation sauces, milk puddings, etc., are taught in elementary large-scale cookery. Others are less standard and more involved, and thus more difficult to remember, and for these a recipe book or file usually has to be consulted. There are, of course, published books of recipes for quantity catering, but many organisations develop their own recipes, using quantities that fit in with any prescriptions or recommendations about quantities of basic foods to be used. New recipes are constantly being developed, and bodies such as the Dairy Produce Advisory Service, the New Zealand Lamb Advisory Bureau, the White Fish Authority and several food manufacturing firms make a point of helping the caterer by suggesting new recipes. The professional caterer, as we have seen, often keeps his own file of recipe cards. It is important that when new recipes are added to the repertoire the amounts of basic ingredients are adjusted to harmonise with the chart of basic quantities used in a particular establishment. Consider one example. The new recipe calls for a much greater quantity of meat than is usually included. Unless this is adjusted the cost per portion will rise steeply, and the clients, although they may welcome the larger amount of meat in the new recipe, may become dissatisfied with the smaller amounts in other dishes. On the other hand, if the amount served is smaller than usual, dissatisfaction will be immediate. When the proportions of main ingredients are altered the recipe's balance may be upset, and so other adjustments may be necessary before the recipe is added to the file.

There may be other reasons for modifying a recipe from time to time. Sometimes there are slight changes in the properties of basic ingredients. For example, different brands and grades of flour absorb different amounts of moisture, and so small temporary adjustments to pastry or bread recipes should be made accordingly. The thickening property of different custard powder brands varies slightly, so a change of brand may mean that a different amount has to be used. If the price of a particular ingredient rises a recipe may well be adapted by the use of a less expensive substitute. For example, in made-up meat dishes textured vegetable protein may replace part of the meat, and then some further adaptation—perhaps the addition of tasty vegetables such as onions or mushrooms—may be desirable. In recent years milk powder has been used increasingly in place of liquid milk because it is cheaper.

The caterer is, of course, as much concerned about quantities of cooked food as he is with raw weights. With some foods there is a great difference between the weight of food as purchased and the amount of edible food available for service. This applies particularly to meat, where the difference varies according to the cut and the amount of trimming necessary, so that if the caterer works to a certain weight per portion of cooked meat the amount he has to order will vary according to the cut chosen. The quantities given in Table 13 indicate the different amounts appropriate for bone-in and boneless joints, but it is desirable for the caterer to compile his own information about cooked yield from raw weight, and to record this on his standard recipe cards. Methods of preparing, cooking and carving should be such as to ensure that the right number of portions as recorded on the cards is yielded.

With many dishes portion size is related to volume rather than weight. The use of containers of standard dimensions was discussed in Chapter 14 as a way of making the best use of oven and hot cupboard space, and arbitrary reference was made to the number of portions they contained. It is, of course, for catering management to decide the yield, expressed in the number of portions, per standard container, and to instruct staff accordingly. The use of standard containers is a very important element in portion control. Certain items, such as cold sweets, pre-packed butter, cheese, sauces and preserves, may be individually portioned.

When the number of portions per container has been settled, it must be decided whether all clients are to receive equal portions. Practice varies according to the nature of the establishment, the catering style and the clients' needs. When individual items on the menu are priced separately, the size of individual portions is usually expected to be consistent. The hearty eater is able to buy more items, and the smaller eater buys fewer. Each obtains comparable value for his money, and the portion yield of cooked food can be forecast accurately. However, not all caterers offering *à la carte* menus subscribe entirely to this system of portion control. In some establishments the client helps himself, without limit, to less expensive items. There are two possible reasons for this: first, client satisfaction is greater; second, savings in staff labour may justify any extra amount of food consumed.

Where *table d'hôte* meals are served, the caterer assumes that a standard container will yield a given number of portions, but, especially in the case of residential establishments, he does not expect all portions to be of equal size. If they were, some clients would not have enough, but others would have too much and thus food would be wasted. The range of needs and appetites is most marked in schools, or in homes catering for children over a wide range of ages. But even where the system allows for variation in portion size there is likely to be strict control of the upper limit of portion size of expensive protein foods such as meat, fish and poultry. The control of food quantities at every stage—buying, issuing, preparing and serving—is essential to the control of food costs.

Costs

It is not proposed to deal in detail here with methods of costing and cost control, since these are outside the scope of this book. But we shall discuss some general features of cost and cost control, particularly in relation to food costs and the role of the catering manager. This latter varies considerably, but it is always significant so far as the financial success or failure of a catering establishment is concerned.

Catering costs fall naturally into two distinct sections—food and overheads. Salaries and wages and their related costs such as insurance and pension funds are included in the overheads, but there are many others—fuel, cleaning materials, repairs and renewals and so on. The relationship between the two heads is always interesting, and the catering manager usually keeps in mind the percentage of total costs attributable to food and that attributable to overheads.

TABLE 13: Average quantities for foods and beverages

Foods	*Quantity per head/ No of portions per litre*	*Quantity per 100*
Batter (for pancakes or Yorkshire pudding)	10–12 litres	8–10 litres
Cornflakes	20–30 g	2–3 kg
Custard sauce	12–16 litres	6–8 litres
Fish, raw weight:		
with much bone	150–200 g	15–20 kg
with little or no bone	120–150 g	12–15 kg
Fruit:		
for stewing	125–150 g	12·5–15 kg
for pies	100–125 g	10–12·5 kg
dried, prunes, etc.	40–60 g	4–6 kg

TABLE 13 continued

Foods	*Quantity per head/ No of portions per litre*	*Quantity per 100*
Gravy	16/litre	6 litres
Meat, raw weight:		
with bone	100–150 g	10–15 kg
boneless	80–100 g	8–10 kg
Milk pudding	5/litre	20 litres
Pasta	40 g	4 kg
Pastry, flour for	25–35 g (other ingredients in proportion)	2·5–3·5 kg
Porridge	5–7/litre	14–20 litres
Poultry	200–250 g	20–25 kg
Puddings (sponge or suet), flour for	25–30 g (other ingredients in proportion)	2·5–3 kg
Rice	40 g	4 kg
Soup	4–6/litre	16–25 litres
Vegetables:		
green, raw weight	100 g	10 kg
potatoes, raw weight	150–200 g	15–20 kg
potato powder, instant	20–30 g	2–3 kg
roots, raw weight	130 g	13 kg
dried pulses, peas, beans	40–50 g	4–5 kg

Beverages	*Amount per litre*	*Amount per 100 cups*
Coffee, black	6 cups (0·17 litre)	16·6 litres
Coffee, ground (served black)	60 g	990 g
Coffee, ground, with chicory (served black)	40 g	660 g
Coffee, instant (served black)	12 g	200 g
Milk for white coffee (half milk)	12 cups	8·3 litres
Sugar for coffee	50 g	830 g
Tea, brewed	6 cups	16·5 litres
Tea, leaf	10 g	160 g
Milk for tea	40 cups	2·5 litres
Sugar for tea	50 g	830 g

Vended beverages	*Cups (0·14 litre)/kg*
Coffee, instant	600
Chocolate	50
Milk powder	250 cups tea/coffee whitened by 1 kg
Sugar	125 cups tea/coffee sweetened by 1 kg
Tea, instant	1800

The catering budget

So far as running costs are concerned, the caterer is expected to work to a budget (that is, an expenditure plan) for a given period. The budget estimates expenditure on food and overheads for the next financial year (which is the period usually chosen), and there is a separate budget for capital expenditure. The usual method for reaching a figure for the following year's expenditure is to look at spending in the previous year, or years, and to take this as a base, making adjustments for any changes that are expected. In the case of food, a provisional figure is reached by taking the previous year's spending and adding a percentage if price rises are expected, but two other factors must be taken into account. First, will the same number of meals be provided? Obviously, any material changes in meal numbers will have their effect upon food estimates. It is not usually possible to forecast meal numbers with complete accuracy, and so one thinks in terms of a budget figure per meal, or, for residential establishments, per resident per week. In other words, there is a unit cost figure.

Example

$$\frac{\text{Last year's food cost} + \text{y}\,\% \text{ for expected price increases}}{\text{Last year's number of meals}}$$

$$= \text{estimated average food cost per meal for the coming year.}$$

The estimated average food cost per meal times the expected number of meals equals the estimated total spending on food for the next year, but the catering manager is expected to use the unit cost figure as the basis of expenditure.

Secondly, are any policy changes expected next year that will affect food costs? If so, due account should be taken before the figures to be affected are included in the budget. Examples of such changes are: the inclusion of textured vegetable protein in recipes to replace part of the meat, as previously mentioned; the purchase of ready-prepared potatoes instead of potatoes with the peel on.

Another way to estimate food costs is to take specimen menus, recipes and quantity charts and to produce from them a list of commodities to provide meals for a given period—say four weeks—for a given number of meals or residents—say one hundred. The list is costed at current prices, and a percentage is added to cover expected price rises if necessary. The unit cost per meal, or per resident per week, may then be calculated. This method has an obvious use when a new catering concern is to be opened, but it is also useful for existing concerns, for, if results are compared with actual unit costs for the previous year, differences may indicate that there has been either over- or under-spending, and the new budget figures should take this into account.

When menus consist of numbers of *à la carte* items, food costs are estimated according to the first method described, last year's spending being adjusted to allow for any changes in meal demand and food prices, but it is more difficult to be accurate. Also, the idea of a unit cost per meal does not apply.

It is usual, but not invariably so, for catering management to be responsible for the preparation of this part of the budget.

Of the various overheads included in the budget, some will be fixed regardless of the output of meals (for example, rent and rates), and some may vary with the output (for example, fuel, cleaning materials and wages). Overheads are calculated by reference to last year's expenditure—and that of previous years—but the factors that may modify this figure are more numerous and complex than those associated with food. It is essential that any plans for policy changes that will affect this part of the budget shall be made well ahead, and their cost estimated, so that their effects upon the budget may be considered. When the unit cost for overheads is calculated, the estimated number of meals is very significant because, if too high a figure is taken, the estimated unit cost figure will be too low. This happens because of:

(a) non-variable costs such as rent, rates and salaries;
(b) those costs that, while being variable, do not change directly with the number of meals served—for example, wages.

The budget includes also estimates of income (mainly from the sale of meals and refreshments, plus any apportionment of charges made for board residence and any subsidies or grants).

Prices charged

Prices for *table d'hôte* meals are fixed after reference to the following: estimated unit cost of food; estimated unit cost of overheads; income from subsidies or grants. In Britain, however, school catering is an exception, as the price of school meals is fixed by the Government. At times of rapid inflation it is usual to review prices at shorter intervals than a year, perhaps every three months.

For *à la carte* menus the pricing structure is more elaborate. The elements in the prices charged for individual dishes are:

(a) the cost of a portion of food;
(b) a percentage for overheads, but this does not always completely cover them, because the meal may be subsidised.

Sometimes a greater percentage of the overheads is carried by highly saleable items, such as beverages, than by others. Costed recipe cards (see Figure 63) may be used to determine the price to be charged for a specific item once the percentage oncost has been worked out.

Example

Cost of food per portion:	15p
Percentage oncost:	200
Selling price:	45p

This may be expressed in another way:

Selling price per portion:	45p
Food cost:	33·33 % of selling price
Oncost:	66·67 % of selling price.

Where a profit-making establishment is concerned, the term 'target gross profit' (expressed as a percentage of the selling price) is used rather than oncost.

Keeping within the food budget

When an estimated unit cost figure has been fixed, it is up to the catering manager to keep within that budget. He can do this by pre-costing the meals, or the main menu items; if he keeps his costed recipe cards up to date when prices change these will be a great help in pre-costing. But he will also need to know about his historical costs. For *table de'hôte* meals, unit food costs are calculated as follows:

$$\frac{\text{cost of food}}{\text{number of meals}} = \text{unit food cost per meal.}$$

Where accounts are submitted monthly, these costs can be determined for that period, as follows:

1. Estimate the value of stock in hand at the beginning of the period;
2. Total the amount paid for food during the period, and add the estimated value of any outstanding accounts;
3. Estimate the value of closing stocks.

The value of opening stock plus purchases, minus the value of the closing stock, gives the cost of food used. Alternatively, the food cost may be calculated by reference to records of food used. A costed daily issue sheet may be used to give daily cost figures. A consolidated stock record covering a period of a week or a month, of the type shown in Figure 62, may be used in calculating costs.

As well as knowing how his costs compare with the budget figure for each week, or other period concerned, the caterer needs to have information showing his position to date, and for this purpose cumulative figures for food costs and numbers of meals are kept:

$$\frac{\text{cost of food to date}}{\text{number of meals to date}} = \text{cumulative unit food cost.}$$

Similar procedures apply to historical costings for *à la carte* catering, but again the concept of a unit cost figure does not apply.

If it is found that the actual unit cost is higher than the budget figure, corrective action must be taken. For example, procedures should be reviewed to check that:

(a) food is not being over-ordered, and in particular that orders for perishable foods are adjusted to meet any fall in demand;
(b) correct amounts of food are being issued;
(c) there is adequate portion control.

Some adjustment to menus and buying patterns may be indicated, such as the inclusion of more low-cost main dishes, or the use of less expensive fruit or vegetables. But, if the difference has been caused by major price rises emergency action is necessary, including an immediate review of prices charged, if possible. Also, if the actual cost is considerably lower than the budget figure, changes may have to be made. The caterer should check that enough food is being used, and that meal quality reaches the prescribed or target standard, and that this standard is appropriate to the price being charged.

In the case of *à la carte* menus it is usually easy to adjust the prices of individual dishes as necessary, and up-to-date costed recipe cards should be referred to.

Keeping within the overheads budget

As has been mentioned, there are both fixed and variable overhead costs, and obviously the manager must focus his attention on the variable costs in order to keep within the budget. Staffing is the most important single item, and it is of the utmost importance that staff levels are strictly related to output. If too many staff are employed at any time, or if there is no reduction in hours worked to correspond with a fall in output, problems of excess expenditure are bound to arise.

Cost comparisons

Budget figures compared with actual costs are often used to assess the efficiency and performance of an establishment, and to compare one establishment with another. Such assessments and comparisons are made more easily where a unit costing system is used. Of course it is important for like to be compared with like, but one would expect unit food costs to be similar in a group of schools, or homes, or hospitals, especially where supplies are obtained from a common source. The same holds true for overheads, but, because overheads are affected by physical conditions that do not apply to food costs, greater margins of difference are likely. It is usually a duty of senior managers and/or finance officers to investigate marked departures from the average, and to ensure that any necessary corrective action is taken. Both under- and over-expenditure are investigated.

Chapter 22

Economy: cost-effectiveness, cost/benefit and feasibility studies

One of the principal aims of those concerned with catering management is to ensure that their establishments are run as economically as possible. The responsibility for this, so far as day-to-day running is concerned, rests chiefly on the shoulders of the manager or supervisor of the individual unit. But the maximum degree of efficiency that it is possible to achieve is determined to a great extent by the choice of system and plant, and by the working environment.

We shall bring together some of the many details involved in day-to-day kitchen routine, and, since economy here is largely a question of avoiding waste, the subject will be approached from this point of view. We shall then discuss briefly how decisions about the choice of equipment and systems are made, and how the various factors are evaluated. The relationship between kitchen layout and the general working environment to efficiency have been discussed in previous chapters.

Economy in the day-to-day running of a kitchen

In the kitchen materials and energy and labour may be used unprofitably or without adequate return.

Food

Often one of the underlying reasons for waste of food is that staff are not correctly motivated, and they do not necessarily adopt the attitude that they would at home, where they are likely to be very conscious of food costs. Also, when large quantities are handled and some is wasted, the amount may seem so small in relation to the whole that its intrinsic value is not appreciated. Waste of food applies not only to what is visible, but also to unnecessary loss of nutrients during preparation and cooking, through either lack of knowledge or carelessness. Both types of waste are, of course, important, but invisible waste is more likely to be overlooked, not only because it is difficult to detect but also because it does not affect the budget.

The logical way to consider how food may be wasted is to go

through the various processes of buying, storing, preparing, cooking and serving, and to look also at the question of left-over food.

Buying

This subject has been dealt with in detail in Chapter 19. Here it remains to emphasise the importance of careful and informed buying, and the cautious approach necessary when it is proposed to buy large quantities of any particular commodity, either to obtain a more favourable price or against a rising market. The available storage facilities and the possibility of loss of stock through deterioration must be taken into account.

Storing

The question of storage has also been dealt with already, in Chapter 18. Basic points to be borne in mind are that perishable foods must never be kept longer than necessary, nor allowed to deteriorate until they are unfit for use. If a refrigerator breaks down stocks of considerable value may be lost, and sometimes such losses are greater than they need be because too much stock is being held. When an establishment is to be closed for any length of time—for example, during school or college holidays—stocks of semi-perishable foods should be run down, as should any frozen food stocks unless adequate arrangements can be made to check regularly that the freezer store is working properly, or there is an alarm system. It is possible to insure frozen food stocks, and this may be a wise precaution if premises are left unattended at week-ends, so that a freezer store breakdown could go unnoticed. Rotation of stocks and protection from contamination are key points in preventing waste.

Preparing

Some of the greatest waste can occur when meat, potatoes and green vegetables are being prepared. If meat is trimmed or boned in a careless or unskilled way, excessive amounts of lean are left adhering to any surplus fat, gristle or bone, and this is one of the reasons why caterers often buy ready-trimmed meat. There may be further losses after cooking through poor carving.

Potatoes sometimes sustain heavy losses during preparation. They may be left too long in the peeler, and in consequence a great deal of potato flesh is lost. This is not always caused by carelessness, since sometimes the operator does it on purpose in order to remove more of the eyes, and so to reduce the amount of manual work needed afterwards. Often large amounts of potato flesh are removed during the eyeing process because the operator slices it off instead of digging out the eyes with the knife point, which is slightly more difficult.

Green vegetables also are liable to be trimmed excessively during preparation. The dark green outside leaves of cabbage contain a higher proportion of vitamin C and iron than the rest of the plant, and yet they are often thrown away when they are neither blemished nor too coarse to use. If the rib is removed and the leaves are finely chopped the end-product should be entirely acceptable, though cooking times will be slightly longer than they are for more tender leaves. It is fairly common to trim Brussels sprouts excessively, and again the darker outside leaves contain the most vitamin C and iron. It is a mistake to throw away the outside leaves of lettuces just because they are limp; crispness can usually be restored if the washed leaves are put into a tightly-covered vessel inside the refrigerator for from half an hour to an hour. If green vegetables are left to soak in water some of the vitamin C will leach into the water, so this practice should be discouraged.

Cooking

Most of the waste that occurs during cooking is the result of lack of skill or knowledge, or it is due to carelessness, but sometimes better and more economical results could have been obtained if different equipment had been used. And, of course, there is always the possibility of accidents. A textbook gives little help in acquiring skills, and information about cooking processes is outside the scope of this book. The skilled and experienced cook is aware of the critical points in cooking processes, but one with less training and experience may fail to appreciate the importance of temperature control and timing, particularly where certain dishes and cooking methods are concerned. Food that has been cooked at too high a temperature may be unduly dry and shrunken and too dark in colour; the taste also may be affected. As a result it is less palatable and has less appeal to the eye, and either portion size or yield of portions will be smaller than it should be. At worst, the food may be burnt and thus rendered partly or wholly inedible. When the cooking temperature is too low, as a rule the result is less disastrous, but food will not be cooked to anything like perfection. Occasionally the consequences may be extremely serious, as, for example, when undercooked meat or poultry is implicated in cases of food poisoning. Fried food cooked at too low a temperature is particularly unappetising and greasy; also an excessive amount of oil is used in cooking it.

Serving

Food can be wasted at this stage by serving portions that are too large. This may be due to inadequate portion control, so that clients receive either more or less than their due amounts. In the former case, food may be wasted on the plate and also supplies will run out. More has to be produced, if possible, and this is usually expensive convenience food. This represents waste so far as the caterer is concerned, for even though the extra food is eaten it would not have been used had portioning at the service point been correct. When the portions served are too small, unexpected amounts of food are left to be disposed of at the end of the meal, some of which cannot be served again and thus will be wasted. Where children are concerned, a common cause of plate waste is the serving of portions that are too large for their ages and appetites. Food may also be wasted at the serving stage if it is left for too long in the hot cupboard, so that it becomes either dry or soggy according to its nature, and eventually unfit to be served. Green vegetables and potatoes lose much of their vitamin C if they are kept hot for any length of time.

Left-over food

The caterer aims to have as little food as possible left over, and it is good practice to check regularly exactly how much food is left at the end of the service period. Orders and quantity charts should be adjusted where necessary, and it may be that the method of ordering meals or forecasting numbers of meals is unreliable and needs to be improved. However, some left-over food is inevitable from time to time, even though the amount be small. A senior member of staff should be responsible for deciding, immediately the service period has ended, how such food should be disposed of. In the interests of hygiene meat, fish and poultry dishes, and those containing milk or cream, should be discarded if there is any doubt as to whether they have been kept at safe temperatures (that is, at or above 62·7° Celsius or below 10° Celsius) during the service period. On no account should meat, fish and poultry dishes be reheated, but, if they are hot, provided they are cooled immediately it may be possible to offer them as cold dishes at a later meal. Unserved foods such as sponges and stale bread may readily be included in new dishes, for which there are many suitable recipes. In deciding which foods to use and which to discard, hygiene considerations are paramount, but acceptability and the maintenance of good standards are important also. It is good to be thrifty, but it is false economy to serve food that has deteriorated, or to acquire a reputation with clients for being frugal.

Plate waste as well as dish waste should be inspected regularly, and the content as well as the quantity noted. This tells management whether portion sizes have been too large, and which foods are unpopular, or which dishes have fallen below standard on a particular occasion. To look at plate waste in bulk without noticing what has been left on individual plates may sometimes be a little misleading, for a different picture is presented where most clients leave a little from the one where a few clients leave a lot. It is a good practice to weigh total plate waste regularly, and to weigh that from sample plates occasionally. However, when there is a waste-disposal unit in the washing-up area some of its advantages would be lost if all plate waste were collected in a container and weighed before being disposed of. In these circumstances some sort of sampling procedure is appropriate.

Waste food bins

When there is no waste disposal unit in the kitchen waste food, including preparation waste, is disposed of in bins kept outside the kitchen and emptied by a collector. The contents of these bins should be scrutinised at regular intervals to check whether food that ought to have been used has been consigned to the bin.

Although much of the supervisor's duty in preventing waste of food is concerned with the supervision of staff, those staff are unlikely to respond to the continual carping about waste that is sometimes associated with supervision. It is better to have a positive policy, the keystones of which might well be training in the necessary craft and manual skills, motivation, and the provision of specific targets. Targets may be related to the yield expected from given amounts of raw food. This has already been discussed in connection with portion control, but it can be applied to many stages of preparation. Consider potatoes as an example. After preparation the caterer can expect a certain yield from a given quantity if potatoes are of average quality and x kg of potatoes (raw weight) should fill a boiler of y capacity. When dished up they should fill a given number of standard containers. A reasonable figure for plate waste can also be established, though there is a danger that complacency about waste may creep in should the figure be pitched too high. If the average plate waste is calculated over a period of, say, a week or a month, the aim should be to have a lower figure for the following period. When several establishments are under the same management, it is useful to compare amounts of waste.

Fuel and energy

Waste of fuel and energy arises chiefly from inefficient equipment, or inefficiency in the way it is used. Sometimes poor choices of equipment are made in the first instance, or in the course of time a more up-to-date product comes on to the market beside which the existing equipment is inefficient, and it may be that the time for replacement has come. But also equipment may become inefficient because it has not been properly maintained, and sometimes it is just a simple matter of inadequate cleaning. For example, if grease and spilt food are not removed from various surfaces of cooking appliances, charring takes place and the flow of heat is impeded.

Other examples of basic care of equipment are: regular defrosting of the refrigerator (where this is not automatic) to avoid impaired efficiency and wasted energy; oiling moving parts of machinery as necessary. This sort of care is part of the work of kitchen staff, and should be included in their work programmes. But regular maintenance work and checks by qualified staff are needed for all kitchen machinery and for gas equipment; maintenance for the latter should include the cleaning of burners and their adjustment where necessary. In hard water districts maintenance work for some items of equipment includes the removal of scale, which if left can impair efficiency. However, if a certain amount of friction is used in cleaning such things as rinsing sinks and steaming ovens, the build-up of scale—which impedes the transfer of heat—is reduced. Chemical solvents may also be used.

So far as the use of equipment is concerned, most points are obvious and well known; nevertheless, in practice they are often ignored. Probably the commonest cause of waste is the practice—long-established in some cases—of switching on or lighting all or most of the cooking appliances at the beginning of the working session, regardless of whether or not they are to be used, and without reference to the time at which they will actually be needed. This is sometimes done to provide space-heating, though it is a very extravagant method. In other cases it happens simply because no one has worked out the time when cooking should start and the amount of pre-heating time necessary. At the end of the cooking session, often no one turns off the equipment—not necessarily through forgetfulness, but because it is the custom to leave it on. We saw in Chapter 7 that devices are being developed to prevent this sort of misuse or to minimise its effects, and it may be well worth while to have them fitted to existing equipment. But in well-managed and well-supervised kitchens these sorts of practices do not occur regularly.

When gas rings are used, care should be taken to adjust the flames so that no more gas is used than is necessary for the cooking process. With solid-top boiling plates, particular care is needed to prevent waste of fuel. The amount of radiation from these tops is considerable, and, if they are left on when not in use, or if when used they are only partly covered with pans, heat losses are significant. In the case of electrical equipment the fact that electricity cannot be seen means that it is very easy for solid boiling plates to be left on by mistake. Much heat is wasted also when pans without machined bases are used on solid electric boiling-plates. All pans should be kept free from hard-water scale. This is unlikely to accumulate in pans that have to be scoured to keep them clean, but special attention should be given to pans that, so far as the removal of food debris is concerned, need only light cleaning. Scale has to be removed from the bottoms of steamers and from kettles.

The economic use of fuel and energy must be looked at against the historical background. Until recently we have been used in Britain to having ample and cheap supplies of both, and as a result we have learned to be extravagant and wasteful. This applies to caterers and cooks as much as to anyone else. Hence, as well as training new staff to use fuel and energy efficiently, some retraining of experienced staff may be necessary. It is a good plan to tell staff exactly how much is spent on fuel and energy in the establishment, and also the cost of running a particular piece of equipment; target consumption figures, which should not be exceeded, are useful. However, in many institutions gas and electricity are not separately metered for the catering department, and so the cost has to be apportioned. In such circumstances the caterer and his staff tend to be less interested in economy.

Labour

Many aspects of labour costs have already been discussed in Chapters 15 and 16 and elsewhere. One point that particularly concerns the day-to-day running of the kitchen is the planning of suitable work schedules and their adjustment as necessary to suit changes in circumstances. If too much time, or too many people, are allocated to a job, or if more staff than necessary are on duty during slack periods, labour is wasted. This is true also if work sessions begin sooner or end later than is necessary in relation to the times at which meals are served, and careful adjustments of starting and finishing times are necessary. Staff time will be wasted if the workflow from day to day is not even. This depends very much upon the work content of the menu, which should be carefully balanced. If for any reason the amount of work on a particular day is reduced—perhaps by a temporary fall in demand—other necessary routine work, such as cleaning and stocktaking, should be arranged. When conditions change, work schedules should change also. For example, if potatoes are scarce and potato powder is used temporarily, less time should be allocated to vegetable preparation. Similarly, if a later meal time is introduced, the starting and finishing times of work sessions should be adjusted accordingly.

If the available tools and equipment are insufficient, staff time will be wasted. Probably the first that come to mind are major items such as potato machine and dishwasher, since if these break down it is immediately necessary to allocate extra hours. But the cook, the staff serving meals and those preparing vegetables depend in their work upon small tools, the lack of which causes a waste of time quite out of proportion to their cost. Cooks often prefer to provide their own knives and other implements, but where they do not good quality tools should be kept for their exclusive use. All staff should know which implements they should use, and where to find them.

Staff need materials as well as tools, and if they are kept waiting for supplies, either through late delivery or through delay in the issue of stores, their time is wasted. They also need instructions on the menu and numbers to be catered for in good time at the start of the working session. Failure to communicate, or late or inadequate communications, waste time.

Unit costs

We saw in Chapter 21 how unit costs could be used as a management tool for comparing the efficiency of similar establishments, although there we were concerned particularly with food and staffing costs. But similar comparisons may be made for fuel, cleaning materials and replacements. Generally speaking, high unit costs tend to reflect unfavourably to a considerable extent on the capabilities of the supervisory and management staff.

Cost-effectiveness and cost-benefits

When it is proposed to install a new piece of equipment, its cost-effectiveness should be calculated—that is, will the cost involved be justified by savings to be made, usually in running costs? Consider a simple example relating to a proposal to install a timing device on a cooker to prevent its being left on for long periods accidentally or through carelessness. Suppose the cost of supplying and fitting it will be £15, and that the amount of fuel it will save is estimated to be £10 a year. Clearly, if the figure for fuel saving is reliable, the timer will pay for itself in about eighteen months (or sooner if the price of fuel were to rise) and will thus be cost-effective. Apart from the saving of fuel, the timer could have other advantages. First, it might on occasion prevent the burning and consequent waste of food, though this saving would not be quantifiable. Secondly, after the timer had been fitted the supervisor would have less responsibility in checking that fuel was not wasted.

Cost-benefit studies

The example quoted was very simple; not many factors were involved, and only one possible way to reduce fuel costs was considered. When a cost-benefit study is undertaken in connection with major changes in equipment or policy, it is usual to look at several different ways of achieving the defined objective, and to analyse and assess the costs and benefits of each. Both quantifiable and unquantifiable costs and benefits are assessed. A large-scale cost-benefit study is normally undertaken by a team of specialists, which would include a finance expert. The cost benefit technique can, however, be applied by the caterer in a variety of circumstances. The following example deals with the installation of a dishwasher, and illustrates the point.

Cost-benefit study of a proposal to install a dishwasher

Objective: to reduce the cost of washing dishes.

Choices considered: (a) a semi-automatic machine;
(b) a fully-automatic machine.

Capital costs. The same items apply for (a) and (b), but of course the amounts will be different.

Capital cost items: the machine and its installation;
extra tabling and its fixing;
a water softener and its installation;
improvements to the hot water supply;
ancillary equipment;
removal of existing sinks and drainers.

Against this expenditure is set any sum realised from the sale of the old equipment.

Annual running costs. These are calculated for the existing system, and assessed for dishwashers (a) and (b). It is important for all costs to be identified. The financing of the capital and installation costs of the new equipment must be included. Assuming a life of not less than ten years for either dishwasher, a suitable figure for the annual cost of equipment would be one-tenth of the capital cost plus a sum for interest charges.

The following running costs would apply to the existing method:

ancillary consumable items—
teatowels,
dishcloths, etc.;
detergent;
electricity or gas for heated rinsing sink;
fuel for hot water supply;
maintenance of equipment;
labour.

The following running costs would apply to (a) and (b), though again the actual sums involved would be different for most items:

detergent;
electricity for the machine;

fuel for hot water supply;
maintenance of dishwasher, water softener and ancillary equipment;
rinse aid;
tea towels, if needed;
salt for recharging water softener;
labour;

equipment cost per annum (*e.g.*, one-tenth of capital cost plus interest).

Benefits. The following might well be listed:

1. The work involved in using either machine is much lighter than the work of washing up by hand, and machine (b) has the greater advantage here.

2. Staff working conditions would be improved if a machine were installed, because less water would be spilt on the floor and the atmosphere would be less steamy; this would apply equally to either machine.

3. It is to be expected that, with lighter work and improved conditions, staff turnover would be smaller; this would mean a reduction in the expenses associated with the appointment of new staff.

Reaching a decision. A decision is likely to be reached chiefly in relation to costs. Do (a) and (b) offer savings on the existing system, and, if so, which offers the greater saving? But possible benefits should also be considered, particularly where there has been difficulty in recruiting and retaining staff to do washing up by hand.

Feasibility studies

A feasibility study has a wider scope than a cost-benefit study, for it is concerned not only with costs and benefits but also with the techniques involved in any proposed new system, and, after a decision has been made, with preparing a development plan leading to the completion of the project. The study involves research to acquire the information necessary to determine whether the proposed project is feasible, and consideration of the evidence in order to reach a decision. If the project is feasible the next step is to determine, through a study of the costs involved, whether the project is economically sound; any benefits are assessed also. A report is then prepared and referred to the decision-makers (for example, a committee of management). If the decision is favourable, the team responsible for the study prepares a development plan for the project's completion.

When a feasibility study is undertaken, it is essential that sufficient expertise is available to make the study comprehensive. Pilot schemes are often launched as part of the study or as a result of it, to test new techniques and systems and to gain experience before there is a wholesale change of policy.

Chapter 23

Food hygiene

It is essential at the outset of a career in catering to understand fully the importance of food hygiene, and the ways in which hygiene considerations affect the running of a kitchen. The aim is always to ensure that only safe food is served to the client. To achieve this, not only must food be clean in the ordinary sense of the word, but also every effort must be made to avoid contamination of food by pathogenic bacteria—or by other means—and to ensure that there should be no opportunity for bacteria associated with food poisoning to multiply rapidly.

There is a real and continuing need for every care to be taken in the treatment of food, and this is demonstrated by the numbers of cases of food poisoning reported each year, which, on the whole, are increasing (see Table 14). In 1966, 4500 cases were reported, but in 1976 the number was over 9000. At one time outbreaks of food poisoning were quite rare, but there was a rapid rise in the years immediately following World War II. During the war it was government policy to encourage the provision of canteens for schoolchildren, industrial workers and others. Hence there was a big increase in large-scale catering, and this was a principal reason for the increased incidence of food poisoning. At that time caterers were largely ignorant of the causes of food poisoning. It would be only reasonable to expect that since then the improved design of catering establishments, more hygienic equipment and working surfaces, greater knowledge of food hygiene and widespread education on the subject would have brought about an improvement, but this has not happened and so one must look for the reasons.

One reason for the increase is that food, especially meat and poultry, goes through more complicated processes than was common in the past, and highly-processed made-up meat and poultry dishes are often involved in food-poisoning outbreaks. Another reason is that dried feeding stuffs fed to animals are often infected, and as a result—and also through other circumstances—meat and poultry may already be contaminated when they enter the kitchen.

There is no doubt that, when food is prepared and cooked on a large scale, there are more hazards to contend with than when the scale is smaller. But there are subsidiary reasons why food poisoning has come to be associated with institutional catering. If contaminated food is served in a private house, only a few people are affected, but in an institution many may be involved. Food poisoning in the home may not be identified as such, but, if those affected belong to a group in a school, factory or hospital, an outbreak can hardly escape notice and is almost certain to be identified. But this does not necessarily apply to a restaurant, where the customers are likely to have dispersed before symptoms develop, and, unless there were serious illness, it is unlikely that food poisoning would be identified.

Sources of food contamination

Food may be contaminated by either poisonous chemicals or pathogenic bacteria. Chemicals may be present because they have been deliberately added with malicious intent, or accidentally—as when some noxious substance is mistaken for food. Certain toadstools, for example, and some other plants naturally contain substances that cause illness if they are eaten. However, cases of food poisoning of chemical origin are comparatively rare.

Causative organisms

Salmonella. This group is the most common cause of food poisoning, and may be carried in the intestines. Cattle, pigs, ducks, chickens, turkeys, birds, mice, rats, cats and dogs, as well as man, are all potential *Salmonella* carriers. Illness caused by the living bacteria in food develops from twelve to thirty-six hours after contaminated food has been eaten, and the symptoms are: abdominal pain, diarrhoea, vomiting, fever and headache. In severe cases death can result, especially in the old, the very young and the sick.

Staphylococci. These are found in human carriers, and may be present in the nose or throat, or in cuts, burns and any septic lesions. Symptoms of illness are similar to those caused by *Salmonella*, but there is no fever and onset is very rapid, sometimes only two hours after the contaminated food has been eaten, but more usually between four and six hours. The illness is caused by toxins produced by bacteria growing on the food.

Clostridium welchii. Bacteria in this group are carried in human and animal intestines, and are also spread by soil, dust and flies; they grow in anaerobic conditions. The organism is spore-forming. The spores of some strains can survive normal cooking temperatures. Raw meat and poultry are often contaminated by this organism and so are some dehydrated foods. Illness is caused by toxins formed in the intestine by the ingested bacteria. The symptoms, which occur between eight and twenty-two hours after ingestion, are abdominal pain, diarrhoea and nausea, but as a rule there is no vomiting.

Clostridium botulinum. Food poisoning from this source is very rare, but it is often fatal. The organisms may be found in soil and mud, fish, meat and vegetables. *Clostridium botulinum* is spore-bearing and anaerobic. It produces toxins that in pure form are destroyed by boiling, but which, when they are mixed with protein and other food, are heat-resistant. The spores also are heat-resistant. Of the six types of *Clostridium botulinum*, four produce toxins that affect man. Symptoms of fatigue, headache and dizziness occur between twenty-four and seventy-two hours after contaminated food has been eaten, though the incubation period may be shorter. The central nervous system is affected. In the later stages paralysis affects the patient's speech and his breathing.

Bacillus cereus. This bacillus is aerobic and spore-forming. Spores are often present in cereals, and they survive light cooking. Illness may occur within two to fifteen hours, when there is acute vomiting and also diarrhoea. Boiled rice is often associated with outbreaks of poisoning caused by *Bacillus cereus.*

Escherichia coli. Food poisoning from this source is associated particularly with diarrhoea in infants, though it may be that adults also are affected by some strains. The organism is present in many raw foods, and cooked food is readily cross-infected.

Vibrio parahaemolyticus. This may be found in fish and shellfish during warm weather, and any illness it causes has an incubation period of about fifteen hours. Symptoms are diarrhoea, vomiting and fever.

Food-borne illnesses other than poisoning

Food may be infected by pathogenic bacteria other than those that cause food poisoning, and several diseases can be food-borne. Typhoid fever, cholera and dysentry are well-known examples. But, though food may be the vehicle of infection, the causative bacteria do not multiply in food.

How food becomes infected with food-poisoning organisms

It has already been indicated that food may be infected with food-poisoning organisms at the time it reaches the kitchen. This applies particularly to meat and poultry, and their infection may occur in any of the following ways:

1. The animal or bird may have eaten infected food;
2. Infection may have been picked up from other animals or birds;
3. Meat and poultry may become contaminated after slaughter.

Within the kitchen, food may become infected by various organisms in a number of ways.

Salmonella

1. Any staff who are suffering from food poisoning caused by *Salmonella*, or who are carriers, excrete these bacteria, and as a result their hands become contaminated. Unless hands are thoroughly washed after visits to the lavatory, any food handled and any surfaces touched are likely to become contaminated.

2. Infected meat or poultry may contaminate other food either through direct contact with the flesh or through drips and juices that fall on to other food.

3. There may be cross-contamination through contact with such things as slicing machines, working surfaces, knives and other tools, containers and kitchen cloths.

Staphylococcus

1. Food may be contaminated by direct contact with open cuts or boils on the food handler's person, or by contact with hands that have touched nose, mouth, handkerchief, cuts or boils.

2. There may be cross-contamination from implements, working surfaces, kitchen cloths, etc.

Clostridium welchii

1. Contamination may come from soil brought in with vegetables, or from dust.

2. Flies and bluebottles may be carriers.

3. There may be cross-contamination from equipment, utensils, etc.

Bacillus cereus

Contamination may spread from infected cereals by means of cereal dust, or through contact with contaminated surfaces or tools.

The growth of food-poisoning organisms

Some species of pathogenic bacteria are liable to cause illness even if only a few are ingested, but this is not true of most food-poisoning organisms. There has to be a heavy growth of bacteria for food-poisoning to be caused. So one must ask, once food has become contaminated, what conditions favour growth? Conditions are favourable when food and moisture are available—these are obtained from the media on which the organism grows—and when the atmosphere is moderately warm. Pathogenic bacteria multiply at temperatures between 15 and 45° Celsius; they do best at 37° Celsius, with the exception of *Clostridium welchii*, which grows well up to temperatures of 47–50° Celsius. Under ideal conditions bacteria multiply by dividing into two every twenty to thirty minutes; thus a single bacterium can increase to two million in seven hours. Time is therefore an important factor in the increase of food-poisoning bacteria. Growth is inhibited at temperatures below 7·2° Celsius, and bacteria are destroyed at temperatures above 60° Celsius, except for spores. The spores produced by certain types of bacteria can stay alive, but dormant, under adverse conditions, including high temperatures. When conditions improve they become active bacteria.

Foods most likely to be vehicles of food poisoning
Certain foods are more likely than others to be the vehicles of food poisoning, and in Britain meat and poultry are the most common. The percentage of reported cases in which these foods are implicated varies from year to year, but usually it is between eighty and ninety. Reheated meat and cold meat (both processed and fresh) account for most cases; sea foods, milk and cream are also involved from time to time. The following is a list of foods that, in addition to reheated meat, are commonly involved in outbreaks of food poisoning, and therefore need special care:

Made-up meat dishes
Meat pies
Pressed beef
Brawn
Sausages
Ham
Cold sweets, especially trifles
Cream cakes
Soups
Stews
Gravies

It will be noticed that some of these dishes may be subject to much handling—some before cooking, and some again after cooking. In other cases most of the handling occurs after cooking.

Cases of bacterial food poisoning are associated with a chain of circumstances, and in the kitchen they are as follows:

First, an infective organism must be present. Usually it enters the kitchen by means of infected food, or it is brought in by the kitchen staff. Secondly, if it is not already present on food, the infective organism is transferred to it by various means, for example by the food handler or by cross-contamination. Thirdly, once the organism is present on food, conditions must be such that it can grow easily and rapidly. Fourthly, the infected food must be ingested by a susceptible person.

If this chain can be broken at any point, there will be no outbreak of food poisoning. Hence, control is directed at the breaking of the chain at any of these points. So far as the first circumstance is concerned, the caterer cannot prevent infected food from coming into the kitchen, but he can take some reasonable precautions: he can deal only with suppliers who are known to have high hygiene standards, and he can note the condition of delivery vans, trays, etc. It is good practice to consult the Environmental Officer of Health before opening an account with a new firm. The possibility of employing staff who are carriers of infection cannot be eliminated completely, but again certain precautions can be taken. It is possible to require that an employee shall submit a medical certificate of fitness to work as a food handler before he takes up his appointment, and also when he returns to duty after a period of absence. The law provides for staff to be suspended in certain circumstances. The Food Hygiene Regulations, 1970, require that: 'Immediately a person engaged in the handling of food becomes aware that he is suffering from, or is the carrier of, typhoid, paratyphoid or any other *Salmonella* infection or amoebic or bacillary dysentery or any staphylococcal infection likely to cause food poisoning, he shall inform the person carrying on the food business, and that person shall immediately notify the appropriate medical officer of health accordingly.' (Paragraph 13(I).) (The office of Medical Officer of Health no longer exists and notification should be made to the local authority.) If necessary, the person is suspended from duty. However, the control of carriers is difficult because neither the carrier nor his employer may be aware that he is a source of danger until after there has been an outbreak. In the case of *Staphylococci*, whose natural habitat is the mucous membrane and skin of man, a high percentage of the population carries them in the nose, but not all types are associated with food poisoning.

So far as the transfer of organisms to food is concerned, personal hygiene on the part of the food handler has an important part to play; also, the less food is handled the better, particularly after it has been cooked. It is important, too, that incoming foods such as meat and poultry, which may be contaminated, should not come into contact with other food that might be a suitable medium for the growth of organisms. Cross-contamination is controlled chiefly by keeping raw food away from the cooked product, and by establishing effective procedures and routines for cleaning equipment and premises.

The next part of the chain is most important. Food that is susceptible to infection should not be stored for any length of time in conditions that favour the growth of infective bacteria. The Food Hygiene Regulations, 1970, require that all food consisting of meat, fish, gravy or imitation cream, or prepared from or containing any of those substances or any egg or milk, shall either be kept at a temperature of not less than 62·7° Celsius or below 10° Celsius, except when it is to be served for immediate consumption. If the temperature should fall below 62·7° Celsius, the food must be cooled quickly under hygienic conditions to below 10° Celsius. Figure 68 gives a temperature guide for safe food handling.

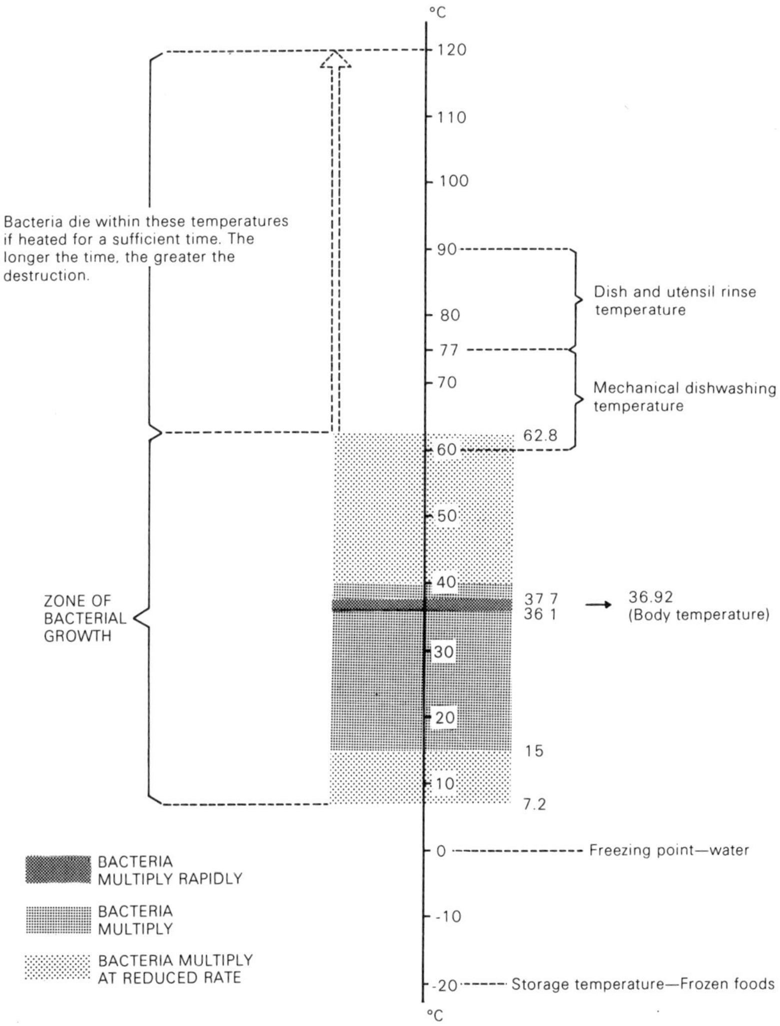

Fig. 68 Temperature guide for safe handling of food

No caterer wittingly allows the fourth circumstance to arise, but he may well have to use his judgment as to whether a food would be likely to cause food poisoning, and so should not be used. The susceptibility of persons to food poisoning is, of course, outside the hands of the caterer. In any group of people some are more susceptible than others. The very young, the elderly, and the sick are particularly vulnerable.

Hygiene in storing, preparing and cooking food

Meat and poultry

1. Because these foods may be infected in their raw state, they should be kept away from cooked foods—especially meat and poultry—and other susceptible foods at all times. They should not be allowed to come into contact with other food in the refrigerator, nor to drip on to it. It is better to have separate tools and equipment for preparing raw meat and poultry, but when this is not possible equipment should be cleaned thoroughly before it is used for other foods.

2. Meat and poultry should be placed in the refrigerator or cold store as soon as it arrives, and should stay there until it is due to be prepared and cooked.

3. Meat and poultry should be thoroughly cooked to ensure that any pathogenic bacteria that may be present are destroyed. Meat is a poor conductor of heat, so it is possible for the outside of a joint to be cooked before the required temperature is reached at the centre. From the hygiene point of view, the practice of serving rare meat must be deprecated.

4. Frozen joints of meat and poultry should be thawed completely before they are cooked; otherwise there is a danger that the required temperature will not be reached at the centre when the outside is done. This is a particular hazard with large turkeys.

5. Unless meat or poultry is to be eaten cold, it should be served as soon as possible after cooking, and in any event within two hours.

6. When meat or poultry is to be served cold, it should be cooled rapidly after cooking and kept at a low temperature until it is needed. Large joints take a long time to cool, and for this reason the size of joints intended for the cold table should not exceed 2·5 kg. In good conditions a joint weighing about 2·5 kg should cool in from one-and-a-half to two hours.

7. Except where the processes of prime cooking, cooling and storing have taken place under controlled conditions, as in a cook-freeze kitchen, cooked meat and poultry should not be reheated.

Milk, cream, artificial cream and eggs: products containing milk, cream and eggs

1. Milk and cream should be stored in the refrigerator.
2. Milk, cream, artificial cream and desserts containing them should not be allowed to stand for long periods on serving counters, especially during warm weather, unless the counter is refrigerated.
3. Desserts, sauces and dressings that are to be served cold should be cooled quickly and stored at a low temperature until they are needed.
4. Great care should be taken to keep equipment used for finishing cold sweets scrupulously clean and disinfected. Any non-disposable piping bags should be boiled after use.
5. Because duck eggs are fairly often infected with *Salmonella typhi-murium* they should always be very well cooked—for example, boiled for ten minutes—and it is better not to use them for lightly-cooked dishes such as omelettes.

Frozen foods

Frozen food, as we have seen, should be stored consistently at a temperature of −20° Celsius or lower. When it has been thawed, it should be treated as fresh food. Problems sometimes arise when a storage freezer breaks down and the contents thaw. Is the food safe to use? This depends upon several factors: the length of time for which it has been thawed, and the temperatures involved. If the centre of the food is still frozen, the temperature on the outside should be low enough to prevent the growth of bacteria, and the food should be fit for use. Thawed food should not be refrozen, as this practice constitutes a hygiene hazard—the quality also would suffer.

Chilled foods

Foods that are chilled with the intention of their being reheated subsequently (for example in microwave ovens) should be chilled promptly and rapidly to between two and four degrees Celsius. Subsequently they should be held at that temperature until they are reheated. Preferably the holding time should not exceed forty-eight hours and in no circumstances should it exceed six days.

Fruit and salad vegetables

In *Food Poisoning and Food Hygiene* Betty C. Hobbs recommends that dessert fruits eaten with the peel should have been washed in water containing a little sodium hypochlorite. The amount to be used varies with the strength of the sodium hypochlorite, but should be such that the amount of available chlorine is approximately sixty to eighty parts per million. This applies also to salad vegetables that are to be eaten raw—for example lettuce, tomatoes and watercress. So far as imported fruits are concerned, it should be borne in mind that in many of the exporting countries the incidence of intestinal pathogenic bacteria is high, and that infection is spread by flies.

General care of food

1. Open foods should be protected from dust, flies, droplets from sneezes, etc. When perishable food, such as meat, is cooling or is in the kitchen during preparation, butter muslin is a suitable covering because it allows air circulation. Food on display in service areas should be protected by so-called sneeze plates. Particular care should be taken to see that no food is left exposed when the floor, or any other surface, is being swept.

2. Food in store should be kept covered and protected from vermin.

3. Open food should not be left in the kitchen overnight because it may attract vermin and be contaminated by them.

4. Food should be protected from contamination by chemicals; this has already been discussed in Chapter 18 in connection with food storage. Occasionally food becomes contaminated because unsuitable equipment has been used. For example, acid fruit prepared in galvanised iron containers has caused zinc poisoning.

Food hygiene and the food handler

It is an important precept that the less food is handled the better, but a certain amount of handling is necessary, and food inevitably comes into contact with equipment and tools that have been touched by food handlers. The aim is to control the transfer of bacteria from the handler to food, or to any other object or surface in the kitchen. The person, habits and clothing of the handler are all involved, as are the procedures he uses in handling food.

It goes without saying that the food handler's person should be clean—this is a requirement of the Food Hygiene Regulations—but the most important point is the cleanliness of hands. Those who handle food should know that it is essential for hands to be washed thoroughly, and for fingernails to be clean, immediately before they start work. If, during a food-preparation task, work is suspended and hands are used for another purpose, they should be washed before the worker returns to his task; this is particularly important after visits to the lavatory.

It is important also that hands are in good condition and free from cracks. The food handler should look after his hands, using hand cream or lotion if necessary. Any skin lesions caused by cuts and burns are likely to harbour *Staphylococci*, and it is a requirement of the Food Hygiene Regulations, 1970, that any such lesions shall be covered with waterproof dressings to prevent the passage of bacteria.

Adequate facilities for hand-washing are, of course, necessary. A wash basin with a supply of hot water, together with soap, nailbrush and towels or other means of drying hands, is required near the water closet, and also in the food preparation area of the kitchen. Cross-contamination of hands is less likely if the W.C. is flushed by means of a foot pedal, and if the wash-basin taps are designed for operation by the elbow rather than the hand. Towels used for drying hands are potential sources of infection and re-infection, and for this reason disposable paper towels or hot-air driers are preferable. The first-aid box—which should be readily accessible—should contain suitable waterproof dressings. The Food Hygiene Regulations, 1970, lay down what hand-washing facilities are to be provided, and require a notice to be fixed near every sanitary convenience asking users to wash their hands afterwards. The provision of first-aid materials is mandatory, as is the use of waterproof dressings on cuts.

The food handler needs to wear clean protective clothing to cover his own clothes, and to cover or restrain his hair. This is donned before the food preparation area is entered, and removed before the premises are left. Although it is usual for the employer to provide such clothing, the Food Hygiene Regulations place the onus on the food handler to wear 'sufficient clean and washable overclothing'. The style of cap should become the wearer, since otherwise there may be extreme reluctance to wear it. Ideally hair should be completely covered, for hair and dandruff can be sources of infection. But one object of the wearing of a cap is to keep hair tidy and away from the face, so that it is not necessary for the wearer to touch his hair while he is at work. Caps are often provided that fulfil this function without completely confining the hair.

Touching the skin round the mouth and nose is an extremely undesirable habit. Hence smoking is not allowed in kitchens, because it involves touching the mouth. Smoking is prohibited under the Food Hygiene Regulations. So far as touching the nose goes, special mention should be made of the handkerchief as a medium for the transfer of infection. It is much more hygienic to use paper handkerchiefs rather than cotton ones, provided that they are disposed of immediately after use.

When hands are washed thoroughly, coliform bacteria (which are associated with faeces) are effectively removed or reduced in number, but *Staphylococci* may still remain in considerable—though reduced—force, lodged in skin crevices. Hence it is particularly important to avoid handling those foods such as cooked meats, cream and cooked seafoods, on which *Staphylococci* grow readily.

The following equipment is useful in reducing the handling of cooked food:

Carving fork: to steady the joint when meat is carved by hand;
Cook's fork: for many items, including sliced meat;
Electric meat slicer:
Fish slice or similar implement: for removing sliced meat from the meat slicer;
Pastry servers and tongs: for use at the service counter and elsewhere;
Plastic disposable gloves: for miscellaneous use, and for handling frozen foods during packing in cook-freeze kitchens.

Cleaning and disinfecting utensils, equipment and working surfaces
The aim in cleaning such items is to remove visible dirt and food debris and to remove, so far as possible, all sources of infection. This does not mean that after cleaning equipment will be sterile (that is, free from all microbial life), but it does mean that the presence of micro-organisms has been reduced to a level that is not likely to be harmful. In this context the term 'disinfection' as opposed to 'sterilisation' is often used. In addition to disinfection by cleaning, heat or chemicals may be used, but they must not be regarded as a substitute for cleaning, which always comes first; it is then followed by any further method of disinfection considered necessary.

Any consideration of cleaning and disinfection must take into account not only the actual processes, but also for which items the use of heat or chemicals is particularly important, and how often cleaning and disinfection should take place. Usually the answer to the last question is straightforward: equipment should be cleaned at the end of use, or at the end of a process. But if it is in continuous use for a long period there must be a break for cleaning to prevent the build-up of bacteria. For example, a meat-slicing machine should not be used continuously for longer than two hours. At the end of this time there should be a break for thorough cleaning.

Items needing special care and attention

Slicing machines. The design should allow for easy dismantling for cleaning, and every part of the machine should be cleaned. Wherever practicable, parts should be immersed after washing in a heated sink. A disinfectant such as hypochlorite should be used for fixed parts. To avoid cross-contamination, disposable cloths should be used for wiping.

Containers used for carrying hot food. Specially-designed sterilising jets for disinfecting this type of container after it has been washed are available.

Can openers, mincing machines and their attachments and piping bags. These are other articles needing special care.

The general cleaning of equipment and utensils

When equipment and utensils are cleaned, at least two distinct processes are involved. First soil is removed by means of the washing water, and second the article is dried. A method often used in the home is to wash in a sink of water, and then to dry with an absorbent cloth. Some of the washing water is transferred to the cloth during the drying process. As the washing water becomes dirty, the cloth in turn becomes contaminated and infects all articles subsequently dried by it. Hence, this method does not produce articles that are really clean, and when the washing water contains a considerable amount of soil the amount of contamination remaining on a clean article is considerable. There are two ways of keeping down the level of soil in the washing water, and both should be used. First, heavy soil is removed before washing by scraping and/or pre-rinsing; second, the washing water is changed frequently. A washing sink should be emptied and refilled at intervals of not more than twenty minutes.

When rinsing is introduced between washing and drying, the amount of soil remaining on washed items is reduced considerably; still better results are obtained if the rinsing water is capable of destroying most of the remaining bacteria. There are two ways of achieving this. One is to maintain the temperature of the rinsing water at not less than 77° Celsius, and the second is to dose it with a measured amount of a suitable chemical disinfectant. Hypochlorites and quaternary ammonium compounds are often used for this purpose, but the one chosen must be compatible with the detergent used. The rinsing will not be effective unless all food and grease have been removed during the washing. Where a heated rinsing sink is used, articles should be immersed for at least two minutes.

An improvement on the cleaning method first described is to eliminate the use of drying cloths so far as possible, so that there is less possibility of contamination from that source. But, as we saw in Chapter 12, this is not always practicable for all items. Any cotton or linen cloths used should be changed often and washed and boiled regularly, though a better method is to use disposable paper towels.

It is as important to rinse pots, pans, tools and utensils as it is to rinse tableware, though this point is sometimes overlooked. Any containers in which food has remained for some time need very careful cleaning.

Detergents for washing up

When the removal of soil was discussed in Chapter 12 in relation to dishwashing machines, mention was made of detergents. A detergent suitable for washing up should possess a number of properties:

1. It can dissolve some food materials, particularly protein.
2. It acts as a wetting agent by reducing the surface tension of the water so that soil is more readily softened.
3. It emulsifies grease, breaking up fat and holding it in suspension in the water. The temperature of the water is important here because this melts the fat, but the detergent breaks it up into small particles and prevents its being re-deposited on articles, or forming scum on the surface of the water.
4. It should be able to break up any solid food matter of whatever nature.
5. Where water is hard, the detergent chosen should prevent the formation of scum and scale.
6. It should be harmless, and, if it is to be used for washing up by hand, it should not have a bad effect upon the skin.
7. It should be easy to rinse away.

Several ingredients are combined in detergents to give all the necessary properties.

The nature of detergents

Strictly speaking, soap is a detergent, but the term is popularly used to denote soapless synthetic detergents. Soap is seldom used for washing up because it is less effective than are synthetic detergents, and when it is used in hard water scum is formed. The scum consists of soil and magnesium or calcium salts—the cause of hardness—which are thrown out of solution by the soap. Most detergents contain a sequestering agent to keep hardness salts in solution, and thus to prevent scum formation.

Detergents may be either organic or inorganic. Inorganic detergents are often strongly alkaline, and may contain caustic ingredients such as sodium hydroxide. They are obviously unsuitable for manual use, because they harm the skin. Their low-foaming properties make them suitable for dishwashing machines, since foaming impairs the efficiency of spray-type machines. Organic detergents fall into three groups: anionic (negatively charged), cationic (positively charged) and non-ionic (neither negatively nor positively charged).

Anionic detergents are not as a rule alkaline, and so are suitable for washing up by hand. Most of them create considerable amounts of foam, which makes them unsuitable for dishwashing machines. They may be used in conjunction with soap, which is also anionic. The group possesses most properties required from a washing-up detergent.

Cationic detergents include the quaternary ammonium compounds. These act as bactericides for some organisms, but their range is limited. They are often used purely as disinfectants, but they do have detergent properties, and in combination with other ingredients of an inorganic nature they are used to produce combined detergents and bactericides. These detergents cannot be mixed with soap.

Non-ionic detergents have good wetting properties in cold water, and they are used in many specialised cleaning agents. They are stable in hard water, and also in the presence of acids and alkalis.

Some detergents intended for use in washing-up machines are formulated to control staining of tea and coffee cups.

Detergents for cleaning surfaces and articles other than pots and pans

Detergents intended for washing up by hand are suitable also for such purposes as washing working surfaces and performing other light cleaning operations. But many cleaning tasks present special features for which manufacturers have developed specially-formulated products, some of which contain caustic ingredients. Detergents available include those designed for: the removal of carbonised grease from ovens and fish fryers; cleaning drains; general heavy-duty work, such as the cleaning of floors and canopies.

Chemical disinfectants

As has been mentioned, chemical disinfectants are sometimes used in the rinsing water in washing-up processes, and also for disinfecting machines, or parts of them, *in situ* if they cannot be taken to the sink. They may also be used on working surfaces and any equipment for which heat treatment is unsuitable. The disinfectant chosen should be compatible with the detergent used—for example, if the detergent is anionic an anionic disinfectant, such as hypochlorite, must be used, since otherwise the disinfectant will be inactive.

Various types of organic material render chemical disinfectants inactive, and if food debris is present in the washing water or on the equipment the disinfectant will be ineffective. It is an important precept, therefore, that articles should be clean before they are disinfected. Disinfectants do not kill all types of bacteria, though they usually destroy *Staphylococci*. Some do not destroy, but merely inhibit growth.

Chemical disinfection takes time. Articles should remain in contact with the disinfectant for at least two minutes, and up to thirty minutes' contact is necessary in the case of slow-acting products. Disinfectant solutions are more effective at high temperatures than at low ones. Disinfectants have a place in kitchen hygiene, but they need to be used with thought and discretion, and their individual properties should be studied. Only those suitable for use in connection with food operations should be used.

Cleaning the kitchen premises

In the cleaning of kitchen premises, three types of soil are involved:

Loose dirt. If this is allowed to remain it harbours germs. One source of bacteria in dust is the droplets that are scattered by people when they talk, and especially when they cough or sneeze. These droplets fall to the ground, or elsewhere, and mingle with the dust. There is dust also from fine food particles—for example cereal dust, and soil from vegetables (which may contain pathogenic bacteria) is often present.

Grease. This type of soiling is caused by splashing, and by particles of fat or greasy substances that are dropped on the floor. Grease easily becomes impacted and other soil tends to stick to it. Also the oil and fat used in cooking, and the fat on meat that is being roasted, have a tendency to sublime; hence grease is deposited on walls, ceilings, canopies, light fittings and other surfaces.

Food debris. The third type consists of particles of food of all types, some of which will be greasy.

Grease and food particles are attractive to vermin and to many kinds of insect pests, and they also harbour pathogenic organisms. Grease and dust collect more readily on horizontal and sloping surfaces such as floors, canopies and cupboard tops than on vertical surfaces. They adhere most readily to rough surfaces.

Cleaning the floor

While all surfaces must be cleaned, the floor needs the most frequent attention and the greatest amount of labour. There is no doubt that, if it were possible for staff to do their work without allowing any solid food particles or any liquids to fall to the ground, the work of cleaning the floor would be greatly eased. But it is not possible to achieve this ideal. Nevertheless, the aim should always be to work neatly and tidily. If this is done, floor cleaning will be much easier, and standards of comfort and safety will be higher. Spilt food should always be swept or mopped up immediately to avoid its being spread by footwear or trodden in.

Sweeping. The practice of dry sweeping to remove dust and food debris is sometimes criticised because dust, and consequently germs, may be spread by this means. However, it is often the only effective way of dealing with spilt food, and, if the floor is not swept before it is washed, food debris tends to be pushed to the edge of the floor and left there. Vacuum cleaning is a more hygienic alternative, but it is not always practicable in a kitchen. If the floor is swept regularly so that there is no great accumulation of dust, if it is washed daily, and if sweeping is done carefully, the process should on the whole improve rather than detract from hygiene standards. But it is important that no open food is left exposed while sweeping is in progress, and care should be taken to avoid raising dust.

Cleaning by washing and scrubbing. The kitchen floor should be cleaned daily by either washing or scrubbing, and an especially thorough clean is necessary at regular intervals—not less than once a week. When soiling is not heavy and the floor surface is good, washing alone is often adequate for the daily clean, but scrubbing at least once a week is usually necessary to remove impacted soil. In both washing and scrubbing the floor should be rinsed with clean water after the soil has been removed, but the amount of water used for rinsing should be strictly controlled; otherwise a great deal of moisture enters the atmosphere during the drying.

Long-handled mops are usually used for washing. These have heads of synthetic sponge or cotton or other fibre. The first have self-squeezing devices, and the others are used in conjunction with special buckets with wringing devices. Wringers consisting of upper and lower rollers are particularly efficient. Specially-designed trolleys for use in floor washing are fitted with wringers and accommodate buckets of washing and rinsing water. It is very important to keep mops clean, and cotton mop-heads should be easily detachable for washing and disinfecting.

Usually either a long-handled brush known as a deck scrubber or a machine is used for scrubbing, but in most kitchens there are some areas that are inaccessible to either, and for these a hand scrubbing brush must be used. A deck scrubber is best used in combination with a squeegee, which consists of a rubber blade fitted to a long handle, by means of which dirty washing water is sucked along the floor, leaving a comparatively dry area behind it. A certain amount of skill is needed to use either of these implements effectively. Those to be used by women should be light in weight. Floor scrubbing machines are efficient and labour-saving, but they are not suitable for use in all kitchens because of difficulties in manoeuvring round equipment and fixtures.

Any grids and floor gullies should be cleaned at the same time as the floor, and grids should be removed from the gullies for the purpose.

Walls and ceilings

Walls and ceilings must be cleaned regularly, but it is not reasonable to expect catering staff to do more than a limited amount of this work. Usually staff are asked to clean only what is within reach—but the reach can be greatly extended by the use of long-handled tools. Other cleaning should be done either by maintenance staff or by outside firms.

Canopies, electric light fittings, windows and fly screens must all be given regular routine attention, and in the case of windows and fly screens this is necessary not only for ordinary reasons of cleanliness, but because dirty windows and screens cut out light. These tasks are often outside the scope of the catering staff, in which case, unless maintenance staff are employed, it is advisable to make standing arrangements with an outside firm. There are several well-known firms that specialise in this sort of maintenance cleaning.

The kitchen entrance and yard

Yards and entrance areas should be kept swept and washed to ensure that the indoor premises are not soiled unnecessarily by dirt trampled in from outside. Gullies, grids and any grease traps or peel traps should receive regular attention. Areas around bins need to be clean and free from scraps that could attract flies, vermin or dogs, and the insides of the bins must also be kept clean. Now that waste-disposal units are commonly used, fewer kitchens have waste food bins. Where they are still used, they should be cleaned and disinfected each time they are emptied, which should be at least three times a week. It is easier to keep the area round bins clean if they are raised from the ground on platforms of slatted metal about 300 mm high.

High-pressure cleaning

Cleaning premises and plant takes a great deal of labour when traditional methods are used. In the hospital kitchens studied and reported upon in Management Services (NHS), *Study of Work in Hospital Kitchens to Determine Staffing Ratios*, twenty-three per cent of the time of unskilled staff was spent on cleaning floors, walls and fixed equipment. It is therefore not surprising that attention has been turned recently towards improving cleaning methods and bringing them up to date. One development is cleaning by means of high-pressure jets; this has proved highly successful in removing impacted dirt at great speed and with very little labour. It has the additional advantage that areas that are difficult to reach and clean successfully by other methods are within easy range of a jet. The basic components for high-pressure cleaning are: the pump, which may be operated by air pressure or electricity; the water tank; the detergent tank; and the lance through which the pressurised cleaning agent is ejected. Pressure cleaners may be portable, or there may be a built-in system with several lances available at various points. Cleaners can operate at either 3400 kN/m^2 or 6900 kN/m^2. High-pressure equipment can be used only on suitable impervious surfaces, and the design of equipment must be suitable also. Cabinet-type equipment such as refrigerators, fryers and ovens should have drain plugs that can be removed easily. When new catering establishments are planned, the possibility of installing high-pressure jets should be considered at the outset. Before portable machinery is used, a competent person should check that it is safe to do so, and that no electricity cables are likely to come into contact with water.

Control of pests and domestic animals

Rats and mice. Infestations must be dealt with promptly and effectively, and the local authority should be consulted at an early stage. It is obviously preferable, however, to prevent infestations wherever possible.

1. Premises should be kept in good repair, and there should be no means by which pests may readily gain access to kitchens or storerooms. Attention should be given to gaps under doors, which are often overlooked as means of access.
2. Food scraps should be removed from the premises promptly.
3. Rodent-proof containers with well-fitting lids should be provided for food in stores.
4. Open foods should not be left lying about in the kitchen, and in no circumstances should they be left out overnight.

Flies. The fly is the most common insect pest in the kitchen. Flies are frequenters of manure heaps and decaying refuse. They can transmit bacteria mechanically on their feet, and also in their excreta. When flies are a serious nuisance the cause may be a nearby rubbish tip that is not properly controlled, so the local authority should be informed. The following are methods of control.

1. Windows and ventilators in stores should be screened to prevent flies from entering.
2. Open food should be protected with fly-proof covering.
3. Scraps of food should not be left lying about.
4. Lids should be kept on waste bins, and waste-food bins should be emptied and cleaned regularly so that they do not provide breeding-places for flies.
5. Electrically-operated fly killers may be installed. These have ultra-violet fluorescent tubes to attract the insects, an electrified grid to kill them, and a collecting tray.

The use of the knock-down type of aerosol insecticides is not recommended because the insects so knocked down may well fall into food and remain there undetected.

Cockroaches. These pests are associated particularly with steam-operated kitchens. They are nocturnal in habit and occupy crevices in walls and floors, especially in warm places. Although they are susceptible to most insecticides, complete elimination is difficult once there has been an infestation. Either the local authority or a firm that specialises in pest control should be consulted.

Ants. These insects are often a nuisance, but they are not believed to be a hygiene hazard. They are extremely difficult to get rid of, but cleanliness in removing food particles, especially of sugar, helps to avoid attracting them in the first place. When there is an infestation insecticidal sprays, or a lacquer that is painted round cracks in walls and floors, etc., may be effective.

Cats and dogs. These animals may carry *Salmonella*, and so may excrete *Salmonella* organisms. It is therefore necessary to exclude them from all parts of the catering premises. They should not be allowed access to waste bins, dishes, utensils or any food. It is extremely undesirable that food should be left outside the premises for any reason, for example by a delivery man, since it might be fouled by dogs or cats (or from other sources).

Design of catering premises, plant and equipment, and their state of repair

There have been frequent references in earlier parts of the book to hygiene in relation to the design of premises and plant, and the materials used. It is sufficient to say here that in general terms the design should allow easy access for cleaning, and that the materials used must be such that they may be thoroughly and easily cleaned; this is a requirement of the Food Hygiene Regulations.

Regulations and codes of practice

Although many references have been made to the Food Hygiene Regulations, 1970, all their requirements have not been mentioned. However, it is essential that the caterer should be familiar with them all, and the obligations they impose upon those who carry on a food business, or who have control or management of persons engaged in handling food, and upon the food handler himself. Likewise, the caterer has a duty to see that food handlers for whom he is responsible are aware of the Regulations and what is required of them. Penalties for offences are laid down in the Regulations, which also specify that each local authority (that is, the District Council) shall enforce and execute the provisions of the Regulations in its district. The Environmental Health Officer has the duty of inspecting catering establishments, and he also offers advice and help. Legislation passed in 1976 gives District Councils power to close catering premises.

Many catering concerns—including the National Health Service—

issue food hygiene codes to food handlers to help them to understand and remember key points. The Department of Health and Social Security, in conjunction with the Ministry of Agriculture, Fisheries and Food, publishes food hygiene codes of practice from time to time relating to specific sections and aspects of the food trade. It also issues a general code for food trade workers.

Ten-point code for food trade workers

1. Wash your hands always before touching food, and always after using the W.C.
2. Tell your supervisor at once of any skin, nose, throat or bowel trouble.
3. Cover cuts and sores with waterproof dressings.
4. Wear clean clothing, and be clean.
5. Remember smoking in a food room is illegal and dangerous. Never cough or sneeze over food.
6. Clean as you go in food rooms.
7. Keep food clean, covered and either cool or piping hot.
8. Keep your hands off food as far as possible. Keep food utensils clean.
9. Keep the lid on the dustbin.
10. Remember the law requires clean, fully-equipped, well-lit and airy conditions for food preparation.

TABLE 14: Numbers of cases of reported food poisoning, England and Wales

Year	*Number*
1966	4531
1967	5018
1968	5955
1969	7338
1970	7566
1971	6720
1972	5484
1973	7059
1974	6225
1975	8863
1976	9050

Source: *Annual Abstract of Statistics*, Central Statistical Office, HMSO, 1977, Table 3.51, Notifications of Infectious Diseases.

Appendix 1: Schedule of recommended equipment, storage and accommodation for school kitchens, *Educational Building Note 14, School Kitchens*, Scottish Education Department

No.	*Description*	*No. or Measure*	*Meals Capacity of Kitchen*																*Comments*
			30	50	75	100	150	200	250	300	350	400	450	500	550	600	800	1000	
1	Boiling rings	No	—	1	—	—	—	—	—	—	—	—	—	—	—	—	—	—	
2	Boiling tables	No	—	—	1	—	—	—	—	—	—	—	—	—	—	—	—	—	
3	RANGES Single oven	No	1	1	1	—	—	—	—	—	—	—	—	1	1	1	1	—	
	Double oven	No	—	—	—	1	1	1	1	1	1	1	1	1	1	1	1	2	
4	Grills	No	—	—	—	—	—	—	—	—	1	1	1	1	1	1	1	1	Secondary schools only
5	OVENS, GENERAL PURPOSE 1 Tier	No	—	—	—	—	—	—	—	—	1	1	—	—	—	—	—	—	
	2 Tier	No	—	—	—	—	—	—	—	—	—	—	1	1	1	1	2	2	
6	STEAMING OVENS 5 Shelf	No	—	—	—	1	1	1	1	1	1	—	—	—	2	2	—	—	
	6 Shelf	No	—	—	—	—	—	—	—	—	—	1	1	1	—	—	2	3	
7	FRYERS 60 lb per hour (27 kilos per hour)	No	—	—	1	1	1	1	—	—	—	1	1	—	—	—	—	—	
	120 lb per hour (54 kilos per hour)	No	—	—	—	—	—	—	1	1	1	1	1	2	2	3	3	4	

8	BOILING PANS Single purpose	Litres	— — —	— — —	— — —	— 45 —	— 45 —	— 45 —	— 90 —	— 90 —	— 90 —	— 90 —	90 — 45	90 — 45	90 — 45	90 — 45	90 45 45	90 90 45	
	Dual purpose	Litres	—	—	—	—	—	45	45	45 45	45 45	45 45	45 45	45 45	45 45	90 45	90 45	90 45	
9	HOT CUPBOARDS Self service	Metre Run	0·600	0·600	0·600	1·200	1·800	1·800	2·400	2·400	3·000	3·600	4·200	4·800	5·400	5·400	*	*	* Metre run will vary according to the number and seating capacity of dining rooms.
	Family service	Metre Run	0·600	0·600	1·200	1·800	2·400	3·000	3·600	—	—	—	—	—	—	—	—	—	
10	MACHINERY Vegetable preparation machine	No	—	—	—	—	—	—	—	—	—	1*	1*	1*	1*	1	1	1	* Including chip blade
	Food mixer	Litres	—	11*	14*	14*	14*	22*	22*	22*	33*	33**	33**	33**	33**	33** 14	33** 14	33** 14	* Complete with attachments for crumbing, shredding, slicing and mincing. ** With mincing attachments only

No.	Description	No. or Measure	Meals Capacity of Kitchen																Comments
	Potato chipper	No	—	—	—	—	—	—	—	—	—	—	—	—	—	1	1	1	
	Meat slicer (Gravity feed)	No	—	—	1*	1*	1	1	1	1	1	1	1	1	1	1	1	1	* 0·175 m blade
	Waste disposal units	No	Motor rating will depend on the type of waste for disposal																
11	STORAGE	Minimum																	
	Vegetables	Metre Run of	0·900	0·900	1·200	1·200	1·500	2·100	2·700	3·000	3·600	3·900	4·500	4·800	5·400	5·700	6·900	7·800	
	Dry goods	Lower	2·700	3·000	3·000	3·300	3·600	3·900	4·200	4·500	4·800	5·400	5·700	6·300	6·900	7·200	8·400	9·600	
	Larder	Shelves	0·600	0·600	0·900	1·200	1·200	1·500	1·800	1·800	2·100	2·100	2·400	2·400	2·700	2·700	3·300	3·900	
12	Refrigerators	m^3	0·20	0·28	0·28	0·42	0·42	0·57	0·71	0·71	0·71	0·85	0·85	—	—	—	—	—	
13	Cold rooms	m^3	—	—	—	—	—	—	—	—	—	—	—	6·00	6·00	6·00	7·00	7·00	
14	CUPBOARDS																		
	Utensils	Total	—	—	—	—	0·900	1·200	1·500	1·800	2·100	2·400	2·700	3·000	3·300	3·600	4·800	6·000	
	Reserve equipment	Metre	To be provided in dead storage space																
	Brooms	Run of	0·600	0·600	0·600	0·600	0·750	0·750	0·750	0·900	0·900	0·900	1·050	1·050	1·200	1·200	1·200	1·200	
	Cook's store	Shelves	—	—	—	—	—	—	0·600	0·600	0·600	0·900	0·900	0·900	0·900	0·900	0·900	0·900	
	Linen		2·400	2·400	2·400	3·000	3·000	3·000	3·000	3·600	3·600	3·600	3·600	3·600	4·000	4·000	4·000	4·000	
15	Preparation benching	Minimum Metre Run	1·800	1·800	1·800	1·800	2·400	3·000	3·600	4·200	4·800	5·400	6·000	6·600	7·200	7·800	9·000	10·800	
16	Scales (platform)	No	—	—	—	—	—	1	1	1	1	1	1	1	1	1	1	1	
17	Scales	No	One in every kitchen																
18	Wash hand basin	No	One in every kitchen																

	Cook's desk only	No	—	—	—	—	1	1	—	—	—	—	—	—	—	—	—	—	
	Supervisor's office	No	—	—	—	—	—	—	1	1	1	1	1	1	1	1	1	1	
	Staff acc. inl. toilet	m²	4·0	4·0	4·0	7·0	7·0	9·0	9·0	11·0	11·0	12·0	12·0	13·0	13·0	13·0	23·5	23·5	
20	SERVICE OPENINGS																		
	Service counters (for all types of service)	Minimum Metre Run	1·200	1·200	1·800	1·800	2·400	3·000	3·600	4·200	5·400	6·000	6·000	7·200	7·200	9·000	2 × 9·000	2 × 9·000	
	Returns		0·900	0·900	0·900	0·900	0·900	0·900	0·900	0·900	1·800	1·800	1·800	1·800	1·800	1·800	2 × 1·800	2 × 1·800	
21	WASH-UP UNITS																		
	Small	No	1	1	1	1	—	—	—	—	—	—	—	—	—	—	—	—	* Dependent on the number of dining rooms.
	Standard	No	—	—	—	—	1	1	1	1	2	2	2	2	2	*	*	*	
22	Vegetables sinks	No	1 Small				1 Medium		2 Medium		2 Large		3 Large				4 Large		
23	Preparation sinks	No	—	—	—	—	—			1 dual purpose				1 Standard			2 Standard		
24	Pot-wash sinks	No	—	—	—	—	—	—	—	—	—	—	—	1	1	1	1	2	
25	Hot water storage Cylinders	Litres	275	275	350	350	450	450	650	650	650	900	900	1·100	1·100	1·300	1·300	1·500	These capacities are for kitchens not fitted with dish-washing machines. Where these machines are installed the manufacturer's recommendations should be followed regarding extra hot water capacity required, if not supplied as an integral part of the machine.

Appendix 2: List of equipment for finishing kitchens (*i.e., kitchens in which frozen and other convenience foods are chiefly used*)

Item	Capacity of kitchen expressed in daily output of meals: 150	200	250	300	350	400	450	500	550	600
Forced-convection ovens	1 × 200 litres	1 × 200 litres	2 × 200 litres	2 × 200 litres	2 × 200 & 1 × 113 litres	3 × 200 litres	3 × 200 litres	3 × 200 & 1 × 113 litres	4 × 200 litres	4 × 200 litres
Boiling tables, 0·7 m deep	1 × 0·9 m	1 × 0·9 m	1 × 0·9 m	1 × 1·8 m	1 × 1·8 m	1 × 1·8 m	1 × 1·8 m	1 × 1·8 m; 1 × 0·9 m	1 × 1·8 m; 1 × 0·9 m	2 × 1·8 m
Fish fryers (output of chips, 20 kg/hour)	1	1	2	2	3	3	4	4	5	5
Water boilers	27 litres	36 litres	45 litres	54 litres	2 × 36 litres	2 × 36 litres	2 × 45 litres	2 × 45 litres	2 × 54 litres	2 × 54 litres
Hot cupboards, 0·6 m deep (metre runs)	1·8 m	2·4 m	3·0 m	3·6 m	4·3 m	4·8 m	5·4 m	6·0 m	6·6 m	7·2 m
Freezer storage units	0·76 m³	1·0 m³	1·3 m³	1·6 m³	1·9 m³	2·0 m³	2·3 m³	2·6 m³	2·9 m³	3·0 m³
Refrigerators	0·15 m³	0·15 m³	0·25 m³	0·25 m³	0·35 m³	0·35 m³	0·42 m³	0·42 m³	0·57 m³	0·57 m³
Electric mixers	1 × 12 litres	1 × 12 litres	1 × 20 litres	1 × 20 litres	1 × 20 litres	1 × 20 litres	1 × 20 litres	1 × 20 litres	1 × 20 litres	1 × 20 litres
Meat slicers	—	—	—	1	1	1	1	1	1	1
Dishwashers	—	—	1	1	1	1	1	1	1	1
Sinks:										
Washing-up unit, 3·6 m long	1	1	—	—	—	—	—	—	—	—
Cook's sink	1 × 0·6 m	1 × 0·6 m	1 × 0·76 m	1 × 0·76 m	1 × 0·76	1 × 0·76 m	1 × 0·76 m	1 × 0·76 m	1 × 0·76 m	1 × 0·76 m
Salad sink, 0·6 m long	1	1	1	1	1	1	1	1	1	1
Wash-hand basin	1	1	1	1	1	1	1	1	1	1

Notes:

1. This list is planned for simple two-course meals.
2. Water boilers are intended for the provision of hot drinks, and as ready sources of hot water for instant potatoes etc.
3. The freezer storage units relate to one main meal each day, and capacity is calculated on the assumption that frozen food deliveries will be made twice weekly.

Appendix 3.1: Basic foods that supply the necessary daily nutrients

For adults:	0·3 litre of milk 1 egg 25 g cheese 10 g cocoa powder 1 small orange or other vitamin C-rich food 150 g (6 slices) bread 1 knob of butter or margarine plus: meat or fish and vegetables twice a day, bacon three times a week, liver and fat fish once a week.
For children:	additional protein foods are necessary so milk is increased to 0·6 litre and cheese to 50 g.

Energy requirements depend on individual needs.

Source: Second Book of Food and Nutrition, Wendy Mathews and Dilys Wells, third edition, 1976.
Note: Quantities of milk have been converted from Imperial measures and rounded off.

Appendix 3.2: Information about basic foods and quantities published by the Department of Health and Social Security in *Catering in Homes for Elderly People*

Qualities of certain foods

Elderly persons are an especially vulnerable group. Malnutrition is possible in people coming into residential care who have been living on their own. Through infirmity, apathy and reduced sense of taste they tend to eat less food and very often the type of food they do eat is less nutritious. Tea and biscuits are often substituted for normal meals.

As people grow old they require fewer calories as their basic metabolism decreases and as they expend less effort in various activities than they did when young, they will therefore need less to eat. This can easily be seen in the table of recommended intakes Appendix 1.* However, it is important to realise that though their calorie needs are certainly reduced, their need for vitamins, minerals and protein is not less. As their appetite may be poor these have to be given in a more concentrated form.

Foods for repair

These are foods containing protein *e.g.*, milk, meat (including offal), ham, bacon, cheese and eggs. To make these foods, which are the most expensive, go further and to get the best nutritional value from our diet, we also use vegetable protein from pulses, bread and cereal.

Approximately 50% of the budget should be allowed for animal protein.

Milk

Use can be made of full cream dried milk for cooking purposes; this is cheaper than fresh milk and has the same nutritional value if correctly reconstituted (1 lb. to 1 gal.). [100 g per litre]

Meat, Offal, Bacon and Ham

As these are expensive foods it is important to specify the cut of meat required *i.e.*, sirloin or topside of beef for roasting and chuck or shin for stewing. It should also be remembered that the nutritional value of stewing steak is the same as the cuts for roasting. Though it is not always popular, liver is a valuable source of minerals and vitamins. Calf or pig liver is more acceptable than ox liver and it is often more popular in the form of liver sausage or paté rather than braised or fried.

* See Appendix 3.7 of *The Kitchen in Catering*.

Cheese

Though most cheese is a good source of protein, hard cheeses such as Cheddar have a higher proportion than cheese spreads. It should be remembered that cream cheese has a very low protein content but it may be useful occasionally to give variety.

Fish

Fresh fish is becoming more expensive and difficult to obtain especially in rural areas, but frozen fish is widely available. As many residents have faulty eyesight and cannot always see the bones, filleted fish is preferable to whole fish.

Fish fingers have a higher protein than purchased fish cakes.

Eggs

It is reasonable to use the medium and small eggs for cooking and the larger ones for boiled eggs.

Suggested quantities

Food	*Suggested quantities per head per week*
Milk	5–7 pts. (including dried milk used for cooking) [3–4 litres]
Meat (including offal, sausages etc.)	$1\frac{1}{4}$–$1\frac{1}{2}$ lbs. boneless [570–680 g]
Bacon and Ham	6 ozs. [170 g]
Cheese	3–4 ozs. [85–110 g]
Fish	6 ozs. [170 g]
Eggs	4–5 (this number will be less if cakes are purchased and sponge ready-mixes are used).

These items are interchangeable and the following portions all contain the same amount of protein:–

1 egg
$1\frac{1}{2}$ ozs. cooked fish [43 g]
1 oz. cooked meat [28 g]
1 oz. cooked bacon [28 g]
1 oz. hard cheese [28 g]

The menu should contain at least 4 portions per day.

e.g. 1 egg for breakfast = 1 portion
2 ozs. meat for lunch = 2 portions
1 oz. cheese for tea = 1 portion

If the majority of residents do not take 'a portion' of protein daily at breakfast, care should be taken to provide extra at other meals.

Vitamin-containing foods

These foods, principally vegetables and fruit, contain essential vitamins and mineral salts and will cost approximately 20–25 % of the total allowance.

Care needs to be taken in the storage and cooking of vegetables as the nutrients can easily be destroyed by long storage, over-cooking or the addition of bicarbonate of soda to the cooking water. Frozen vegetables contain as much Vitamin C as fresh vegetables purchased from a wholesaler or retailer.

Fresh fruit should be provided at least twice a week preferably one of which should be an orange. Many residents find difficulty in eating oranges so advantage should be taken of fruits such as tangerines and satsumas when in season, or alternatively canned or frozen orange juice may be used twice weekly.

Food	*Suggested quantities per head per week*
Tomatoes	4–6 ozs. (fresh or canned) [110–170 g]
Green vegetables and salads	$1\frac{1}{4}$–$1\frac{1}{2}$ lbs. [570–680 g]
Root and other vegetables	8–12 ozs [230–340 g]
Cooked fruit (fresh and dried) as part of the sweet course	3 times weekly at least
Raw fruit	1–2 pieces per week

Foods for activity and warmth

e.g., fats, bread, sugar, jam, cakes, cereals etc.

These foods will cost approximately 25–30 % of the total cost. They are cheaper than other types of food and are often taken in excess when old people live alone. For the elderly too much of these foods is most undesirable because they can cause unwanted increase in weight and also spoil the appetite for the more valuable foods mentioned above.

The suggested quantity of fats is 12 ozs. [340 g] per person per week including that required for cooking and baking.

If the majority of cakes are purchased less will be used.

When margarine is used, care should be taken to see that it is fortified with Vitamins A and D. These Vitamins are not always added to the cheaper cooking brands.

Note: Metric quantities in brackets are not given in *Catering in Homes for Elderly People.*

Appendix 3.3: Information about basic foods and quantities published by the Department of Health and Social Security in *Catering in Community Homes*

Quantities of certain foods

Though the amounts of nutrients required differ for each child they all need the same types of food but in varying amounts.

A table of requirements is shown in Appendix 1.* It can be quickly seen that the energy requirement for the 15–18 year olds is double that of the 2 year olds.

Foods for growth

These are foods containing protein *i.e.*, milk, meat, fish, ham, bacon, cheese and eggs. To make these foods, which are the most expensive, go further and to get the best nutritional value from our food we also use vegetable protein from pulses, bread and cereal.

Approximately 50% of the budget should be allowed for animal proteins.

Milk

Use can be made of full cream dried milk for cooking purposes; this is cheaper than fresh milk and is almost as good nutritionally.

Tinned milk is relatively expensive but is a useful and popular accompaniment to fruit and other sweet dishes.

Suggested quantities

One pint [0·57 litre] of fresh milk daily per child. This allows for some children who require a little more and others who will take less.

Meat, Offal, Bacon and Ham

As these are expensive foods it is important to include both the cheaper cuts such as neck of mutton for Irish stew as well as the prime roasting joints such as leg of lamb. Because some children may spend several months in residential care it is important that they should be aware of the various cuts such as lamb chops or steak which can be introduced in the menu for special occasions.

Though it is not always popular, children should be encouraged to eat liver because it is a valuable source of minerals and vitamins. Calf or pig liver is more acceptable than ox liver.

* See Appendix 3.7 of *The Kitchen in Catering*.

Cheese

Though most cheese is a good source of protein, hard cheeses such as Cheddar have a higher proportion than cheese spreads. It should be remembered that cream cheese has a very low protein content but it may be useful occasionally to give variety.

Fish

Fresh fish is becoming more expensive and difficult to obtain especially in the rural areas, but frozen fish is widely available.

Fried fish is very popular and occasionally advantage might be taken of the fish and chip van or the local fish and chip shop.

Fish fingers have a higher protein content than fish cakes.

Eggs

It is reasonable to use the medium and small eggs for cooking and the larger ones for boiled eggs.

Suggested quantities (for one week)

Food	*3–5 years*	*5–10 years*	*11–18 years*
Meat and offal	1 lb. of boneless [450 g]	1–1¼ lb. boneless [450–570 g]	1¼–1½ lb. boneless [570–680 g]
Poultry	4–6 ozs. [110–170 g]	6–8 ozs. [170–230 g]	6–8 ozs. [170–230 g]
Bacon and Ham	2 ozs. [60 g]	4–6 ozs. [110–170 g]	4–6 ozs. [110–170 g]
Cheese (hard)	2 ozs. [60 g]	3 ozs. [90 g]	4 ozs. [110 g]
Fish	3 ozs. [90 g]	4 ozs. [110 g]	6 ozs. [170 g]
Eggs	4–5	4–5	5–6

These items are interchangeable and the following portions all contain the same amount of protein:

1 egg
1½ ozs. cooked fish [43 g]
1 oz. cooked meat [28 g]
1 oz. cooked bacon [28 g]
1 oz. hard cheese [28 g]

It will be seen that these quantities do not provide 21 meals (*i.e.*, 3 protein meals daily) but the remainder of portions will come from items such as tinned fish, fish fingers, bought pies, sausages etc.

As a rough guide the menu should include 2 portions a day for the children under 5 and 4–5 portions a day for the children between 5 and 18.

e.g., child aged 7 years

1 egg for breakfast	= 1 portion
2 ozs. meat for lunch	= 2 portions
1 oz. cheese for tea	= 1 portion
Total	4 portions

Foods for vitality

These foods, principally vegetables and fruit, contain essential vitamins and mineral salts and will cost 20–25% of the total allowance.

The older children should get sufficient vitamin C from potatoes, green vegetables and fresh fruit. Children between 2–5 years do not have large appetites for vegetables and fruit, so it is necessary to see that a concentrated form, such as blackcurrant or orange juice is available for this age group.

All children should be encouraged to eat plenty of green and root vegetables and these should not be restricted.

Care needs to be taken in the storage and cooking of vegetables as the nutrients can easily be destroyed by long storage, over-cooking or the addition of bicarbonate of soda to the cooking water. Frozen vegetables contain as much vitamin C as fresh vegetables purchased from a wholesaler or retailer.

Fresh fruit should be provided at least 2 to 3 times weekly, one of which should be an orange. They can be part of a meal or often children enjoy having a piece of fruit whilst watching television.

Suggested quantities (for one week)

Food	*3–5 years*	*5–10 years*	*11–18 years*
Tomatoes	4 ozs. [110 g]	6 ozs. [170 g]	8 ozs. [230 g]
Green vegetables and salad	1 lb. [450 g]	1½ lbs. [680 g]	1½ lbs. [680 g]
Root vegetables	4 ozs. [110 g]	6 ozs. [170 g]	8 ozs. [230 g]
Fresh fruit	8 ozs. [230 g]	12 ozs. [340 g]	12 ozs. [340 g]

Foods for activity and warmth

These foods include fats, bread, sugar, jam, cakes, cereals, etc.

These foods will cost approximately 25–30% of the total budget.

The quantities of these foods will vary considerably, as even children of the same age and weight have different calorie requirements, depending on their build and general activity.

When margarine is used care should be taken to see that it is fortified with vitamins A and D. These vitamins are not always added to the cheaper cooking brands.

The suggested quantity of fats to include cooking and table use is 8–16 ozs. [230–450 g] a week depending on the age and energy requirement of the child.

Note: Metric quantities in brackets are not given in *Catering in Community Homes.*

Appendix 3.4: Recommended quantities of foods, Department of Education and Science Circular 3/66, Appendix

TABLE 1—Recommended quantities of foods (as purchased)

Food	*Quantity for 100 meals a day for 4 weeks, i.e., 500 meals a week, 2,000 meals in 4 weeks*	
Fresh meat	See details in Table 2(a) and (b)	215¾ lbs (97·9 kg)
Bacon and ham		13¾ lbs (6·2 kg)
Tinned meat		12½ lbs (5·7 kg)
Liver		12½ lbs (5·7 kg)
Sausages		18¾ lbs (8·5 kg)
Fish		42 lbs (19 kg)
Cheese		12½ lbs (5·7 kg)
Eggs (standard)		200 eggs
Main dish	100 eggs	
Culinary	100 eggs	
Milk		
Dried		62½ lbs (28·4 kg)
Fresh		30 gallons (136·5 litres)
Fats		78 lbs (35·4 kg)
Margarine	54¾ lbs (24·8 kg)	
Cooking fat	15½ lbs (7 kg)	
Cooking oil	7¾ lbs (3·5 kg)	
Potatoes		1000 lbs (453·6 kg)
Vegetables		469 lbs (212·7 kg)
Green	250 lbs (113·4 kg)	
Root	188 lbs (85·3 kg)	
Pulses		
i.e., Peas (tinned or dried)	12 lbs (5·4 kg)	
Split peas	12 lbs (5·4 kg)	
Haricot beans	3½ lbs (1·6 kg)	
Butter beans	3½ lbs (1·6 kg)	
Fruit		146 lbs (66·2 kg)
Fresh	83 lbs (37·7 kg)	
Tinned	31½ lbs (14·3 kg)	
Dried (large)	10½ lb (4·8 kg)	
Dried (small) *e.g.*, currants raisins sultanas	21 lbs (9·5 kg)	
Sugar		63 lbs (28·6 kg)
Preserves		25 lbs (11·3 kg)
Flour (culinary)		156 lbs (70·8 kg)

Cereals		
Oatmeal	1 lb (0·5 kg)	30 lbs (13·6 kg)
Custard / Cornflour	12 lbs (5·4 kg)	
Rice, etc.	16 lbs (7·3 kg)	
Macaroni/Spaghetti	1 lb (0·5 kg)	

Note: This Table illustrates the different quantities of food which would be used over a four-week period. These figure *must* be read in conjunction with the changes set out in Tables 2(a) and 2(b), and the revised incidence of the various cuts and kinds of meat For example, on looking at the first item, *i.e.*, meat, this does not mean a reduction in the portion quantity. Whereas under circular 290, 275 lbs of meat was used for 16 meals and gave an average portion (as purchased) of $2\frac{3}{4}$ ozs, what is proposed is $215\frac{3}{4}$ lbs for 12 meals with an average portion of $2\frac{7}{8}$ ozs; even this comparison cannot be taken literally, because of the changed incidence of bone-in and boneless meat).

TABLE 2(a)—Summary of recommended pattern of main dishes

Food	*No. of meals per 4-week period*	
Fresh meat		
(a) ROAST		
Beef	2	12
Lamb or mutton	1	
Pork	1	
(b) STEWING, BRAISING, BOILING		
Beef	5	
Lamb or mutton	2	
Pork or veal	1	
Bacon and ham		4
Liver		
Sausages		
Tinned meat		
Eggs		2
Cheese		
Fish		2
Total		20

TABLE 2(b)—Recommended detailed pattern of main dishes over a 4-week period and quantities purchased for 100 portions

This table indicates the various types of main dishes recommended for a 4-week period. It will be noted that several alternatives are given for a number of items in order to provide flexibility and variety.

	Main dish		*No. of meals*	*Purchased quantity for 100 portions*	
FRESH MEAT				lbs	(kg)
	ROASTING				
BEEF	Rib	Boneless	1	18¼	(8·3)
	Sirloin	Boneless	1	17½	(7·9)
LAMB OR MUTTON	Shoulder, Leg	Bone in	1	22	(9·9)
	Loin	Bone in		25	(11·3)
PORK	Leg, Shoulder, Hand or Spare Rib	Bone in	1	15½	(7)
	STEWING, BRAISING, BOILING				
BEEF	Silverside, Topside	Boneless	1	13½	(6·1)
	Chuck, Shoulder Steak	Boneless	2	16	(7·3)
	Clod and Sticking, Neck, Flank	Boneless	1½	16	(7·3)
	Brisket	Boneless	½	18¾	(8·5)
MUTTON	Shoulder, Leg	Bone in	2	20	(9)
LAMB OR MUTTON	Loin, Best End	Bone in		25	(11·3)
VEAL	Chuck	Boneless	½	17¼	(7·8)
PORK	Shoulder, hand or spare rib	Bone in	½	14¾	(6·7)
	Total number of Fresh Meat dishes		12		
OTHER ITEMS					
BACON AND HAM	Back and Streaky	Boneless	1	12	(5·4)
	Fore End	Bone in		15½	(7)
TINNED MEAT	Corned Beef, Pork Luncheon Meat		1	12½	(5·7)
LIVER	Ox, Lamb		1	12½	(5·7)
SAUSAGES	Beef, Pork		1	18¾	(8·5)
FISH			2	21	(9·5)
CHEESE			2	12½	(5·6)
EGGS				100	eggs
	TOTAL MEALS		20		

Notes: The annual reasonable unit cost grant limitation* will be based on
(a) an average of the above items. (The total quantity of fresh meat in Table 1 is similarly based on average use);
(b) home killed and imported as follows:

Roasting Beef, all Lamb and Mutton	50% home killed 50% imported
Stewing, Braising or Boiling Beef	25% home killed 75% imported
Veal	Imported
Pork	Home killed

* The reference to 'unit cost grant limitation' is now out of date.

Appendix 3.5: List of some good sources* of essential minerals and vitamins†

(Extracted from *Nutrition in Schools*, Department of Education and Science, 1975)

Calcium	*Iron*	*Riboflavin*	*Vitamin A*	*Vitamin C§*	*Vitamin D*
Liquid and dried milk*	Liver*: kidney*: heart*	Cheese* Liver: kidney	Liver*: kidney	Blackcurrants* and blackcurrant syrup*	Fortified margarine*
Cheese*	Black pudding*		Butter: fortified margarine: eggs: cheese	Rose hip syrup*: Tinned guavas	Fatty fish*: fresh or tinned
Yoghurt	Beef: lamb: chicken	Liquid and dried milk	Carrots: watercress: spinach: tomatoes: lettuce	Red and green peppers	Fortified dried milk
Wheat flour products, including white and brown bread	Sardines: pilchards: herrings	Yoghurt	Apricots (fresh or dried): prunes	Oranges and orange juice: grapefruit and grapefruit juice	Eggs
Most fish but especially sardines and pilchards		Eggs		Strawberries	Butter
Watercress: sprouting broccoli	Haricot beans: baked beans: lentils: peas: broad beans	Beef: lamb: pork: poultry: tongue: bacon and ham: tinned meat	Liquid and full cream dried milk	Sprouts: spinach: kale: new potatoes: mustard and cress: watercress	Liver

Appendix 3.5 *continued*

Calcium	*Iron*	*Riboflavin*	*Vitamin C§*
Baked beans: haricot beans	Dried apricots and prunes	Fatty fish	Gooseberries: redcurrants
Cabbage	Bread: crispbread: oatmeal	Spinach: sprouts: mushrooms	Cabbage: cauliflower: tomatoes and tomato juice
Soya flour	Green vegetables: potatoes	Peas and beans	Fresh and frozen broad beans: peas: lettuce
	Cocoa: curry powder	Concentrated yeast extract	Main crop potatoes: runner beans
	Black treacle: peanuts: mincemeat		Bananas

* Foods which are particularly rich sources of nutrients are marked with an asterisk.
† Foods are arranged in roughly descending order of value.
§ The amount of vitamin C in fruits and vegetables will always be lower after cooking.

Appendix 3.6: Suggested pattern of main dishes

(Extracted from *Nutrition in Schools*, Department of Education and Science, 1975)

The Table following suggests a pattern for including in the school dinner meat and other protein foods for the main course. It indicates the size of portion on the plate which experience over the years has shown to be necessary if the meal is to be acceptable to pupils and also the amount of protein which is on average likely to be derived from the size of serving. It will be appreciated that the servings suggested in the table are intended for pupils of average age. For older or younger pupils the amount would need scaling up or down in proportion to the overall recommended quantities of protein for the different age groups.

The Table also suggests the frequency with which fresh meat and the other commodities listed might be served. The pattern followed here is similar to the one recommended by the 1965 Working Party namely that fresh meat should on average be served on three days a week, the other main dishes being provided by other foods of animal origin.

Suggested pattern of main dishes showing size of portion and frequency of serving

	Edible portion ready to serve (*oz.*)	(*grams*)	*Protein content per portion** (*grams*)	*Number of meals per 20-day period*
Fresh meat (Roasting, boiling, stewing etc.)				
Beef, Lamb or Mutton, Pork, Veal, Poultry	$1\frac{3}{4}$–$2\frac{1}{4}$	50–65	11–15	12
Bacon and ham	2–$2\frac{1}{2}$	55–70	11–14	4 (Bacon and ham, Offal, Tinned Meat, Sausages)
Offal	2	55	15	
Tinned Meat	$1\frac{1}{2}$–$2\frac{1}{2}$	40–70	8–13	
Sausages	3	85	11	
Fish	$2\frac{3}{4}$–$3\frac{1}{4}$	80–90	15–18	4 (Fish, Cheese, Eggs)
Cheese	2	55	14–15	
Eggs	2	55	7	

* These quantities are based primarily on *The Composition of Foods*—Medical Research Council Special Report Series No. 297 by McCance, R. A. and Widdowson, E. M. (1967): London, HMSO, but later information has been used where this is available.

Note: In Circular 3/78 (Department of Education and Science), Circular No. 12/78 (Welsh Office), 20/1/78, the following statement about the use of vegetable protein foods was made: 'There is no objection to the use of vegetable protein foods (suitably fortified) provided they replace no more than 10 per cent of the meat or other animal protein in a meal. Alternatively, for convenience, and where there is a menu cycle, vegetable protein foods could substitute for the meat in a meat dish in up to 10 per cent of the meals served. . . .'

Appendix 3.7

Recommended daily intakes of energy and nutrients for the United Kingdom. *Recommended Intakes of Nutrients for the United Kingdom, Reports on Public Health and Medical Subjects No 120*, Department of Health and Social Security, 1969

(a) Age range	Occupational category	*(c)* Body	*(d)* Energy		*(f)* Protein	*(g)* Thiamine	Ribo-flavine	Nicotinic acid	Ascorbic acid	Vitamin A	*(j)* Vitamin D	Calcium	Iron
		kg	*kcal*	*(e)* *MJ*	*g*	*mg*	*mg*	*(h)* *mg equivalents*	*mg*	*(i)* *µg retinol equivalents*	*µg cholecal-ciferol*	*mg*	*mg*
BOYS AND GIRLS												(1)	(1)
0 up to 1 year (b)		7·3	800	3·3	20	0·3	0·4	5	15	450	10	600	6
1 up to 2 years		11·4	1200	5·0	30	0·5	0·6	7	20	300	10	500	7
2 up to 3 years		13·5	1400	5·9	35	0·6	0·7	8	20	300	10	500	7
3 up to 5 years		16·5	1600	6·7	40	0·6	0·8	9	20	300	10	500	8
5 up to 7 years		20·5	1800	7·5	45	0·7	0·9	10	20	300	2·5	500	8
7 up to 9 years		25·1	2100	8·8	53	0·8	1·0	11	20	400	2·5	500	10
BOYS													
9 up to 12 years		31·9	2500	10·5	63	1·0	1·2	14	25	575	2·5	700	13
12 up to 15 years		45·5	2800	11·7	70	1·1	1·4	16	25	725	2·5	700	14
15 up to 18 years		61·0	3000	12·6	75	1·2	1·7	19	30	750	2·5	600	15
GIRLS													
9 up to 12 years		33·0	2300	9·6	58	0·9	1·2	13	25	575	2·5	700	13
12 up to 15 years		48·6	2300	9·6	58	0·9	1·4	16	25	725	2·5	700	14
15 up to 18 years		56·1	2300	9·6	58	0·9	1·4	16	30	750	2·5	600	15
MEN													
18 up to 35 years	Sedentary	65	2700	11·3	68	1·1	1·7	18	30	750	2·5	500	10
	Moderately active		3000	12·6	75	1·2	1·7	18	30	750	2·5	500	10
	Very active		3600	15·1	90	1·4	1·7	18	30	750	2·5	500	10
35 up to 65 years	Sedentary	65	2600	10·9	65	1·0	1·7	18	30	750	2·5	500	10
	Moderately active		2900	12·1	73	1·2	1·7	18	30	750	2·5	500	10
			[illegible]	[illegible]	[illegible]	[illegible]	[illegible]	18	30	750	2·5	500	10

75 and over	sedentary life	63	2100	8·8	53	0·8	1·7	18	30	750	2·5	500	10
WOMEN													
18 up to 55 years	Most occupations	55	2200	9·2	55	0·9	1·3	15	30	750	2·5	500	12
	Very active		2500	10·5	63	1·0	1·3	15	30	750	2·5	500	12
55 up to 75 years	Assuming a	53	2050	8·6	51	0·8	1·3	15	30	750	2·5	500	10
75 and over	sedentary life	53	1900	8·0	48	0·7	1·3	15	30	750	2·5	500	10
											(k)	(m)	
Pregnancy, 2nd and 3rd trimester			2400	10·0	60	1·0	1·6	18	60	750	10	1200	15
Lactation			2700	11·3	68	1·1	1·8	21	60	1200	10	1200	15

Notes:

(a) The ages are from one birthday to another: *e.g.*, 9 up to 12 is from the 9th up to, but not including, the 12th birthday. The figures in the Table in general refer to the mid-point of the ranges, though those for the range 18 up to 35 refer to the age 25 years, and for the range 18 up to 55, to 35 years of age.

(b) Average figures relating to the first year of life. Energy and minimum protein requirements for the four trimesters are given in Tables 2 and 3 respectively.

(c) The body weights of children and adolescents are averages and relate to London in 1965. (Taken from Tanner, Whitehouse & Takaishi, 1966; Tables IV A and IV B, 50th centile). The body weights of adults do not represent average values; they are those of the FAO (1957) reference man and woman, with a nominal reduction for the elderly.

(d) Average requirements relating to groups of individuals.

(e) Megajoules (10^6 joules). Calculated from the relation 1 kilocalorie = 4·186 kilojoules, and rounded to 1 decimal place.

(f) Recommended intakes calculated as providing 10 per cent of energy requirements (see paragraph 64). Minimum protein requirements given in Table 3.

(g) The figures, calculated from energy requirements and the recommended intake of thiamine of 0·4 mg/1000 kcal, relate to groups of individuals.

(h) 1 nicotinic acid equivalent = 1 mg available nicotinic acid or 60 mg tryptophan.

(i) 1 retinol equivalent = 1 μg retinol or 6 μg β-carotene or 12 μg other biologically active carotenoids.

(j) No dietary source may be necessary for those adequately exposed to sunlight, but the requirement for the housebound may be greater than that recommended.

(k) For all three trimesters.

(l) These figures apply to infants who are not breast fed. Infants who are entirely breast fed receive smaller quantities; these are adequate since absorption from breast milk is higher.

(m) For the third trimester only.

Appendix 3.8: Table of quantities taken from *Catering in Community Homes*, Catering and Dietetic Branch, Department of Health and Social Security

Meat	
Roast Beef	4 to 5 portions to 1 lb. [9–11 to 1 kilo]
Roast Lamb or Pork	4 portions to 1 lb. [9 to 1 kilo]
Neck of Mutton	3 portions to 1 lb. [7 to 1 kilo]
Stewing, boiling, or mince beef	5 portions to 1 lb. [11 to 1 kilo]
Liver, tripe, sweetbreads or hearts	5 portions to 1 lb [11 to 1 kilo]
Bacon or ham	
Shoulder, gammon or collar	
(a) Main meal	4 portions to 1 lb. [9 to 1 kilo]
(b) Tea meal	5 portions to 1 lb. [11 to 1 kilo]
Rashers alone—breakfast or tea	8 portions to 1 lb. [18 to 1 kilo]
Breakfast or tea	10 portions to 1 lb. [22 to 1 kilo]
Poultry	
Chicken, boiled or roast	2 to 3 portions to 1 lb. [4–7 to 1 kilo]
Rabbit, baked or stewed	2 to 3 portions to 1 lb. [4–7 to 1 kilo]
Fricassee or creamed (no bone)	7 to 8 portions to 1 lb. [15–18 to 1 kilo]
Fish	
White or smoked	
(a) Filleted	4 portions to 1 lb. [9 to 1 kilo]
(b) With bone	3 portions to 1 lb. [7 to 1 kilo]
Cod roe, or herring roe	5 to 6 portions to 1 lb. [11–13 to 1 kilo]
Herrings or kippers	4 portions to 1 lb. [9 to 1 kilo]
Vegetables	
Raw weight	
Potatoes (old) baked, roast or boiled	3 to 4 portions to 1 lb. [7–9 to 1 kilo]
Potatoes new, or creamed	4 to 5 portions to 1 lb. [9–11 to 1 kilo]

Greens or sprouts	4 portions to 1 lb. [9 to 1 kilo]
Cauliflower	4 portions to 1 lb. [9 to 1 kilo]
Spinach	3 portions to 1 lb. [7 to 1 kilo]
Roots, onions, or leeks	3 to 4 portions to 1 lb. [7–9 to 1 kilo]
Tomatoes (8 in 1 lb.)	8 portions to 1 lb. [18 to 1 kilo]
Dried peas, beans, etc.	10 to 12 portions to 1 lb. [22–26 to 1 kilo]
Tinned carrots, peas or beans	30 portions to 1 A 10 tin
Fruits	
Fresh apples, gooseberries, plums etc.	4 portions to 1 lb. [9 to 1 kilo]
Dried prunes, apricots, mixed etc.	10 portions to 1 lb. [22 to 1 kilo]
Tinned peaches, apricots, pineapple etc.	30 portions to 1 A 10 tin

Notes

1. Metric quantities in brackets are not given in *Catering in Community Homes*.

2. *A similar table appears in Catering in Homes for Elderly People*, Catering and Dietetic Branch, Department of Health and Social Security.

Appendix 4

International metric system

The International System of Units (SI) is a coherent system and is built up from three kinds of units—base units, supplementary units and derived units.

Base units

There are seven base units:

Physical Quantity	*Unit*	*Symbol*
length	**metre**	m
mass	**kilogram**	kg
time	**second**	s
electric current	**ampere**	A
thermodynamic temperature	**kelvin**	K
luminous intensity	**candela**	cd
amount of substance	**mole**	mol

Supplementary units

There are, in addition to the base units, two supplementary units:

Physical Quantity	*Unit*	*Symbol*
plane angle	**radian**	rad
solid angle	**steradian**	sr

Derived units

Units for measuring other physical quantities are derived from the base units and the supplementary units by multiplication or division, without the introduction of conversion factors.

Some examples are:

Physical Quantity	*Derived Unit*	*Symbol*
area	**square metre**	m^2
volume	**cubic metre**	m^3
density	**kilogram per cubic metre**	kg/m^3
speed	**metre per second**	m/s
acceleration	**metre per second squared**	m/s^2

Some derived units have special names and symbols, for example:

Physical Quantity	*Derived Unit*	*Derivation*	*Symbol*
force	**newton**	kg m/s^2	N
pressure and stress	**pascal**	N/m^2	Pa
work, energy, quantity of heat	**joule**	N m	J
power	**watt**	J/s	W
electrical potential, PD and EMF	**volt**	W/A	V
electric resistance	**ohm**	V/A	Ω
luminous flux	**lumen**	cd sr	lm

Prefixes

An essential feature is the systematic use of prefixes to designate decimal multiples and submultiples of all the units. The prefixes in most common use are:

Prefix		*Symbol*
mega	one million times (10^6)	M
kilo	one thousand times (10^3)	k
hecto	one hundred times (10^2)	h
deca	ten times (10)	da
deci	one tenth of (10^{-1})	d
centi	one hundredth of (10^{-2})	c
milli	one thousandth of (10^{-3})	m
micro	one millionth of (10^{-6})	μ

Thus:
MJ = megajoule = one million joules
km = kilometre = one thousand metres
mg = milligram = one thousandth of a gram
μV = microvolt = one millionth of a volt

The kilogram, not the gram, is the coherent base unit of mass for SI and the name is retained for continuity reasons even though it contains a prefix. Names of decimal multiples and submultiples of this unit are formed by attaching prefixes to gram.

Certain multiples and submultiples of units have long-established special names, such as:

Physical Quantity	*Special Name*	*Definition*	*Symbol*
length	**micron**	10^{-6}m	μm
area	**hectare**	$hm^2 = 10^4m^2$	ha
volume	**litre**	$dm^3 = 10^{-3}m^3$	l*
mass	**tonne**	$Mg = 10^3kg$	t*
pressure	**bar**	$10^5N/m^2 = 10^5Pa$	bar

* The symbol 'i' can be confused in typescript with the figure 'one'. Similarly the symbol 't' can be mistaken for an abbreviation for the imperial ton. It is customary, therefore, to write the units 'litre' and 'tonne' in full.

Units used with SI

Time

The everyday units of time are so well established throughout the world that they remain in use, although not decimal multiples of the base unit, the second.

Physical Quantity	*Unit*
Time	**minute**
	hour
	day
	month
	year

Temperature

The degree Celsius, at present widely known as the degree Centigrade, is used for most general purposes. It is a unit of temperature interval identical with the kelvin. The zero of the Celsius scale is the temperature of the ice point (273·15K).

Physical Quantity	*Unit*	*Symbol*
Temperature	**degree Celsius**	°C

Plane angle

The degree continues to be used in many applications.

Physical Quantity	*Unit*	*Symbol*
Plane angle	**degree**	°

The degree $= \pi/180$ radians.

Bibliography

Advisory Conciliation and Arbitration Service, *Code of Practice 1, Disciplinary Practice and Procedures in Employment*, HMSO, London, 1977

Automatic Vending Association of Britain, *Vending*, The Automatic Vending Association of Britain, London, 1972

Bender, Arnold E., *Dictionary of Nutrition and Food Technology*, (4th edn), Newnes-Butterworth, London, 1975

British Gas, *A Student's Guide to Gas Catering*, British Gas, Marketing Division, 326 High Holborn, London WC1V 7PT, 1975

British Gas, *Systematic Layout Planning for Commercial Catering*, British Gas, London, 1975

Central Statistical Office, *Annual Abstract of Statistics, 1977*, HMSO

City of Canterbury, *Thought for Food*, City of Canterbury, 1976

Clay, H. H., *Clay's Public Health Inspector's Handbook* (13th edn revised by F. G. Davies), H. K. Lewis, London, 1972

Curson, Christopher, *'Education' Guide to Industrial Relations*, Swift Publications for Councils and Education Press, London, 1977

Department of Education and Science, *Nutrition in Schools, Report of the Working Party on the Nutritional Aspects of School Meals*, HMSO, London, 1975

Department of Employment, various leaflets and booklets on employment legislation, Department of Employment, London

Department of Health and Social Security, *Recommended Intakes of Nutrients for the United Kingdom, Reports on Public Health and Medical Subjects, No. 120*, HMSO, London, 1969

Department of Health and Social Security, Catering and Dietetic Branch,
Health Service Catering, Catering for Patients in Long Stay Hospitals
Catering in Community Homes
Catering in Homes for Elderly People
Health Service Catering, Clean Food
Health Service Catering Manual, vol. 2, Hygiene in Catering Departments and Food Services Areas 1974 : vol. 4, Fresh Fruit and Vegetables, 1976: *vol. 5, Safety at Work*, 1976

Department of Health and Social Security, Catering and Dietetic Branch, London

Department of Health and Social Security, Welsh Office, Scottish Home and Health Department, *Management Services (NHS), Study of Work in Hospital Kitchens to determine Staffing Ratios, 7*, HMSO, London, 1973

Department of Health and Social Security, Ministry of Agriculture, Fisheries and Food, Welsh Office, *Food Hygiene Codes of Practice, 9: Hygiene in Microwave Cooking*, HMSO, London, 1972

Electricity Council, *Finishing Kitchen Planning Guide*, Electricity Council, London, 1977

Evans, Judith, *Catering in Schools and Colleges*, Barrie and Jenkins, London, 1974

Food Hygiene (General) Regulations, 1970, HMSO, London

Health and Safety at Work etc. Act, 1974, HMSO, London

Hobbs, Betty C., *Food Poisoning and Food Hygiene* (3rd edn), Edward Arnold, London, 1974

Home Office, *Sex Discrimination, A Guide to the Sex Discrimination Act 1975*, Home Office, London

Hotel and Catering Industry Training Board, *Industrial Relations, A Guide for Managers*, HCITB, Wembley

Leeds University, The Catering Research Unit, *A Manual on Cook-Freeze Catering*, Local Government Training Board, Luton, 1975

Mathews, Wendy and Wells, Dilys, *Second Book of Food and Nutrition*, (3rd edn) *Home Economics* in association with the Flour Advisory Bureau, London, 1976

Meat and Livestock Commission in conjunction with the Department of Health and Social Security, *Cutting and Preparing Beef*, DHSS, London, 1974

McCance and Widdowson, *The Composition of Foods, Medical Research Council, SR 297,* HMSO, London 1978

Millross, Speht, Holdsworth and Glew, *The Utilisation of the Cook-freeze Catering System for School Meals*, The University of Leeds, 1973

Millward, J. G., *Municipal Work Study*, British Institute of Management, London

Ministry of Agriculture, Fisheries and Food, *Food Standards Committee, Report on Novel Protein Foods*, London, 1974

Ministry of Agriculture, Fisheries and Food, *Manual of Nutrition*, (eighth edn) HMSO, London, 1976

Ministry of Health and Ministry of Agriculture, Fisheries and Food, *Food Hygiene Codes of Practice 7: Hygiene in the operation of coin operated food vending machines*, HMSO, London, 1967

New Zealand Meat Producers Board, *Profitable Catering with Lamb*, New Zealand Meat Producers Board, c/o New Zealand Lamb Information Bureau, London

Oakley, Stan, *ABC of Work Study*, Pitman Publishing, London, 1973

Riley, Michael, *Understanding Food Cost Control, a Programmed Approach*, Edward Arnold, 1976

Royal Society for the Prevention of Accidents, *Accident Prevention in Large-Scale Catering*, Royal Society for the Prevention of Accidents, Birmingham

Scottish Education Department, *Educational Building Note 14, School Kitchens*, HMSO, Edinburgh, 1976

Strank, R. H. D., *Ergonomics: Functional Design for the Catering Industry*, Edward Arnold for Luncheon Voucher Catering Research Institute London, 1971

Taylor, David, of the Electricity Council, *Freeze Production Catering Unit Design Guide*, Electricity Council, 1975

University Grants Committee, *University Building Notes, Kitchen Planning*, HMSO, London, 1973

White Fish Authority, Herring Industry Board and Torry Research Station, *Specifications for the Purchase of Fish*, The White Fish Authority, Edinburgh